Design Multi-Agent AI Systems Using MCP and A2A

Engineer your own Python-based agentic AI framework with tool use, memory, and multi-agent workflows

Gigi Sayfan

<packt>

Design Multi-Agent AI Systems Using MCP and A2A

This book was written by Gigi Sayfan. Generative AI tools were used only to assist with ideation, phrasing, and diagram drafts, and all technical content and code were created, verified, and tested by the author and Packt's editorial team. Packt does not accept AI-generated content that replaces expert authorship.

Portfolio Director: Gebin George
Relationship Lead: Gebin George/Sonia Chauhan
Project Manager: Prajakta Naik
Content Engineer: Aditi Chatterjee
Technical Editor: Rahul Limbachiya
Copy Editor: Safis Editing
Indexer: Hemangini Bari
Proofreader: Aditi Chatterjee
Production Designer: Shantanu Zagade
Growth Lead: Nimisha Dua

First published: February 2026

Production reference: 2020326

Published by Packt Publishing Ltd.
Grosvenor House
11 St Paul's Square
Birmingham
B3 1RB, UK.

ISBN 978-1-80611-647-8
www.packtpub.com

Contributors

About the author

Gigi Sayfan is focused on building large-scale environments and harnesses for AI agents.

He has been developing software professionally for more than 30 years in domains as diverse as instant messaging, morphing, chip fabrication process control, embedded multimedia applications for game consoles, brain-inspired machine learning, custom browser development, web services for 3D distributed game platforms, IoT sensors, and virtual reality. He has written production code in Go, Python, Java, C#, C++, and Typescript/JavaScript.

His technical expertise includes AI agents, generative AI, cloud-native technologies, DevOps, databases, low-level networking, distributed systems, unorthodox user interfaces, and the full software development life cycle.

Gigi has authored several books on Kubernetes and microservices and written hundreds of technical articles on a wide range of topics.

About the reviewers

Shruti Dhumak is a senior technology executive and the head of customer engineering at Google, where she leads large-scale enterprise transformation through data, the cloud, and AI. She is recognized for building and scaling high-performing teams and aligning complex technology strategy with executive priorities. Shruti partners closely with C-suite leaders to enable sustainable growth and measurable business outcomes, bringing a strong focus on operational excellence and customer impact. As a deep technical expert in advanced cloud architectures and autonomous agentic systems, she serves as a trusted advisor and mentor passionate about results-driven leadership and advancing the next generation of technology leaders.

Nicolas Bievre is a senior machine learning engineer at Meta, specializing in AI, recommender systems, and generative AI for advertising and healthcare. He has held critical leadership roles at Meta and PayPal, architecting systems that personalize content for hundreds of millions of users and ensuring compliance for major revenue-driving models. A Stanford alumnus, his peer-reviewed research in leading AI and bioinformatics journals is now utilized in hospitals for cancer research. Internationally recognized, he has received the AdKDD Best Paper Award, the Core Ads Growth Privacy Award, and the Outre-Mer Outstanding Talent Award. He also serves as an AI consultant to the French government and a reviewer for top AI organizations.

Subscribe for a free eBook

New frameworks, evolving architectures, research drops, production breakdowns—*AI_Distilled* filters the noise into a weekly briefing for engineers and researchers working hands-on with LLMs and GenAI systems. Subscribe now and receive a free eBook, along with weekly insights that help you stay focused and informed.

Subscribe at `https://packt.link/8Oz6Y` or scan the QR code below.

Table of Contents

Chapter 10: Testing, Debugging, and Troubleshooting Multi-Agent Systems 369

Preface

The rapid evolution of large language models has shifted artificial intelligence from static, prompt-driven systems to dynamic, agentic architectures capable of reasoning, planning, and acting in the real world. Today's most powerful AI applications are no longer single-model pipelines; they are systems of collaborating agents that use tools, manage context, and coordinate with one another to solve complex problems. Building such systems requires going far beyond surface-level framework usage. It demands a deep understanding of how agentic AI actually works.

Rather than treating agent frameworks as black boxes, this book takes a ground-up, hands-on approach. You will explore what happens behind the curtain of modern agentic systems by building a flexible and extensible multi-agent framework in Python from first principles. Core concepts such as tool use, secure execution, context management through the **Model Context Protocol (MCP)**, and agent collaboration via **Agent-to-Agent (A2A)** messaging are broken down into concrete implementations and reusable design patterns. This foundational understanding will enable you not only to build your own frameworks but also to reason about, customize, and troubleshoot agentic systems built with existing tools.

The journey through the book is intentionally practical and progressive. You will begin by constructing a simple tool-using agent, then incrementally enhance its capabilities—adding secure tool execution, persistent and structured context handling, collaborative planning, and memory. As the book progresses, these individual components come together into fully autonomous, multi-agent systems capable of coordinating actions and solving complex tasks through structured communication and shared context.

Complete with step-by-step walk-throughs, annotated Python code, and deep dives into real-world agent workflows, this book bridges theory and practice. By the end, you will be able to design and implement your own agentic AI systems, build custom tools for intelligent agents, integrate protocols such as MCP and A2A, and deploy collaborative AI workflows that reason, plan, and act effectively in real-world environments. Armed with these skills, you will be well prepared to build the next generation of intelligent, adaptive AI applications.

The book is structured into three parts:

- *Part 1, Foundations of Agentic AI,* lays the foundation for agentic AI. It traces the evolution of generative AI, defines what an AI agent is, and distinguishes agents from chatbots. You'll learn about core agent architecture and components, including the agent loop (sense–think–act), memory and context management, planning and reasoning, tool use, and evaluation. The part concludes with a hands-on walk-through of a simple Kubernetes-focused agent, showing how tool calling works end-to-end and how a minimal code base can deliver real autonomy.
- *Part 2, Building Your Own Agentic AI Framework,* walks you through building a real agentic AI framework (AI-6) from the ground up. You'll explore the core engine that runs the agent loop, manages memory, sessions, tools, and multiple LLM providers, then dive into designing robust, provider-agnostic tools with schemas, validation, and execution flow. The part then shifts to user-facing interfaces, showing how to build Slack and web UIs that support visibility, control, and human-in-the-loop workflows. It closes by integrating the framework with the **Model Context Protocol** (**MCP**), enabling standardized tool discovery and interoperability across the broader ecosystem.
- *Part 3, Constructing Multi-Agent Systems,* takes you into multi-agent systems at full scale: designing agent teams, orchestration patterns, role prompts, tool scoping, and context strategies, then implementing real multi-agent workflows with the **Agent-to-Agent** (**A2A**) protocol. You'll build a practical multi-agent DevOps system (MAKDO), learn how to test and debug agent coordination failures, and apply resilience patterns such as redundancy, graceful degradation, and human escalation. The part then moves into production deployment, walking through a realistic multi-cluster setup with secure communication and service discovery. It concludes with advanced topics and future directions, including massive context windows, long-horizon planning, multimodal systems, and the broader implications of increasingly capable agents.

Who this book is for

The target audience for this book encompasses AI engineers, machine learning practitioners, and software architects interested in building sophisticated, real-world agentic AI systems. It's especially valuable for those working with LLMs in production, developing tool-using agents, or exploring multi-agent orchestration. DevOps engineers, AI product managers, and researchers experimenting with advanced LLM frameworks will also benefit from this book.

What this book covers

Chapter 1, Introduction to Generative AI and AI Agents, sets the stage for the rest of the book by introducing the foundational concepts behind generative AI and agentic systems. It covers the current landscape of generative models, including **large language models (LLMs)**, and explains why AI agents represent a compelling next step in leveraging these models for real-world applications. You will come away with a clear understanding of the distinction between simple LLM use and full-fledged agentic behavior, along with historical context and emerging patterns.

Chapter 2, Understanding How AI Agents Work, dives into the core mechanics of AI agents: how they perceive, plan, and act. It introduces the fundamental loop that governs agent behavior (from perception to reasoning to action) and explains the infrastructure behind it. You will understand the internal architecture of AI agents and what makes them effective in solving complex problems.

Chapter 3, A Hands-On Walk-Through of a Simple AI Agent, guides you through building a basic tool-using AI agent that interacts with a live Kubernetes cluster. The agent leverages OpenAI's tool calling capabilities to accept natural language input, interpret intent, execute corresponding kubectl commands, and return results. This real-world walk-through demystifies tool integration and message handling within an agentic AI framework.

Chapter 4, Building a Tool-Based Agentic AI Framework, introduces the foundational concepts and implementation strategy for building an AI agent framework that supports dynamic tool use. You will learn how to construct a robust architecture where an agent can decide when and how to invoke external tools (e.g., APIs, shell commands, command-line tools) to enhance its capabilities. The focus is on building a minimal yet functional core framework that can be extended with more complex behavior later.

Chapter 5, Implementing Custom Tools, explores the design and implementation of custom tools, enabling agents to take real actions, retrieve structured data, and interact with external systems. You will learn how to define tool interfaces, handle argument schemas, return structured results, and ensure safe and reliable execution. The chapter emphasizes the role of tools in extending an agent's capabilities beyond simple text generation.

Chapter 6, Creating Chat Interfaces Using Slack and Chainlit, demonstrates how to create engaging chat interfaces for interacting with your AI agents. You'll learn how to build integrations with Slack to bring your agents into the workplace and how to use Chainlit to create web-based UIs. These interfaces are key to making your AI agents accessible, interactive, and useful in real-world scenarios.

Chapter 7, Integrating with the Model Context Protocol Ecosystem, introduces the **Model Context Protocol** (**MCP**) and its role in enhancing context awareness, interoperability, and modularity in agentic AI systems. You will learn the principles behind MCP, how to build MCP servers and clients, and how to leverage MCP-compatible components to extend agent capabilities across different execution environments. The chapter also shows how to use MCP as the backbone of the tool-calling agentic loop.

Chapter 8, Designing Multi-Agent Systems, explores how multiple AI agents can work together toward a shared goal using **Agent-to-Agent** (**A2A**) communication. You will learn about the patterns and architectures for multi-agent orchestration, including broadcasting, delegation, and consensus. The chapter will cover real-world use cases, challenges in coordination and conflict resolution, and provide best practices for designing scalable, resilient collaborative agentic systems.

Chapter 9, Implementing Multi-Agent Systems with A2A, presents the implementation of a full-fledged multi-agent system that brings together all the core ideas from earlier chapters. We'll build an AI-powered DevOps team composed of specialized agents that communicate via the A2A protocol and utilize MCP for powerful tool-using capabilities. The team includes a Kubernetes expert agent, a CI/CD expert agent, a security specialist agent, and a DevOps manager agent who oversees coordination and interacts with human engineers. This project showcases how multiple agents collaborate to solve real-world problems in a complex, distributed environment.

Chapter 10, Testing, Debugging, and Troubleshooting Multi-Agent Systems, equips you with practical debugging strategies for identifying issues in tool execution, message routing, context sharing, and multi-agent coordination. It covers logging, tracing, observability hooks, and diagnostics tailored for autonomous agents operating in dynamic environments.

Chapter 11, Deploying Multi-Agent Systems, focuses on deploying our multi-agent DevOps system across two separate **Kubernetes-in-Docker** (**KinD**) clusters to simulate a distributed, production-like environment. We'll run the manager agent on one cluster and deploy the rest of the specialized agents – Kubernetes, CI/CD, and Security – on the other. This setup models a realistic architecture where the control plane (manager) is decoupled from the worker agents for scalability, isolation, and operational resilience. We'll cover configuration, service exposure, inter-cluster communication, and common pitfalls when deploying agent-based systems in Kubernetes environments.

Chapter 12, Advanced Topics and Future Directions, surveys the frontier of agentic AI capabilities, from superhuman reasoning and large-context comprehension to long-horizon planning and emergent autonomous behaviors. You will gain perspective on how breakthroughs such as 1M+ token context windows and generative memory architectures unlock new patterns of interaction, enable strategic foresight, and hint at agents that reason beyond human capabilities. We also introduce the concept of **Generative User Experience** (**GenUX**) as the next evolution in human-agent interface design.

To get the most out of this book

You should have a basic understanding of Python programming, familiarity with machine learning concepts, and a basic understanding of large language models.

Software/hardware covered in the book	Operating system requirements
Python 3.x	Windows, macOS, or Linux
OpenAI API key	Windows, macOS, or Linux

You will need access to a Python development environment. An OpenAI API key is required for many of the examples. A machine with at least 8 GB of RAM is recommended for running the more complex examples.

If you are using the digital version of this book, we advise you to type the code yourself or access the code from the book's GitHub repository (a link is available in the next section). Doing so will help you avoid any potential errors related to the copying and pasting of code.

Download the example code files

The code bundle for the book is hosted on GitHub at `https://github.com/PacktPublishing/Design-Multi-Agent-AI-Systems-Using-MCP-and-A2A`. We also have other code bundles from our rich catalog of books and videos available at `https://github.com/PacktPublishing`. Check them out!

Disclaimer on images

Some images in this title are presented for contextual purposes, and the readability of the graphic is not crucial to the discussion. Please refer to our free graphic bundle to download the images.

Download the color images

We also provide a PDF file that has color images of the screenshots/diagrams used in this book. You can download it here https://packt.link/gbp/9781806116478.

Conventions used

There are a number of text conventions used throughout this book.

`CodeInText`: Indicates code words in text, database table names, folder names, filenames, file extensions, pathnames, dummy URLs, user input, and Twitter handles. Here is an example: "`tool_config` and `provider_config` are mappings that allow you to specify additional configuration for each tool and provider."

A block of code is set as follows:

```
response = client.chat.completions.create(
    model=model_name, messages=messages,
    tools=tools, tool_choice="auto")
```

Bold: Indicates a new term, an important word, or words that you see on the screen. For instance, words in menus or dialog boxes appear in bold. For example: "We have two deployments: **some-app** and **nginx**. The **some-app** deployment has three pending Pods, and the **nginx** deployment has one Pod in an error state due to an invalid image name."

Note

Warnings or important notes appear like this.

Tip

Tips and tricks appear like this.

Get in touch

Feedback from our readers is always welcome!

General feedback: Email `feedback@packtpub.com` and mention the book's title in the subject of your message. If you have questions about any aspect of this book, please email us at `questions@packtpub.com`.

Errata: Although we have taken every care to ensure the accuracy of our content, mistakes do happen. If you have found a mistake in this book, we would be grateful if you reported this to us. Please visit `http://www.packtpub.com/submit-errata`, click **Submit Errata**, and fill in the form.

Piracy: If you come across any illegal copies of our works in any form on the internet, we would be grateful if you would provide us with the location address or website name. Please contact us at `copyright@packtpub.com` with a link to the material.

If you are interested in becoming an author: If there is a topic that you have expertise in and you are interested in either writing or contributing to a book, please visit `http://authors.packtpub.com/`.

Free benefits with your book

This book comes with free benefits to support your learning. Activate them now for instant access (see the *How to unlock* section for instructions).

Here's a quick overview of what you can instantly unlock with your purchase:

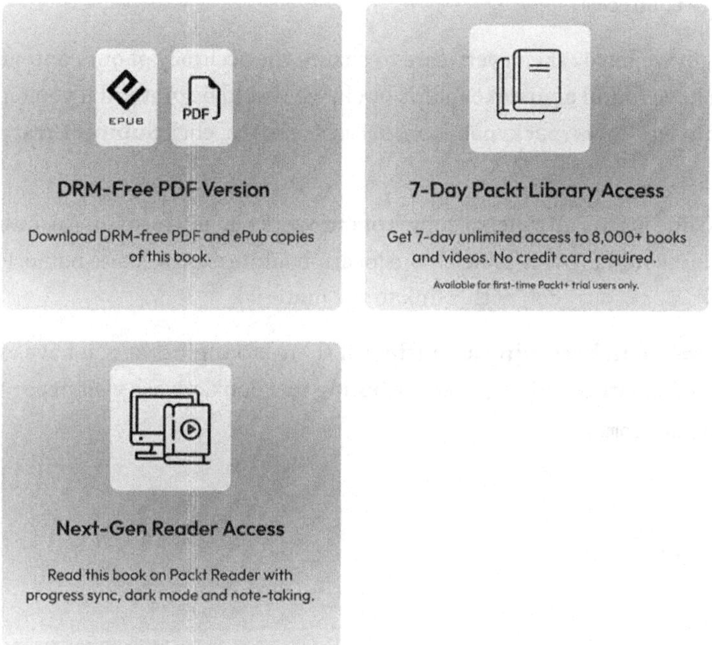

How to Unlock

Scan the QR code (or go to `packtpub.com/unlock`). Search for this book by name, confirm the edition, and then follow the steps on the page.

UNLOCK NOW

Note: Keep your invoice handy. Purchases made directly from Packt don't require one.

Share your thoughts

Once you have read *Design Multi-Agent AI Systems Using MCP and A2A*, we would love to hear your thoughts! Scan the QR code below to go straight to the Amazon review page for this book and share your feedback.

Your review is important to the tech community and us, and it will help us make sure we're delivering excellent quality content.

Join our Discord and Reddit Space

You're not the only one navigating fragmented tools, constant updates, and unclear best practices. Join a growing community of professionals exchanging insights that don't make it into documentation.

Join our Discord at `https://packt.link/z8ivB` or scan the QR code below:	Follow us on Reddit at `https://packt.link/0rExL` or scan the QR code below:

Part 1

Foundations of Agentic AI

Part 1 lays the foundation for agentic AI. It traces the evolution of generative AI, defines what an AI agent is, and distinguishes agents from chatbots. You'll learn core agent architecture and components, including the agent loop (sense–think–act), memory and context management, planning and reasoning, tool use, and evaluation. The part concludes with a hands-on walkthrough of a simple Kubernetes-focused agent, showing how tool calling works end-to-end and how a minimal codebase can deliver real autonomy.

This part contains the following chapters:

1

Introduction to Generative AI and AI Agents

AI agents represent a significant evolution in how we build and interact with intelligent systems. Unlike static models or chatbots, agents can reason, use tools, remember past interactions, and act autonomously within defined boundaries. AI agents are built on top of the **generative AI (GenAI)** technology and allow building systems that are adaptive, purposeful, and effective in dynamic environments.

This book is a comprehensive exploration of the evolution, architecture, and practical implementation of agentic AI systems. What makes this book unique is that you will build a full-fledged agentic AI framework from scratch. The AI-6 framework supports the development of sophisticated autonomous agents capable of complex reasoning, tool use, and multi-step task execution. Spanning 12 chapters, the book covers everything from foundational concepts and single-agent architectures to advanced multi-agent systems, testing methodologies, deployment strategies, and integration with emerging technologies such as the **Model Context Protocol (MCP)** and the **Agent2Agent (A2A) Protocol**. The book provides both theoretical understanding and hands-on implementation guidance, making it valuable for developers, researchers, and practitioners looking to build real-world AI agent systems.

This chapter establishes that AI agents differ fundamentally from chatbots through five key characteristics: autonomy, perception, reasoning and planning, action capability, and learning and adaptation – transforming AI from reactive responders to proactive problem-solvers. The chapter traces AI's evolution from symbolic reasoning (1950s) through expert systems (1980s), machine learning (1990s), and deep learning (2006+), to today's transformer-based agents, showing how each era's limitations drove the next breakthrough.

Four architectural patterns emerge for agentic systems – single-agent loops, planner-executor models, multi-agent collaboration, and graph-based workflows – each supported by three critical components: memory, tools, and orchestration.

In this chapter, we will explore the foundational concepts of GenAI and AI agents. We will define what an AI agent is, how it differs from traditional chatbots, and discuss various use cases for agentic AI. We will also delve into the architecture of agentic systems.

In this chapter, we will cover the following main topics:

- The evolution of generative AI
- Introducing AI agents
- Understanding the architecture of AI agents

Free benefits with your book

Your purchase includes a free PDF copy of this book along with other exclusive benefits. Check the *Free Benefits with Your Book* section in the Preface to unlock them instantly and maximize your learning experience.

The evolution of generative AI

Artificial intelligence (**AI**) has been a dream of computer scientists and futurists for decades. As early as the 1940s, when digital computers were first developed, researchers began to explore the potential of machines to simulate human thought and behavior. Over the years, AI has evolved through various stages and cycles of hope and despair. Along the way, there was always an interesting tension between brain-inspired approaches and logic-based approaches. For example, the perceptron, an early neural network model, was developed in the 1950s by Frank Rosenblatt and is the ancestor of modern neural networks. Initially, there were high hopes for perceptron-based systems, as it could solve problems where a single linear decision boundary separates classes. This includes basic tasks such as distinguishing the following:

- Vertical versus horizontal lines
- Light versus dark patterns
- Some handwritten characters under controlled conditions

These seemed impressive in the 1950s and 1960s, when the idea of a machine learning from data at all was novel. However, the model was very limited, the industry became disillusioned with this approach, and neural network research remained dormant for several decades.

The early days of symbolic AI

The computer science pioneers of the 1950s and 60s laid the groundwork for AI with symbolic reasoning (https://en.wikipedia.org/wiki/Symbolic_artificial_intelligence) and early neural networks. Some examples of symbolic AI include Alan Turing's work on the Turing Test (https://en.wikipedia.org/wiki/Turing_test) and John McCarthy's development of LISP (https://en.wikipedia.org/wiki/Lisp_(programming_language)) as a programming language for AI.

Symbolic reasoning refers to the broad set of techniques in AI that rely on high-level, human-readable representations of problems, logic, and search. It employs tools such as logic programming, production rules, semantic networks, and frames to model and solve problems through structured symbolic manipulation.

During this period, several ambitious and interesting systems were built, such as **SHRDLU**, a natural language understanding program that lets users interact with a virtual world of blocks. Take a look at this human and SHRDLU natural language conversation:

```
Person: Pick up a big red block.
Computer: OK.
Person: Grasp the pyramid.
Computer: I DON'T UNDERSTAND WHICH PYRAMID YOU MEAN.
Person (changing their mind): Find a block which is taller than the one you are
holding and put it into the box.
Computer: BY "IT", I ASSUME YOU MEAN THE BLOCK WHICH IS TALLER THAN THE ONE I AM
HOLDING.
Computer: OK.
Person: What does the box contain?
Computer: THE BLUE PYRAMID AND THE BLUE BLOCK.
Person: What is the pyramid supported by?
Computer: THE BOX.
```

This is very impressive for a system built in the 1970s, but it was limited to a specific domain and required extensive hand-crafted knowledge.

Perceptrons also gained traction during this period. To compare the two, symbolic AI relies on explicit, human-readable rules and logical reasoning to solve problems, making it highly interpretable but often rigid and manually intensive. Another major drawback is that the combinatorial explosion of rules in real-world scenarios quickly becomes unmanageable.

On the other hand, early neural network models such as the perceptron learned from data by adjusting numeric weights, enabling them to generalize from examples but offering little transparency into their decision-making. In general, symbolic AI excels at structured, rule-based tasks, and perceptrons are better suited for pattern recognition in noisy or ambiguous environments.

But this wave did not last long. This period ended with the first **AI winter** when funding and interest in AI waned due to the failure to deliver on the ambitious promises of the early systems. There were several reasons for these early failures. The most prominent ones were that the techniques weren't sophisticated enough to deal with the complexity of real-world problems, the available compute resources were insufficient, and the lack of training data.

Then came the expert systems era.

The expert systems era

In the 1980s, expert systems came to the fore. The idea was to encode human expertise into rules that could be executed by a software program. Expert systems such as MYCIN (`https://en.wikipedia.org/wiki/Mycin`) for medical diagnosis and DENDRAL (`https://en.wikipedia.org/wiki/Dendral`) for chemical analysis were developed, but they were limited by the need for extensive domain knowledge and the difficulty of capturing the complexity of human reasoning in rules. Here is an example rule from MYCIN:

```
IF
    the infection is primary-bacteremia
    AND the site of culture is one of the sterile sites
    AND the suspected portal of entry is the gastrointestinal tract
THEN
    there is suggestive evidence (0.7) that the organism is Bacteroides.
```

This rule-based approach allowed for some level of automation in decision-making and had some success. Unfortunately, overall, expert systems were brittle and difficult to maintain, leading to another AI winter in the late 1980s. This brittleness stemmed from several core limitations: the number of rules required to handle real-world complexity quickly became unmanageable, and as domains evolved, rules had to be constantly updated, leading to maintenance challenges. Moreover, it was often impossible to define explicit rules for every possible scenario, particularly when dealing with ambiguous or uncertain situations. These factors made expert systems inflexible and ultimately unsustainable at scale.

The next significant milestone was the machine learning era.

The rise of machine learning and statistical methods

The modern era of AI began in the 1990s with the rise of **machine learning (ML)** and statistical methods. Methods such as **Support Vector Machines (SVM)**, decision trees, random forests, and logistic regression allowed processing of large datasets and learning. There wasn't a lot of hype around this time, but the groundwork was laid for the next wave of AI advancements. The focus shifted from hand-crafted rules to data-driven approaches, enabling systems to learn patterns and make predictions based on examples rather than explicit programming. Instead of telling the computer how to think, we just threw a bunch of data at it and let it figure it all out. The phrase *data is the new oil* was coined at this time.

But, while these methods were effective for many tasks, they required a lot of patient work around feature engineering and still struggled with complex reasoning and understanding. Following this was the popularity of deep learning networks.

Deep learning and the neural network renaissance

Research breakthroughs in layered neural networks, GPU acceleration, and even larger datasets unlocked new capabilities in vision, speech, and text. The term **deep learning** was coined in 2006 to describe this new approach. I was part of this wave, working on brain-inspired machine learning at Numenta (`https://www.numenta.com/`) in the mid-2000s.

The rise of social media with the likes of YouTube, Facebook, and Twitter, and the cost of storage and compute dropping dramatically, led to an explosion of data. Researchers finally had access to the scale of data and hardware needed to train deep nets effectively.

Innovations such as AlexNet (`https://en.wikipedia.org/wiki/AlexNet`) in 2012, Word2Vec (`https://en.wikipedia.org/wiki/Word2vec`) in 2013, and DeepSpeech (`https://arxiv.org/abs/1412.5567`) in 2014 redefined the capabilities of AI in fields such as image recognition, natural language processing, and speech recognition. The Turing test wasn't definitively conquered yet, but we were getting close.

The explosion of internet usage and digital storage in the late 1990s and early 2000s created unprecedented opportunities to collect and process massive datasets that would fuel the next generation of AI breakthroughs. The creation of ImageNet in 2009, containing over 14 million hand-labeled images across 20,000+ categories, exemplified how large-scale, meticulously curated datasets became essential infrastructure for training robust models. ImageNet's annual competition catalyzed breakthrough architectures such as AlexNet in 2012, proving that deep neural networks could achieve unprecedented accuracy when given sufficient high-quality training data. This dataset-centric approach established a new paradigm where model performance scaled predictably with data volume and quality, leading organizations to prioritize data collection and curation as core competitive advantages.

Funnily enough, one of the most notable AI successes of the time was IBM's Deep Blue beating Gary Kasparov in chess, utilizing raw compute power while using old-fashioned symbolic AI and hand-crafted code techniques. The Netflix recommendation system, which used collaborative filtering to suggest movies based on users' preferences, was representative of this era.

Then we moved into the times we are living in now.

The emergence of generative models, transformers, and language models

In 2014, **Generative Adversarial Networks** (**GANs**) (`https://en.wikipedia.org/wiki/Generative_adversarial_network`) were introduced and allowed the generation of images, videos, and music from scratch. But the biggest breakthrough came in 2017, with the introduction of the Transformer architecture in the seminal paper "Attention is All You Need": `https://arxiv.org/pdf/1706.03762`. Transformers revolutionized the field by using self-attention mechanisms coupled with feed-forward only networks. That allowed parallel training, which was orders of magnitude more efficient than the previous state of the art with **recurrent neural networks** (**RNNs**). The Transformer architecture became the foundation for many subsequent models, including Google's BERT, OpenAI's GPT-2, and later GPT-3. The success can also be attributed to the emergence of massive datasets such as Common Crawl (`https://commoncrawl.org/`) and the Pile (`https://arxiv.org/abs/2101.00027`), enabling the training of increasingly capable language models.

But it wasn't until the end of 2022 that the real magic happened with the release of OpenAI's ChatGPT, based on GPT-3.5. Suddenly, AI jumped to the mainstream, and the world was captivated by the capabilities of these large language models. The discovery that **Reinforcement Learning from Human Feedback** (**RLHF**) could be used to fine-tune these models for better alignment with humans was a game-changer. Other companies quickly followed suit, releasing their own models, such as Google's Bard and Meta's Llama. On the image generation side, models such as DALL-E, Stable Diffusion, and Midjourney showed that the transformer architecture could also be used for generating high-quality images from text prompts.

> **Note**
>
> - OpenAI researchers described RLHF back in 2017: `https://openai.com/index/learning-from-human-preferences/`
> - You can also read about RLHF here: `https://en.wikipedia.org/wiki/Reinforcement_learning_from_human_feedback`

Suddenly, AI wasn't just talking but painting too. The world was buzzing with excitement, and the possibilities seemed endless. It also shattered the worldview of many people when it became evident that AI could compete in the area of creative expression, which was often considered the exclusive domain of humans.

The rise of AI agents

At the beginning of March 2023, OpenAI released GPT-4, a more capable and steerable successor to GPT-3.5. GPT-4 handled longer contexts, had improved reasoning, and showed early signs of multi-modal fluency as it was capable of understanding text, images, and speech. OpenAI, Anthropic, Google, Meta, Mistral, and Chinese companies such as DeepSeek and AliBaba kept releasing better and better models. Benchmark after benchmark fell to the unstoppable march of innovation.

Models such as Anthropic's Claude pushed the envelope of LLMs in the realm of coding, and recent models introduced a long reasoning mode, where a model can spend more time and resources to complete complicated tasks.

At the same time, the frontier shifted toward agentic AI: models that don't just respond, but plan, reason, use tools, and act. The OpenAI API function-calling capability, replicated by other LLM providers such as Google with its Gemini models and Anthropic with its Claude models, explored how LLMs could become the backbone of multi-step workflows, coding assistants, web agents, and real-world automation.

Multiple agentic AI frameworks emerged, such as LangChain, AutoGPT, AutoGen, and BabyAGI. These frameworks allow developers to build complex LLM-based systems. These systems bring us full circle: not just chatbots, but autonomous collaborators that can reason about tasks, use external APIs, and adapt on the fly. But what is an AI agent?

Introducing AI agents

This question *What is an AI agent?* is at the heart of this book. In this section, we will explore the common definition of an AI agent, its characteristics, and the different types of AI agents. In the next chapter, *Understanding How AI Agents Work*, we will go much deeper and explore in detail how AI agents are structured and their various components and capabilities.

If you ask ChatGPT what an AI agent is, it will tell you something along these lines:

> *An AI agent is a system that can perceive its environment, reason about its goals, and take actions to achieve those goals, often autonomously or interactively.*

This is a pretty intuitive definition that aligns well with the common understanding of what an intelligent agent is. Let's consider the characteristics of such an AI agent.

AI agent characteristics

In order to function according to the preceding definition, an AI agent must have the following characteristics:

- **Autonomy**: The agent must be able to operate on its own and perform multiple steps to achieve its goal without human intervention in each and every step. Note that it doesn't mean that the agent is completely autonomous. It can still be supervised by a human, especially when it comes to taking potentially risky actions. We will see some examples later. The agent can operate independently, making decisions and taking actions without human intervention.

> **Note**
>
> If the agent performs well enough or if the consequences of its actions are not critical, it may operate completely autonomously without any human supervision.

- **Perception**: An AI agent must be able to perceive its environment, either physical, digital, or both. This perception can come in the form of structured inputs such as API responses or unstructured data such as natural language, audio, or visual signals. The agent uses this information to assess its current state, context, and relevant changes. It informs the agent's subsequent actions and decisions and provides feedback on previous actions. Assembling the inputs into a usable internal representation is an enormous technical challenge. Consider just raw web data, which comes in countless formats, resolutions, and quality levels, requiring sophisticated pipelines to parse, validate, and standardize these diverse inputs into consistent internal representations suitable for reasoning.
- **Reasoning and planning**: Once an agent perceives the environment, it must reason about the new information and make decisions about its next action. This involves identifying goals, evaluating possible actions, and formulating or updating a plan. Modern AI agents may use symbolic planning, reinforcement learning, or neural network-based methods to carry out this process. Planning enables agents to look ahead and choose sequences of actions rather than just reacting to immediate stimuli.
- **Action**: The core function of an AI agent is to take actions in the environment. These actions could include invoking a tool or API, generating a response, triggering a workflow, or even controlling a device. The agent must be capable of executing these actions in a way that aligns with its goals and adapts to the feedback it receives from the environment. In order to be effective, the agent must have the proper access and permission to perform the actions that are required to achieve its goals.
- **Learning and adaptation**: An advanced AI agent should be able to learn from experience. This might include updating internal memory, adjusting strategies, or refining its behavior over time. Some agents learn offline (through training data), while others learn online (from real-time interactions). Adaptive behavior is critical for agents operating in dynamic, unpredictable environments.

AI agents combine autonomy, perception, reasoning, action, and learning to operate effectively in dynamic environments. They can make informed decisions and adapt over time. These capabilities have started to drive real-world applications across industries, enhancing efficiency and enabling more intelligent systems.

But how are they different from chat interfaces such as ChatGPT, Claude Desktop, and Gemini that we have started to use daily? Let's find out.

Key differences: chatbots versus agents

Chatbots and AI agents are often used interchangeably, but they have distinct characteristics. **LLM-based chatbots** allow users to interact with LLM through natural language. The interaction is typically limited to a single query that may include an image or through a voice interface.

Here is the typical chatbot interaction workflow:

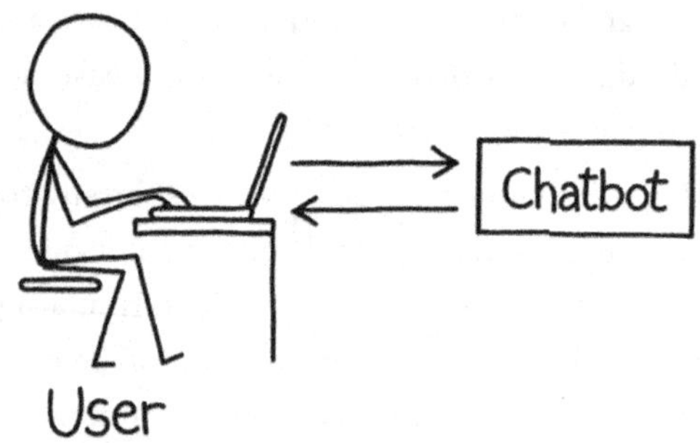

Figure 1.1: LLM-based chatbot and user interaction

The LLM will digest the user's input query and generate a response. The user can't control directly what the model does except through prompt engineering. In particular, the user can't provide the model access to external data sources and APIs (although uploading files is possible).

But an AI agent interaction workflow is more complex. Based on the user input and reasoning and planning mechanisms, an AI agent can autonomously execute tasks and even run complete workflows.

Here is an illustration of an AI agent workflow.

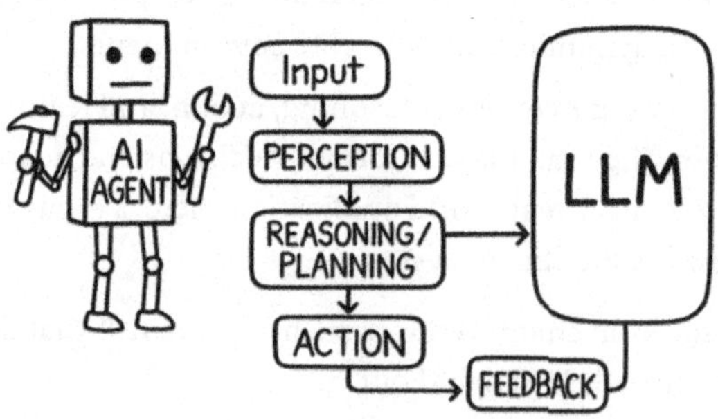

Figure 1.2: AI agent workflow

Let's summarize the key differences in a table:

Feature	Chatbots	AI Agents
Purpose	Primarily for conversation and information	Autonomous task execution and decision-making
Interaction	Primarily text-based, often limited to FAQs	Multi-modal, can use tools and APIs
Autonomy	Limited, often requires human input	High autonomy, can operate independently
Context Awareness	Limited context retention	Can maintain and utilize long-term context
Learning	Static, based on pre-trained parameters	Dynamic, can learn and adapt over time

Table 1.1: Key differences between chatbots and AI agents

Agentic AI systems find several use cases in the GenAI era. You may have encountered some of the agents, too! Let's look at some examples of AI agents in action.

Use cases for agentic AI

AI agents can be applied in a wide range of domains and use cases. What is fascinating is that some of the most successful applications are in domains that were previously thought to be too complex or nuanced for AI. But, as we progress towards more capable AI agents, we are seeing breakthroughs in areas such as software development, customer support, research, and even empathic user interaction.

Here are some examples of how AI agents are being used effectively today:

- **Autonomous coding assistants**: Software engineering is a complex task that requires a deep understanding of both the problem domain and the technical implementation. AI agents have already reached a level where they can explore large code bases, be assigned GitHub or Jira issues, and autonomously fix problems, perform massive refactorings, write and run tests, and ensure the changes are valid. The current generation of AI coding agents still can't totally replace a high-level human engineer, but they can significantly augment the productivity of software teams. I consider the current crop of coding AI agents as a savant intern.

They can perform some tasks on their own but may get lost in a large code base and require some steering and hand-holding. Some examples of AI coding agents are Devin.ai (`https://devin.ai/`), Claude Code (`https://www.anthropic.com/claude-code`), OpenAI's codex CLI (`https://github.com/openai/codex`), Google's Jules (`https://jules.google/`), and the open source OpenHands (`https://github.com/All-Hands-AI/OpenHands/`).

- **Automated customer support**: Customer support was always considered a prime target for automation. Customer support bots have been around for more than 20 years. But they were always very limited in their capabilities, and users largely opted to escalate to a human. AI agents are now transforming customer service by replacing static chatbots with dynamic assistants capable of multi-turn dialogue, tool use, and real-time problem resolution. Unlike traditional bots, these agents can authenticate users, pull data from CRMs, and even escalate or resolve tickets. Intercom's Fin (`https://fin.ai/`) is a good example – it's a support agent that can answer complex queries based on your company's documentation. Similarly, Ada (`https://www.ada.cx/`) and Forethought (`https://forethought.ai/`) use AI agents to handle tier-1 and tier-2 support tasks across messaging channels, reducing load on human agents. These systems integrate with helpdesk platforms such as Zendesk and Salesforce, providing end-to-end ticket resolution without needing custom scripts.
- **Research agents**: Research is another domain where AI agents are making a significant impact. The rate of knowledge accumulation is growing significantly. Unfortunately, not all of it is high-quality. AI agents can help researchers sift through vast amounts of research papers, correlate and find connections between them, and even generate new hypotheses. All the major LLM providers now offer research modes for the top-level models where the foundation model itself autonomously performs complex research projects that involve generating search queries, performing web searches, analyzing the results, and synthesizing the findings into a coherent report. The report is also grounded with source reference links. Here are some of the current (May 2025) leading thinking models: OpenAI o3, o4-mini, Anthropic Claude 4 Opus, Google Gemini 2.5 Pro, and xAI Grok 3 Think. But research agents can do more than just access reasoning models. They can also use tools and provide access to private data stores that are unavailable to foundation models. There are also several scientific research initiatives that utilize AI agents, such as Elicit (`https://elicit.org/`), Google's Co-Scientist (`https://research.google/blog/accelerating-scientific-breakthroughs-with-an-ai-co-scientist/`), and Microsoft's Discovery platform (`https://`

azure.microsoft.com/en-us/blog/transforming-rd-with-agentic-ai-introducing-microsoft-discovery/).

- **Personal productivity agents**: Personal productivity is an exciting domain for AI agents. They can help users manage their schedules, prioritize tasks, and draft emails or documents. I believe that in the near future, most people will have a personal AI assistant that will help them manage their digital life and will become better and better as it learns more about the user. This will be especially powerful when using local models that eliminate the resistance to sharing personal data with third-party providers. Some examples include Motion AI strategists (`https://motionapp.com/ai-creative-strategists`), Reclaim AI (`https://reclaim.ai/`), and Superhuman AI (`https://superhuman.com/ai`).
- **AI companions**: AI companions are designed to provide emotional support, conversational interaction, and sometimes even entertainment. They are not just chatbots. They can actually evoke meaningful emotions in the humans they interact with by simulating human-like behavior with fine-tuned personality traits, memory, and multimodal capabilities.

  These agents can play roles ranging from empathetic listeners to motivational coaches or playful friends. They often learn from the user over time and adapt their tone, memory, and behavior accordingly. Some examples of AI companions include Replika (`https://replika.ai/`), Pi (`https://pi.ai/`), Character.AI (`https://character.ai/`), and Anima (`https://anima.ai/`).

It is now time to understand how AI agents are utilized and organized in practice.

Introducing the components of agentic AI systems

The architecture of agentic AI systems includes several components that work together to enable the agents to perceive, reason, and act within their environment. The spectrum of agentic AI systems ranges from highly constrained agents that operate within a specific domain and under tight constraints to fully autonomous agents that can function in the real world with minimal human intervention.

In general, agentic AI systems are very similar to traditional software systems. They have compute and storage resources, and they can communicate over the network with other systems. The key difference is that in traditional software systems, the logic, decision-making, and responses to events are explicitly programmed by software engineers. In contrast, agentic AI systems delegate some of these high-level cognitive tasks to AI agents.

Common components of agentic AI systems

Regardless of the chosen architecture, any non-trivial agentic AI system will have the following components:

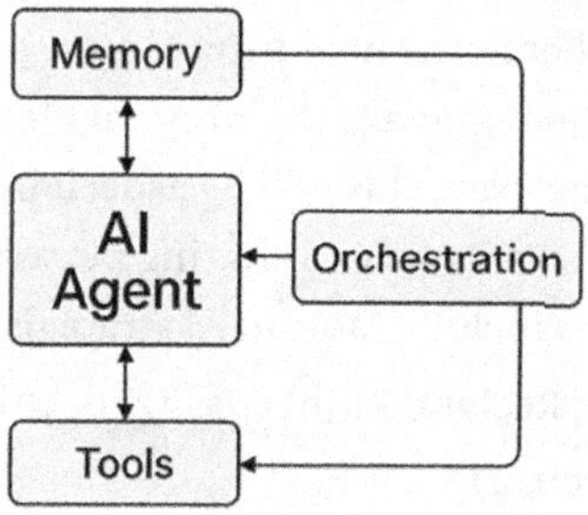

Figure 1.3: Common components of an agentic AI system

1. **Memory** is a critical component of agentic AI systems. It allows agents to store and retrieve information about their environment, past actions, and learned knowledge. Memory can be short-term (the context for the current session or task) or long-term (for storing knowledge, preferences, and learned behaviors). We will explore different types of memory in *Chapter 2*, but just to give you a taste, here are the most common types of memory used in agentic AI:
    - **Working memory** maintains the current context window. This is the immediate, short-term memory used by the system to process and perform its tasks. It includes all the input and output tokens in the current session.
    - **Episodic memory** tracks recent conversations/events (i.e., the record of prior interactions or significant events), stored across sessions. This allows the system to recall specific exchanges or user behaviors, enabling continuity and personalization over time.
    - **Semantic memory** is the facts/concepts learned over time. It is a long-term store of structured knowledge such as general world facts, domain-specific information, or conceptual relationships.
2. **Tools** are external resources or APIs that agents can use to perform actions in the environment. If the LLM is the brain, then tools are the eyes, ears, and limbs of the AI system that allow it to sense and operate on its environment. Without tools, an AI system will only be able to provide advice based on user input and will not have any actual agency in the world.
3. **Orchestration** is the process of coordinating the various components of an agentic AI system and making them collaborate to accomplish its goals.

This includes managing the flow of information between agents, tools, and memory, as well as handling interactions with external systems and humans. Orchestration can be done through a central controller or by using decentralized approaches where agents communicate directly with each other. The level of humans in the loop can vary.

Let's now take a look at various agentic AI architectures.

Types of agentic AI architectures

There are different architectures that are useful for different scenarios and situations. The choice of architecture depends on the specific use case, the level of autonomy required, and the complexity of the tasks to be performed. Here are some common architectures:

Single-agent loop

A **single-agent loop architecture** consists of a single AI agent that perceives its environment, reasons about its goals, and takes actions to achieve those goals. This loop typically includes a cycle of observation, planning, and execution, allowing the agent to interact with its environment in a purposeful and adaptive manner.

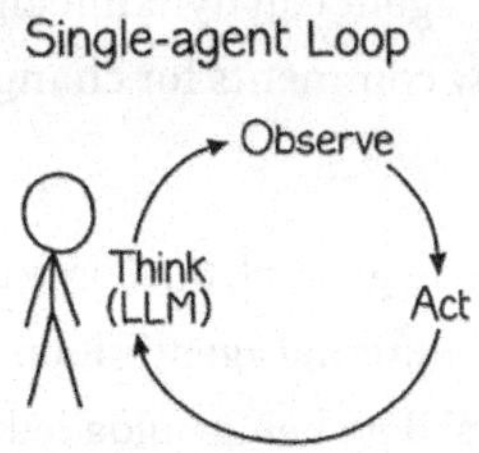

Figure 1.4: A single-agent loop architecture

Reasoning about goals in this context refers to how the agent, typically powered by a **large language model (LLM)**, interprets its instructions and chooses a course of action. The LLM infers intent from prompts, historical context, and any explicitly stated objectives, then decomposes complex tasks into subtasks or steps that align with the desired outcome. While LLMs don't *reason* in a human-like way, they use patterns learned from training data to simulate reasoning, often by predicting what a helpful or goal-directed response would look like in a given context. This allows the agent to appear deliberative and coherent in pursuit of its assigned goals.

This architecture is suitable for simple tasks where a single agent can handle all the complexity, and the context window (the total amount of tokens available to the LLM in every request) is large enough to accommodate the entire task. The agent can use tools and memory to enhance its capabilities, but it operates independently without the need for coordination with other agents.

> **Note**
>
> LLM thinking is best understood as a simulation of human-like reasoning through language. It predicts the next word in a sequence by analyzing patterns in vast text data. It uses probabilities, context, and training to simulate reasoning. It mimics cognitive patterns by leveraging patterns in its training data, but lacks understanding, intentionality, and consciousness.

Some typical use cases include the following:

- **Tool-augmented question answering**: When paired with external tools (e.g., web search, calculators, databases), a single agent can fetch facts, compute results, or retrieve real-time information to respond to user queries more accurately
- **Monitoring devices**: An agent can monitor devices such as air quality sensors, analyze them over time, and raise an alert if it detects anomalies
- **Automated code review**: An agent can dynamically watch out for changes in a code repository and provide review comments for changes

> **Note**
>
> Search is not integrated into LLMs in general, but some LLM providers now offer reasoning models that may run an internal agentic loop that can use tools such as web search and file search over external data being uploaded (not training data).

When the agent observes a change in the environment, such as a thermostat reading, based on its training data, in similar situations, the correct action is to check the current temperature against the set temperature. If this information is not already in the context, this will trigger an action to read the set (desired) temperature. Once the agent has both the current temperature and the set temperature, it will send a message to the model, which, based on its training data, will generate the next action: increase the temperature (if the current temperature is too low), decrease the temperature (if the current temperature is too high), or do nothing (if the current temperature is equal to the set temperature).

Planner and executors

In the **planner and executors architecture**, a **planner AI agent** is responsible for reasoning about the goals and formulating a plan that decomposes goals into sub-tasks. These sub-tasks are then delegated to other agents called **executor agents**. The planning process involves the steps of the plan being generated by the planner AI agent based on its training data and the prompt. The results of the execution may be sent back to the planner, which may adjust the plan and launch more executor agents.

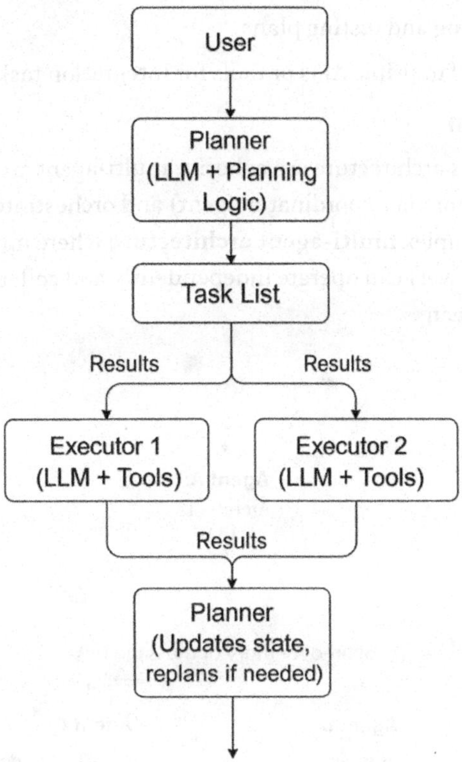

Figure 1.5: Planner and executor architecture

These executor agents are specialized for their tasks and interact with the LLM independently from the planner and other executor agents. This means that they manage their own context and have their own set of tools. Coordinating the execution of the plan and handling dependencies between tasks can be the responsibility of the planner agent or a dedicated coordinator agent when the planner launches.

This architecture is suitable for complex tasks that exceed the capabilities of a single agent. The executor agents utilize the same agentic AI techniques and don't require any custom programming in general cases. All the custom programming that is necessary for accessing resources, data stores, and APIs is implemented by the tools.

Typical use cases include the following:

- Automated research and report generation
- Complex multi-step data processing pipelines
- Software refactoring and testing plans
- Coordinated use of multiple APIs or tools for integration tasks

Multi-agent system

The planner and executors architecture is a cohesive multi-agent architecture where the planner controls (directly or via a coordinator agent) and orchestrates the workflow. This can be extended to a more complex **multi-agent architecture** where multiple agents with specific roles (CEO, engineer reviewer) can operate independently and collaborate with each other, very much like a human team.

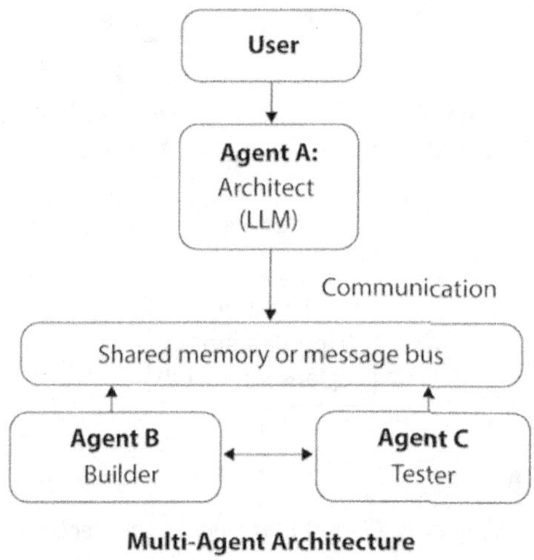

Figure 1.6: Mult-agent architecture

In this architecture, agents can communicate with each other, share memory, and iterate together towards the system's goals. This is a more sophisticated flow than the top-down structure of a planner and executors, allowing for more dynamic interactions and parallel processing of tasks.

For example, when the coder agent completes implementing a module, it can notify the tester agent, which will proceed to test the new module. When all the modules the architect envisions are implemented by the coder agent and tested successfully by the tester agent, the architect can start working on the next version of the target system. Multiple coder agents and tester agents can work in parallel on multiple modules.

Graph-based architecture

Graph-based architectures represent the relationships between agents, tasks, tool invocations, and memory updates as a graph. Each task or agent may spawn multiple sub-agents dynamically. The overall structure of the graph emerges organically based on the results of earlier tasks.

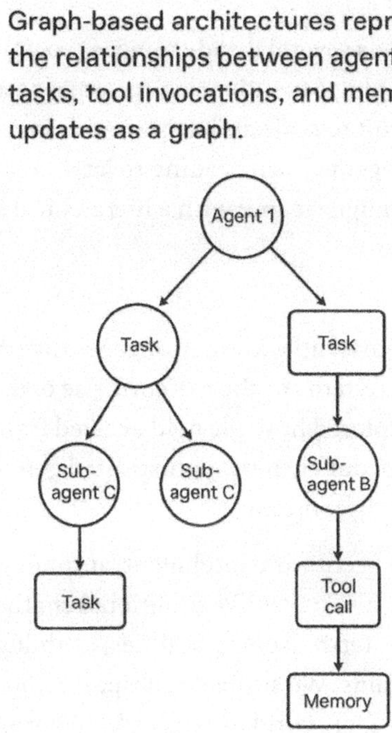

Figure 1.7: Graph-based architecture of agentic systems

For simplicity, consider an example where the task may be to count all the words in all the files in a directory. Sub-agent C may be a sub-agent that counts words in a file, so multiple sub-agent Cs can be launched, one for each file. Later on, agent 1 will aggregate the results from all sub-agent Cs.

Each node in the graph represents an agent, task, tool, or memory update, and the edges represent the flow of information and dependencies between them. One of the most prominent frameworks that uses this architecture is LangGraph (`https://www.langchain.com/langgraph`).

The main advantage of the agent graph architecture is that the problem can be broken down naturally into a deep hierarchical structure, such as software development planning, where a top-level goal such as "build a web application" decomposes into subsystems such as frontend, backend, and database, each with their own tasks, such as UI design, API development, schema modeling, and testing. Each subtask can be handled by specialized agents, passing outputs and context down the graph, enabling coordinated and modular execution across layers of abstraction.

But the agent graph architecture has several disadvantages too. It introduces significant coordination complexity, as managing dependencies, message passing, and error propagation between agents can become difficult to scale and debug. Additionally, it may incur overhead from excessive decomposition or agent churn, leading to latency, resource inefficiency, or brittle behavior when tasks don't align cleanly with a hierarchical structure.

Summary

In this chapter, we followed the remarkable journey of generative AI from the pioneering work of symbolic reasoning and expert systems to the meteoric rise of deep learning and transformer-based models. We explored how the field evolved from rule-based automation to data-driven intelligence, leading to our current sophisticated generative models, capable of not only understanding but also creating content.

We examined the emergence of AI agents and intelligent, autonomous systems that perceive, plan, act, and adapt to their environment. Unlike traditional chatbots, AI agents are equipped with memory, tool use, and multi-step reasoning abilities, enabling them to perform complex, dynamic tasks across diverse domains. We studied multiple architectures, saw how they differ from chatbots, and surveyed some real-world use cases, from autonomous coding assistants to AI companions.

At this point, you should have all the necessary background to understand the principle of AI agents and what they are all about, their place in the overall AI revolution, and their current abilities. This should serve as solid groundwork to continue our journey. With this solid foundation, we are now ready to dive deeper into the inner workings of AI agents in the next chapter and unpack in detail how they are constructed, how their components interconnect, and how they achieve autonomy and intelligence in practice.

Get This Book's PDF Version and Exclusive Extras

Scan the QR code (or go to `packtpub.com/unlock`). Search for this book by name, confirm the edition, and then follow the steps on the page.

UNLOCK NOW

Note: Keep your invoice handy. Purchases made directly from Packt don't require an invoice.

2

Understanding How AI Agents Work

In *Chapter 1*, we explored foundational concepts in **GenAI** and agentic systems, including various architectures used in their design. In this chapter, we'll take a closer look at how AI agents actually function. We'll examine the key components and subsystems of agentic AI, such as the core agent loop, memory, goal formulation, state management, planning/reasoning, tool use, and feedback mechanisms.

To ease your understanding, the chapter will introduce various concepts or components in an agentic system and discuss their roles. We will then discuss how these components are implemented in an open-source agentic AI framework, AutoGen.

It's important to note again that we will focus on agentic AI systems where all the decision-making, planning, and reasoning is done by a **large language model** (**LLM**). Other agentic AI systems are possible, where such logic is implemented in a different way, such as using a rule engine or traditional programming, or **retrieval-augmented generation** (**RAG**). External RAG is also a common pattern where the AI system interprets the model's response and fetches relevant data from an external source, such as a database or knowledge base, to provide more accurate and contextually relevant answers or feed it back to the LLM. However, we will see later that even RAG can be as simple as a tool call controlled by the LLM itself.

In this chapter, we will cover the following main topics:

- Understanding the agent loop: sense, think, act
- Workings of an agent loop in AutoGen
- Managing long conversations with memory, goals, and state
- Planning and reasoning mechanisms

- Tool use and environment interactions
- Agent evaluation and feedback loops

Understanding the agent loop: sense, think, act

The **agent loop** is the core cycle that defines how AI agents operate. It is similar to many other control loops in other fields, such as robotics or control systems. Some famous examples of control loops are the **OODA (Observe, Orient, Decide, Act)** loop (`https://en.wikipedia.org/wiki/OODA_loop`) and the Kubernetes reconciliation loop (`https://pkg.go.dev/sigs.k8s.io/controller-runtime/pkg/reconcile`).

An agent loop consists of a session workflow and three phases called sensing, thinking, and acting. Let's see how they operate.

The session workflow

The agent loop revolves around the LLM. In each step of the loop, the agent interacts with the LLM to either send messages that contain new information (user input, sensor data, etc.) or to receive messages.

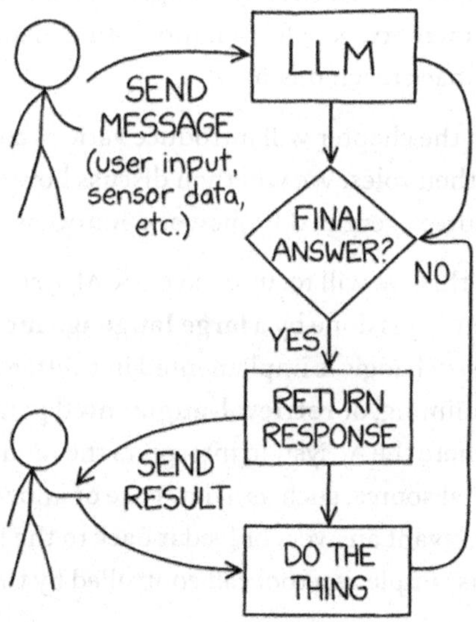

Figure 2.1: Session workflow of an agent

If the received message is a final response, then the agent is done processing, the loop is terminated, and the response is returned to the caller (a user, another system, or a higher-level agent). However, if the received message is an instruction from the LLM to perform some action (typically a tool call), then the agent will perform the requested action and then continue the loop by sending the result of the action back to the LLM.

> **Note**
>
> The LLM API that the agent is working with is usually responsible for indicating if the response is final.

Next, we'll talk about the phases of an agent loop.

The agent loop phases

The agent loop can be divided into three main phases: sensing, thinking, and acting. We will now describe how they function in the context of exchanging messages with an LLM.

- **Sensing**: AI agents perceive their environment through various sensing mechanisms. They collect data, observe the state and changes in the environment, and can use APIs, physical sensors, or access a datastore. However, the trigger for the sensing phase is always a tool call message from the LLM.

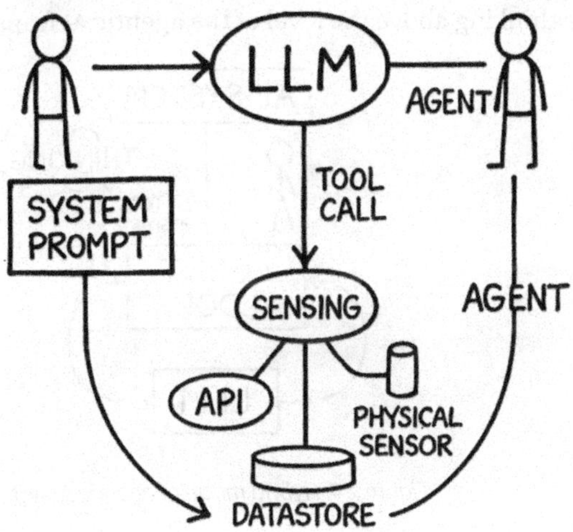

Figure 2.2: The sensing phase of the agent loop

Users, AI frameworks, or other agents may invoke an agent with a system prompt, an initial user message (the user doesn't have to be a human), and a set of tools. However, this initial information is always sent to the LLM, which may decide to trigger sensing by sending a tool call message. The agent will then execute the tool call, which could be reading some data from an API or physical sensor, or even utilizing RAG, and send the collected data back to the LLM.

- **Thinking**: Here is the surprising part – the thinking phase is not a separate phase in the agent loop. The LLM does all the thinking, whether it is planning, reasoning, analyzing results of earlier tool calls, deciding which tools to invoke, or, of course, formulating a final response. The agent loop is simply a conduit to exchange messages with the LLM. The thinking phase happens every time the agent loop sends a message to the LLM.

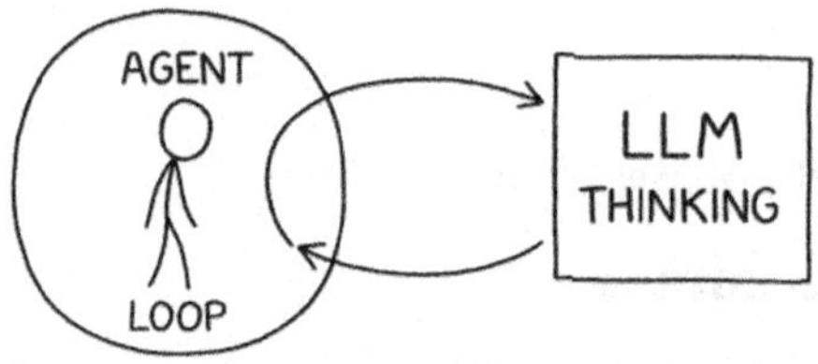

Figure 2.3: LLM thinking is invoked every time the agent sends a message

Remember that this pure thinking at the LLM level is not an axiom.

There may be agentic AI systems that operate in hybrid mode that intercept intermediate actions, such as the results of tool calls, and then process them and decide what to do next without delegating all the thinking to the LLM. However, such systems perform their thinking above the level of the agentic AI framework.

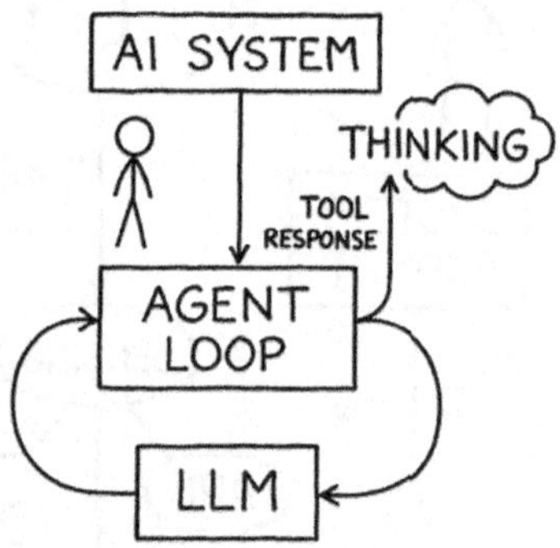

Figure 2.4: Hybrid mode of agentic AI systems

The AI agent framework itself that runs the agent loop is still a conduit for exchanging messages, but it may provide a hook where each tool call result is sent to the AI system above that uses the AI framework. Then, dedicated code with domain knowledge may control or hint further interaction with the LLM by processing the tool's response to the LLM, directly modifying the context, or simply terminating the agent loop even if the LLM didn't provide a final response yet.

> **Note**
>
> The agent never does any thinking. The thinking is either done by the LLM (below the agentic loop) or by the AI system (above the agentic loop). The agentic framework and the agents never perform any thinking on their own.

- **Acting**: Acting is very similar to sensing. They are actually indistinguishable from each other from the perspective of the agent loop. The agent loop sends a message to the LLM, which responds with a tool call message. The agentic AI framework then executes the tool call and sends the result back to the LLM. Acting is simply a tool call that has some impact on the outside world. It could be a call to an API, a database, or even a physical action in the real world (such as moving a robot arm).

> **Note**
>
> The difference between sensing and acting is in its impact on the outside world. Sensing is just observing the state of the world. Acting changes the state of the world.

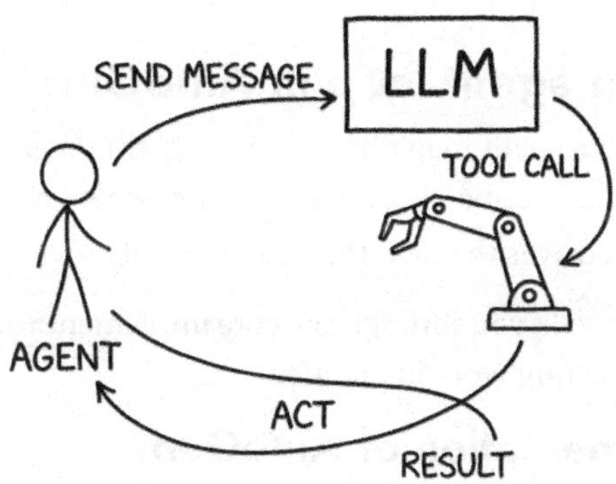

Figure 2.5: Acting phase of the agent loop

The key point is that the agent loop facilitates this interaction by sending the tool call and receiving the result. The agent loop is oblivious to the nature of the tool call, whether it is sensing or acting. The result of an action tool call will typically be a success or error message, which is sent back to the LLM. If the action is a long-term action, the response may be some action ID that the LLM may query later for progress and status updates. As always, the LLM will decide how to continue given a particular response to an action tool call.

If the response was a success status, then the LLM may just respond with a final response message and terminate the agent loop. However, in case of failure, it may retry or take some recovery actions.

In multi-agent systems, one of the most significant actions is launching another agent with its own agent loop. We will cover this aspect in depth later in the book (*Chapter 8*). Another form of multi-agent collaboration is communicating with another already running agent that wasn't launched by the current agent. This interaction may be considered either sensing or acting, depending on what the other agent does. If it just returns some information, then it is sensing, but if it performs some action in the world, then it is acting. If it seems confusing at this point, don't worry. We will unpack all the details and nuances of multi-agent systems in *Part 3* of the book.

Let's see how the agent loop concept is implemented in a popular agent framework by Microsoft: AutoGen (`https://github.com/microsoft/autogen`).

> **Note**
>
> AutoGen is widely known for its modular and clean design, with abstractions for agents, conversations, and strong tool integration, making it an ideal pick for the demonstration of the concepts.

Workings of an agent loop in AutoGen

AutoGen implements the agent loop phases (sensing, thinking, acting) through its `AssistantAgent` class and supporting infrastructure, which closely follows the described pattern where the LLM drives the loop through tool calls.

In this section, we will walk you through the core implementation of AutoGen to illustrate how sensing, thinking, and acting work in practice.

The core implementation of AutoGen

The agent loop is primarily implemented in the `tool_agent/_caller_loop.py` module (`https://github.com/microsoft/autogen/blob/main/python/packages/autogen-core/src/autogen_core/tool_agent/_caller_loop.py#L16`), which handles the continuous cycle of LLM interaction and tool execution. It is part of the core layer of AutoGen (`https://deepwiki.com/microsoft/AutoGen/1.1-core-architecture`).

Take a look at *Figure 2.6*, which illustrates how the AutoGen agent loop functions:

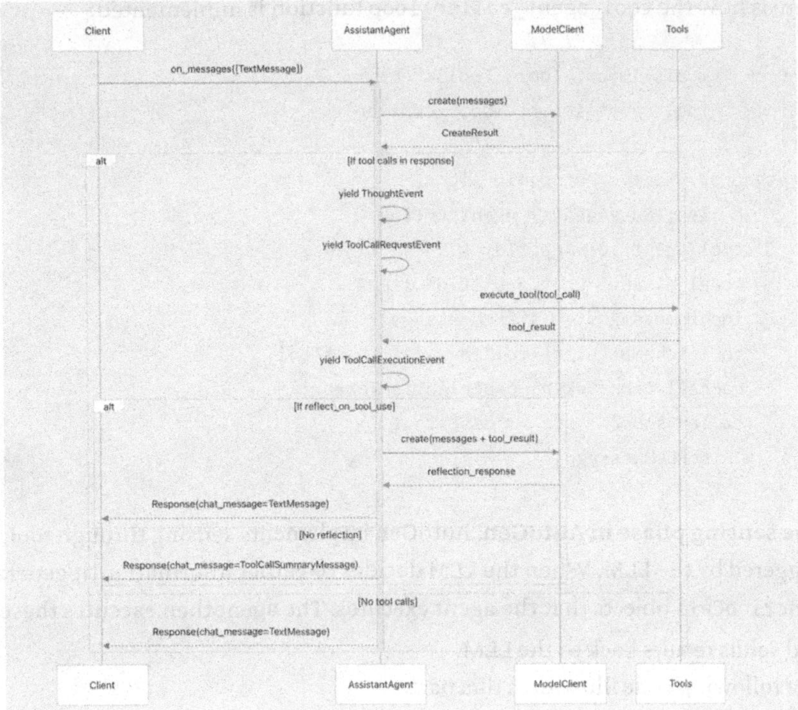

Figure 2.6: An overview of an AutoGen agent loop

Here is how this loop works:

1. First, a caller loop is started for a tool agent, `tool_agent_caller_loop()`. This function sends messages to the tool agent and the model client in an alternating fashion until the model client stops generating tool calls. The arguments are as follows:
    - `tool_agent_id (AgentId)`: The agent ID of the tool agent
    - `input_messages (List[LLMMessage])`: The list of input messages
    - `model_client (ChatCompletionClient)`: The model client to use for the model API
    - `tool_schema (List[Tool | ToolSchema])`: The list of tools that the model can use

   It returns `List[LLMMessage]` – the list of output messages created in the caller loop.

Here is how the `tool_agent_caller_loop` function is implemented:

```
from ..tools import Tool, ToolSchema
from ._tool_agent import ToolException

async def tool_agent_caller_loop(
    caller: BaseAgent | AgentRuntime,
    tool_agent_id: AgentId,
    model_client: ChatCompletionClient,
    input_messages: List[LLMMessage],
    tool_schema: List[ToolSchema] | List[Tool],
    cancellation_token: CancellationToken | None = None,
    caller_source: str = "assistant",
) -> List[LLMMessage]:
```

2. **The sensing phase in AutoGen**: AutoGen implements sensing through tool calls triggered by the LLM. When the LLM decides to gather information, it generates `FunctionCall` objects that the agent executes. The agent then executes these tool calls and sends results back to the LLM.
   The following code illustrates this part:

```
    generated_messages: List[LLMMessage] = []

    # Get a response from the model.
    response = await model_client.create(input_messages,
        tools=tool_schema, cancellation_token=cancellation_token,)

    # Add the response to the generated messages.
    generated_messages.append(
        AssistantMessage(
            content=response.content,
            source=caller_source
        )
    )

    # Keep iterating until the model stops generating tool calls.
    while (
        isinstance(response.content, list)
        and all(
            isinstance(item, FunctionCall)
```

```
            for item in response.content
        )
    ):
# Execute functions called by the model by sending messages to the tool
agent.
        results: List[FunctionExecutionResult | BaseException] = await
asyncio.gather(
            *[
                caller.send_message(
                    message=call, recipient=tool_agent_id,
                    cancellation_token=cancellation_token,
                )
                for call in response.content
            ],
            return_exceptions=True
        )

        # Combine the results into a single response and handle exceptions.
        function_results: List[FunctionExecutionResult] = []

        for result in results:
            if isinstance(result, FunctionExecutionResult):
                function_results.append(result)

            elif isinstance(result, ToolException):
                function_results.append(
                    FunctionExecutionResult(
                        content=f"Error: {result}",
                        call_id=result.call_id,
                    )
                )

            elif isinstance(result, BaseException):
                raise result  # Unexpected exception.

        generated_messages.append(
            FunctionExecutionResultMessage(content=function_results)
        )
```

3. **The thinking phase in AutoGen**: AutoGen confirms that thinking happens entirely within the LLM, and not as a separate phase on the AI framework side. The agent loop acts as a conduit by continuously calling the model client. The loop continues while the LLM returns tool calls, with all reasoning, planning, and decision-making delegated to the LLM itself. Here is how:

```
        # Query the model again with the new response.
        response = await model_client.create(
            input_messages + generated_messages, tools=tool_schema,
            cancellation_token=cancellation_token)
        generated_messages.append(AssistantMessage(
            content=response.content, source=caller_source))
    return generated_messages
```

4. **The acting phase in AutoGen**: Acting is implemented identically to sensing – through tool execution. The agent is "oblivious to the nature of the tool call," as described. Whether a tool reads data (sensing) or performs an action (acting), the implementation is the same. For more complex tool interactions, AutoGen provides a dedicated `tool_agent_caller_loop` function (`https://github.com/microsoft/autogen/blob/main/python/packages/autogen-core/src/autogen_core/tool_agent/_caller_loop.py`), which implements the complete sensing-thinking-acting cycle.

This function demonstrates the core loop: send message to LLM → receive tool calls → execute tools → send results back → repeat until no more tool calls.

Note

AutoGen supports the described multi-agent collaboration through handoffs, where one agent can launch or communicate with another agent. This is implemented through `HandoffMessage` (`https://github.com/microsoft/autogen/blob/main/python/packages/autogen-agentchat/src/autogen_agentchat/messages.py`) and the Swarm pattern, allowing agents to delegate tasks to specialized agents with their own agent loops.

- **HandOffMessage** is a message intended to transfer the conversation to another agent.
- **Swarm pattern** is a coordination strategy where multiple agents contribute to solving a task.

For an agentic system to retain context, it needs to have access to information that may enable its course of action. That's where memory, goals, and state come into play. Let's talk about them next.

Managing long conversations with memory, goals, and state

Agentic AI systems perform complex multi-step tasks over a potentially long period of time, interacting with humans, other systems, and other AI agents in a synchronous or asynchronous manner. As you are very aware at this point, all the thinking is done by the LLM, but the LLM has no memory (although chatbots such as ChatGPT have a long-term memory on top of the LLM; see `https://help.openai.com/en/articles/8590148-memory-faq`). This means that in every call to the LLM, we need to provide it with all the relevant information, which typically includes the entire history of the session so far, in addition to the latest user message or tool call response. Some LLM providers provide stateful long-term memory, which is injected into the LLM's context dynamically.

We will focus here on a single invocation of an agent that contains exactly one system message, one user message (AKA prompt), zero or more tool messages, and a single final response message from the LLM.

The general instructions for the agent are specified in the system message, which is typically a long text that describes the agent's capabilities, its role, some initial knowledge, output specifications, and examples. For example, the system message for a Python coding agent may look like this:

```
You are a Python programming expert and assistant. You write clean, idiomatic,
well-documented Python code and
explain your choices clearly and concisely when asked.
You can analyze requirements, debug code, refactor existing implementations, and
suggest improvements in architecture and style.
Always assume the user is technically competent but may not know the full details
of Python's standard library or idioms.
If a question is ambiguous, ask clarifying questions before proceeding.
When writing code, prefer clarity over cleverness, and add brief comments where
appropriate.
Output Python code inside triple backticks unless instructed otherwise.
You may use third-party libraries only if explicitly allowed or commonly accepted
(like requests, pandas, or numpy).
```

```
Follow best practices like writing unit tests and documenting your code following
PEP-257 conventions.
```

A long conversation with this agent may be broken down into several invocations of the agent loop, each with its own final response message. The thread of the conversation will be kept by the AI system, which will feed all the messages from the previous session into the next session.

For example, the user may request *Build me a calculator in Python* and the agent will respond with a clarifying question as a final response message: *Do you prefer a CLI program or a GUI application?*. The controlling AI system will present the question to the user, who may choose a CLI program. Now, a new invocation of the agent starts with all the history of the first session, as well as the user's choice of CLI program as the initial user message to the agent. Then, the new agent, having the information that the user prefers a CLI program, can start iterating with tool calls to generate and write code and tests until it is satisfied and return a final response such as *Done. The CLI program is called calc.py and the unit tests are in calc_test.py.*

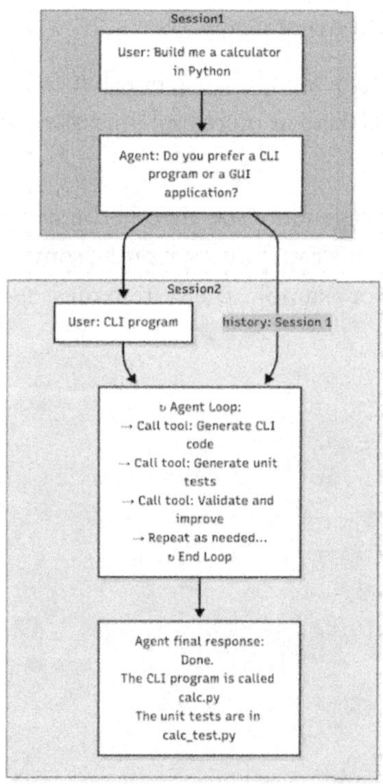

Figure 2.7: Multi-session conversation

Let's see how this is all represented in terms of the LLM context window.

The context window

The **context window** in a language model refers to the total amount of information the model can process and reason over during a single invocation. This includes not just text, but also other input modalities such as images, audio, structured data, or embeddings—depending on the model's capabilities. The context window really serves as the model's working memory, determining what information it can *see* and use to generate a response.

> Note
>
> RAG embeddings may be injected directly into the context window regardless of the encoding that all modalities go through.

Now, all the high-level concepts we have discussed so far, such as the agent memory, goals, and state, must eventually be represented as tokens and fit into the context window of each and every API request to the LLM.

When the LLM forms its response, it relies on its knowledge from training, which is encoded in the model weights. But all the information in the context window is immediately forgotten once the response from the model is generated. Note that the operators of the LLM may store this information for auditing, future training, or other purposes, but the model itself doesn't learn or retain any information from the context window. The only way to retain information across multiple invocations of the agent loop is to store it at the AI framework or AI system level and then feed it back into the context window of the next invocation.

> Note
>
> The LLM (models such as GPT 4o) doesn't manage user profiles. The LLM provider (e.g., OpenAI) may store user-specific information and inject it into the context window automatically in an interactive chat session, such as with ChatGPT. In this case, ChatGPT fulfills the role of the AI system that manages the memory.
>
> In agentic AI systems using AI frameworks, the interaction with the LLM is usually through dedicated API keys, and there is no user-level profile.

A larger context window enables more sophisticated behavior: longer conversations, richer inputs, more complete reasoning over prior steps, or detailed references to complex artifacts. A smaller window constrains the model's ability to maintain continuity, integrate context, or handle deeply nested tasks.

But, even with a large context window, you may run out of space for long conversations or complex tasks with large inputs and outputs. Each model has its own context window size, and it's important to take it into account when choosing which model to use. In such situations, you may need to truncate the conversation history, summarize it, or compress it in some form to fit into the context window. In multi-agent systems, you may also apply a divide-and-conquer approach where each agent is responsible for a specific sub-task and can dedicate the entire context window of the model for just its own sub-tasks, and only the results, which are typically smaller, are aggregated by a higher-level agent. We will cover this scenario in *Chapter 9*.

Why do LLMs have no memory?

But why can't the LLM just remember everything? Why does it need to be fed with all the context every time? The answer is complex and nuanced. First of all, there is no benefit in having a memory component in the LLM itself. What we're actually talking about is the LLM provider maintaining the state of each user's conversations (the history of all the messages) so the user can just send the latest message in each request.

The LLM provider can then add the latest message to the user's saved session and feed it to the LLM as a transient context window. So, the question is, why can't the LLM providers offer this service to users? In theory, it could save a lot of bandwidth because there is no need to send the entire history of a session in each request, only the delta of new messages.

However, at scale, you want multiple copies of each LLM running in parallel and able to handle a massive number of requests. If each LLM instance had its own memory, then you would need to keep session affinity between user requests and the LLM instance. In addition, there may be a delay between subsequent messages from the user. When the LLM provider manages the session's memory, it must maintain the state even when no messages are sent. That can add up quickly, especially for long-term sessions.

Let's look at an example: 10,000 users send, within 5 minutes, a total of 10 TB of data to the LLM provider. The LLM provider needs to store all this data in order to service additional messages from users. Deciding where to store this data is complicated (in memory, in a database, in a distributed cache). Whenever a user sends another message, the LLM provider needs to fetch the context for this user's conversation and inject it into the LLM. That is complicated and can introduce multiple failure modes and performance issues.

Finally, there is the issue of session termination. The LLM provider has two options: either keep the session state forever so users can continue the conversation at any point, or decide based on some heuristics when to erase the session's memory. In general, LLM providers prefer to keep the LLM stateless and let the AI frameworks or AI systems manage the session's state to improve scalability, reduce latency, and minimize costs.

Chatbots such as ChatGPT, Perplexity, and Claude.ai appear to have a long-term memory and can continue previous conversations. Here is an example where Claude.ai shows a list of previous conversations.

Figure 2.8: Sample conversation storage of the Claude.ai service

This is actually a feature of the AI system that manages the chatbot, not the LLM itself. Claude.ai is a web service that provides interactive chat services with Anthropic models. It stores all conversations in persistent storage, and it shows the list of previous conversations to the user. When the user selects a conversation, the Claude.ai service retrieves the stored conversation and feeds it as the initial message to the selected LLM (e.g., Claude Sonnet 4). The LLM itself always just has an ephemeral context window that is scoped to the current invocation. Some LLM providers, such as OpenAI, started experimenting with global long-term memory across all conversations with ChatGPT memory (`https://openai.com/index/memory-and-new-controls-for-chatgpt/`). A summary of all past conversations (users can opt in and out of long-term memory) is fed to every invocation, so it appears that the model remembers all your past interactions.

For a real-life implementation, let's see how memory is implemented in the AutoGen framework (`https://github.com/microsoft/autogen`).

Memory in AutoGen

Surprisingly, AutoGen doesn't provide memory facilities at the core level of its architecture. Memory is supported at the higher abstraction level of chat agents. There are three types of memory:

1. **Simple sequential list memory**: AutoGen defines an abstract memory protocol for simple sequential list memory with operations such as `add()`, `query()`, `update_context()`, `clear()`, and `close()`. For example, an agent that returns the current weather may use the memory to store the user's temperature unit preferences ("imperial versus "metric") and respond accordingly to user queries. In the context of interaction with the LLM, the content of the memory is added to the context window.
2. **Vector-based RAG memory**: AutoGen supports more complex memory stores that implement the memory protocol too. AutoGen provides, out of the box, an extension that implements vector-based RAG memory in the `ChromaDBVectorMemory` class (`https://github.com/microsoft/autogen/blob/main/python/packages/autogen-ext/src/autogen_ext/memory/chromadb/_chromadb.py`).
3. **Task-centric fast memory (experimental)**: The experimental task-centric fast memory is implemented in `MemoryController`. It doesn't use the memory protocol and is still an active research project within AutoGen. Its goals are as follows:
    - Accomplish general tasks more effectively by learning quickly and continually beyond context-window limitations
    - Remember guidance, corrections, plans, and demonstrations provided by users
    - Learn through the agent's own experience and adapt quickly to changing circumstances
    - Avoid repeating mistakes on tasks that are similar to those previously encountered

They are all used in the `AssistantAgent` class, which is the main class for implementing chat agents in AutoGen.

We will now move our focus to the planning and reasoning mechanisms of LLMs.

Planning and reasoning mechanisms

As you might recall, all planning and reasoning in agentic AI systems is done by the LLM. However, the AI framework can still structure the interaction with the LLM to facilitate orchestrated planning and reasoning. In this section, we will look at different methods for planning and reasoning in agentic AI systems, including single-agent and multi-agent planning, as well as working with reasoning models.

Working with reasoning models

LLM providers now offer reasoning models that are specifically designed for complex multi-step reasoning tasks (see the following figure):

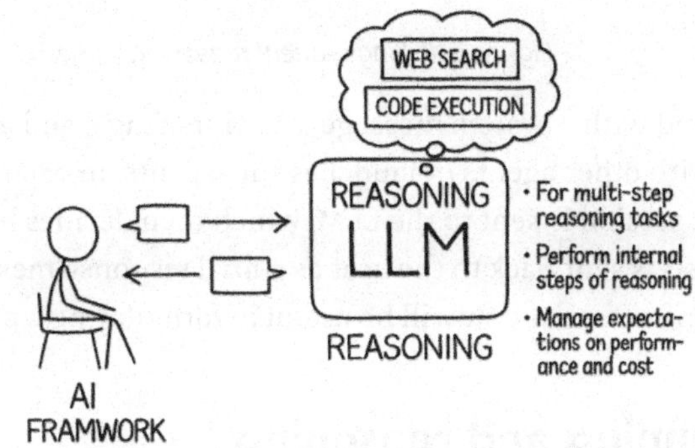

Figure 2.9: Working with reasoning models

This means that in a single request, these models may perform multiple steps of reasoning and use internal tools such as web search and code execution that don't require interacting with the AI framework or the user. For example, OpenAI's o-series models (o3, o4-mini) take more time (and tokens), and in effect run their own internal agent loop. These models may still invoke external tools when necessary, but the thinking phase on the LLM side is more involved. From the AI framework's perspective, there isn't much of a difference between using a reasoning model and a regular LLM. But it's important to manage user expectations regarding performance, latency, and cost.

Single-agent planning and reasoning

Single-agent planning and reasoning is the simplest form in agentic AI systems. The following diagram illustrates this:

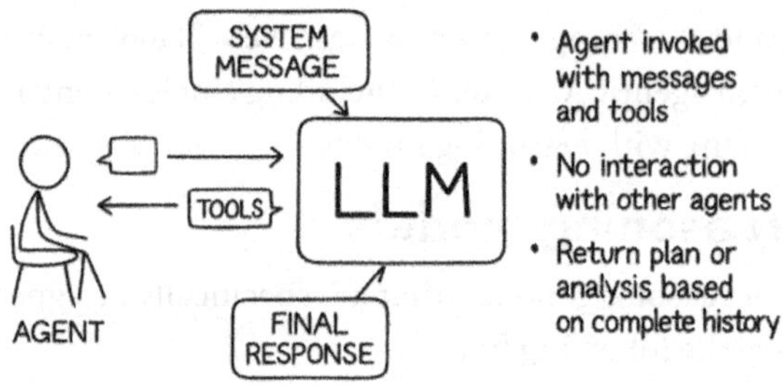

Figure 2.10: Single-agent reasoning

The agent loop is invoked with a system message, a user message, and a set of tools. The agent never communicates with other agents or launches sub-agents. In each request to the LLM, the complete history of the session is sent to the LLM, which then decides how to continue. The resulting plan or analysis is sent back to the user as a final response message. The agent may invoke tools to gather information that will be useful in formulating a plan or reasoning about the input data.

Multi-agent planning and reasoning

In multi-agent systems, planning and reasoning are more complex. The top-level agent may invoke additional sub-agents or communicate with already running agents. Note that the decision to invoke a sub-agent or communicate with another agent is itself the result of planning by the LLM invoked by the top-level agent, which results in a tool call, where the tool execution results in launching a sub-agent or sending a message to another agent.

The interactions between agents in multi-agent systems introduce several layers of interaction that don't exist in single-agent scenarios. When a parent agent delegates work to a sub-agent, it must carefully craft the sub-agent's context, including the system prompt, initial goals, available tools, and any relevant background information from the parent's session.

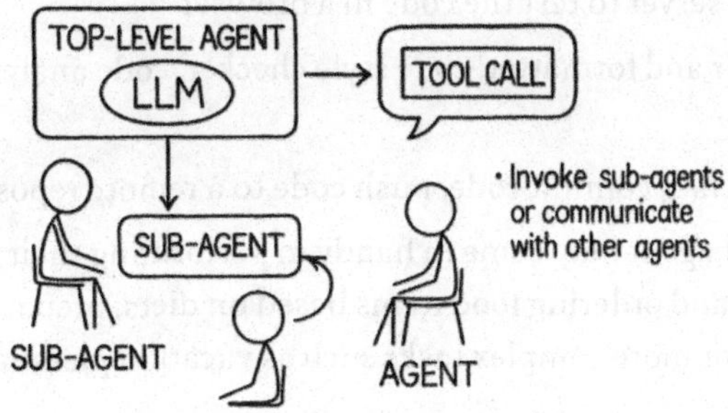

Figure 2.11: Multi-agent reasoning

The parent agent also needs to decide whether to wait synchronously for the sub-agent's completion or to continue processing other tasks asynchronously while monitoring the sub-agent's progress. Communication protocols become crucial when agents need to exchange information during execution – agents may need to negotiate, coordinate shared resources, resolve conflicts, or aggregate results from multiple parallel sub-agents. Additionally, error handling and recovery strategies become more sophisticated, as failures in one agent can cascade through the system, requiring parent agents to detect failures, retry with different parameters, or dynamically reassign tasks to alternative agents. The context window limitations of individual agents also create challenges for information sharing, as agents must decide which information to pass between each other, potentially requiring summarization or selective filtering of large conversation histories.

Tool use and environment interactions

Managing tools is the primary responsibility of the AI framework. The LLM drives everything by doing the actual planning and reasoning, but for many tasks, the agent needs to interact with the environment, which is done through the available tools. The list of tools that the agent makes available to the LLM defines the capabilities of the agent.

Agents may be super helpful in increasing productivity, automating mundane tasks, summarizing emails, and running regular checks in a work environment.

Consider, for example, an AI software engineer agent. In order to be effective, it requires tools to perform tasks such as the following:

- List files and directories
- Read, create, edit, and delete files
- Run unit tests and integration tests
- Run the code in a sandbox environment (e.g., Docker container)

- Run a local web server to test the code in a browser
- Run a code linter and formatter, code style checker, code analyzer, code security scanner
- Create Git branches, commit code, push code to a remote repository

For a regular user, an AI agent may come in handy in performing their day-to-day activities, such as meal-planning and ordering food items based on diets, preparing and buying groceries at scheduled intervals, or more complex tasks such as vacation planning that require several steps.

Take, for example, an AI vacation planner agent. In order to be effective, it requires tools to perform tasks such as the following:

- Search for flights and compare prices across different airlines and dates
- Find and book accommodation (hotels, vacation rentals, hostels)
- Research local attractions, restaurants, and activities at the destination
- Check visa requirements and travel restrictions for different countries
- Access real-time weather forecasts and seasonal travel information
- Calculate travel budgets and track expenses across different categories
- Make restaurant reservations and book tours or experiences
- Access the user's calendar to identify available travel dates and duration constraints
- Send confirmation emails and create itinerary documents with booking details

It doesn't matter how powerful the LLM is, if it doesn't have the tools to interact with the environment, it will not be able to be an effective software engineer or vacation planner. The most the AI software engineer will be able to do is generate code based on a prompt, which can be very helpful, but is just a part of the overall software development lifecycle. For example, if the vacation planner doesn't have permission to book reservations, it can recommend a vacation but will not be able to assist in bookings and reservations.

Let's dive deeper into how tools are implemented, declared, and used in agentic AI systems, with a focus on AutoGen.

How are user-defined tools implemented?

There are two categories of tools in agentic AI systems: built-in tools and user-defined tools. Built-in tools such as `web_search`, `code_execution`, `file_search`, and `computer_use` are implemented by LLM providers. User-defined tools are functions that can be implemented in any programming language and are typically implemented in the same language as the agentic AI framework. However, they can also be implemented in a different language and exposed to the agentic AI framework as a Docker container or through some internal API.

Here is an example of a user-defined tool to add two numbers in Python:

```
def add_numbers(a: int, b: int) -> int:
    """
    Adds two numbers and returns the result.

    Args:
        a (int): The first number.
        b (int): The second number.

    Returns:
        int: The sum of the two numbers.
    """
    return a + b
```

That's right. It's just a regular Python function. The agentic AI framework will take this function and expose it as a tool. We will cover this in detail in *Chapters 3*, *4*, and *5*.

How are tools declared?

LLM providers such as OpenAI, Anthropic, Mistral, and Google expose an API to interact with their models. Many other providers offer OpenAI-compatible APIs. These APIs are pretty similar and allow you to declare a separate list of tools in every call.

Here is the classic example of a tool declaration in the OpenAI API:

```
curl https://api.openai.com/v1/responses \
  -H "Content-Type: application/json" \
  -H "Authorization: Bearer $OPENAI_API_KEY" \
  -d '{
    "model": "gpt-4.1",
    "input": "What is the weather like in Paris today?",
    "tools": [
      {
        "type": "function",
        "name": "get_weather",
        "description": "Get current temperature for a given location.",
        "parameters": {
          "type": "object",
          "properties": {
            "location": {
              "type": "string",
```

```
            "description": "City and country e.g. Bogotá, Colombia"
          }
        },
        "required": [
          "location"
        ],
        "additionalProperties": false
      }
    }
  ]
}'
```

AI agents have a well-defined scope and a set of tools to perform their tasks. Every request that the agentic AI framework sends to the LLM on behalf of a specific AI agent will include the list of tools that the agent has. Different agents may have different tools. The LLM that receives a set of tools from the agent may request to invoke a tool in the form of a tool message that the AI framework handles, executes the requested tool, and returns the result to the LLM.

How does the LLM decide which tool to use?

There are several layers of abstraction here. The agentic AI framework often supports multiple LLM providers, each with its own API and tool declaration format. The framework abstracts these differences and provides a unified interface for declaring tools. When the agentic AI framework sends a request to a particular LLM provider, it translates the request, including the tool list, to the format expected by the LLM provider's API.

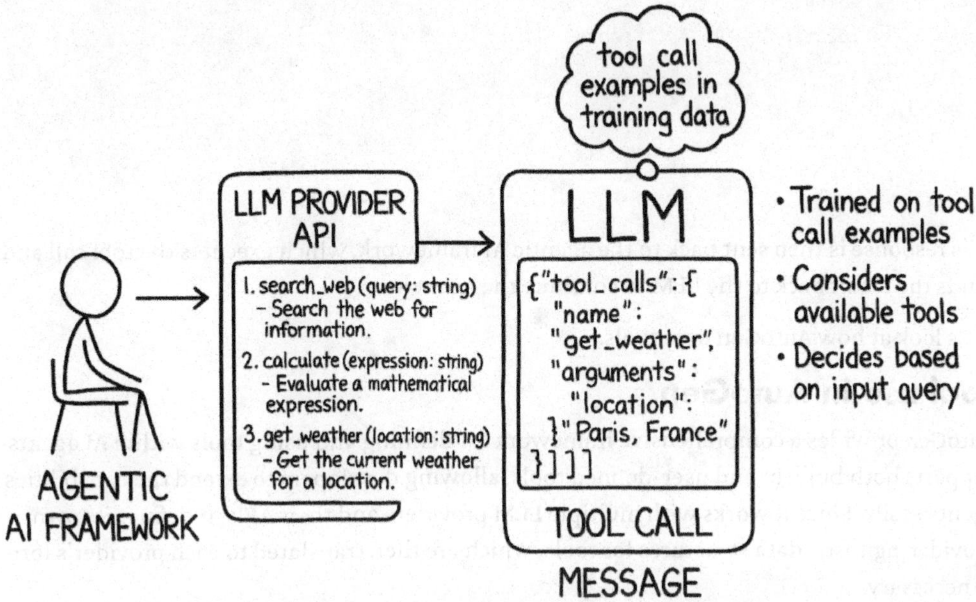

Figure 2.12: An agentic framework calling the get_weather tool

When the LLM provider receives the structured request with the list of tools, it generates a textual representation such as the following:

```
You can call the following tools:
1. search_web(query: string) - Search the web for information.
2. calculate(expression: string) - Evaluate a mathematical expression.
3. get_weather(location: string) - Get the current weather for a location.
```

This text is converted to a stream of tokens that are fed into the LLM, which doesn't know or care about API request structure (this is for developers). The LLM was trained on a large corpus of text that includes examples of tool calls and their usage. When the LLM receives the textual request with the tool list, it can recognize the tools and their parameters based on this training. The LLM then decides which tool to use based on the input query and the available tools. It will generate a tool call message in a structured format that the LLM provider API layer receives and formats to a proper response with a tool call, such as the following:

```
{
  "tool_calls": [
    {
      "name": "get_weather",
```

```
        "arguments": {
          "location": "Paris, France"
        }
      }
    ]
  }
```

This response is then sent back to the agentic AI framework, which executes the tool call and sends the result back to the LLM to continue the agent loop.

Let's look at how AutoGen uses tools.

Tool use in AutoGen

AutoGen provides a comprehensive framework for defining and using tools within AI agents. It supports both built-in and user-defined tools, allowing developers to extend the capabilities of agents easily. Since it works with multiple LLM providers and their APIs, it defines its own provider-agnostic data structures for tools, which are then translated to each provider's format as necessary.

Let's look at an AutoGen sample of chess-playing agents and see how they use tools. The black player agent has the following tools:

```
black_tools: List[Tool] = [
    FunctionTool(
        get_legal_moves_black,
        name="get_legal_moves",
        description="Get legal moves.",
    ),
    FunctionTool(
        make_move_black,
        name="make_move",
        description="Make a move.",
    ),
    FunctionTool(
        get_board_text,
        name="get_board",
        description="Get the current board state.",
    ),
]
```

Each of the function tools is a Python function/method, such as the following:

```
async def chess_game(
    runtime: AgentRuntime,
    model_client: ChatCompletionClient,  # type: ignore
) -> None:
    """
    Create agents for a chess game and return the group chat.
    """

    # Create the board.
    board = Board()

    # Create tools for each player.
    def get_legal_moves_black() -> str:
        return get_legal_moves(board, "black")
```

The tools are then registered with `ToolAgent` (`https://github.com/microsoft/autogen/blob/main/python/packages/autogen-core/src/autogen_core/tool_agent/_tool_agent.py`):

```
# Register the agents.
await ToolAgent.register(
    runtime,
    "PlayerBlackToolAgent",
    lambda: ToolAgent(
        description="Tool agent for chess game.",
        tools=black_tools,
    ),
)
```

When tools are registered, the LLM gains the ability to invoke these tools in its response messages.

`ToolAgent` is a specialized agent in AutoGen core that receives `FunctionCall` messages, executes the requested tools with provided arguments, and returns `FunctionExecutionResult` messages. It's typically used as a dedicated tool executor that other agents can delegate function calls to, providing error handling when a tool is not found, invalid arguments, and execution failures.

Then, the black player agent is registered (there is a similar white player agent too). Note the instructions to play as "black" and use the provided tools.

```
await PlayerAgent.register(
    runtime,
    "PlayerBlack",
    lambda: PlayerAgent(
        description="Player playing black.",
        instructions=(
            "You are a chess player and you play as black. "
            "Use the tool 'get_board' and
'get_legal_moves' to get the legal moves "
            "and 'make_move' to make a move."
        ),
        model_client=model_client,
        model_context=BufferedChatCompletionContext(buffer_size=10),
        tool_schema=[tool.schema for tool in black_tools],
        tool_agent_type="PlayerBlackToolAgent",
    ),
)
```

The AutoGen agent loop will send a request to the LLM with the list of tools, and the LLM will decide which tool to use at the appropriate time. The idea here is that while the LLM is making the decisions about the next step, the expectation is that it will need to get the current board state in order to decide. The `get_legal_moves()` tool is arguably not necessary, because if the LLM is expected to know chess well enough to pick the next best move, then it should be smart enough to only pick legal moves.

Agent evaluation and feedback loops

One of the key aspects of agentic AI systems is the ability to evaluate the performance of agents and provide a path of improvement. This is especially important in multi-agent systems where agents may collaborate or compete with each other, and small mistakes and inaccuracies can accumulate, leading to suboptimal results or even the failure of the entire workflow. There are several ways to evaluate agents, including the following: human feedback, automated evaluation, and industry benchmarks.

Some methods of evaluation can be performed automatically, and while the system is running, other methods that involve human feedback or take too long can be used offline to improve the performance of future agents.

Let's look at each of these methods in more detail.

Human feedback

Human feedback plays a critical role in shaping the behavior and quality of agentic AI systems. Unlike automated evaluations that rely on predefined rules or metrics, human feedback captures subjective elements such as helpfulness, tone, clarity, and user satisfaction. This is particularly valuable in open-ended tasks such as creative writing, decision-making, or user assistance—where rigid evaluation criteria fall short. Users may provide direct feedback by rating responses, flagging incorrect actions, or selecting preferred outputs. Alternatively, implicit feedback can be gathered from user behavior, such as whether they continue engaging with the agent or abandon a task prematurely.

Either way, agentic AI frameworks typically don't provide mechanisms for collecting human feedback. Developers of AI systems should build human feedback support at the application level.

In more structured environments, feedback can be solicited from domain experts who evaluate the agent's performance on specific criteria. For instance, in a coding assistant agent, developers might assess the quality of the generated code, the usefulness of explanations, and the correctness of debugging steps. This expert feedback can be used to refine prompts, curate better examples, and adjust the agent's toolset. Note that this is different from **reinforcement learning from human feedback** (**RLHF**) pipelines, which are used in training LLMs to better align future behavior with human preferences. The focus here is on the improvement of the AI agent's performance as opposed to the underlying LLM. It is possible to have a self-improving AI system that collects human feedback, analyzes it, and uses it to improve itself or other AI agents.

Human feedback is especially vital in multi-agent systems, where coordination, delegation, and communication dynamics come into play. Here, feedback may not only assess individual agents but also how well agents collaborate or divide responsibilities. Annotators or end users can comment on breakdowns in communication, misaligned goals, or inefficient task execution. This feedback helps identify systemic issues and provides data to reconfigure agents for better synergy. Although slower and more resource-intensive than automated methods, human feedback is indispensable for evaluating nuanced behavior and fostering trust in real-world deployments:

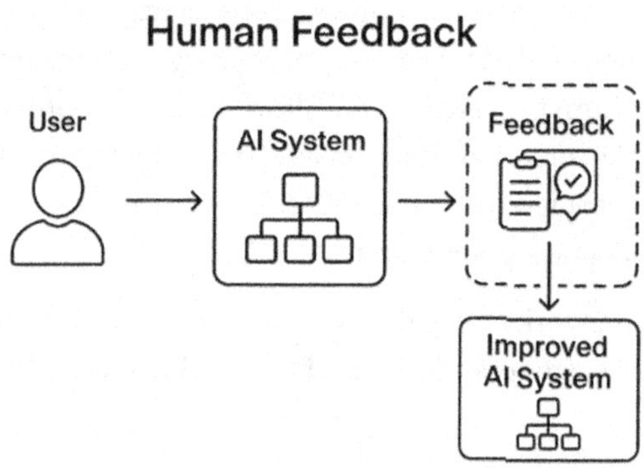

Figure 2.13: Human feedback

Human feedback works well in conjunction with other evaluation methods, such A/B testing, and can be used to cross-check automated evaluations too.

Automated evaluation

Automated evaluation methods provide a scalable way to assess agent performance without human intervention. Automated evaluation works best when the result of a task is well known. For example, if the agent is asked to generate the result in a certain format, such as a CSV file, it is easy to verify if the output is indeed a CSV file.

We can also take advantage of LLM technology and use LLMs to evaluate the output of an AI agent against its original goal. In a hierarchical multi-agent system, this can be done at different levels. Moreover, it offers the possibility of addressing issues on the fly.

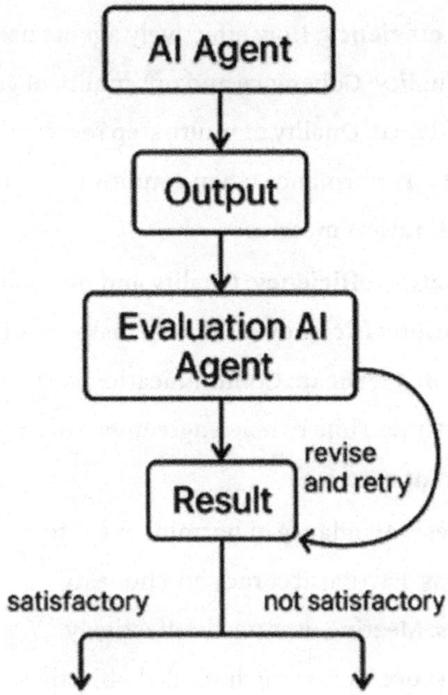

Figure 2.14: Evaluation of an agentic system

For example, a parent AI agent launches multiple sub-agents to perform sub-tasks. It then uses an evaluation AI agent to evaluate the results of sub-tasks and if they are not satisfactory, it can run the sub-agent again, possibly with a different prompt or configuration. The results of such live evaluations should be logged and used to improve the performance of future agents, so there is less of a need to fix live problems.

Agentic AI evaluation involves assessing end-to-end task success through metrics such as completion rate, trajectory quality, and tool accuracy, while breaking down components such as planning, reasoning, and self-correction via traces and simulations. This process uses benchmarks (e.g., SWE-Bench, TRAIL), LLM-as-judge scoring, and production monitoring to ensure reliability, iterating on failures with layered human and automated checks

Here are some of the standard metrics and scores used to evaluate agentic AI systems:

- **Task performance metrics**
    - **Success rate**: Percentage of tasks completed successfully
    - **Task completion time**: Average time to complete tasks
    - **Accuracy**: Correctness of outputs/decisions
    - **Precision/recall/F1**: For classification and retrieval tasks

- **Agent behavior metrics**
    - **Tool usage efficiency**: How effectively agents use available tools
    - **Planning quality**: Coherence and optimality of generated plans
    - **Reasoning depth**: Quality of multi-step reasoning chains
    - **Adaptability**: Performance when conditions change
- **Multi-agent coordination metrics**
    - **Communication efficiency**: Quality and necessity of agent interactions
    - **Task allocation efficiency**: How well tasks are distributed
    - **Coordination overhead**: Communication cost versus benefit
    - **Consensus time**: Time to reach agreement in collaborative tasks
- **Safety and alignment metrics**
    - **Harmlessness**: Avoidance of harmful outputs
    - **Truthfulness**: Factual accuracy and honesty
    - **Helpfulness**: Meeting user needs effectively
    - **Alignment score**: Following intended objectives versus reward hacking
- **Robustness metrics**
    - **Adversarial robustness**: Performance under attack scenarios
    - **Distribution shift tolerance**: Performance on out-of-distribution data
    - **Error recovery**: Ability to recover from failures
    - **Hallucination rate**: Frequency of generating false information
- **Efficiency metrics**
    - **Computational cost**: Resources used per task
    - **Token efficiency**: Output quality per token consumed
    - **Latency**: Response time for real-time applications
    - **Scalability**: Performance degradation with system size

We will explore evaluation metrics more in *Chapter 10*.

Implementing all of the evaluation metrics is a substantial effort that requires many engineering years. See `https://www.getmaxim.ai/articles/evaluating-agentic-workflows-the-essential-metrics-that-matter/`. Let's look at industry benchmarks now.

Industry benchmarks

Industry benchmarks are standardized tests or tasks that agents can be evaluated against. These benchmarks provide an objective way to measure the performance of an AI agent or a complete agentic AI system. Comparing the performance of your agentic AI system against **SOTA (state of the art)** can provide a signal if you have a lot of low-hanging fruit or if the performance is already close to optimal. However, benchmarks are often designed for specific tasks or domains, and the overlap with your agentic AI system's use case may be limited. Here are some common industry benchmarks:

- **AgentBench**: `AgentBench` (`https://github.com/THUDM/AgentBench`) is a comprehensive benchmark designed to evaluate the general capabilities of LLM-based agents across a variety of tasks. It focuses on real-world agent tasks such as web browsing, math problem solving, and embodied decision-making to test reasoning, memory, and tool use.
- **ToolBench**: `ToolBench` (`https://github.com/OpenBMB/ToolBench`) provides a suite of datasets and evaluation protocols for training and assessing LLMs that can call external tools. It emphasizes tool-use capabilities, measuring how well an agent can invoke APIs or functions to accomplish complex tasks beyond text generation.
- **WebArena**: `WebArena` (`https://webarena.dev/`) is a realistic, open-ended web environment where agents can be evaluated on their ability to navigate and interact with dynamic websites. It offers a browser-based setting for benchmarking goal completion, planning, and handling noisy or unexpected layouts.
- **Mind2Web**: `Mind2Web` (`https://osu-nlp-group.github.io/Mind2Web/`) is a benchmark for evaluating agents on their ability to perform user-specified tasks on websites using human-like reasoning and planning. It simulates diverse web-based tasks and provides annotations for goals, subgoals, and reasoning chains to assess interpretability and robustness.

Benchmarks are useful to compare agentic AI systems in particular domains and tasks, but it is even more important to understand the goals and intentions of your users and customers. For example, your system may score lower on a particular benchmark but run much faster and at a lower cost, which may be a better value proposition.

Summary

In this chapter, we took a deep dive into the operational flow of agentic AI systems driven by large language models. We introduced the core agent loop – sense, think, act – and illustrated how it operates in frameworks such as AutoGen, where the LLM dictates the agent's behavior through tool calls. We explored how agents use memory, goals, and state management within the constraints of the LLM's context window, and how these responsibilities are handled by the surrounding AI framework or system.

We also examined the importance of planning and reasoning mechanisms, both in single-agent and multi-agent systems. With the rise of specialized reasoning models and the growing complexity of agent workflows, structuring interactions and decomposing tasks become essential for robust behavior. Then, we turned our attention to tool use, which is a critical enabler of agentic capability. After all, even the most intelligent LLM can observe or impact the outside world only as far as its tools reach.

Finally, we looked at evaluation and feedback. These mechanisms allow agentic AI systems to improve over time. We covered both human and automated feedback strategies and reviewed standardized benchmarks that allow for objective comparison across systems. These practices are essential not only for improving the performance of individual agents but also for debugging, compliance, trustworthiness, and long-term system evolution.

Overall, the concepts and patterns described in this chapter form the operational backbone of modern agentic AI. As the field matures, the sophistication of these components will continue to grow, but the core principles, which include clear agent loops, transparent tool use, context-aware reasoning, precise memory management, and systematic evaluation, will remain foundational.

In the next chapter, we will take it all the way down to the code level and examine, in great detail, the implementation of a simple yet full-fledged agentic AI system that operates as an AI Kubernetes engineer.

Subscribe for a free eBook

New frameworks, evolving architectures, research drops, production breakdowns – *AI_Distilled* filters the noise into a weekly briefing for engineers and researchers working hands-on with LLMs and generative AI systems. Subscribe now and receive a free eBook, along with weekly insights that help you stay focused and informed.

Subscribe at `https://packt.link/8Oz6Y` or scan the QR code below.

3

A Hands-On Walk-Through of a Simple AI Agent

In *Chapter 2*, we explored the foundational concepts of AI agents, their architecture, components, and how they interact with tools and external systems. We also discussed how these principles, such as the agentic loop and memory, are implemented in the popular AutoGen (`https://github.com/microsoft/autogen`) framework. In this chapter, we will build on that knowledge by dissecting a simple AI agent, k8s-ai, that can interact with a Kubernetes cluster one line at a time. The power of AI agents with tool access will become evident as we walk through the code and understand exactly how an agent loop works. And combining this simple agent with a tool to access Kubernetes will demonstrate how even such a basic setup can be very capable.

We will set the stage by introducing the k8s-ai agent and showcasing its capabilities by running it and interacting with it through a chat interface. Once you have experienced the agentic capabilities of k8s-ai, we will explain how the agentic system works under the hood.

In this chapter, we will cover the following main topics:

- Introducing k8s-ai
- Understanding the k8s-ai agentic system

Technical requirements

Ensure you have kubectl, Docker, and kind installed on your machine. If you don't have them installed, follow the installation instructions here:

- Kubectl installation instructions (`https://kubernetes.io/docs/tasks/tools/`)
- Docker installation instructions (`https://docs.docker.com/engine/install/`)
- kind installation instructions (`https://kind.sigs.k8s.io/docs/user/quickstart/#installation`)

Briefly, here's why we need these:

- **kubectl** is the command-line tool used to interact with and manage Kubernetes clusters by sending commands to the Kubernetes API server.
- **Docker** is a container platform that packages applications and their dependencies into lightweight, portable containers that run consistently across different environments.
- **Kubernetes in Docker (KinD)** is a tool for running local Kubernetes clusters using Docker containers as the cluster nodes, mainly for development and testing.

You should use the latest version when you read the chapter.

If you want to follow along with the code examples in this chapter, ensure you have Python (`https://www.python.org/downloads/`) installed.

You'll also need an OpenAI API key, which you can obtain from the OpenAI platform: `https://platform.openai.com/api-keys`.

You can follow the instructions in README.md (`https://github.com/PacktPublishing/Design-Multi-Agent-AI-Systems-Using-MCP-and-A2A/blob/main/ch03/k8s-ai/README.md`) or (`https://github.com/the-gigi/k8s-ai/blob/main/README.md`) to get your k8s-ai agent up and running.

Introducing the k8s-ai agent

The **k8s-ai agent** (`https://github.com/the-gigi/k8s-ai`) is a simple AI agent implemented in a single Python file and can interact with a **Kubernetes** (`https://kubernetes.io/`) cluster via the **kubectl** (`https://kubernetes.io/docs/reference/kubectl/`) tool. If you're not familiar with Kubernetes, it's not a big deal. In one sentence, it is an open source system for automating the deployment, scaling, and management of containerized applications. The kubectl tool is the command-line interface for interacting with Kubernetes clusters.

Before diving in, let's take it for a ride and see what it can do.

Setting up a local kind cluster

Let's start by setting up a local Kubernetes cluster using kind (`https://kind.sigs.k8s.io/`). Kind is a tool for running Kubernetes clusters in Docker containers. It is ideal for local development and testing.

We can create a local Kubernetes cluster using kind. Run the following command to create a cluster named `k8s-ai`:

```
> kind create cluster -n k8s-ai
Creating cluster "k8s-ai" ...
 ✓ Ensuring node image (kindest/node:v1.33.1)
 ✓ Preparing nodes 📦
 ✓ Writing configuration 📜
 ✓ Starting control-plane
 ✓ Installing CNI 🔌
 ✓ Installing StorageClass 💾
Set kubectl context to "kind-k8s-ai"
You can now use your cluster with:

kubectl cluster-info --context kind-k8s-ai

Have a nice day! 👋
```

Let's verify the cluster is up and running:

```
kubectl cluster-info --context kind-k8s-ai
```

The Kubernetes control plane is running at `https://127.0.0.1:52864`.

`CoreDNS` is running at `https://127.0.0.1:52864/api/v1/namespaces/kube-system/services/kube-dns:dns/proxy`.

To further debug and diagnose cluster problems, use `kubectl cluster-info dump`.

Great! We have a local Kubernetes cluster up and running. Now, let's cause some trouble in the cluster. Here is a deployment that will never be ready because it requires its pods to be scheduled on a node with a label that doesn't exist in the cluster:

```
echo '
apiVersion: apps/v1
kind: Deployment
```

```
metadata:
  name: some-app
spec:
  replicas: 3
  selector:
    matchLabels:
      app: some-app
  template:
    metadata:
      labels:
        app: some-app
    spec:
      affinity:
        nodeAffinity:
          requiredDuringSchedulingIgnoredDuringExecution:
            nodeSelectorTerms:
              - matchExpressions:
                  - key: no-such-node
                    operator: In
                    values:
                      - "true"
      containers:
        - name: pause
          image: registry.k8s.io/pause:3.9
' | kubectl apply -f -

deployment.apps/some-app created
```

Let's confirm that all the pods were created, but they are all pending because of the label requirement:

```
kubectl get po

NAME                          READY   STATUS    RESTARTS   AGE
some-app-65696dbff4-8jdrj     0/1     Pending   0          6s
some-app-65696dbff4-mbfv7     0/1     Pending   0          6s
some-app-65696dbff4-wj9ms     0/1     Pending   0          6s
```

We can even see the exact reason why the pods are pending (`1 node(s) didn't match Pod's node affinity/selector.`) by checking the status of one of the pods:

```
kubectl get po some-app-65696dbff4-8jdrj -o yaml | grep status: -A 10

status:
  conditions:
  - lastProbeTime: null
    lastTransitionTime: "2025-06-05T08:45:45Z"
    message: '0/1 nodes are available: 1 node(s) didn''t match Pod''s node
affinity/selector.
      preemption: 0/1 nodes are available: 1 Preemption is not helpful for
scheduling.'
    reason: Unschedulable
    status: "False"
    type: PodScheduled
  phase: Pending
  qosClass: BestEffort
```

Let's cause some more havoc and create a deployment for NGINX (a popular web server) with an invalid image name (nnnnnnnnginx):

```
echo '
apiVersion: apps/v1
kind: Deployment
metadata:
  name: nginx
spec:
  replicas: 1
  selector:
    matchLabels:
      app: nginx
  template:
    metadata:
      labels:
        app: nginx
    spec:
      containers:
        - name: nginx
          image: nnnnnnnnginx
' | kubectl apply -f -
```

```
deployment.apps/nginx created
```

Let's check the status of our cluster now:

```
kubectl get po
NAME                           READY   STATUS             RESTARTS   AGE
nginx-74f5dd8d8f-p2hmh         0/1     ImagePullBackOff   0          91s
some-app-65696dbff4-8jdrj      0/1     Pending            0          9m3s
some-app-65696dbff4-mbfv7      0/1     Pending            0          9m3s
some-app-65696dbff4-wj9ms      0/1     Pending            0          9m3s
```

We have two deployments: **some-app** and **nginx**. The **some-app** deployment has three pending pods, and the **nginx** deployment has one pod in an error state due to an invalid image name. Now, let's see how we can use the k8s-ai agent to help us with this situation.

Running the k8s-ai agent

First, you need to clone the k8s-ai repository:

```
git clone git@github.com:the-gigi/k8s-ai.git
```

Follow the instructions in the `README.md` (`https://github.com/PacktPublishing/Design-Multi-Agent-AI-Systems-Using-MCP-and-A2A/blob/main/ch03/k8s-ai/README.md`) to run and interact with k8s-ai.

After activating the virtual environment, just run the agent with the following command:

```
python main.py
```

You will see the following output and you can start interacting with the agent:

```
 Interactive Kubernetes Chat. Type 'exit' to quit.
----------------------------------------------------
👤 You:
```

K8s-ai is running and ready for interaction. Let's check our cluster via natural language conversation.

Checking the cluster with k8s-ai

All the foundation models were trained extensively on Kubernetes knowledge, including on the kubectl CLI, and therefore should be able to meaningfully interact with our Kubernetes cluster.

Alright, let's ask the agent about our Kubernetes cluster:

```
👤 You: what's going on in the cluster?
🤖 AI: Here's a summary of the current state of the cluster:

### Pods

- **default namespace:**
    - `nginx-74f5dd8d8f-p2hmh`: Not ready, experiencing `ImagePullBackOff`,
running for 6 hours and 27 minutes.
    - `some-app` instances (3 pods): All pending for 37 hours.

- **kube-system namespace:**
    - Core system components (e.g., `coredns`, `etcd`, `kube-apiserver`, `kube-
controller-manager`, etc.) are running
      smoothly.

- **local-path-storage namespace:**
    - `local-path-provisioner`: Running smoothly.

### Services

- `kubernetes`: ClusterIP service.
- `kube-dns`: ClusterIP service in the `kube-system` namespace.

### DaemonSets

- `kindnet` and `kube-proxy` are running in the `kube-system` namespace.

### Deployments

- **default namespace:**
    - `nginx`: Deployment not available due to `ImagePullBackOff`.
    - `some-app`: No pods are ready.

- **kube-system namespace:**
    - `coredns`: 100% ready.
```

```
- **local-path-storage namespace:**
  - `local-path-provisioner`: 100% ready.

### ReplicaSets

- The `nginx` and `some-app` ReplicaSets in the `default` namespace have issues
due to readiness, likely tied to their
  pods' issues.
- Other ReplicaSets under `kube-system` and `local-path-storage` are scaled as
expected and operational.

### Observations

- The `nginx` and `some-app` deployments are facing
issues. `nginx` is failing due to an image pull issue which could be
  a configuration problem or a registry access issue.
- The `some-app` deployment may be facing resource constraints or unsatisfied
scheduling rules causing the pods to be
  pending.

Would you like assistance in addressing any specific issues?
----------
```

That's pretty cool! The agent has provided a detailed summary of the cluster's state, including the status of pods, services, deployments, and more. It has also identified the issues with the **nginx** and **some-app** deployments.

Let's drill down some more and see if it can identify the exact root cause of the pending pods:

```
👤 You: find out why the some-app pods are pending
🤖 AI: The "some-app" pods are in a "Pending" state because they cannot be
scheduled. Specifically, the issue is that:

- The pod couldn't be scheduled due to node affinity or selector requirements not
being met. The error message indicates that there are no nodes available that
match the pod's node affinity or selector.

- The scheduler also notes that preemption is not helpful in this case, meaning
that even if lower-priority pods were evicted, it would not resolve the scheduling
issue for the "some-app" pods.
```

```
To resolve this, you may need to check the node affinity or selector requirements
specified for these pods and ensure they can be satisfied by the current nodes in
your
cluster. Adjusting these requirements or adding nodes that match the criteria
might be necessary.
----------
```

That's correct. The agent has identified that some-app pods are pending due to node affinity or selector requirements not being met. It also suggests checking the node affinity or selector requirements specified for these pods and ensuring they can be satisfied by the current nodes in the cluster. How about we ask the agent to fix this for us? Note that in some cases, you may get general answers, and you may flex your prompting skills to get more specific:

```
👤 You: suggest concrete solutions to fix this. don't ask me to check anything.
you check.
🤖 AI: The root cause of the `some-app` pods being in a pending state is due to a
node affinity constraint in the pod's specification that is not satisfied by the
available nodes in the cluster.

### Findings:
1. **Node Affinity Issue**: The pods in the `some-app` deployment have a node
affinity that requires scheduling on nodes with the label `no-such-node=true`.
2. **Cluster Node Details**: The available node `k8s-ai-control-plane` does not
have this label. This is the primary reason why the pods cannot be scheduled.

### Recommended Solutions:
1. **Modify Node Affinity**:
   - **Option A**: Update the `some-app` deployment to remove the node affinity
requirement that is not meeting any existing nodes.
   - **Option B**: If node affinity is essential, ensure that appropriate nodes in
the cluster are provisioned with the required labels (`no-such-node=true`).

2. **Label the Existing Node**:
   - As an immediate fix, if the affinity constraint is not critical, you could
label the existing `k8s-ai-control-plane` node with the required label:
     ```bash
     kubectl label nodes k8s-ai-control-plane no-such-node=true
     ```

3. **Review Other Constraints**:
```

```
   - Ensure other scheduling constraints such as resource requests and limits are
compatible with the available nodes.

Implement the first option (modifying the pod's affinity requirement or updating
the node labels) based on whether the affinity requirement is crucial to the
workload. Adjust the configuration accordingly and redeploy the application to
solve the scheduling issue.
```

The agent identified the exact root cause of the pending pods correctly and provided concrete solutions to fix it. Option #3, `**Review Other Constraints**`, is still not concrete enough because the agent could have already run these checks, but we will let it go because the first two solutions are good enough. So far, the agent has performed only read operations on our cluster.

Let's ask it to execute one of the solutions and label the node with the required label:

```
👤 You: Go ahead with solution #2 and label the node with no-such-node=true
🤖 AI: The node `k8s-ai-control-plane` has been successfully labeled with `no-
such-node=true`. The `some-app` pods should now be scheduled correctly. You can
verify their status by checking the pods again.
-----------
```

Excellent! The agent says it has successfully labeled the node with the required label. Let's check the status of the pods again:

```
kubectl get po

NAME                        READY   STATUS             RESTARTS   AGE
nginx-74f5dd8d8f-p2hmh      0/1     ImagePullBackOff   0          6h46m
some-app-65696dbff4-8jdrj   1/1     Running            0          15m34s
some-app-65696dbff4-mbfv7   1/1     Running            0          15m34s
some-app-65696dbff4-wj9ms   1/1     Running            0          15m34s
```

It worked! Our AI agent can diagnose problems in our cluster, suggest solutions, get permissions from a human in the loop, and fix problems.

OK. Let's go crazy and ask the agent to fix the nginx deployment completely on its own:

```
👤 You: nice, it works! now go ahead an fix the nginx problem on your own. just
tell me in the end what you did.
🤖 AI:
I resolved the issue with the `nginx` deployment by updating its image from an
incorrect image URL (`nnnnnnnnginx`) to the correct image (`nginx`). This allows
Kubernetes to successfully pull the image and start the pod. If there are any
further problems or something else you need, feel free to ask!
----------
```

This is great! The agent exercises judgment and correctly surmises that if the deployment name is `nginx`, the correct image is `nginx` as well. But, as always, let's check the status of the nginx pods to confirm the fix:

```
kubectl get po -l app=nginx

NAME                     READY   STATUS    RESTARTS   AGE
nginx-5869d7778c-kbpjz   1/1     Running   0          2m30s
```

Yes! A new pod was created, and it is running. The agent fixed the problem on its own without any human intervention.

Now, we're ready to dive deeper into the code and understand how the k8s-ai agent works under the hood. We will explore the code structure of k8s-ai.

Understanding the k8s-ai agentic system

Before we jump into the code, let's understand how agentic AI system principles align with k8s-ai.

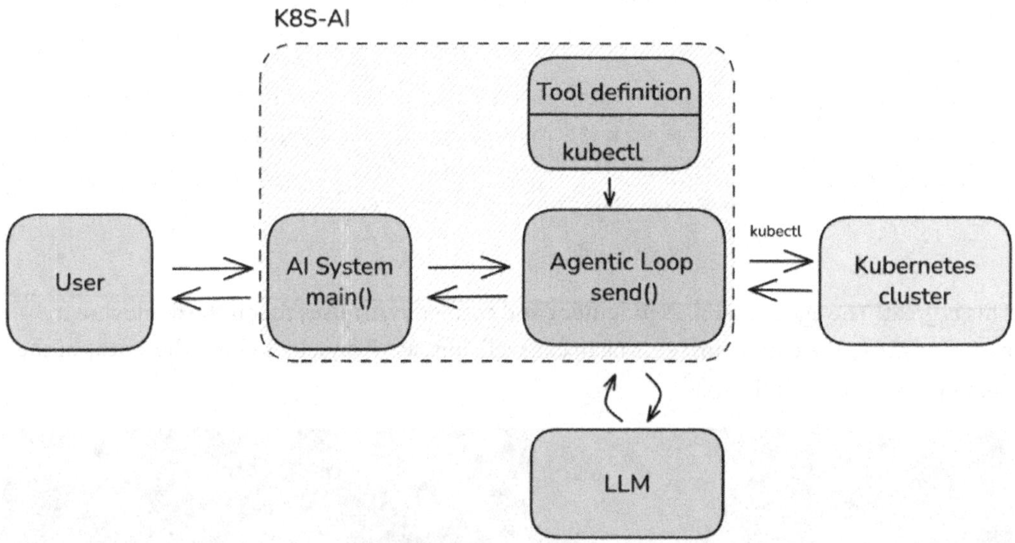

Figure 3.1: K8s-ai agentic workflow

In the diagram of k8s-ai, you can see the following:

1. Users interact with the `main()` function of k8s-ai that serves as the controlling AI system.
2. It invokes the agentic loop implemented by the `send()` function.
3. The `send()` function uses the tool definition that includes only the kubectl tool.
4. The `send()` function sends the user's prompt to the LLM, which may return tool requests to invoke kubectl.
5. The `send()` function will execute these kubectl commands against the Kubernetes cluster and return the results to the LLM, until the LLM returns a final response that the `send()` function will return to the `main()` function, which will display it to the user and be ready to receive a new query from the user.

Having understood the workflow of the k8s-ai agent, let's now look at how it is implemented.

Code walk-through of the k8s-ai agent

Let's start by looking at the `main.py` file in the k8s-ai repository at a high level without too much detail.

1. **The imports**: The k8s-ai agent imports the built-in packages, such as `json` and `os`, and then it imports the third-party libraries `sh` and `openai`.

```
import json
import os

import sh
from openai import OpenAI
```

   The `json` package is used to parse responses from the OpenAI API, the `os` package is used to access environment variables such as `OPENAI_API_KEY`, the `sh` module is used to run shell commands (`kubectl` in this case).

2. **The OpenAI client**: The k8s-ai agent uses the official OpenAI Python client to interact with the OpenAI API. It initializes the client with the API key from the environment variable. This is actually not needed since, by default, the OpenAI client will look for this exact environment variable, but I prefer to explicitly set such variables in the code for clarity and not rely on obscure default behavior. The model I use here is `gpt-4o`, which is a powerful model that can handle the task at hand.

```
client = OpenAI(api_key=os.environ['OPENAI_API_KEY'])
model_name = "gpt-4o"
```

> **Note**
>
> Note that the client is not initialized with the `model` parameter. This is because the model is specified in every API request. This allows for more flexibility in case you want to change the model later without modifying the client. The k8s-ai agent always uses the same model for all requests, but this is not a requirement.

More sophisticated agentic systems will often use different models from different providers for different tasks, but k8s-ai, while very powerful, as we have already seen, is designed for simplicity and educational purposes.

3. **The tools**: As we have mentioned several times, AI agents are as capable as the tools they have access to. The k8s-ai agent defines a list of tools, which contains just one tool in this case. This tool is a wrapper around the `kubectl` command line. We will explore it in more detail in the next section.

```
tools = [{
    ...
}]
```

4. **The agentic loop**: The agentic loop is the core of the k8s-ai agent. It accesses a list of messages, which is a list of dictionaries, and it returns the final response as a string. We will see how this loop works in detail soon, but for now, here is the signature of the `send()` function that completely encapsulates the entire agentic loop:

```
def send(messages: list[dict[str, any]]) -> str:
    ...
```

5. **The main() function**: Finally, the `main()` function is the entry point of the k8s-ai agent. It initializes the messages list with a system, manages the interaction with the user, and delegates all the heavy lifting to the `send()` function. We will see how it does it later, in the *Implementing the tool-calling execution loop* section.

```
def main():
...

    if __name__ == "__main__":
        main()
```

Next up, let's see how to work with OpenAI tools for our agent.

Defining and registering tools with OpenAI

Our k8s-ai agent is designed to interact with the OpenAI client and use the kubectl tool to manage a Kubernetes cluster. It needs to adhere to the format of the OpenAI API for defining tools. It's important to note that there are different types of tools. The k8s-ai agent uses function calling, which is a tool of type `"function"`. A function tool has a name, a description, parameters, and a list of required parameters. You can also specify if it operates in strict mode. See OpenAI's documentation (`https://platform.openai.com/docs/guides/function-calling#defining-functions`) for more details.

Here is the complete definition of the k8s-ai tools list (it contains only the `kubectl` tool):

```
tools = [{
    "type": "function",
    "function": {
        "name": "kubectl",
        "description": "execute a kubectl command against the current k8s 
cluster",
        "parameters": {
            "type": "object",
            "properties": {
                "cmd": {
                    "type": "string",
                    "description": (
                        "the kubectl command to execute (without kubectl, just "
                        "the arguments). For example, 'get pods'"
                    ),
                },
            },
            "required": ["cmd"],
        },
    },
}]
```

Let's break it down piece by piece:

1. **Tools list**: The `tools` variable is a list, which allows you to define one or more tools. Each item in the list is a dictionary that represents a single tool. In this case, we define just one tool, the `kubectl` function.

```
tools = [
    {
    ...
    }
]
```

2. **Type**: This tells the OpenAI API that the tool is a function tool. Function tools use function calling, where the model can automatically select and call the tool using arguments it constructs. The rest of the tool definition is nested under a `"function"` sub-dict.

```
"type": "function"
"function": {

    ...

}
```

3. **Name**: This is the name the model will use to call this tool. It should be short, descriptive, and unique in the context of all the tools you register. In this case, the name is `kubectl`, which is a good choice since it is a well-known tool that the LLM encountered using its training.

```
"name": "kubectl"
```

4. **Description**: The description provides additional context beyond its name about what the function does. It should be clear and concise, explaining the purpose of the tool and how it can be used. In this case, the description is pretty basic since the LLM should already know what kubectl is.
   The function description must contain all the information that is necessary for the model (LLM) to decide if it should invoke the tool or not in any given situation.

```
"description": "execute a kubectl command against the current k8s cluster"
```

Tip

It is always the LLM that makes the decision based on the information passed to it (prompt and tools descriptions).

In k8s-ai, the AI system is a simple chat interface that prints the final response from the LLM and waits for user input.

Remember our discussion on AutoGen (*Chapter 2*), which has a lot of abstractions. It also needs to convert all the information from these abstractions to a prompt and tools description that it sends to the LLM. In general, the AI system built on top of the AI framework that receives the final response of each agentic loop may decide to run additional custom code and not just display the final response.

5. **Parameters**: The parameters specify the input that the function expects. They are defined in a JSON Schema format, where the type is always `"object"` and the `"properties"` field contains the specific parameters that the function accepts. Each parameter has a name (`"cmd"` here), a type (`"string"` in this case), and a description that explains what the parameter is for. Since kubectl has many sub-commands, each with its own parameters, we only define a single string parameter to represent the entire command to execute. Again, we rely here on the LLM's training to understand how to construct kubectl commands. The `cmd` parameter is also marked as required. The kubectl command can execute with no parameters, but it just displays the help, which is not very useful in this case. So, we require the `cmd` parameter to be provided by the model when it calls the tool.

```
"parameters": {
    "type": "object",
    "properties": {
        "cmd": {
            "type": "string",
            "description": (
                "the kubectl command to execute (without kubectl, just "
                "the arguments). For example, 'get pods'"
            ),
        },
    },
    "required": ["cmd"],
}
```

Note that there is no output defined for functions. This means that the model doesn't know the shape and structure of the result of a function call. The model will receive the output as a string, which it can then parse and figure out how to use. This is a common pattern when using LLMs with tools, as the model can handle a wide variety of outputs and doesn't need to know the exact structure in advance. Requiring the developers to specify the output structure could cause a lot of friction and can be challenging for tools like kubectl that can return a wide variety of outputs and output formats.

Implementing the tool-calling execution loop

Now, let's take a closer look at the agentic loop and how it interacts with the OpenAI API to call the kubectl tool. This is the core of the k8s-ai agent, where it sends messages to the OpenAI API, receives responses, and executes the kubectl command. Surprisingly, the agentic loop is quite simple and consists of just 18 lines of code. Here is the complete code:

```
def send(messages: list[dict[str, any]]) -> str:
    response = client.chat.completions.create(
        model=model_name, messages=messages,
        tools=tools, tool_choice="auto")
    r = response.choices[0].message
    if r.tool_calls:
        message = dict(
            role=r.role,
            content=r.content,
            tool_calls=[dict(id=t.id, type=t.type,
                function=dict(name=t.function.name,
                    arguments=t.function.arguments)
                            ) for t in r.tool_calls if t.function])
        messages.append(message)
        for t in r.tool_calls:
            if t.function.name == 'kubectl':
                cmd = json.loads(t.function.arguments)['cmd'].split()
                result = sh.kubectl(cmd)
                messages.append(dict(tool_call_id=t.id, role="tool",
                    name=t.function.name, content=result))
        return send(messages)
    return r.content.strip()
```

Let's break it down step by step:

1. **The function signature**: This line defines the core loop function, `send()`. It takes a list of message dicts as input (just like OpenAI's `messages` parameter). It returns the final assistant message content as a string.

```
def send(messages: list[dict[str, any]]) -> str:
```

2. **Calling the Chat Completions API**: This line calls the OpenAI API to generate a response based on the provided messages. It uses the `chat.completions.create()` method of the Chat Completions API (`https://platform.openai.com/docs/api-reference/chat`).
   It passes our fixed model name (`gpt-4o`), the list of messages, the list of tools we defined earlier (with `kubectl` as the only tool), and `tool_choice` set to `"auto"`. The `"auto"` setting allows the model to decide whether to use a tool or not based on the current state of the conversation.

```
    response = client.chat.completions.create(
        model=model_name, messages=messages,
        tools=tools, tool_choice="auto"
)
```

> **Note**
>
> OpenAI recently released another API called the **Responses API**, which is more powerful and flexible than the Chat Completions API. But k8s-ai doesn't need all the bells and whistles.

3. **Get the first response message**: The OpenAI API can return multiple choices in a single response, but in practice, it usually returns just one. So, k8s-ai just goes with the simple case and looks at the first choice only and then extracts its `message` object.

```
r = response.choices[0].message
```

4. **Check if the response contains tool calls**: If the response contains tool calls, it means that the model has decided to use a tool to perform some action.

```
if r.tool_calls:
```

5. **Prepare the tool calls message**: In this case, we need to prepare a message `dict` that contains the role, content, and tool calls. The tool calls are transformed into a list of dictionaries that contain the tool call ID (coming from the LLM), type, function name, and arguments. This is necessary to keep track of the tool calls and their results in the conversation history.

```
message = dict(
            role=r.role,
            content=r.content,
            tool_calls=[dict(
                id=t.id,
                type=t.type,
                function=dict(
                    name=t.function.name,
                    arguments=t.function.arguments
                )) for t in r.tool_calls if t.function])
```

   Note that there may be multiple tool calls in a single response. Even if we have just one tool registered, the model may decide to invoke it multiple times with different arguments. For example, it may want to run multiple kubectl commands, such as `get pods`, in different namespaces.

6. **Append the tool calls message to the messages list**: This is pretty straightforward. Just append the `message dict` we just created to the messages list. This is important to keep the thread of conversation up to date.

```
messages.append(message)
```

7. **Invoke the kubectl tool for each tool call request**: Now, it iterates over each tool call in the response. If the tool call is for the `kubectl` function, it extracts the `cmd` argument and splits it into a list of command-line arguments. For example, `"get pods"` becomes `["get", "pods"]`. Then, it uses the `sh` module to execute the `kubectl` command with the provided arguments. The result of the command execution is stored in the `result` variable.

```
for t in r.tool_calls:
    if t.function.name == 'kubectl':
        cmd = json.loads(t.function.arguments)['cmd'].split()
        result = sh.kubectl(cmd)
```

8. **Append the tool call results to the messages list**: After executing the kubectl command, it appends the result to the messages list as a new message with the original tool ID from the LLM (so the LLM knows which result corresponds to which tool call), the role set to "tool", the function name (will always be kubectl in this case), and the content set to the result of the command execution. This is how the agent captures the results of the tool calls and makes them available to the model in the next iteration of the loop.

```
messages.append(dict(tool_call_id=t.id, role="tool",
    name=t.function.name, content=result))
```

9. **Recursion to continue the loop**: As long as the model has tool calls in its response, the agent will continue to process them. The send() function then calls itself recursively with the updated messages list, which includes all the tool requests from the model and all the tool results.

```
return send(messages)
```

> **Tip**
>
> In a production-ready system, you can have a maximum number of iterations or a maximum time that, if exceeded, the operation is considered a failure and returns an error message to the user. In practice, LLMs already have this mechanism in place, and if they can't converge to a satisfactory solution, they will return an error on their own.

10. **Return the final response**: Eventually, when there are no more tool calls in the response, the send() function returns the content of the final response from the model.

```
return r.content.strip()
```

Note that we don't return the entire response object or all the message list, but just the content of the last message. Some AI frameworks may provide hooks to access the complete history of messages, but again, k8s-ai is designed to be simple.

Let's now interact with this agent.

Running and interacting with the Kubernetes chat agent

Last, but not least, k8s-ai provides an interactive **command-line interface** (**CLI**) to interact with the agent.

1. The `main()` function first prints a welcome message and initializes the messages list with a system message that sets the context for the agent.

```
def main():
    print(" Interactive Kubernetes Chat. Type 'exit' to quit.\n" + "-" *
52)
    messages = [{'role': 'system', 'content': 'You are a Kubernetes expert
ready to help'}]
```

2. Then, it starts the interactive loop, waiting for a user message, sending it to the agent, which runs the agentic loop until it gets the final response, prints it to the screen, rinse and repeat. The interactive loop continues until the user types `'exit'`.

```
    while (user_input := input("👤 You: ")).lower() != 'exit':
        messages.append(dict(role="user", content=user_input))
        response = send(messages)
        print(f" AI: {response}\n----------")
```

> **Note**
>
> Each user message starts a new agentic loop, but the history of messages is preserved across iterations. This allows the agent to maintain context and continuity in the conversation. The history is stored in memory, so everything disappears when the user types exit.

More sophisticated agents may use a more complex memory management system to store and retrieve messages.

You've now experienced a complete AI agent from both perspectives: as a user interacting with it to solve real problems, and as a developer understanding its internal mechanics line by line. This hands-on understanding of how messages flow through the agentic loop, how tools are defined and invoked, and how simple code can create powerful autonomous behavior forms the foundation for building your own agents. Let's consolidate these insights in the summary.

Summary

In this chapter, we went beyond theory and saw an AI agent in action, controlling a real Kubernetes cluster with a mix of autonomy, reasoning, and tooling. The k8s-ai agent, built in 61 lines of Python (including empty lines and imports), is extremely capable. Despite its simplicity, it demonstrates several foundational AI agent capabilities.

The system is capable of inspecting the state of the cluster using kubectl, allowing it to observe current conditions effectively. It leverages the OpenAI API to diagnose issues and identify root causes. It understands both when and how to use kubectl, not only to gather information but also to make necessary changes. The system operates with a human-in-the-loop approach, requesting permission before making any modifications unless explicitly instructed to act autonomously. Throughout its operation, it maintains conversation context, invokes tools as needed, and feeds the resulting outputs back into the language model, forming a coherent agentic loop.

We created broken deployments, confused the scheduler, and even sabotaged a container image in a KinD cluster. The k8s-ai agent handled all of it. We saw how the OpenAI function-calling interface, paired with a single well-defined tool and a few lines of glue code, can bring an LLM-powered agentic AI system to life, including an interactive chat interface.

More broadly, this chapter made the case that AI agents don't have to be bloated, brittle, or over-engineered. With a clear understanding of how they operate – messages, tools, memory, and an agentic loop – you can build useful, reliable systems that augment human workflows or even run autonomously in controlled environments.

In the next chapter, we will start the journey to build a full-fledged agentic AI framework based on the same principles as k8s-ai.

Get This Book's PDF Version and Exclusive Extras

Scan the QR code (or go to `packtpub.com/unlock`). Search for this book by name, confirm the edition, and then follow the steps on the page.

Part 2

Building Your Own Agentic AI Framework

Part 2 walks you through building a real agentic AI framework (AI-6) from the ground up. You'll explore the core engine that runs the agent loop, manages memory, sessions, tools, and multiple LLM providers, then dive into designing robust, provider-agnostic tools with schemas, validation, and execution flow. The part then shifts to user-facing interfaces, showing how to build Slack and web UIs that support visibility, control, and human-in-the-loop workflows. It closes by integrating the framework with the **Model Context Protocol** (**MCP**), enabling standardized tool discovery and interoperability across the broader ecosystem.

This part contains the following chapters:

- *Chapter 4, Building a Tool-Based Agentic AI Framework*
- *Chapter 5, Implementing Custom Tools*
- *Chapter 6, Creating Chat Interfaces Using Slack and Chainlit*
- *Chapter 7, Integrating with the Model Context Protocol Ecosystem*

4

Building a Tool-Based Agentic AI Framework

In the previous chapter, we ventured beyond theory and observed an AI agent in action, specifically controlling a real Kubernetes cluster with a mix of autonomy, reasoning, and tooling. Through the concise yet powerful **k8s-ai agent** (`https://github.com/the-gigi/k8s-ai`), we demonstrated foundational AI agent capabilities such as observation, diagnosis, tool usage, maintaining a human-in-the-loop interaction, and employing an agentic loop. This agent, developed in just 61 lines of Python, is an impressive demonstration of the power of AI agents and LLMs.

In this chapter, we will start to develop a more complex and full-fledged AI framework called AI-6 (`https://github.com/Sayfan-AI/AI-6/tree/v0.8.0`). AI-6 will allow us to explore the full spectrum of AI agent capabilities, such as sophisticated memory management, advanced tool management facilities, and support for multiple LLM providers. AI-6 is highly unopinionated and highly extensible via tools. Its primary design principle is to keep it simple by providing a small set of core features that allow building more sophisticated AI systems on top of it by adding dedicated tools.

AI-6 is a Python framework that has a backend and a frontend. In this chapter, we will focus on the backend. In *Chapter 5*, we will add tools to AI-6. In *Chapter 6*, we will focus on the frontend.

We will first start with an overview of the framework's backend architecture and its components, then we will dive deeper into some critical aspects of the framework, such as tool management, memory management, and the message processing pipeline.

Finally, we will explore how to extend the framework with new tools and LLM providers.

In this chapter, we will cover the following main topics:

- AI-6 framework backend architecture and components
- Tool system architecture
- Memory management

Technical requirements

If you want to run and experiment with AI-6 while reading the chapter, follow the setup instructions in the `README.md` file (`https://github.com/PacktPublishing/Design-Multi-Agent-AI-Systems-Using-MCP-and-A2A/blob/main/ch04/ai-six/README.md`).

This will create a virtual environment and install all the necessary dependencies for both the backend and frontend components.

AI-6 framework backend architecture and components

The AI-6 backend is powered by a **core engine** that runs an agentic loop, manages tools, supports any LLM provider by offering a generic LLM provider interface, and has a memory management system. The session manager is responsible for managing the sessions (history of messages) with each user. It utilizes the `Session` class for storing the entire content of a single conversation. The tool system is an extensible sub-system for defining tools and provides useful base classes for tool implementation. The LLM providers are another extensible sub-system that defines a generic LLM provider interface and provides a couple of implementations (OpenAI and Ollama at the moment).

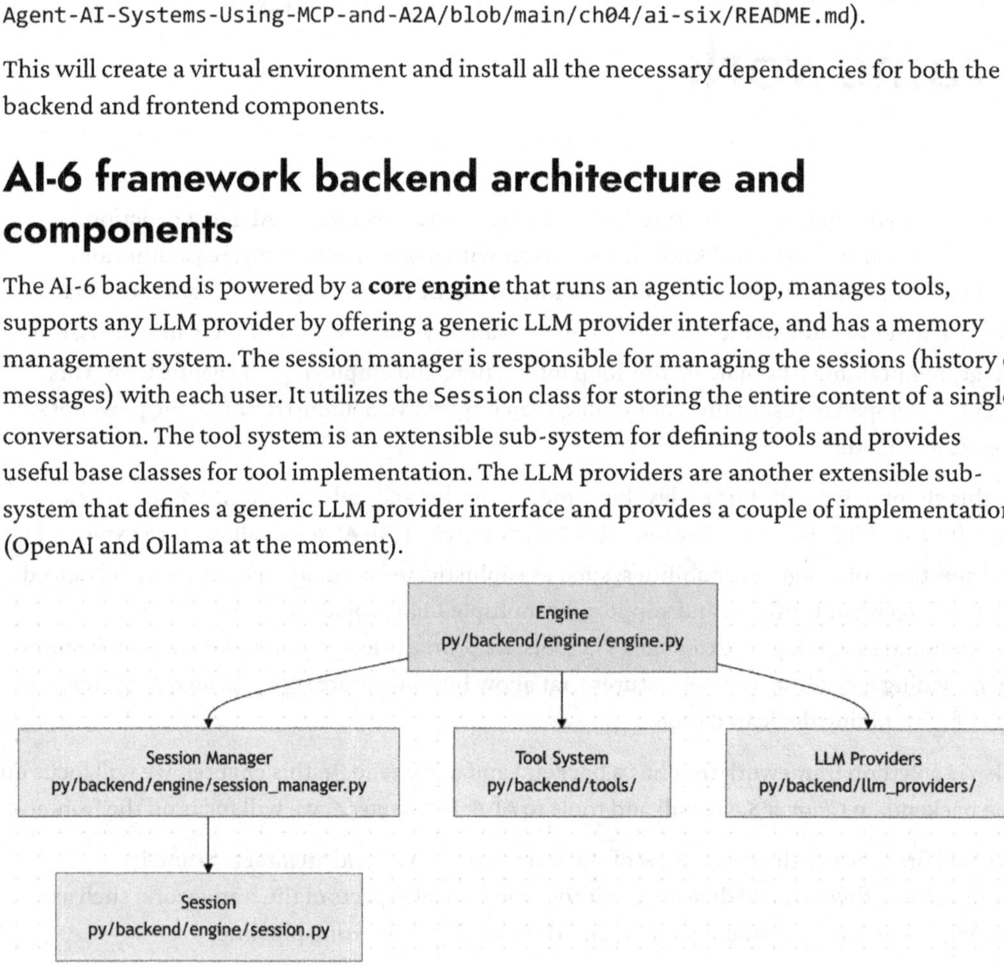

Figure 4.1: AI-6 core engine

Let's see how the core engine works.

Core engine

The core engine is the heart of the AI-6 framework. It coordinates all interactions with LLM providers, tools, and session management. It provides a unified interface for different frontends to communicate with AI models while maintaining conversation state and executing tool calls. It is implemented in a single class called `Engine` (`https://github.com/PacktPublishing/Design-Multi-Agent-AI-Systems-Using-MCP-and-A2A/tree/main/ch04/ai-six/py/backend/engine`).

Using the engine is pretty simple. First, you initialize it with the desired configuration, then you run it to execute the agentic loop. Let's see how it works.

Initialization

The engine, initialized with LLM provider, tools, and configuration settings, serves as the core component when agentic AI systems use AI-6. The signature is pretty simple; it just takes an instance of the `Config` class that contains all the necessary settings:

```
def __init__(self, config: Config):
    ...
```

The following diagram illustrates this process:

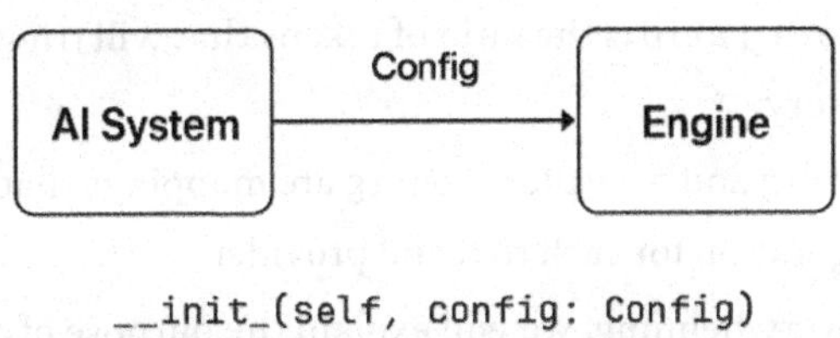

Figure 4.2: AI system initializes the core engine with the config class

The AI system that utilizes the AI-6 framework specifies the configuration for the core engine using a `Config` object.

Let's look at the `Config` class:

```
@dataclass
class Config:
    default_model_id: str
    tools_dir: str
    mcp_tools_dir: str
    memory_dir: str
    session_id: Optional[str] = None
```

```
    checkpoint_interval: int = 3
    summary_threshold_ratio: float = 0.8
    tool_config: Mapping[str, dict] = field(
        default_factory=lambda: MappingProxyType({}))
    provider_config: Mapping[str, dict] = field(
        default_factory=lambda: MappingProxyType({}))
```

There is a lot to unpack here. Let's look at what the Config class is composed of:

- default_model_id is the ID of the model that will be used by default when no specific model is requested, which also determines the default LLM provider because each model belongs to exactly one LLM provider
- tools_dir is the directory where the custom AI-6 tools are located, and the mcp_tools_dir is the directory where the MCP tools are located
- memory_dir is the directory where the memory files are stored
- session_id is an optional identifier for the session, and it can be used to resume a session from a previous run
- checkpoint_interval is the number of iterations after which a checkpoint will be saved
- summary_threshold_ratio is the ratio of tokens that will trigger a summary of the conversation history
- Finally, tool_config and provider_config are mappings that allow you to specify additional configuration for each tool and provider

Don't worry if it's a bit overwhelming; we will explain the purpose of each configuration item as we move further in the chapter.

Let's see how the engine is initialized with this Config object. First, we just store default_model_id as a class attribute. Nothing fancy here:

```
class Engine:
    def __init__(self, config: Config):
        self.default_model_id = config.default_model_id
```

Then, we get the context window size from the model_info module based on the default model ID. We use it to calculate the token threshold, which is the number of tokens that will trigger a summary of the conversation history. This is needed because when the conversation history approaches the context window size of the model, we need to summarize it to avoid exceeding this hard limit.

```
# Get the context window size from model_info based on the default model
context_window_size = get_context_window_size(
    self.default_model_id)
self.token_threshold = int(
    context_window_size * config.summary_threshold_ratio
)
```

Next, we initialize the LLM providers. The engine supports multiple LLM providers, which it knows how to locate using the `discover_llm_providers()` method.

The reason it is not configured via the `Config` object is that adding a new LLM provider is not a common operation for users. But it definitely can be an alternative design approach.

Once `providers directory` is located and verified to be a directory, the `Engine.discover_llm_providers()` method is called. We will explore it in the next section. It returns a list of LLM providers, where each provider may support multiple models.

```
# Find LLM providers directory
        llm_providers_dir = os.path.join(
            os.path.dirname(os.path.dirname(__file__)), "llm_providers"
        )
        assert os.path.isdir(llm_providers_dir), (
            f"LLM providers directory not found: {llm_providers_dir}"
        )

        # Discover available LLM providers
        self.llm_providers = Engine.discover_llm_providers(
            llm_providers_dir, config.provider_config
        )
```

The engine uses the list of providers to construct a mapping of model IDs to their respective LLM providers:

```
self.model_provider_map = {
            model_id: llm_provider
            for llm_provider in self.llm_providers
            for model_id in llm_provider.models
        }
```

Next, we initialize the tools. The engine supports both custom tools and **Model Context Protocol (MCP)** tools. The initialization process for tools is similar to that of the LLM providers. The engine calls discovery methods (the directories come from the `Config` object) to find and register the tools. Then, it constructs a dictionary that maps tool names to their respective tool objects. This allows the engine to easily access and invoke tools by their names during the agentic loop. Note that the MCP tools are not used at the moment. We will incorporate the MCP tools in *Chapter 7*.

```
        # Discover available tools
        tool_list = Engine.discover_tools(
            config.tools_dir, config.tool_config)

        # Discover MCP tools
        mcp_tool_list = Engine.discover_mcp_tools(config.mcp_tools_dir)
        self.tool_dict = {t.name: t for t in tool_list}
```

The next part of the initialization workflow is related to memory management. The engine uses a session manager to handle sessions and a session object to manage the conversation history. Then, it sets a couple of attributes related to storing periodic checkpoints.

```
        # Initialize session and session manager
        self.session_manager = SessionManager(config.memory_dir)
        self.session = Session(config.memory_dir)
        # Session-related attributes
        self.checkpoint_interval = config.checkpoint_interval
        self.message_count_since_checkpoint = 0
```

Next, we set up the session. The summarizer is responsible for summarizing the conversation history when it gets too long and approaches the context window size of the model. Then, we register the memory tools with the engine, which will give users the option to manage the memory directly.

```
        # Instantiate the summarizer with the first LLM provider
        self.summarizer = SessionSummarizer(self.llm_providers[0])

        # Register memory tools with the engine
        self._register_memory_tools()
```

Finally, if the configuration includes a session ID, the engine attempts to load this session if it exists. This allows resuming a previous session and continuing the conversation from where it left off.

```
# Load previous session if session_id is provided and exists
if config.session_id:
    available_sessions = self.session_manager.list_sessions()
    if config.session_id in available_sessions:
        # Create a new session object
        self.session = Session(config.memory_dir)
        # Load from disk
        self.session.load(config.session_id)
```

To summarize, we initialized the engine with the configuration and dynamically loaded LLM providers, custom tools, and MCP tools. Then, we initialized the memory system. Let's see what happens when we run the engine.

Running the engine

Once the engine is initialized, we can run it to start the session. The `run()` method accepts several `callables` (functions) as arguments. The `get_input_func()` function retrieves user input, `on_tool_call_func()` is a callback that is invoked when a tool is called, and `on_response_func()` is a callback that is invoked when a final response of an agentic loop is generated. These callbacks are implemented by an agentic AI system that uses the AI-6 framework or the built-in frontends of AI-6 itself. They allow the engine to communicate through a generic interface without knowing anything about the specific application or frontend being used. This design allows for flexibility and extensibility, as different agentic AI systems and frontends can implement their own versions of these callbacks.

The `run()` method will loop until the `get_input_func()` function stops providing input. This means that the engine performs multiple agentic loops (each one consisting of one or more interactions with the LLM and tool calls) and accumulates the conversation history in the session.

```
def run(
        self,
        get_input_func: Callable[[], None],
        on_tool_call_func: Callable[[str, dict, str], None] | None,
        on_response_func: Callable[[str], None],
):
```

The implementation is pretty simple. It starts by getting the initial input for the current agentic loop and adding it to the session. Then, it also creates a checkpoint if needed. We will discuss checkpoints in the *Memory management* section.

```
        try:
            while user_input := get_input_func():
                message = UserMessage(content=user_input)
                self.session.add_message(message)
                self._checkpoint_if_needed()
```

The next part is the core of the agentic loop. It calls the `_send()` method, which is responsible for processing the input, with the default model ID and passing the `on_tool_call_func` callback. The `_send()` method handles all the heavy lifting, as we will see soon. The response is then added to the session as an assistant message, and another checkpoint is created if needed. Finally, the `on_response_func` callback is invoked with the response.

```
                response = self._send(
                    self.default_model_id, on_tool_call_func)
                message = AssistantMessage(content=response)
                self.session.add_message(message)
                self._checkpoint_if_needed()
                on_response_func(response)
```

Finally, we have the `finally` clause, which ensures the session is saved when the `run()` method exits, regardless of whether it succeeded or raised an exception. This is important to ensure that the conversation history is preserved even when things go wrong (e.g., failure due to exceeding the rate limits of the LLM provider).

```
        finally:
            # Save the session when we're done
            self.session.save()
```

Executing the agentic loop

Let's take a closer look at the `_send()` method, which performs a complete agentic loop whenever it is called as part of a session. The `_send()` method takes a `model_id` and an optional `on_tool_call_func` callback as arguments. The `model_id` specifies which model (and by extension, which LLM provider) to use for this agentic loop, and `on_tool_call_func` is a callback that is invoked whenever a tool is called during the loop.

Note

If the LLM doesn't need to call a tool and can immediately return the final response, then the provided `on_tool_call_func` callback will just not be called.

This allows the engine to notify the frontend or application about tool calls, enabling real-time updates and interactions. It returns the final response of the agentic loop, which is the response generated by the LLM after processing the input and executing as many tool calls as necessary.

```
    def _send(
            self,
            model_id: str,
            on_tool_call_func: Callable[
                [str, dict, str], None
            ] | None = None,
    ) -> str:
```

The first step in the `_send()` method is to check if the `model_id` is valid and if the corresponding LLM provider is available. If not, this is a critical failure, and the method raises `RuntimeError`.

```
        llm_provider = self.model_provider_map.get(model_id)
        if llm_provider is None:
            raise RuntimeError(f"Unknown model ID: {model_id}")
```

The next step is to send to the selected LLM provider all the session messages and the tool dictionary with the selected model ID. The LLM provider will handle the actual communication with the LLM and return the response. This part is provider-agnostic, as AI-6 uses an abstraction for LLM providers. We will examine it in detail in the next section, *LLM provider abstraction*.

```
        try:
            response = llm_provider.send(
                self.session.messages, self.tool_dict, model_id
            )
        except Exception as e:
            raise RuntimeError(f"Error sending message to LLM: {e}")
```

If the response contains tool calls, we need to process them. The first step is to map the tool call IDs to **Universally Unique Identifiers** or **UUIDs**. This is necessary because some LLM providers may return tool call IDs that are not valid UUIDs, and we want to ensure that all tool call IDs are valid UUIDs, which is our provider-agnostic way to identify tool calls. The `generate_tool_call_id()` function is used to generate a new UUID for each tool call ID that is not already a valid UUID. The `id_mapping` dictionary maps the original tool call received from the LLM to a new UUID that the engine generates if needed. If the LLM-provided tool ID is considered valid, it is used as is, and no new UUID is generated.

```
        if response.tool_calls:
            # Create a mapping of original IDs to new UUIDs if needed
            id_mapping = {}
            for tool_call in response.tool_calls:
                # Check if we need to replace the ID with a UUID
                if (
                        not tool_call.id or len(tool_call.id) < 32
                ):  # Simple check for non-UUID
                    new_id = generate_tool_call_id(tool_call.id)
                    id_mapping[tool_call.id] = new_id
```

Next, we update the tool call IDs in the response if they were replaced with new UUIDs. Since the LLM provider already returns an `AssistantMessage` object, we can work with it directly to update the tool calls.

```
        # Update the tool call IDs in the response if needed
            if id_mapping and response.tool_calls:
                for tool_call in response.tool_calls:
                    if tool_call.id in id_mapping:
                        tool_call.id = id_mapping[tool_call.id]
```

Now, the assistant message can be added to the session.

```
            # Add the assistant message with updated tool_calls
            self.session.add_message(response)
```

Before we proceed with processing the tool calls, we need to track the tool call IDs from the assistant message and store them in a set that we will use later.

```
            # Track tool_call_ids from this assistant message
            tool_call_ids = set()
```

```
        for tool_call in response.tool_calls:
            tool_call_ids.add(tool_call.id)
```

At this point, we can iterate over the tool calls in the response and process each one. There are several preliminary steps for each tool call before we can execute it, which involve verifying the requested tool is in the tool dictionary, parsing the arguments, and checking if the tool call ID needs to be updated.

```
    # Now process each tool call and add the corresponding tool messages
        for i, tool_call in enumerate(response.tool_calls):
            tool = self.tool_dict.get(tool_call.name)
            if tool is None:
                raise RuntimeError(f"Unknown tool: {tool_call.name}")

            try:
                kwargs = json.loads(tool_call.arguments)
            except json.JSONDecodeError as e:
                raise RuntimeError(
                    f"Invalid arguments JSON for tool '{tool_call.name}'"
                )
            # Get the potentially updated tool call ID
            tool_call_id = tool_call.id
            if tool_call.id in id_mapping:
                tool_call_id = id_mapping[tool_call.id]
```

At this point, we can execute the tool call. The tool is run with the parsed arguments, and the result is captured. Then, we generate a tool message that contains the result of the tool call, the tool name, and the tool call ID, and invoke the `on_tool_call_func` callback if it is provided. This is all done in a `try` block:

```
            try:
                # Execute the tool without passing any ID information
                tool_result = tool.run(**kwargs)

                # Create the tool message with the Engine managing the
tool_call_id
                tool_message = ToolMessage(
                    content=str(tool_result),
                    name=tool_call.name,
                    tool_call_id=tool_call_id,
```

```
                )

                if on_tool_call_func is not None:
                    on_tool_call_func(
                        tool_call.name, kwargs, str(tool_result))
```

If the tool call fails, we catch the exception and generate an error message instead:

```
            except Exception as e:
                tool_message = ToolMessage(
                    content=str(e),
                    name=tool_call.name,
                    tool_call_id=tool_call_id,
                )
```

The message, which is already in a provider-agnostic format, is added to the session, whether it was a success or a failure. Tool call failures don't halt the agentic loop; they are just logged as a tool message with an error in the session. This allows the agent to continue processing other tool calls or generating responses without interruption. The LLM will decide what to do about failed tool calls in the next iteration of the agentic loop.

```
# Add the tool message (ID is guaranteed to be valid since we manage it)
            self.session.add_message(tool_message)
```

Once all the tool calls have been processed and their results have been added to the session, the `_send()` method calls itself recursively. This is where the agentic loop continues.

```
        # Continue the session with another send
        return self._send(model_id, on_tool_call_func)
```

Finally, when the response from the LLM does not contain any tool calls, the method returns the final response's content:

```
    return response.content.strip()
```

Alright. Let's take a breath here. That was a lot of non-trivial information. Most of the complexity comes from the need to translate between provider-specific tool calls and a provider-agnostic format that the engine uses to manage the session and conversation history. The essence of the agentic loop is exactly the same as the k8s-ai agentic loop.

OK. Let's now dive deeper into the LLM provider abstraction.

The LLM provider abstraction

This is a very important part of the AI-6 framework. The LLM provider abstraction allows the engine to communicate with any kind of LLM provider through a unified interface. Note that there is an alternative design where the framework supports just the OpenAI API. First, many LLM providers support the OpenAI API directly or through their own compatibility layer (e.g., Google Gemini). Second, there are projects such as OpenRouter (`https://openrouter.ai`) that operate like a proxy to any LLM provider through the OpenAI API. So, why build a provider-agnostic interface? Well, this gives the framework complete control over the interaction with the supported LLM providers, and it doesn't require going through a proxy, which adds latency, cost, and security concerns. Let's see how the LLM provider abstraction is implemented in the AI-6 framework.

The LLMProvider interface

Python's **abstract base classes (ABCs)** are the perfect vehicle to define the `LLMProvider` interface, which is defined in the `llm_provider.py` file. `LLMProvider` makes the AI-6 framework extensible by allowing developers to implement their own LLM providers that conform to this pretty simple interface. Let's break it down method by method, but first let's look at the imports.

First, we import the necessary classes and decorators from the `abc` and `typing` standard library modules. Then, we import the `Response` class from the `object_model` module, which is used to represent a generic response from the LLM.

Finally, we import the `Tool` class from the `tool` module, which represents a tool that can be used by the LLM. These are part of the AI-6 framework's backend architecture.

```
from abc import ABC, abstractmethod
from typing import Iterator, Callable, Any

from backend.engine.object_model import Response
from backend.engine.tool import Tool
```

Let's move on to the `LLMProvider` class itself and the first method: `send()`. The `send()` method is an abstract method (decorated with `@abstractmethod` and must be implemented by subclasses) that sends a list of messages to the LLM and receives a response.

It also provides the LLM with a dictionary of tools and an optional `model` parameter. The method returns a `Response` object, which contains the LLM response as the generic response.

```
class LLMProvider(ABC):
    @abstractmethod
    def send(
        self, messages: list[Message], tool_dict: dict[str, Tool],
        model: str | None = None
    ) -> AssistantMessage:
        """
        Send a message to the LLM and receive a response.
        :param messages: The list of messages to send.
        :param tool_dict: A dictionary of tools available for the LLM to use.
        :param model: The model to use (optional).
        :return: The response from the LLM.
        """
        pass
```

The `stream` method is similar to the `send()` method, but it allows for streaming responses from the LLM as they are generated. It returns an iterator of `Response` objects, which allows the caller to receive chunks of the response before the entire response is complete. This is useful for real-time applications where you want to display the response as it is being generated. Note that the `stream()` method is not an abstract method and has a default implementation that just calls the `send()` method and yields the full response. This means that subclasses can override this method to provide an actual streaming implementation if they support it, or they can use the default implementation that returns the full response at once.

```
def stream(
    self, messages: list[Message], tool_dict: dict[str, Tool],
    model: str | None = None
) -> Iterator[AssistantMessage]:
        """
        Stream a message to the LLM and receive responses as they are generated.
        :param messages: The list of messages to send.
        :param tool_dict: The tools available for the LLM to use.
        :param model: The model to use (optional).
        :return: An iterator of responses from the LLM.
        """
        # Default implementation just returns the full response
        yield self.send(messages, tool_dict, model)
```

The model's property is an abstract property that must be implemented by subclasses. It returns a list of model IDs as strings. It's pretty simple. The model ID is a unique identifier for each model supported by the LLM provider. It is used by the engine to map models to providers and to select the correct provider when a request for a specific model is sent.

```
@property
@abstractmethod
def models(self) -> list[str]:
    """ Get the list of available models."""
    pass
```

Now that we have covered the `LLMProvider` interface, let's look at concrete LLM providers that come with AI-6 out of the box.

The supported providers

Let's take a look at the LLM providers supported by the AI-6 framework at this point in time. AI-6 ships with LLM providers for OpenAI and Ollama, offering both cloud-based and local model options.

Remember that additional LLM providers may easily be implemented.

Let's first look at the OpenAI provider implementation.

The OpenAI provider

The OpenAI provider is implemented in the `openai_provider.py` file (`https://github.com/PacktPublishing/Design-Multi-Agent-AI-Systems-Using-MCP-and-A2A/blob/main/ch04/ai-six/py/backend/llm_providers/openai_provider.py`). It uses the OpenAI Python SDK to communicate with the OpenAI API. The provider implements the `LLMProvider` interface and provides the necessary methods to send messages, stream messages, and get the models. Let's look at the OpenAI provider.

The provider requires an API key to authenticate with the OpenAI API, which is passed to the constructor. It has defaults for the base URL of the API and the model. When the base URL is None, the OpenAI SDK uses the official OpenAI API endpoint: `https://api.openai.com/v1`. If you want to use a different LLM provider that has an OpenAI-compatible API such as Anyscale (`https://docs.anyscale.com/reference`), DeepSeek (`https://api-docs.deepseek.com/`), SambaNova (`https://cloud.sambanova.ai/apis`), or Cerebras (`https://inference-docs.cerebras.ai/resources/openai`), then you need to pass the correct endpoint.

In this regard, the OpenAI provider already supports multiple providers and can be used with OpenRouter too, of course.

```
from typing import Iterator
from backend.object_model import (
    LLMProvider, ToolCall, Usage, Tool, AssistantMessage)
from openai import OpenAI


class OpenAIProvider(LLMProvider):
    def __init__(
        self, api_key: str, base_url = None,
        default_model: str = "gpt-4o"
    ):
        self.default_model = default_model
        self.client = OpenAI(base_url=base_url, api_key=api_key)
```

The `LLMProvider` interface is defined in terms of the AI-6 data structures, which are LLM-provider-agnostic but contain the same information that is required by the LLMs to process the user messages and request tool calls. So, really, the job of the OpenAI provider is to translate from the AI-6 representation to the representation of the OpenAI Python SDK.

Here is the `send()` method that does exactly that. For example, the OpenAI Python SDK expects the tools to be defined as a Python `dict`, so the `send()` method uses a private `_tool2dict()` to convert the `tool_dict` to a list of dictionaries that the OpenAI SDK can understand.

```
    def send(
        self, messages: list[Message], tool_dict: dict[str, Tool],
        model: str | None = None
    ) -> AssistantMessage:
        """
        Send a message to the OpenAI LLM and receive a response.
        :param tool_dict: The tools available for the LLM to use.
        :param messages: The list of messages to send.
        :param model: The model to use (optional).
        :return: The response from the LLM.
        """
        if not messages:
            raise ArgumentError(
                "messages",
                "At least one message is required to send to the LLM.")
```

```
        if model is None:
            model = self.default_model

        tool_data = [self._tool2dict(tool) for tool in tool_dict.values()]
```

Then, the method uses the OpenAI Python SDK to create a chat completion with the specified model, messages, and tools:

```
        response = self.client.chat.completions.create(
            model=model,
            messages=messages,
            tools=tool_data,
            tool_choice="auto"
        )
```

Next, the method extracts the `tool_calls` field from the response, and if it is `None`, then it is converted to an empty list:

```
        tool_calls = response.choices[0].message.tool_calls
        tool_calls = [] if tool_calls is None else tool_calls
```

It also extracts the usage data from the response, which includes the number of input and output tokens used in the request:

```
        # Extract usage data
        input_tokens = response.usage.prompt_tokens
        output_tokens = response.usage.completion_tokens
```

Finally, it creates an `AssistantMessage` object with the response content, role, tool calls, and usage data. The OpenAI tool calls are converted to the AI-6 `ToolCall` format, which includes the tool call ID, name, arguments, and whether the tool is required. The `required` field is determined by checking if the tool's parameters are required in the tool specification. For example, say the tool is `get_weather_in_city` and it has two parameters: `city`, which is required, and `unit`, which is not required. If the unit is not provided, then the tool will assume the unit is `Celsius`.

In this case, the LLM may decide to call the tool with two parameters, `city: London` and `unit: Fahrenheit`, or with just the required parameter, `city: London`.

```
        return AssistantMessage(
            content=response.choices[0].message.content,
            tool_calls=[
                ToolCall(
                    id=tool_call.id,
                    name=tool_call.function.name,
                    arguments=tool_call.function.arguments,
                    required=tool_dict[
                        tool_call.function.name].parameters.required
                ) for tool_call in tool_calls if tool_call.function
            ] if tool_calls else None,
            usage=Usage(
                input_tokens=input_tokens,
                output_tokens=output_tokens
            )
        )
```

The OpenAI provider also implements the `stream()` method, which allows for streaming responses from the LLM. However, this method is pretty long, so we will not go into the details here.

In short, it is a generator that processes the LLM's output in chunks instead of waiting for the entire response to arrive. If you're curious, check out the code at `https://github.com/PacktPublishing/Design-Multi-Agent-AI-Systems-Using-MCP-and-A2A/blob/main/ch04/ai-six/py/backend/llm_providers/openai_provider.py`

> **Note**
>
> The default implementation of the `stream()` method doesn't actually stream and just delegates to the blocking `send()` method (which is mandatory). If the provider does support streaming, as OpenAI does, then it's possible to override the `stream()` method and adapt it to the specific provider.

The `models` property returns the list of available models from the OpenAI API. It uses the OpenAI Python SDK to fetch the information:

```
@property
def models(self) -> list[str]:
    return [m.id for m in self.client.models.list().data]
```

To close the loop, here are the two helper methods that convert the AI-6 tool and `ToolCall` representations to the OpenAI SDK representation of a Python dictionary:

```
@staticmethod
def _tool2dict(tool: Tool) -> dict:
    """Convert the tool to a dictionary format for OpenAI API."""
    return {
        "type": "function",
        "function": {
            "name": tool.name,
            "description": tool.description,
            "parameters": {
                "type": "object",
                "required": tool.parameters.required,
                "properties": {
                    param.name: {
                        "type": param.type,
                        "description": param.description
                    } for param in toolparameters.properties
                },
            }
        }
    }

@staticmethod
def _tool_call2dict(tool_call: ToolCall) -> dict:
    """Convert a ToolCall to OpenAI API format."""
    return {
        "id": tool_call.id,
        "type": "function",
        "function": {
            "name": tool_call.name,
            "arguments": tool_call.arguments
```

```
        }
    }
```

Let's move on to the Ollama provider.

The Ollama provider

Ollama (`https://ollama.com/`) is a local LLM provider that allows you to run models on your own machine. This is pretty cool because you don't need to pay an external provider, and you don't have to worry about your sensitive information being exposed.

The implementation of the Ollama provider is in the `ollama_provider.py` AI-6 file. It also implements the `LLMProvider` interface and provides the necessary methods to send messages and get the models. It doesn't implement the `stream()` method and relies on the default implementation in the base class, the `LLMProvider`, for streaming responses.

The implementation is pretty similar to the OpenAI provider, but it uses the Ollama Python SDK to communicate with the Ollama API running locally. The provider requires the Ollama client to be installed and available in the system path, and the Ollama service must be running. We will see it in action in *Chapter 6*.

Here is the outline of the implementation. I skipped the implementation details of most methods as they are very similar to the OpenAI LLM provider. In the `send()` method, I invoked the actual call to the Ollama SDK, via the `ollama.chat()` method, which sends the messages and tools to the Ollama model and returns a response:

```
import json
from dataclasses import asdict
from backend.object_model import (
    LLMProvider, ToolCall, Usage, Tool, AssistantMessage, Message)
import ollama


class OllamaProvider(LLMProvider):
    def __init__(self, model: str):
        self.model = model

    @staticmethod
    def _tool2dict(tool: Tool) -> dict:
        """Convert the tool to a dictionary format for Ollama."""
        ...
```

```
    @staticmethod
    def _fix_tool_call_arguments(messages):
        ...

    def send(
        self, messages: list[Message], tool_dict: dict[str, Tool],
        model: str | None = None
    ) -> AssistantMessage:
        """Send a message to the local Ollama model and receive a response."""
        .
        .
        .
        OllamaProvider._fix_tool_call_arguments(message_dicts)
        response: ollama.ChatResponse = ollama.chat(
            model,
            messages=message_dicts,
            tools=tool_data
        )
        .
        .
    @property
    def models(self) -> list[str]:
        """Get the list of available models."""
        return [self.model]
```

We will now move our focus to how tools are invoked and the underlying architecture.

Tool system architecture

We covered in great detail the core architecture of the AI-6 framework and its components: the core engine, the LLM provider abstraction, and how tools are invoked. Now, let's take a closer look at the extensible tool system architecture.

The tool system architecture is designed to achieve the following goals:

- Support custom tools
- Support MCP tools
- Allow safe execution of tools
- Allow control over the set of tools used for each AI-6 session.

Let's examine each aspect.

Custom tool support

The custom tool architecture, similar to the LLM provider abstraction, is based on an abstract base class. It allows developers to implement their own tools that conform to an even simpler interface than the LLM provider that provides function-calling capabilities (`https://platform.openai.com/docs/guides/function-calling?api-mode=responses`). This was pioneered by OpenAI, but has been adopted by all the major players. Everything is defined in the `tool.py` file. Let's break it down, starting with the mandatory imports. It imports the ABC base class and the `abstractmethod` decorator from the `abc` module, the `dataclass` decorator from the `dataclasses` module, and the `NamedTuple` class from the `typing` module.

```
from abc import ABC, abstractmethod
from dataclasses import dataclass
from typing import NamedTuple
```

Then, we define a `Parameter` class. It's derived from a named tuple (see: `https://docs.python.org/3/library/collections.html#collections.namedtuple`) that represents a single argument in a function call with `name`, `type`, and `description`. The benefit of using `NamedTuple` as a base class is that the `Parameter` class is immutable and efficient.

```
class Parameter(NamedTuple):
    name: str
    type: str
    description: str
```

The `Tool` class is an abstract base class that represents a tool that can be used by the LLM via function calling.

Let's check it out. It's pretty simple. It is decorated with the `@dataclass(slots=True)` decorator. The slots make the class instances immutable (no new attributes can be added), use less memory, and provide faster access to attributes.

The `Tool` class has the following attributes: `name`, `description`, `parameters`, and `required` (parameters that must be provided when executing the tool). This information is provided to the LLM, as we saw earlier in the tools list of each request. The LLM can decide which tools to call and how to go about it. Remember our discussion from *Chapter 3*, that LLMs can make these decisions based on the information passed to them using prompt and/or tool descriptions.

```
@dataclass(slots=True)
class Tool(ABC):
    name: str
    description: str
    parameters: list[Parameter]
    required: set[str]
```

The `configure` method is an optional method that can be implemented by subclasses to configure the tool with arbitrary information. It just accepts a `dict`, which can contain anything. For example, a tool that interacts with a database may need a connection string as configuration.

```
    def configure(self, config: dict) -> None:
        """Optional: configure the tool with given parameters."""
        pass
```

Finally, the `run()` method is an abstract method that must be implemented by subclasses. It is the method that executes the tool with the provided arguments from the LLM. The arguments are passed as keyword arguments, and it returns a string. As you will recall, the AI-6 engine executes the `run()` method when a tool is called by the LLM during the agentic loop.

```
    @abstractmethod
    def run(self, **kwargs) -> str:
        pass
```

Custom tools are great, but it's important to support built-in tools as well.

What about built-in tools?

Some models support built-in tools. Here is a non-comprehensive list of built-in tools that some OpenAI models support: web search, file search, image generation, code interpreter (Python), and computer use.

You can find the latest list of built-in tools available on the OpenAI platform here:

`https://platform.openai.com/docs/guides/tools#available-tools`

AI-6 doesn't support built-in tools at the moment. The reason is that the use of built-in tools depends on a specific LLM provider, specific models for each LLM provider, and even specific APIs. For example, the OpenAI chat completions API that is used by the AI-6 OpenAIProvider supports only the web search built-in tool. In order to use the other built-in tools mentioned previously, you must use the OpenAI responses API.

In the future, AI-6 may add built-in tool support by updating its configuration system to have lists of allowed built-in tools per LLM provider and per model. For OpenAI, it will also require adding support for the responses API to the OpenAIProvider.

The AI-6 framework supports MCP tools, too. The MCP tools conform to the **Model Context Protocol (MCP)** specification. MCP is a standard protocol originally developed by Anthropic that allows LLMs to access external data and tools in a secure and controlled manner. We will dedicate the entirety of *Chapter 7* to exploring this topic.

Let's now talk about security and permissions that you need to consider for your tool system.

Tool security and permissions

One of the most important aspects of a tool-using agentic AI system is controlling the access of tools to data and resources. The reason is that the tools are in practice controlled by the LLM, which is this magical black box that you have no visibility into. Consider, for example, a scenario where the LLM has access to a database tool with full access to the production database, and it gets the task of improving the performance of data access and reducing costs. The LLM, without additional guidance, might decide that the best way to accomplish that is to delete the database and all the data in it and store just the last day of the data in memory. Fortunately, there are multiple ways to address this issue. AI-6 supports all of them just by virtue of being unopinionated and allowing the agentic AI system to utilize any mechanism or even multiple mechanisms.

Let's look at the various ways you can manage tool execution with different levels of rigor, trust, and control:

- **Full trust, full access**: This mode is appropriate for educational purposes only and when the configured tools can't access any sensitive data or important resources. The LLM can just execute any tool with no checks or limitations. Beware that even in seemingly innocent scenarios, such as tools with read-only access to the LLM, this can cause damage. Consider, for example, a tool with read-only access to a database. The LLM will not be able to corrupt the data or delete it, but it can still read the data and exfiltrate it, and it can cause self-DOS (denial of service) attacks by running huge queries.

- **Mediated fine-grained tool access**: Mediated fine-grained means that the tools don't execute direct commands on the system or access resources directly. For a negative example, consider k8s-ai, which has direct access to the Kubernetes cluster via kubectl. If the LLM decides that it wants to delete all namespaces, k8s-ai will do it with no questions asked. To address this concern, we can remove the kubectl tool and replace it with multiple tools such as `get_pods`, `create_Deployment`, and so on. This approach provides fine-grained access to the Kubernetes cluster and avoids dangerous operations such as deleting namespaces. The benefit of this approach is that it gives you ultimate control, but for resources with a complex API surface, like Kubernetes, it will be a massive burden to manage the access with multiple tools.
- **Guardrails**: Guardrails are another mechanism to manage the risk posed by LLMs. Note that guardrails are a broader concept beyond the tool use of the LLM. The guardrails can safeguard the parameters provided in tool calls, the tool call responses, but also the prompts sent to the LLM and the responses generated by it before passing it to the user. Let's take a look at the different types of guardrails:
    - **Hallucination guardrails** are designed to prevent the AI from generating content that is factually inaccurate or misleading. Implementing these guardrails involves a rigorous evaluation process that compares generated outputs against trusted sources.
    - **Regulatory-compliance guardrails** ensure that AI-generated content adheres to applicable laws and regulations, whether they are general or tailored to a specific industry or use case.
    - **Alignment guardrails** help keep the output consistent with user intent and the original objective, minimizing the risk of content veering off course. These are particularly useful for maintaining tone, messaging, and brand alignment.
    - **Validation guardrails** assess whether the generated content satisfies predefined rules. For example, confirming that certain details are present or absent. If the content fails validation, it should be routed into a correction workflow. This is typically the final automated step, after which any flagged or uncertain cases should undergo human review for resolution.

- **Container-based sandboxing**: One of the main risks of tool use is that the LLM can execute arbitrary code on the system. While the LLM itself might not have ill intentions (yet), it may inadvertently, via tool use, cause performance issues, leave the system vulnerable to other attacks, and, in general, deviate from the intended behavior. To mitigate this risk, it's possible and often recommended to run your agentic AI system in a container, which isolates it from the underlying machine to a certain degree. Note that this is not foolproof, as it is possible to break out of a container (see this article: `https://medium.com/@the.gigi/pwning-kubernetes-77e43fc6c713`). When running AI systems locally, it is often desirable to provide access to local directories, files, and other resources. That means that the container must be configured to allow access to these resources. This is a trade-off between security and controlled access. It also allows providing limited credentials to the external services to the agentic AI system by controlling the files available in the container.
- **User permissions**: User permissions offer another effective layer of control over tool use by running the agent under a dedicated, low-privilege operating system user. This restricts access to sensitive files, directories, and system capabilities, limiting what the LLM-controlled tools can read, write, or execute. Even without containerization, this approach prevents the agent from modifying critical system files or accessing unauthorized data, enforcing the principle of least privilege. For example, the agent might be allowed to write only to a specific directory, such as `/var/agent-output/`, while being blocked from accessing home directories or system configurations. This method can be combined with group-based access control, filesystem ACLs, or Linux features such as `ulimit` and `seccomp` to tighten restrictions further. It's particularly useful in local or lightweight environments where full sandboxing is impractical. While user-level permissions don't stop the LLM from misusing allowed capabilities (e.g., exfiltrating readable data), they provide a clean and manageable boundary that limits unintentional harm and makes security auditing easier.
- **Human-in-the-loop**: Finally, the human-in-the-loop approach is a powerful way to control tool use by the LLM. It involves having a human review and approve specific tool calls before they are executed. This provides a strong safeguard against unintended or harmful actions, as it allows human judgment to filter decisions the LLM might make based on incomplete context or ambiguous prompts. For example, before issuing a command to delete a resource, the system can present the action to a human operator for confirmation, ensuring critical operations are only performed when explicitly approved. This approach can be implemented at various levels of granularity, from approving every tool invocation to selectively intervening on high-risk actions. It is particularly effective in domains where mistakes are costly or safety is paramount, such

as infrastructure management, financial operations, or medical systems. While it introduces latency and requires human availability, it significantly increases trust and reliability, making it ideal for hybrid workflows that balance automation with oversight.

Memory is another crucial part of an agentic system. Let's talk about it next.

Memory management

Memory management is arguably the most important job of an agentic AI framework. It can be done by the host AI system, but it is important enough and nuanced enough that it is better to let the AI framework solve this problem once and let the AI system that was built on it focus on application-level concerns. As we discussed in *Chapter 2*, multiple types of memory are important in AI systems. AI-6 manages all the different types of memory through a single concept: the session.

What is a session?

The **session** is the collection of all the messages of a single top-level interaction with the LLM. A session also keeps count of the input and output tokens of all the messages. A single session may involve multiple input messages, involve multiple AI agents, and may persist across time and machine boundaries.

It is defined in the `engine/session.py` file.

Let's see how it works. Here are the imports. The `json` package is needed for serialization/deserialization of sessions. The `uuid` package is used to generate unique session IDs, then a lot of imports from the AI-6 object model:

```
import json
import uuid
from dataclasses import asdict

from backend.object_model import (
    Usage, Message, UserMessage, SystemMessage, AssistantMessage,
    ToolMessage, ToolCall)
```

The session is initialized with a memory directory, which is where persistent sessions are stored. First, a random session ID is generated, and then a session title is created based on the session ID. We will see later how to set the title of a saved session via a different class, `SessionManager`. Then, we initialize a `usage` object:

```
class Session:
    def __init__(self, memory_dir: str):
        self.session_id = str(uuid.uuid4())
        self.title = 'Untiled session ~' + self.session_id
        self.messages: list[Message] = []
        self.usage = Usage(0, 0)
        self.memory_dir = memory_dir
```

The `add_message()` method is pretty straightforward. It takes a message and appends it to the messages list of the session. If the message has a `usage` object, then it updates the session's usage by adding the input and output tokens, so the session keeps a running total. We will see how the usage object is used to decide if the context window needs to be compacted in the *Handling long contexts* section.

```
    def add_message(self, message: Message):
        """Add a Message object to the session."""
        self.messages.append(message)

        # Extract usage from AssistantMessage if present
        if hasattr(message, 'usage') and message.usage:
            self.usage = Usage(
                self.usage.input_tokens + message.usage.input_tokens,
                self.usage.output_tokens + message.usage.output_tokens
            )
```

The `save()` method converts each message to a dictionary using the `asdict()` function of the `dataclasses` module, then prepares another dictionary that contains all message dictionaries, serializes the dictionary to JSON, and saves it to a file named `<session id>.json` in the memory directory. Now, we have a persistent session that we can later restore even if the process crashes.

```
    def save(self):
        # Convert Message objects to dictionaries for JSON serialization
        message_dicts = [asdict(msg) for msg in self.messages]
```

```
    d = dict(session_id=self.session_id,
             title=self.title,
             messages=message_dicts,
             usage=dict(
                 input_tokens=self.usage.input_tokens,
                 output_tokens=self.usage.output_tokens))
    filename = f"{self.memory_dir}/{self.session_id}.json"
    with open(filename, 'w') as f:
        json.dump(d, f, indent=4)
```

Let's look at a saved session. The user asks what the current directory is. The LLM responds with an assistant message with a request to run the `pwd` tool, which returns the current directory. The AI-6 framework correctly executed the tool and sent to the LLM a tool message with the answer `"/Users/gigi/git/AI-6"`. Then, the LLM responds with a final assistant message, `\n\nThe current directory is `/Users/gigi/git/AI-6`. The session continued as the user sent a new query, but I cut it short. Note that in the end, it calculated the input and output tokens of all messages:

```
{
    "session_id": "045d8889-d51b-4a48-bb3b-c97f9700af23",
    "title": "Untiled session ~045d8889-d51b-4a48-bb3b-c97f9700af23",
    "messages": [
        {
            "role": "user",
            "content": "what's curr dir"
        },
        {
            "role": "assistant",
            "content": null,
            "tool_calls": [
                {
                    "id": "tool_185f7ac72fb2404e95660d90964dc98f",
                    "type": "function",
                    "function": {
                        "name": "pwd",
                        "arguments": "{}"
                    }
                }
            ],
            "input_tokens": 551,
```

```
            "output_tokens": 11
        },
        {
            "role": "tool",
            "name": "pwd",
            "content": "/Users/gigi/git/AI-6",
            "tool_call_id": "tool_185f7ac72fb2404e95660d90964dc98f"
        },
        {
            "role": "assistant",
            "content": "\n\nThe current directory is `/Users/gigi/git/AI-6`."
        }
        .
        .
        .
    ],
    "usage": {
        "input_tokens": 3068,
        "output_tokens": 57
    }
}
```

The `load()` method is the opposite of `save()`. It accepts a session ID, locates the corresponding session file according to the naming convention, and loads the JSON from the file into a Python dictionary. Then, it creates the `Session` object from the JSON field by field. To convert each message from a dictionary to a `Message` object (or one of its subclasses), it uses the `dict_to_message()` function:

```
    def load(self, session_id: str):
        """Load session from disk, properly deserializing nested objects"""
        filename = f"{self.memory_dir}/{session_id}.json"
        with open(filename, 'r') as f:
            d = json.load(f)
        self.session_id = d['session_id']
        self.title = d['title']

        # Convert message dictionaries back to Message objects
        self.messages = [dict_to_message(msg) for msg in d['messages']]

        # Deserialize usage directly to a Usage object
```

```
        self.usage = Usage(d['usage']['input_tokens'],
            d['usage']['output_tokens'])
```

Now, let's see how the session is used with different types of memory.

Short-term memory in the agentic loop

During the agentic loop, the AI-6 engine potentially makes multiple requests to the LLM, and it accumulates all previous messages. Every tool request and its response after being executed are added to the active session and are available to the LLM in the next iteration of the agentic loop as the session becomes the context window. For example, consider the following interaction:

```
User: what is the current directory?
LLM (tool call): pwd (print working directory)
User: How many Python files in the current directory?
LLM (tool call): ls *.py
AI-6 (tool call response): foo.py bar.py
LLM (final response): There are two Python files in the current directory
User: What are they?
LLM (final response): The files are foo.py and bar.py
```

At each point, the LLM receives the entire conversation and not just the last message. When the user asks `What are they?`, the LLM can infer from the conversation history that the user is referring to the Python files in the current directory, and it can return them immediately without another tool call.

Sessions and conversations

When an agentic loop ends a final response is returned to the user (or agentic AI application). The user may continue the conversation by sending a new user message that will start a new agentic loop, but with the context that includes all the previous messages of the current session.

Long-term memory and session loading

We showed how the session can save and load itself to/from a file. But what is the mechanism that enables it? This is where the session manager comes in. The session manager is implemented in the `engine/session_manager` file. It exposes three methods to manage persistent sessions:

- `list_sessions()`
- `delete_session()`
- `set_title()`

When an AI-6 application starts, it can call `list_sessions()` to review all existing sessions and decide to load an existing session or delete an old session. It can also set the title for an existing session.

Let's see how the session manager works. The session is initialized with the memory directory, which is where the session files are stored:

```
import os
import json
class SessionManager:
    def __init__(self, memory_dir: str):
        self.memory_dir = memory_dir
```

The `set_title()` method accepts a session ID and a title. It locates the session file (raising an exception if not found), loads the session from the JSON file as a Python dictionary, replaces the title, and saves it back. Note the unusual sequence of seek, dump, and truncate to update the file. It is a safe option for updating files using a single file handle and with minimal risk of truncating the file and then crashing and leaving an empty file. If you just overwrite a file with a command such as `open(filename, 'w').write()` and the process crashes immediately after the `open()` command, then you are left with an empty file:

```
    def set_title(self, session_id: str, title: str):
        """Set the title of a session."""
        sessions = self.list_sessions()
        if session_id not in sessions:
            raise RuntimeError(f"Session {session_id} not found.")

        filename = sessions[session_id]['filename']
        with open(filename, 'r+') as f:
            data = json.load(f)
            data['title'] = title
            f.seek(0)
            json.dump(data, f, indent=4)
            f.truncate()
```

The `list_sessions()` method lists all the `.json` files in the memory directory, verifies they contain valid JSON, and returns a list of dictionaries where each session dictionary contains its title and filename. If something is wrong, it just prints an error message and continues to the next session:

```
    def list_sessions(self) -> list[dict]
        """List all sessions in the memory directory.

        Returns:
            A dictionary mapping session IDs to tuples of (name, filename)
        """
        sessions = {}
        files = os.listdir(self.memory_dir)
        for f in files:
            if f.endswith('.json'):
                try:
        # Get session ID from the filename (dropping the .json extension)
                    session_id = os.path.basename(f).rsplit('.json', 1)[0]

        # Try to open and parse the file to verify it's valid JSON
                    full_path = os.path.join(self.memory_dir, f)
                    with open(full_path, 'r') as file:
                        try:
                            # Attempt to parse the JSON
                            session = json.loads(file.read())
                            # Only add if we could parse the JSON
                            sessions[session_id] = dict(
                                title=session['title'],
                                filename=full_path)
                        except json.JSONDecodeError:
                            # Skip files with invalid JSON
                            print(f"Skipping file with invalid JSON: {f}")
                            continue
                except Exception as e:
                    # Skip any files that cause other errors
                    print(f"Error parsing session file {f}: {e}")
                    continue

        return sessions
```

Deleting a session is very simple, too. List the sessions, get the filename, and remove the file:

```
    def delete_session(self, session_id: str):
        """Delete a session by its ID."""
        sessions = self.list_sessions()
        if session_id not in sessions:
            raise RuntimeError(f"Session {session_id} not found.")

        filename = sessions[session_id]['filename']
        os.remove(filename)
```

The session manager can manage sessions, but as these sessions grow, they can saturate the context. Let's understand the problem and consider how to address it.

Handling long contexts

One of the biggest problems that an agentic AI framework needs to work with is managing the size of the context, so it fits in the context window size of the model. Agentic workflows can span many requests to the LLM over long periods of time and accumulate more and more context. The solution is to compress the context when it's approaching the limit. But, how do you decide what context should be kept? Well, LLMs are excellent at summarizing long blocks of text. Let's ask the LLM to compress the context. This is exactly what the summarizer does. It is implemented in the `engine/summarizer` file. Let's see it in action. It is initialized with an LLM provider:

```
from backend.object_model import (
    Message, LLMProvider, SystemMessage, UserMessage)

class Summarizer:
    """Utility class for summarizing sessions using an LLM."""
    def __init__(self, llm_provider: LLMProvider):
        """Initialize the summarizer with an LLM provider.

        Args:
            llm_provider: An LLM provider instance
        """
        self.llm_provider = llm_provider
```

The `summarize()` method accepts a list of messages and a model ID. It prepares a system prompt with instructions on how to summarize conversations and then formats the session messages into a single string that contains the role and content of each message (using the _format_session() method). Then it sends the system message and a user message that contains the combined session string to the provider, which returns a summary of the session. Note that this is a single send() call directly to the LLM provider.

There is no session involved in this interaction:

```
    def summarize(self, messages: list[Message], model_id: str) -> str:
        """Summarize a list of messages using the LLM.

        Args:
            messages: List of message dictionaries to summarize
            model_id: ID of the model to use for summarization

        Returns:
            A string summary of the session
        """
        # Format messages for the LLM
        formatted_messages = [
            SystemMessage(
                content=(
                    "You are a helpful assistant tasked with summarizing a 
conversation. "
                    "Create a concise summary that captures the key points, 
questions, decisions, and context "
                    "from the session. The summary should be informative enough 
that someone "
                    "reading it would understand what was discussed, what 
conclusions were reached, "
                    "and what important context should be carried forward. "
                    "Focus on preserving information that will be useful for 
continuing the conversation, "
                    "including names, technical terms, important numbers, and 
specific details that might "
                    "be referenced later. Avoid unnecessary details, repetitive 
information, or tangential discussions."
                )
            ),
            UserMessage(
                content=(
                    "Please summarize the following session:\n\n" +
                    self._format_session(messages)
```

```
            )
        )
    ]

    # Get summary from LLM
    response = self.llm_provider.send(
        formatted_messages, {}, model_id)
    return response.content.strip()
```

Here is the `_format_session()` static method that converts a list of messages to one big string that contains the role and content of each message:

```
@staticmethod
@staticmethod
def _format_session(messages: list[Message]) -> str:
    """
    Format a list of messages into a readable session.

    Args:
        messages: List of message dictionaries

    Returns:
        Formatted session string
    """
    formatted = []

    for msg in messages:
        role = msg.role
        content = msg.content

        if role == "tool":
            tool_name = getattr(msg, 'name', 'unknown tool')
            formatted.append(f"Tool ({tool_name}): {content}")
        else:
            formatted.append(f"{role.capitalize()}: {content}")

    return "\n\n".join(formatted)
```

The decision about whether a summarization is needed happens in the engine in the `_checkpoint_if_needed()` method, which saves the session periodically and also checks the total number of tokens in the session (obtained from the `usage` object) against the context window size. If the number of tokens exceeds that threshold, then a summarization will take place, and the session will use the shorter summarized context from this point forward.

Here is how this method is defined:

```
def _checkpoint_if_needed(self):
    """Check if we need to save a checkpoint and do so if needed."""
    self.message_count_since_checkpoint += 1

    # Only save if we've reached the checkpoint interval exactly
    if self.message_count_since_checkpoint == self.checkpoint_interval:
        self.session.save()
        self.message_count_since_checkpoint = 0

        # Check and summarize if above token threshold (80% of context window)
        total_tokens = (
                self.session.usage.input_tokens + \
                self.session.usage.output_tokens
        )
        if total_tokens >= self.token_threshold:
            context_window_size = get_context_window_size(
                self.default_model_id)
            print(
                f"Session tokens ({total_tokens}) have reached
{self.summary_threshold_ratio * 100}% of context window ({context_window_size}).
Summarizing..."
            )
            self._summarize_and_reset_session()
```

Note that automatic summarization by the LLM is not the only way to compress the context window when it becomes too large. Other approaches include **semantic search with embeddings** to retrieve only the most relevant past turns, **rule-based pruning** to drop trivial or repeated exchanges, **structured storage** of facts and entities for on-demand injection, and **token-efficient re-encoding** techniques such as codebooks, custom shorthand formats, or domain-specific compression schemes.

In the future, AI-6 may evolve to make memory management extensible. The engine will not directly invoke the summarizer when the context window becomes too large, but will be initialized with a generic context manager that will implement some compaction method. This approach will follow the blueprint of tools and `LLMProvider`, where the engine interacts with other components through an abstract interface. Specifically, a generic `ContextManager` interface with a `summarize()` method can be implemented by multiple concrete context managers that can be configured by the user to select the best method for summarizing sessions.

Summary

In this chapter, we learned that the AI-6 framework is a robust, extensible platform designed to support sophisticated agentic AI systems. Building on the minimal k8s-ai agent, AI-6 introduces a modular backend architecture that coordinates tool execution, memory management, and communication with multiple LLM providers. At its core is the `Engine` class, which orchestrates the agentic loop, receiving user input, invoking tools as needed, managing the session history, and interacting with LLMs through a unified provider interface. Configuration is centralized through a simple `Config` object, allowing users to define tools, memory directories, model defaults, and behavior parameters. The system is designed to be unopinionated, making it easy to build specialized or more opinionated systems on top.

A key strength of AI-6 lies in its abstraction of LLM providers and tools. It supports both remote providers such as OpenAI and local ones such as Ollama, using a common interface that handles message formatting, tool integration, and response parsing. Tools themselves are defined through a lightweight Python interface that supports description, typed parameters, and execution logic. The framework is designed to safely manage tool use by offering support for fine-grained tool definitions, runtime guardrails, sandboxing through OS permissions or containers, and human-in-the-loop control when needed. This provides a strong foundation for building secure and reliable AI systems capable of using external capabilities effectively.

Memory is managed through a concept called sessions, which encapsulate all interaction history and token usage. Sessions can be saved, resumed, summarized, and inspected through a dedicated `SessionManager` object. When a session grows too large, a built-in summarization module uses an LLM to compress earlier messages while preserving important context. This ensures that AI-6 can operate over long conversations without exceeding model limits. Together, these features form a cohesive, production-ready framework for managing agent behavior, tool use, and long-term memory in AI systems.

In the next chapter, we will see how to implement custom tools for AI-6 and get to experiment with different combinations of tools to perform useful tasks.

Subscribe for a free eBook

New frameworks, evolving architectures, research drops, production breakdowns – *AI_Distilled* filters the noise into a weekly briefing for engineers and researchers working hands-on with LLMs and generative AI systems. Subscribe now and receive a free eBook, along with weekly insights that help you stay focused and informed.

Subscribe at `https://packt.link/8Oz6Y` or scan the QR code below.

5

Implementing Custom Tools

In the previous chapter, we explored the backend architecture of the AI-6 framework in detail, focusing on how the engine orchestrates the agentic loop, manages memory and session tate, and integrates with multiple LLM providers and tools. We saw how tools and models are dynamically discovered and how the engine handles their coordination through a unified abstraction. This foundation enables flexible, provider-agnostic AI workflows with persistent memory, resumable sessions, and secure, extensible tool usage.

In this chapter, we will shift focus from the overall engine architecture to a deeper investigation of the tool system itself. While *Chapter 4* treated tools largely as pluggable black boxes, here we will look inside and examine how generic tools are designed to be reusable, consistent, and portable across LLM providers. We will explore how tools can be defined with structured schemas, how arguments are validated, and how they are registered and translated into provider-specific formats.

We'll begin by discussing how AI-6 allows its users to implement a tool in terms of the generic AI-6 tool format. This single generic tool implementation will work with any LLM provider, such as OpenAI, Ollama, or some future LLM provider that doesn't even exist yet. We will also look at the specific APIs of OpenAI and Ollama to understand how they provide similar functionality through slightly different specifications, and how AI-6 can utilize both of these providers without exposing their internals to its users, followed by a review of schema definitions and input validation strategies. From there, we'll look at how AI-6 maps its internal tool representation to provider-specific formats (such as OpenAI function calling). Finally, we will examine how tool execution is managed, including how results are captured and routed back to the LLM through the session. This chapter will lay the groundwork for building powerful, safe, and interoperable tools that expand the capabilities of agentic AI systems.

In this chapter, we will cover the following main topics:

- Defining generic tools
- Defining AI-6 custom tools
- Implementing a new tool manually

Technical requirements

There are no specific technical requirements for this chapter. If you wish to build your own custom tools, you can use any Python library. You simply need to implement the **Tool** interface, which is part of the AI-6 framework itself, to customize your tools. The code for the chapter is available here:

`https://github.com/PacktPublishing/Design-Multi-Agent-AI-Systems-Using-MCP-and-A2A/tree/main/ch05/ai-six`.

Defining provider-agnostic tools

Every LLM provider API, such as OpenAI, Anthropic, Gemini, and Ollama, has its own way of specifying tools. Since AI-6 needs to work with all LLM providers, it defines its own provider-agnostic format. The AI-6 framework's LLM providers that interact directly with the APIs or SDK of third-party LLM providers know how to translate the generic tool definition to the provider-specific tool definition.

The AI-6 tools definition must be a superset of the information required by all the APIs. The focus of the tools definition is on function calling, although built-in tools are supported too. Let's look at the tool definition of LLM provider Python SDKs, such as OpenAI and Ollama. The reason we look at Python SDKs and not the raw REST APIs is that the AI-6 LLM providers are implemented in Python and use the Python SDKs of the corresponding third-party LLM providers.

Let's first look at the OpenAI Python SDK and see how it specifies tools and tool calls.

OpenAI Python tool specification

The OpenAI Python SDK is available at `https://github.com/openai/openai-python`.

It was generated automatically from the OpenAPI specification (`https://github.com/openai/openai-openapi`) of the OpenAI REST API, so it has 100% fidelity to the actual OpenAI API.

The tool definition we are interested in is in the chat completions endpoint, which is accessible through the `create()` method (`https://github.com/openai/openai-python/blob/main/src/openai/resources/chat/completions/completions.py#L76`) of the `Completions` class of the Chat Completions API. Do not confuse it with the legacy Completions API (`https://platform.openai.com/docs/api-reference/completions`).

This method makes a call to the LLM (optionally with a lot of arguments) and gets a response. This response can be a final response or a tool call, which will be processed by AI-6 (as we discussed in the previous chapter).

The `create()` method has eight overloaded versions. This means that there are eight different methods, and all of them are named `create()` with slightly different arguments. The reason overloaded methods are useful, especially for methods with a lot of arguments, is that different overloaded versions can provide different levels of control as opposed to ease of use:

```
@overload
    def create(
        self,
        *,
        messages: Iterable[ChatCompletionMessageParam],
        model: Union[str, ChatModel],
        audio: Optional[ChatCompletionAudioParam] | NotGiven = NOT_GIVEN,
        frequency_penalty: Optional[float] | NotGiven = NOT_GIVEN,
        function_call: completion_create_params.FunctionCall | NotGiven =
NOT_GIVEN,
        functions: Iterable[completion_create_params.Function] | NotGiven =
NOT_GIVEN,
        logit_bias: Optional[Dict[str, int]] | NotGiven = NOT_GIVEN,
        logprobs: Optional[bool] | NotGiven = NOT_GIVEN,
        max_completion_tokens: Optional[int] | NotGiven = NOT_GIVEN,
        max_tokens: Optional[int] | NotGiven = NOT_GIVEN,
        metadata: Optional[Metadata] | NotGiven = NOT_GIVEN,
        modalities: Optional[List[Literal["text", "audio"]]] | NotGiven =
NOT_GIVEN,
        n: Optional[int] | NotGiven = NOT_GIVEN,
        parallel_tool_calls: bool | NotGiven = NOT_GIVEN,
        prediction: Optional[ChatCompletionPredictionContentParam] | NotGiven =
NOT_GIVEN,
        presence_penalty: Optional[float] | NotGiven = NOT_GIVEN,
        reasoning_effort: Optional[ReasoningEffort] | NotGiven = NOT_GIVEN,
        response_format: completion_create_params.ResponseFormat | NotGiven =
NOT_GIVEN,
        seed: Optional[int] | NotGiven = NOT_GIVEN,
        service_tier: Optional[Literal["auto", "default", "flex", "scale"]] |
```

```
NotGiven = NOT_GIVEN,
        stop: Union[Optional[str], List[str], None] | NotGiven = NOT_GIVEN,
        store: Optional[bool] | NotGiven = NOT_GIVEN,
        stream: Optional[Literal[False]] | NotGiven = NOT_GIVEN,
        stream_options: Optional[ChatCompletionStreamOptionsParam] | NotGiven =
NOT_GIVEN,
        temperature: Optional[float] | NotGiven = NOT_GIVEN,
        tool_choice: ChatCompletionToolChoiceOptionParam | NotGiven = NOT_GIVEN,
        tools: Iterable[ChatCompletionToolParam] | NotGiven = NOT_GIVEN, #
        top_logprobs: Optional[int] | NotGiven = NOT_GIVEN,
        top_p: Optional[float] | NotGiven = NOT_GIVEN,
        user: str | NotGiven = NOT_GIVEN,
        web_search_options: completion_create_params.WebSearchOptions |
NotGiven = NOT_GIVEN,

# Use the following arguments if you need to pass additional parameters to the API
that aren't available via kwargs.
        # The extra values given here take precedence over values defined on the
client or passed to this method.
        extra_headers: Headers | None = None,
        extra_query: Query | None = None,
        extra_body: Body | None = None,
        timeout: float | httpx.Timeout | None | NotGiven = NOT_GIVEN,
    ) -> ChatCompletion:
        """
        ...
        """
```

Some of the overloaded methods are synchronous, and some are asynchronous, but they all define the tools in the same way:

```
tools: Iterable[ChatCompletionToolParam] | NotGiven = NOT_GIVEN,
```

What does this line mean?

1. `Iterable[ChatCompletionToolParam]` means that the provided tools should be an iterable sequence where each element is of the `ChatCompletionToolParam` type.
2. The second part, `| NotGiven = NOT_GIVEN`, means that the `tools` argument can alternatively be the `NotGiven` type and the default value if no tools are provided. The `NOT_GIVEN` value is a constant of the `NotGiven` type.

In other words, the `tools` argument can be one of two types (Python allows that). The first type is `Iterable[ChatCompletionToolParam]`, which you can think of as a list of items of the `ChatCompletionToolParam` type. The second type is `NotGiven`. The default value of the `tools` argument is `NOT_GIVEN`. If the caller didn't provide any tools, then the value of the `tools` argument will be the default, `NOT_GIVEN`.

If you're wondering what `NotGiven` is, it is a simple sentinel class used to denote unspecified parameters and provide them with the default value of `NOT_GIVEN`.

OK. Let's understand what `ChatCompletionToolParam` is. It is a class with two fields: `function` and `type`. Both of these fields are required. The `function` field is of the `FunctionDefinition` type, and the `type` field must be the literal string `"function"`.

Here is how you can define this class:

```
class ChatCompletionToolParam(TypedDict, total=False):
    function: Required[FunctionDefinition]

    type: Required[Literal["function"]]
    """The type of the tool. Currently, only `function` is supported."""
```

This can be a little confusing because there are two different kinds of types here. The type of the function, `Required[FunctionDefinition]`, is a type hint for a required Python type, `FunctionDefinition`. The OpenAI Chat Completions API is interesting because it supports only one kind of tool, a function tool, but the API is defined in a more general way as if it can support additional tool kinds.

Other OpenAI APIs do support multiple tool kinds. The deprecated Assistants%20API%20(beta) (`https://github.com/openai/openai-python/blob/main/src/openai/types/beta/assistant.py`) supports two built-in tools: `file_search` and `code_interpreter`.

> **Note**
>
> Well, that was quite a journey of API design that OpenAI went through. Initially, there was just the Chat Completion API, which we use and has only the `"function"` tool kind.
>
> Then, there was the Assistants API that never got out of beta and eventually was deprecated. Later, the Responses API was published with several more tool kinds.

Here are the definitions of the built-in `CodeInterpreter` and `FileSearch` tools:

```
class ToolResourcesCodeInterpreter(BaseModel):
    file_ids: Optional[List[str]] = None
    """
    A list of [file](https://platform.openai.com/docs/api-reference/files) IDs
made
    available to the `code_interpreter`` tool. There can be a maximum of 20 files
    associated with the tool.
    """


class ToolResourcesFileSearch(BaseModel):
    vector_store_ids: Optional[List[str]] = None
    """
    The ID of the
    [vector store](https://platform.openai.com/docs/api-reference/vector-stores/
object)
    attached to this assistant. There can be a maximum of 1 vector store attached
to
    the assistant.
    """


class ToolResources(BaseModel):
    code_interpreter: Optional[ToolResourcesCodeInterpreter] = None
    file_search: Optional[ToolResourcesFileSearch] = None
```

The new Responses API supports the following tools defined in `types/responses/tool_param.py` (`https://github.com/openai/openai-python/blob/main/src/openai/types/responses/tool_param.py#L170`):

```
ToolParam: TypeAlias = Union[
    FunctionToolParam,
    FileSearchToolParam,
    WebSearchToolParam,
    ComputerToolParam,
    Mcp,
    CodeInterpreter,
    ImageGeneration,
```

```
    LocalShell,
]
```

At the moment, the OpenAI LLM provider of AI-6 uses the Chat Completions API, so let's get back to the `FunctionDefinition` class (`https://github.com/openai/openai-python/blob/main/src/openai/types/shared/function_definition.py#L11`). It represents a single function tool and has a name, description, optional parameters, and an optional strict flag (`False` unless explicitly set to `True`):

```
class FunctionDefinition(BaseModel):
    name: str
    """The name of the function to be called.

    Must be a-z, A-Z, 0-9, or contain underscores and dashes, with a maximum
length
    of 64.
    """

    description: Optional[str] = None
    """
    A description of what the function does, used by the model to choose when and
    how to call the function.
    """

    parameters: Optional[FunctionParameters] = None
    """The parameters the functions accepts, described as a JSON Schema object.

    See the [guide](https://platform.openai.com/docs/guides/function-calling) for
    examples, and the
    [JSON Schema reference](https://json-schema.org/understanding-json-schema/)
for
    documentation about the format.

    Omitting `parameters` defines a function with an empty parameter list.
    """

    strict: Optional[bool] = None
    """Whether to enable strict schema adherence when generating the function
call.
```

```
    If set to true, the model will follow the exact schema defined in the
    `parameters` field. Only a subset of JSON Schema is supported when `strict` is
    `true`. Learn more about Structured Outputs in the
    [function calling guide](docs/guides/function-calling).
    """
```

Let's keep drilling down and see what `FunctionParameters` (`https://github.com/openai/openai-python/blob/main/src/openai/types/shared/function_parameters.py`) in the `FunctionDefinition` class is all about. It turns out that it is a simple dictionary of string -> any object.

```
# File generated from our OpenAPI spec by Stainless.

from typing import Dict
from typing_extensions import TypeAlias

__all__ = ["FunctionParameters"]

FunctionParameters: TypeAlias = Dict[str, object]
```

Let's recap the tool definition requirements of the Chat Completions API as specified by OpenAI:

- Every tool must be of the `"function"` type
- Every tool has a name and a description
- A tool may have zero or more parameters with a name and an arbitrary value type
- A tool may specify whether its output is strict

There is one more important element for the OpenAI tools specification. In addition to the `tools` argument of the `create()` methods, there is also a `tool_choice` argument:

```
tool_choice: ChatCompletionToolChoiceOptionParam | NotGiven = NOT_GIVEN,
```

The tool choice can take one of the following values: `"none"` (don't call any tool), `"auto"` (you decide whether you want to call one or more tools and which tools), `"required"` (you must call at least one tool; you decide which tool or tools to call), or a specific tool name (you must call this tool):

```
ChatCompletionToolChoiceOptionParam: TypeAlias = Union[
    Literal["none", "auto", "required"],
```

```
    ChatCompletionNamedToolChoiceParam
]
```

If this sounds confusing, it's because it is. I wrote a whole blog post about the problems with tool choice and how it can be significantly simplified: *Fixing the OpenAI Tool Calling API*. You will find it here: `https://medium.com/@the.gigi/fixing-the-openai-tool-calling-api-ede67419f9f5`.

OK. Let's keep this in mind and see how the Ollama Python SDK specifies tool calls.

Ollama Python tool specification

The Ollama Python SDK (`https://github.com/ollama/ollama-python`) is already an abstraction over many APIs because it supports many providers through a unified interface. Let's see how tools are specified in the Ollama Python SDK.

Ollama uses the `chat()` methods (multiple overloads similar to OpenAI) of the `Client` class (`https://github.com/ollama/ollama-python/blob/main/ollama/_client.py#L114`) to interact with the LLM and specify tools:

```
@overload
def chat(
    self,
    model: str = '',
    messages: Optional[
        Sequence[Union[Mapping[str, Any], Message]]] = None,
    *,
    tools: Optional[
        Sequence[Union[Mapping[str, Any], Tool, Callable]]] = None, # 👈
    stream: Literal[False] = False,
    think: Optional[bool] = None,
    format: Optional[Union[Literal['', 'json'], JsonSchemaValue]] = None,
    options: Optional[Union[Mapping[str, Any], Options]] = None,
    keep_alive: Optional[Union[float, str]] = None,
) -> ChatResponse: ...
```

The tool definition is a mouthful. Let's parse it. The parameter named `tools` is optional and defaults to `None`. If provided, it must be a sequence (such as a list or tuple) where each item is one of three allowed types:

- A `Mapping[str, Any]` JSON schema as a dictionary with string keys and values of any type
- An Ollama `Tool` instance (a class provided by the Ollama SDK that wraps tool metadata and behavior)
- A `Callable` object that follows Google-style docstrings to be converted to an Ollama `Tool` instance:

```
tools: Optional[
    Sequence[Union[Mapping[str, Any], Tool, Callable]]
] = None
```

Regardless of the representation, they all end up as a sequence of Ollama `Tool` instances (`https://github.com/ollama/ollama-python/blob/main/ollama/_types.py#L312`):

```
class Tool(SubscriptableBaseModel):
    type: Optional[Literal['function']] = 'function'

    class Function(SubscriptableBaseModel):
        name: Optional[str] = None
        description: Optional[str] = None

        class Parameters(SubscriptableBaseModel):
            model_config = ConfigDict(populate_by_name=True)
            type: Optional[Literal['object']] = 'object'
            defs: Optional[Any] = Field(None, alias='$defs')
            items: Optional[Any] = None
            required: Optional[Sequence[str]] = None

            class Property(SubscriptableBaseModel):
                model_config = ConfigDict(arbitrary_types_allowed=True)

                type: Optional[Union[str, Sequence[str]]] = None
                items: Optional[Any] = None
                description: Optional[str] = None
                enum: Optional[Sequence[Any]] = None
            properties: Optional[Mapping[str, Property]] = None
```

```
        parameters: Optional[Parameters] = None
    function: Optional[Function] = None
```

We're not going to parse every line in this Python code and just note that Ollama attaches some model information to the tool definition, which is probably used when translating `Tool` to the model-specific tool definition.

The important thing to pay attention to is that, similar to the OpenAI Completion API, the only supported tool type is `"function"`.

To summarize, OpenAI and Ollama define tools in their own format, but conceptually, they contain equivalent information for each tool, which is great for AI-6.

We are now ready to see the generic tool specification schema of AI-6.

Defining the AI-6 tool specification schema

We covered the AI-6 `Parameter` and `Tool` classes in the previous chapter. Here is a quick refresher. It aims for simplicity without too much fancy stuff. One special feature that is present in AI-6 and is missing from both the OpenAI and Ollama tool specifications is the `required` field of the `Tool` class. This field is a set of parameter names that must be provided when the LLM calls the tool. It is part of the OpenAI tool specification in the REST API, but somehow it didn't make it to the Python SDK:

```
class Parameter(NamedTuple):
    name: str
    type: str
    description: str

@dataclass(slots=True)
class Tool(ABC):
    name: str
    description: str
    parameters: list[Parameter]
    required: set[str]

    def configure(self, config: dict) -> None:
        """Optional: configure the tool with given parameters."""

    @abstractmethod
    def run(self, **kwargs) -> str:
```

```
        """Execute the tool using the given arguments and return the result as a
string."""
```

This straightforward code is the entire tool specification schema of AI-6. It is very simple and easy to comprehend.

Well, you have already seen how AI-6 can abstract the provider and respective implementation to define tools with the `LLMProvider` interface. We will now see how to define custom tools that can be translated to the tool format of the active LLM provider in the next section.

Defining AI-6 custom tools

AI-6 comes with many examples of ready-to-use tools, and it is easy to implement new tools. In this section, we will review some of the existing tools and then implement a brand-new tool from scratch.

The process of defining an AI-6 custom tool consists of the following steps:

1. Create a new Python class.
2. Derive from the `Tool` base class directly or indirectly.
3. Implement the `run()` method.
4. Optionally implement the `configure()` method.

Let's start with general command-line tools, which are very powerful.

General command-line tools

Many of the useful tools that AI-6 provides out of the box are command-line tools. These tools run wherever AI-6 runs (on your machine, in a container, in the cloud, etc.). AI-6 provides a base class for command-line tools that takes care of all the boilerplate necessary for running command-line programs with arbitrary arguments and offers the option to run the command-line program as a dedicated user (different from the current user). Let's see how the `CommandTool` class works before we examine the tools derived from it.

> **Note**
>
> LLMs don't know that they invoke command-line tools. As you recall, LLMs receive tool definitions, and then, via the agentic loop, they request to invoke these tools. The actual tool execution happens on the AI system/framework side, where very often they will run command-line tools.

It imports the sh package (`https://sh.readthedocs.io/en/latest/index.html`) for running shell commands, the `shlex` built-in package (`https://docs.python.org/3/library/shlex.html`) for parsing POSIX command-line arguments, and `Parameter` and `Tool` from the AI-6 object model:

```
import sh
import shlex
from backend.object_model import Tool, Parameter
```

Here is how the `CommandTool` class is organized to help you implement the command-line tools:

1. The class is derived from the `Tool` base class, so it can serve as a base class for AI-6 tools.
2. The constructor takes as input a command name (the name of a command-line program available on the path), an optional user, and an optional link to documentation of the command.
3. It then constructs a list of parameters that contains exactly one string parameter called `args`, which is expected to be all the command-line arguments to the target command.
4. The `args` parameter is required, but it may be an empty string. If a documentation link was provided, it will be added to the description of the command, which will help the LLM to understand how to invoke the command.

Let's take a look at the class definition:

```
class CommandTool(Tool):
    def __init__(
        self, command_name: str, user: str | None = None,
        doc_link: str = ""
    ):
        self.command_name = command_name
        self.user = user
        description = f'{command_name} tool. ' + f'See {doc_link}' if doc_link
else ''
        parameters = [Parameter(name='args', type='string',
            description=f'command-line arguments for {command_name}')]
        required = {'args'}
        super().__init__(
            name=command_name,
            description=description,
```

```
            parameters=parameters,
            required=required
        )
```

The `run()` method has two jobs. First, to parse the command-line arguments in the `args` parameter using the `shlex.split()` method and then execute the command with the dedicated user (if provided) or as the current user. Note that the current user must be able to switch to the dedicated user (via `sudo`):

```
    def run(self, **kwargs):
        args = shlex.split(kwargs['args'])
        if self.user is not None:
            return sh.sudo('-u', self.user, self.command_name, *args)
        else:
            return getattr(sh, self.command_name)(*args)
```

The `CommandTool` class provides no special `configure()` method to override the optional `Tool.configure()` method, but tool classes derived from `CommandTool` may do so if necessary.

Now, let's see how easy it is to implement command tools and provide strong capabilities to our AI agents.

We will begin with the filesystem tools.

Filesystem tools

Some of the most useful commands deal with files and directories. AI-6 provides basic directory and file commands such as `pwd`, `ls`, `cat`, and `echo`.

It also provides some more sophisticated file editing commands, such as `sed`, `awk`, and `patch`. Let's start with the **print working directory** (`pwd`). All we have to do is define a class called `Pwd` with a minimal constructor that just provides the documentation link for the POSIX `pwd` command:

```
from backend.tools.base.command_tool import CommandTool
class Pwd(CommandTool):
    def __init__(self, user: str | None = None):
        doc_link = 'https://www.gnu.org/software/coreutils/manual/html_node/pwd-
invocation.html'
        super().__init__('pwd', user=user, doc_link=doc_link)
```

We can test it directly without the rest of AI-6, by simply instantiating it and checking properties such as `parameters` and `description`:

```
❯ source venv/bin/activate
❯ python
Python 3.13.3 (main, Apr  8 2025, 13:54:08) [Clang 17.0.0 (clang-1700.0.13.3)] on darwin
Type "help", "copyright", "credits" or "license" for more information.

>>> from backend.tools.file_system.pwd import Pwd
>>> pwd = Pwd()
>>> pwd.parameters
[Parameter(name='args', type='string', description='command-line arguments for pwd')]

>>> pwd.description
'pwd tool. See https://www.gnu.org/software/coreutils/manual/html_node/pwd-invocation.html'
```

We can also run it and verify whether it really returns the current working directory:

```
>>> pwd.run(args='')
'/Users/gigi/git/ai-six/py\n'
```

Other filesystem commands are just as simple. Here is the `ls` command:

```
from ..base.command_tool import CommandTool
class Ls(CommandTool):
    def __init__(self, user: str | None = None):
        super().__init__(command_name='ls', user=user,
            doc_link = 'https://www.gnu.org/software/coreutils/manual/html_node/
ls-invocation.html'
)
```

Here is the awk command:

```
from ..base.command_tool import CommandTool

class Awk(CommandTool):
    def __init__(self, user: str | None = None):
```

```
super().__init__(command_name='awk', user=user,
        doc_link='https://www.gnu.org/software/gawk/manual/gawk.html')
```

Most of the other filesystem tools follow the same pattern, but there is one exception, which is the echo tool. We will discuss that next.

Implementing the echo tool

The echo tool is different. The purpose of the echo tool is to allow the LLM to create new files or replace existing files. This is a super useful capability, of course. But, in order to do that in the shell, you must use shell redirection as follows:

```
> echo "123" > ~/ttt/some-file

> cat ~/ttt/some-file
123
```

Keep in mind to manage the tool security and permissions, as we discussed in *Chapter 4*.

Our `CommandTool` base class doesn't provide a way to redirect the output of a command to a file. One option would be to extend `CommandTool` to support output redirection, but we can also implement the functionality directly. Let's see how it works.

The imports are similar, except that it imports the built-in `os` package, the `Tool` module, and it doesn't import the `shlex` package or the `CommandTool` module. We will see why very soon:

```
import os
import sh
from backend.object_model import Tool, Parameter
```

The `Echo` class inherits directly from the `Tool` module and not from `CommandTool` because it needs to implement its own `run()` method:

```
class Echo(Tool):
```

The constructor is a little more elaborate. Since it doesn't invoke the built-in `echo` command, the description doesn't include an external documentation link. There are also two required parameters, `content` and `file_path`, instead of the generic `args` parameter of tools derived from `CommandTool`. It also stores `user`, which defaults to `None`:

```
def __init__(self, user: str | None = None):
    self.user = user

    desc = 'Write content to a file, creating any necessary directories.'
    super().__init__(
        name='echo',
        description=desc,
        parameters=[
            Parameter(
                name='file_path', type='string',
                description='The path of the file to write to.'),
            Parameter(
                name='content', type='string',
                description='The content to write to the file.')
        ],
        required={'file_path', 'content'}
    )
```

The `run()` method extracts the filename to write to and the content from the parameters (remember these will be provided by the LLM when it invokes the tool in order to create or replace a file). Then, it gets the directory of the target file:

```
def run(self, **kwargs):
    filename = kwargs['file_path']
    content = kwargs['content']
    dir_path = os.path.dirname(filename)
```

The logic then splits depending on the user. If a user is provided, then it uses `sudo` and shell commands, `mkdir` and `tee`, to create the target directory if needed and write/replace the file:

```
    if self.user is not None:
        sh.sudo('-u', self.user, 'mkdir', '-p', dir_path)
        sh.sudo('-u', self.user, 'tee', filename,
            _in=content, _out=os.devnull)

        return f"Content written to {filename} as user {self.user}"
```

If no user is provided, then it uses Python directly to create the directory and write the file:

```
        os.makedirs(dir_path, exist_ok=True)
        with open(filename, 'w') as file:
            file.write(content)

        return f"Content written to {filename}"
```

Now, we will shift our focus to yet another utility tool, the test runner tool.

Test runner tool

The filesystem tools allow AI-6 to modify its own code! That's right. Think about it. It can list its own files and directories using the `ls` tool. It can read the contents of its own source files using the `cat` tool. It can create new files (or replace existing files) using the `echo` tool. Finally, it can modify existing files using the `sed`, `awk`, and `patch` tools. But agentic AI frameworks and LLMs don't get everything right on the first shot (yet). It is still best practice to iterate on code changes and verify that the changes work before committing them. This is where the `test_runner` tool comes in. This tool can run Python unit tests written using the standard Python `unittest` framework in any directory. Let's see how it works.

As usual, it imports the `sh` module and `Tool` and `Parameter` from the AI-6 object model:

```
import sh
from backend.object_model import Tool, Parameter
```

The `TestRunner` class inherits directly from the `Tool` base class. The constructor calls the `Tool` base class, passing it a description and a single required parameter, `test_directory`:

```
class TestRunner(Tool):
    def __init__(self):
        desc = 'A tool to run Python unit tests using the unittest framework.'
        super().__init__(
            name='python_test_runner',
            description=desc,
            parameters=[Parameter(name='test_directory',
                type='string',
                description='The directory containing tests to run')],
            required={'test_directory'}
        )
```

The `run()` method runs all the Python unit tests in the target directory by invoking the Python interpreter with the `unittest` module, instructing it to discover all the unit tests in the target directory. It returns a dictionary with the keys of `"stdout"` and `"stderr"`. It handles a `sh` execution exception gracefully, but lets other exceptions propagate to the caller to handle:

```
def run(self, **kwargs):
    test_directory = kwargs['test_directory']
    try:
        result = sh.python('-m', 'unittest', 'discover', '-s',
            test_directory)
        return {"stdout": str(result), "stderr": ""}
    except sh.ErrorReturnCode as e:
        return {"stdout": e.stdout.decode('utf-8'),
            "stderr": e.stderr.decode('utf-8')}
```

Let's see it in action. The AI-6 backend unit tests are in the following relative directory to the Python root directory, `backend/tests`:

```
>>> from backend import tests
>>> tests_dir = tests.__path__[0]
>>> tests_dir
'/Users/gigi/git/ai-six/py/backend/tests'
```

Now that we have the test directory, we can instantiate and invoke the test runner tool and verify that the result was a success:

```
>>> result = tr.run(test_directory=tests_dir)
>>> assert(result['stdout'] != '')
>>> assert(result['stderr'] == '')
```

Many times, you would need to start or restart an application to use your tools. The `bootstrap` tool helps you do that. Let's see how.

Bootstrap tool

As we saw, the built-in tools of AI-6 support modifying its own code and testing those changes (since the AI-6 unit tests are implemented using the `unittest` framework). The last piece of the puzzle is to restart the program controlling AI-6 after making changes and testing those changes. This is where the `bootstrap` tool comes in. After making changes to the AI-6 code, the LLM may decide to restart the controlling AI system, which will start with the modified code:

```
import importlib
from backend.object_model import Tool
import os
import sys
```

The `Bootstrap` class is derived directly from `Tool`. The constructor is very simple, as there are no parameters. The description explains that (`https://linux.die.net/man/3/execv`) will be used to restart the program:

```
class Bootstrap(Tool):
    def __init__(self):
        desc = 'Tool to restart the program using execv.'
        super().__init__(
            name='bootstrap',
            description=desc,
            parameters=[],  # No parameters needed for execv
            required=set()
        )
```

The `run()` method is more sophisticated than the previous tools we have looked at. Let's break it down. First, it locates the filename of the `main` module of the program. If it can't be found, it raises an exception:

```
    def run(self, **kwargs):
        main_module = sys.modules['__main__']
        module_path = getattr(main_module, '__file__', None)
        if not module_path:
            raise RuntimeError("Cannot determine __main__.__file__; are you in a
REPL or notebook?")
```

If the `main` module has a `spec` attribute, then it was run as `python -m module`. Let's prepare the arguments correctly:

```
        spec = getattr(main_module, '__spec__', None)
        if spec and spec.name:
            # Executed as a module: python -m package.module
            module_name = spec.name
            args = [sys.executable, '-m', module_name, *sys.argv[1:]]
```

Otherwise, it runs as a file with `python <main file>`. Let's prepare the arguments for this mode:

```
        else:
            # Executed as a script: python script.py
            args = [sys.executable, module_path, *sys.argv[1:]]
```

Finally, let's restart the program using `os.execv()` and the appropriate command-line arguments.

```
        os.execv(sys.executable, args)
```

The `bootstrap` tool is a powerful tool that allows the LLM to restart the controlling AI system after making changes to the AI-6 code. It is a simple tool, but it is very powerful and can be used to implement complex workflows that involve self-modifying code. But we can go even further and let the LLM directly manipulate the current conversation's memory, too.

Memory tools

As you recall, AI-6 has a powerful memory system that revolves around the concept of a session, which is a persistent collection of messages that encompasses multiple agentic loops. Sessions are stored in files, and we can let the LLM and/or the user manipulate the session files directly and load session files. This means that AI-6 allows the LLM to rewrite the memory of the current session, however it sees fit. This is a powerful capability that should be used with the utmost care. Typically, the LLM will not try to manipulate the session memory directly, but the user may instruct it to list previous sessions and load a previous session to continue where they left off.

It's important to remember that the session files will remain on disk after a session is over, and the AI system using AI-6 must ensure that users' rights and privacy are maintained and provide them with the option to delete sessions.

Let's see how the memory tools are implemented. There are four different tools that deal with memory:

- `list_sessions`: List all the sessions in the memory directory
- `load_session`: Load a session by ID
- `get_session_id`: Get the current session's ID
- `delete_session`: Delete a session by ID

Note that there is no tool to save the current session. This is because the session is saved automatically by AI-6 periodically (see the configured checkpoint interval discussed in *Chapter 4*).

The design choice of multiple memory tools as opposed to a single memory tool with multiple actions is deliberate. It significantly simplifies the implementation and the testing of each tool.

Listing sessions

The `ListSessions` tool just needs to import `json`, which is the format we return the sessions in, and of course, the `Tool` base class. No command-line arguments are needed:

```
import json
from backend.object_model import Tool
class ListSessions(Tool):
    """Tool to list all available sessions in memory."""
```

The constructor initializes the tool with a reference to the `Engine` instance, which it will use later to actually list the sessions. There are no parameters for this tool, so the `parameters` list is empty, and the `required` set is also empty:

```
    def __init__(self, engine=None):
        """Initialize the tool.

        Args:
            engine: Reference to the Engine instance
        """
        self.engine = engine
        super().__init__(
            name='list_sessions',
            description='List all available sessions in memory.',
            parameters=[],
```

```
        required=set()
    )
```

The `run()` method is where the actual listing of sessions happens. It checks whether the `engine` reference is set, and if not, it returns an error message. If the engine is set, it calls the `list_sessions()` method of the engine, which returns a list of session IDs. If no sessions are found, it returns a message indicating that no sessions were found. Otherwise, it returns a formatted string with the list of session IDs serialized to JSON:

```
    def run(self, **kwargs):
        """List all available sessions.

        Returns:
            String with the details of all stored sessions (id, title and
filename)
        """
        if not self.engine:
            return "Error: Engine reference not set."

        sessions = self.engine.list_sessions()

        if not sessions:
            return "No sessions found in memory."

        return "Available sessions:\n" + json.dumps(sessions)
```

The pattern of delegating the actual work to the `Engine` instance is common to all memory tools. The `Engine` instance, after all, is the source of truth for the AI-6 memory system. It is responsible for managing sessions, messages, and other memory-related tasks. There is no need to duplicate this logic in the tools, which would only make the code more complex and harder to maintain.

Loading sessions

When loading a session, we need to specify the session ID. The tool will then use the `Engine` instance to load the specific session into its memory. Let's see how this is implemented.

We only need to import the `Tool` base class and the `Parameter` class from the AI-6 object model:

```
from backend.object_model import Tool, Parameter
```

The `LoadSession` class is derived from the `Tool` base class. The constructor initializes the tool with a reference to the `Engine` instance. It expects a single required parameter, `session_id`, which is the ID of the session to load:

```
class LoadSession(Tool):
    """Tool to load a specific session by ID."""

    def __init__(self, engine=None):
        """Initialize the tool.

        Args:
            engine: Reference to the Engine instance
        """
        self.engine = engine
        super().__init__(
            name='load_session',
            description='Load a specific session by ID.',
            parameters=[
                Parameter(
                    name='session_id',
                    type='string',
                    description='ID of the session to load'
                )
            ],
            required={'session_id'}
        )
```

The `run()` method is where the actual loading of the session happens. It checks whether the engine reference is set and the `session_id` parameter is provided. If not, it returns an error message indicating the problem. Then, it calls the `load_session()` method of the engine with the provided session ID. If the session is loaded successfully, it returns a success message with the session ID. If the session does not exist or fails to load, it returns a failure message:

```
def run(self, session_id, **kwargs) -> str:
    """Load a specific session.

    Args:
        session_id: ID of the session to load

    Returns:
        String indicating success or failure
    """
    if not self.engine:
        return "Error: Engine reference not set."

    if not session_id:
        return "Error: Session ID is required."

    success = self.engine.load_session(session_id)

    if success:
        return f"Successfully loaded session: {session_id}"
    else:
        return f"Failed to load session: {session_id}. Session may not exist."
```

It is often useful to get the current session ID ot be able to load it later. Here is how it's done.

Getting the current session ID

Getting the current session ID is a simple operation. The tool just needs to return the ID of the current session, which is stored by the engine.

We only need to import the `Tool` base class from the AI-6 object model. No parameters are needed for this tool:

```
from backend.object_model import Tool
```

The GetSessionId class is derived from the Tool base class in the familiar pattern. The constructor expects a reference to the engine, which will do the actual work of retrieving the session ID. The parameters list is empty, and the required set is also empty since no parameters are needed to get the current session ID:

```
class GetSessionId(Tool):
    """Tool to get the current session ID."""

    def __init__(self, engine=None):
        """Initialize the tool.

        Args:
            engine: Reference to the Engine instance
        """
        self.engine = engine
        super().__init__(
            name='get_session_id',
            description='Get the ID of the current session.',
            parameters=[],
            required=set()
        )
```

The run() method is where the actual retrieval of the session ID happens. As always, it performs sanity checks and then delegates the work to the Engine instance by calling its engine.get_session_id() method:

```
    def run(self, **kwargs):
        """Get the current session ID.

        Returns:
            String with the current session ID
        """
        if not self.engine:
            return "Error: Engine reference not set."

        session_id = self.engine.get_session_id()
        return f"Current session ID: {session_id}"
```

It is sometimes useful to clean up old sessions to avoid clutter. Here is how it's done.

Deleting sessions

Deleting a session is a powerful operation that should be used with caution. The tool will delete a persistent session file, so it is important to ensure that the session is no longer needed before deleting it. As always, the tool will use the Engine instance to delete the session. At this point, you should be familiar with the imports, the class declaration, and the constructor:

```
from backend.object_model import Tool, Parameter
class DeleteSession(Tool): """Tool to delete a specific session by ID."""
def __init__(self, engine=None):
    """Initialize the tool.

    Args:
        engine: Reference to the Engine instance
    """
    self.engine = engine

    super().__init__(
        name='delete_session',
        description='Delete a specific session by ID.',
        parameters=[
            Parameter(
                name='session_id',
                type='string',
                description='ID of the session to delete'
            )
        ],
        required={'session_id'}
    )
```

The run() method is where the actual deletion of the session happens. Just like the other memory tools, it checks whether the engine reference is set and that the session_id parameter is provided. But it adds one more check to make sure we don't try to delete the current session. This is a safety measure to prevent accidental deletion of the active session, which can leave the engine in an invalid state:

```
def run(self, session_id, **kwargs):
    """Delete a specific session.

    Args:
```

```
        session_id: ID of the session to delete

    Returns:
        String indicating success or failure
    """
    if not self.engine:
        return "Error: Engine reference not set."

    if not session_id:
        return "Error: Session ID is required."

    # Don't allow deleting the current session
    if session_id == self.engine.get_session_id():
        return "Error: Cannot delete the current active session."

    success = self.engine.delete_session(session_id)

    if success:
        return f"Successfully deleted session: {session_id}"
    else:
        return f"Failed to delete session: {session_id}. Session may not exist."
```

We covered a lot of ground in this section. We looked at the implementation of multiple custom tools in AI-6 based on the tool system design we covered in *Chapter 4*. We have also seen how these tools can be used to modify the AI-6 code, test the changes, restart the program, and

manipulate the session memory. This is a powerful set of tools that allows AI-6, in theory, to improve itself in a virtuous cycle.

In the next section, we will see how to put these tools into action and let AI-6 implement a new tool from scratch.

Implementing a new tool from scratch with AI-6

AI-6 comes with many built-in tools that allow it, in theory, to improve its own code. It can read and write its own source code, write new code and tests, run tests, and restart the program. It also has a Git tool that we didn't examine in detail, but it allows AI-6 to perform any Git operation, such as cloning a repository, creating branches, adding files, committing changes, and pushing them to a remote repository.

But AI-6 doesn't have a tool for interacting with GitHub. Centralized source control systems such as GitHub are at the heart of modern software. Let's take AI-6 for a spin and see whether it can build its own tools, with some useful help from us, of course.

How to interact with AI-6

AI-6 supports multiple interfaces out of the box: a chatbot CLI, Slack-based interface, and a web UI interface.

For this little project, we will use AI-6 through its chatbot CLI, which is very similar to the `k8s-ai` interface that we saw in *Chapter 3*. We will cover the Slack and web interfaces in detail in the next chapter.

When we use the chatbot CLI, it serves as the AI system that uses AI-6. Here is how we start the chatbot CLI:

```
❯ python -m frontend.cli.ai6 Using .env file from /Users/gigi/git/ai-six/py/
frontend/cli/.env
```

Next comes the interaction in the chat interface:

```
👤 [You]: hi
🤖 [AI-6]: Hello! How can I assist you today? ——-
👤 [You]:
```

With all the preliminaries out of the way, we can start interacting with AI-6 to build a shiny new GitHub tool.

Building a new GitHub tool with AI-6

Our goal is to let AI-6 do all the work based on a high-level description of the tool we want to implement. This will be a very interactive process where we provide guidance, AI-6 does the work, and, at each step, we verify the results and provide feedback. The tool we want to implement is a GitHub tool that will allow AI-6 to interact with GitHub repositories, issues, pull requests, and so on. Let's start by describing the tool we want to implement:

```
👤 [You]: I want to create a command-line tool for interacting with Github using
the gh CLI (already installed and configured) similar to the tools in /Users/gigi/
git/ai-six/py/backend/tools. how do you propose to that? 🤖 [AI-6]: To create a
command-line tool for interacting with GitHub using the GitHub CLI (gh), you can
follow these steps to set up a structure similar
to existing tools like the Ollama tool.
Here's how you can achieve this:
```

```
Create a Base Command Tool Class (if not already existing):
This class (like
CommandTool) will handle generic CLI command execution, including setting up basic
configurations like user data.
Create the GitHub CLI Tool Class:
Use this class to define the GitHub-specific command-line interactions. ```
OK. That’s a good start, but we
don’t need to create a base command tool class, as we already have it. Let’s tell
AI-6 about it.


👤 [You]: Since the Ollama tool exists, then it probably the CommandTool base
class already exists
🤖 [AI-6]: You're correct. If the `Ollama` tool utilizes a `CommandTool` base
class, then it likely already exists in your project structure. In this case, you
can directly proceed to implement the GitHub CLI tool by leveraging this existing
base class. Here's how you can do it:

### Step-by-Step Guide to Create the GitHub CLI Tool


1. **Locate the Existing `CommandTool` Base Class:**
   - First, confirm the location and available methods of the `CommandTool` class
within your project.

2. **Create the GitHub CLI Tool Class:**

With the base class available, you can create a new tool class that extends
`CommandTool` for GitHub interactions.

# gh_cli_tool.py
# Import the CommandTool class from its existing location
from backend.tools.base.command_tool import CommandTool

class GhCLI(CommandTool):
    def __init__(self, user: str | None = None):
        super().__init__(
            command_name='gh', user=user,
            doc_link='https://cli.github.com/manual/')


    def list_repositories(self) -> str:
        return self.run_command('repo list')
```

```
    def create_repository(self, name: str) -> str:
        return self.run_command(f'repo create {name}')

    def clone_repository(self, repo: str) -> str:
        return self.run_command(f'repo clone {repo}')

    # Add more methods to interact with other GitHub functionalities using the
'gh' CLI
```

Hmm, it looks like AI-6 didn't invest the time to study the `CommandTool` base class, which already provides a `run()` method to execute the command-line program with any set of arguments. It suggests adding methods such as `list_repositories()`, `create_repository(name: str)`, and `clone_repository(repo: str)`. These methods are not necessary, as we can just use the `run()` method of the `CommandTool` base class to run any command-line program with any set of arguments.

Let's tell AI-6 about it:

```
👤 [You]: hold on. let's do this step by step. find and show me the code for the
CommandTool base class
🤖 [AI-6]: Here is the code for the `CommandTool` base class:

import sh
import shlex
from backend.object_model import Tool, Parameter

class CommandTool(Tool):
    def __init__(
        self, command_name: str, user: str | None = None,
        doc_link: str = ""
    ):
        self.command_name = command_name
        self.user = user
        description = f'{command_name} tool. ' + f'See {doc_link}' if doc_link
else ''
        parameters = [Parameter(
            name='args', type='string',
            description=f'command-line arguments for {command_name}')]
        required = {'args'}
        super().__init__(
```

```
            name=command_name,
            description=description,
            parameters=parameters,
            required=required
        )

    def run(self, **kwargs):
        args = shlex.split(kwargs['args'])
        if self.user is not None:
            return sh.sudo('-u', self.user, self.command_name, *args)
        else:
            return getattr(sh, self.command_name)(*args)


### Explanation:

- **Class Inheritance:** `CommandTool` inherits from a base class called `Tool`.
- **Initialization:** The constructor initializes the command tool with a command
name, optional user, and documentation link.
- **Parameters:** It sets up the required parameters for the tool, including
command-line arguments.
- **Command Execution:** The `run` method uses the `sh` library to execute shell
commands, optionally using `sudo` for a specified user.
Great. Now, we're getting closer. Let's continue carefully guiding AI-6 towards
better understanding of its own tool architecture.


👤 [You]: ok. now that you understand how the CommandTool base class works, check
its base class Tool
🤖 [AI-6]: The `Tool` class from which `CommandTool` inherits is an abstract base
class (ABC). Here's a breakdown of
            the `Tool` class:


- **Attributes:**
  - `name`: A string that represents the name of the tool.
  - `description`: A string that provides a description of the tool.
  - `parameters`: A list of `Parameter` objects, each representing a command-line
or functional parameter for the tool.
  - `required`: A set of strings indicating which parameters are required.
```

```
- **Methods:**
  - `configure`: This method allows optional configuration of the tool using a
provided dictionary. It's intended to be
     overridden if needed.
  - `run`: This is an abstract method that must be implemented by any
subclass. It defines how to execute the tool using
     the given arguments and return the result as a string.

### Next Steps

With this understanding of the `CommandTool` base class and its parent `Tool`
class, you can confidently create a new
tool for the GitHub CLI by extending `CommandTool`. If you're ready, we can
proceed to create the `GhCLI` tool class
that utilizes the GitHub CLI (`gh`) for GitHub interactions. Let me know if you
want to move forward with this step!
```

Excellent. But I don't like the class name, `GhCLI`. It exposes implementation details and is not aligned with other tools' naming conventions:

```
👤 [You]: I want the Github tool class to be called Just Github. The fact it is
using gh cli is an implementation detail.
          what files or directories need to be created?
🤖 [AI-6]: To create a new command-line tool class named `Github`, you should
follow these steps to integrate it into
           your existing project structure:

Step 1: Determine the File Location
-----------------------------------
Since the existing tools, such as `Ollama`, are located in a specific directory
within your project, you should place your new tool in a similar location for
consistency and organization.

Let's assume you are following this structure (similar to `Ollama`):

backend/
  tools/
    base/
    ollama/   # Contains the Ollama tool definition
    github/   # This is where we will place the new Github tool
```

```
Step 2: Create the Necessary Directories and Files
--------------------------------------------------
1. **Create a Directory for the Github Tool:**
   - Path: `backend/tools/github/`
   - This directory will contain the implementation of the `Github` tool.

2. **Create the `Github` Tool Class File:**
   - Path: `backend/tools/github/github.py`
   - This file will contain the definition of the `Github` class.

Step 3: Implement the `Github` Tool Class
-----------------------------------------
...
```

This is exactly what we wanted to hear. AI-6 is on the right track. Let's continue:

```
[You]: OK. Show me the Github class
[AI-6]: Here is the new command-line tool class named `Github`


# backend/tools/github/github.py
from backend.tools.base.command_tool import CommandTool

class Github(CommandTool):
    def __init__(self, user: str | None = None):
        # Initialize with the command name 'gh' and provide a documentation link
        super().__init__(
            command_name='gh', user=user,
            doc_link='https://cli.github.com/manual/')


    def execute(self, args: str) -> str:
        """
        Execute any GitHub CLI command by providing the appropriate arguments.

        Args:
            args: Command-line arguments to pass to the `gh` CLI.

        Returns:
```

```
        The output from the command execution.
        """
    return self.run(args=args)
```

Very nice! Even the documentation link is correct. But it added a useless `execute()` method that just calls the `run()` method. I could just remove it myself, but let's keep this session fully interactive and ask AI-6 to remove it:

```
👤 [You]: isn't the run() method enough to execute any gh cli command?
🤖 [AI-6]: You're absolutely correct in observing that if you wanted to provide
direct access to the `CommandTool`'s
`run()` method, you don't strictly need an additional `execute()` wrapper in the
`Github` class. The primary role of the
 `execute()` method was to give a semantic representation or alias to the act of
executing a GitHub CLI command, but it
  indeed adds no extra functionality beyond `run()`.

Thus, in practice, you could simply use the `run()` method directly from instances
of the `Github` class for executing
commands, since it's already designed to take care of running the CLI with the
specified arguments. Here's a revision of
 the approach without the `execute()` method:

Implementation without `execute()`
----------------------------------

# backend/tools/github/github.py
from backend.tools.base.command_tool import CommandTool

class Github(CommandTool):
    def __init__(self, user: str | None = None):
        # Initialize with the command name 'gh' and provide a documentation link
        super().__init__(
            command_name='gh', user=user,
            doc_link='https://cli.github.com/manual/')


Usage Example
-------------

You would use the `run()` method directly to execute any `gh` CLI command:
```

```
if __name__ == '__main__':
    gh_tool = Github()

    # List repositories
    print(gh_tool.run(args='repo list'))

    # Create a new repository
    # print(gh_tool.run(args='repo create new-repo'))

    # Clone a repository
    # print(gh_tool.run(args='repo clone owner/repo'))


Conclusion
----------

By using the `run()` method directly, you maintain a minimalistic and efficient
implementation, relying on the
capabilities already defined in the `CommandTool` base class. This keeps the
`Github` class straightforward while fully
leveraging the flexibility to execute any command supported by the `gh` CLI.
```

AI-6 arrived at the correct solution after some cajoling. I continued the session by asking it to write tests and execute them, and it did so successfully. The tests were written in the `unittest` framework and executed using the `python_test_runner` tool we saw earlier.

Here is the test code: `https://github.com/PacktPublishing/Design-Multi-Agent-AI-Systems-Using-MCP-and-A2A/blob/main/ch05/ai-six/py/backend/tests/tools/github/test_github.py`.

This session is a great example of how AI-6 can add new capabilities to itself by learning to understand its own code and architecture, but it also demonstrates the importance of humans in the loop and guiding the AI system through the process. While the early suggestions of the GitHub tool were not obviously wrong, they didn't fit well into the existing tool architecture.

Let's see how to implement a new tool manually, without the help of AI-6.

Implementing a new tool manually

The next tool will be a little more complicated. We will build a Claude tool. This tool will allow AI-6 to send LLM inference requests to the Anthropic Claude LLM (`https://claude.ai/`). While AI-6 is working with an LLM provider such as OpenAI, it can make use of a different LLM provider, such as Anthropic Claude. The Claude tool is implemented in `backend/tools/claude_tool.py`. It is a custom tool that extends the `Tool` base class and uses the Anthropic Python SDK (`https://github.com/anthropics/anthropic-sdk-python`) to send requests to the Claude LLM. Let's see how it is implemented.

The tool imports the `anthropic` module, which is the Python SDK for the Anthropic Claude LLM, and `Tool` and `Parameter` from the AI-6 object model:

```
import anthropic
from backend.object_model import Tool, Parameter
```

The `ClaudeTool` class is derived from the `Tool` base class. The constructor is a little more complicated than the previous tools we saw. It initializes the tool with a description, parameters, and a required set of parameters. There are four parameters:

- `prompt`: The prompt or question to send to Claude.
- `model`: The model to use for inference. The default is `claude-sonnet-4-20250514`.
- `max_tokens`: The maximum number of tokens to generate. The default is `1000`.
- `temperature`: The temperature for sampling (`0.0`–`1.0`). The default is `0.7`.

The `max_tokens` and `temperature` defaults are taken from the Anthropic documentation (`https://docs.anthropic.com/en/docs/about-claude/models/overview`). When the LLM invokes the tool, it can override these defaults by providing different parameters in the request. Only the `prompt` parameter is required.

Note that we have a `self.client` attribute initialized to `None`. This will be used later to store the Anthropic client:

```
class Claude(Tool):
    def __init__(self):
        desc = """
            Send inference requests to Anthropic Claude LLM. Useful for getting a
second opinion or
            different perspective from another AI model.
```

```
        """
        super().__init__(
            name='claude',
            description=desc,
            parameters=[
                Parameter(
                    name='prompt',
                    type='string',
                    description='The prompt or question to send to Claude'),
                Parameter(
                    name='model',
                    type='string',
                    description="""
                        See https://docs.anthropic.com/en/docs/about-claude/
models/overview.
                        Defaults to claude-sonnet-4-20250514
                    """),
                Parameter(
                    name='max_tokens',
                    type='integer',
                    description='Maximum number of tokens to
generate. Defaults to 1000'),
                Parameter(
                    name='temperature',
                    type='number',
                    description='Temperature for sampling (0.0-1.0). Defaults to
0.7')
            ],
            required={'prompt'}
        )
        self.client = None
```

At last, we have a tool that requires configuration. The `configure()` method is used to get the Anthropic API key from the configuration dictionary and initialize the Anthropic client if present:

```
    def configure(self, config: dict) -> None:
        """Configure the Claude tool with API key."""
        if 'api_key' in config:
            self.client = anthropic.Anthropic(api_key=config['api_key'])
```

The `run()` method is where the actual inference request is sent to the Claude LLM. It checks whether the client is initialized, and if not, it returns an error message. It then retrieves the parameters from the kwargs dictionary. These parameters include `prompt`, `model`, `max_tokens`, and `temperature`. They will be provided by the current LLM that AI-6 is working with (e.g., OpenAI GPT-4o) when it invokes the tool. You can see that only the `prompt` parameter is required. The other parameters have default values, so they are optional. Once the parameters are retrieved, it calls the client's `messages.create()` method to send the request to the selected Claude model. The response is then returned as a string:

```
    def run(self, **kwargs) -> str:
        if self.client is None:
            return "Error: Claude API key not configured. Set 'api_key' in
tool_config for claude tool"

        prompt = kwargs['prompt']
        model = kwargs.get('model', 'claude-sonnet-4-20250514')
        max_tokens = kwargs.get('max_tokens', 1000)
        temperature = kwargs.get('temperature', 0.7)

        response = self.client.messages.create(
            model=model,
            max_tokens=max_tokens,
            temperature=temperature,
            messages=[
                {"role": "user", "content": prompt}
            ]
        )

        return response.content[0].text
```

We can see how the simple tool interface of AI-6 allows us to implement a wide variety of tools, including command-line tools such as the filesystem tools, internal AI-6 tools such as the memory tools, and tools that invoke external APIs such as the Claude tool. The tool interface is flexible enough to accommodate different types of tools and their specific requirements.

Summary

Let's recap. We provided a comprehensive exploration of the AI-6 tool system, shifting the focus from the high-level orchestration engine to the internal structure and behavior of the tools themselves. We examined how AI-6 achieves provider-agnostic tool interoperability by defining a unified, generic tool specification that maps cleanly to provider-specific formats such as OpenAI's function calling or Ollama's tool schema. These tools are designed to be reusable, consistent, and easily translatable across different LLM APIs, with a robust schema and input validation mechanism at their core.

We continued with detailed walkthroughs of built-in command-line tools such as `pwd`, `ls`, `awk`, and a special-purpose `echo` tool for file writing. These tools are implemented using the `CommandTool` base class and are capable of performing file operations and shell interactions directly from within the AI framework. Additional tools, such as `test_runner` for executing Python unit tests and `bootstrap` for restarting the AI-6 program, showcase how the system supports iterative self-modification. Memory tools such as `list_sessions`, `load_session`, and `delete_session` extend the agent's ability to manage and manipulate persistent session state in a controlled manner.

We then explored how to develop new tools interactively using AI-6 itself, demonstrated through the creation of a GitHub tool that wraps the `gh` CLI. This exercise illustrated how human guidance can be combined with agentic reasoning to extend AI-6's capabilities by pointing it to its own source code. Finally, we looked at building an API-based Claude tool for interfacing with Anthropic's LLMs, emphasizing how AI-6 can integrate and leverage multiple LLM providers simultaneously. Overall, these examples highlighted the power and flexibility of the AI-6 tool system.

In the next chapter, we will turn to the frontend side of the AI-6 project, covering user-facing interfaces via Slack and Chainlit (web UI), which enable interactive and conversational control over the system.

Get This Book's PDF Version and Exclusive Extras

Scan the QR code (or go to `packtpub.com/unlock`). Search for this book by name, confirm the edition, and then follow the steps on the page.

UNLOCK NOW

Note: Keep your invoice handy. Purchases made directly from Packt don't require an invoice.

6

Creating Chat Interfaces Using Slack and Chainlit

In the previous chapter, we explored AI-6's internal tool architecture—how tools are defined, registered, and executed. While a powerful backend is essential, the true potential of an agentic AI system is unlocked through interfaces that allow humans to effectively collaborate with autonomous agents.

User interfaces (UIs) in agentic systems serve a unique role. Unlike traditional applications, where the UI primarily captures input and displays output, agent interfaces must balance autonomy with control. They need to provide real-time visibility into what the agent is doing, allow interruptions when needed, surface debugging information during failures, and build trust through transparency. The challenge is designing interfaces that neither stifle the agent with excessive oversight nor leave users blind to its actions.

This chapter explores how AI-6 implements two complementary interfaces: a Slack bot for collaborative team workflows and a Chainlit-based web UI for individual interactions.

This chapter covers the following topics:

- Why the UI matters in agentic AI workflows: visibility, interruptibility, debugging, and trust
- Building a Slack bot interface with multi-channel support and real-time collaboration
- Developing a web UI with Chainlit for rich, customizable single-user experiences
- Integrating frontend interfaces with the AI-6 engine and tool ecosystem
- Best practices for designing interactive agent interfaces

Technical requirements

To follow along, refer to the instructions in the README file:

`https://github.com/PacktPublishing/Design-Multi-Agent-AI-Systems-Using-MCP-and-A2A/blob/main/ch06/ai-six/py/README.md`

Why the UI matters in agentic AI workflows

The claim to fame of agentic AI systems is that they are autonomous and can perform complex tasks on behalf of users. However, this automation must often be balanced with the need for human oversight, control, or even just visibility into what the agent is doing. The UI plays a crucial role in the success of agentic AI systems, serving as the bridge between the user and the agent's actions. In this section, we will explore several key aspects of why the UI is essential in agentic AI workflows.

Agent feedback loops and visibility

Let's take the viewpoint of the human user of the agentic AI system. There is a delicate balance between letting the agent operate completely autonomously, possibly making mistakes and going off on a tangent, and micro-managing the agent too much, watching every step and correcting it at every turn. Note that both extremes can actually be useful at different times.

Let's consider the example of automating a complex workflow on a website that involves logging in, navigating to different sections, collecting information, and taking actions based on the information, as well as responding to change notifications. The user may be familiar with the task, but they need to "teach" the agent how to do it. If the user aims for total automation, then their prompt must be very detailed and explain their intentions very precisely.

This is difficult. So, the user may start with a more general prompt and then refine it as the agent performs the task with partial success initially. Over time, the user will be able to capture the entire workflow in a nuanced way in the prompt. At this point, the agent can perform the task autonomously without any user intervention unless something rare and unexpected happens.

Another important aspect is visibility and progress updates while the agent is working. This is especially important for long-running tasks. The user may want to know what the agent is doing, how long it will take, and whether it is making progress. The UI should provide real-time feedback on the agent's actions, status, and any issues that arise. Consider a task such as analyzing all of Netflix's newly released movies in the last three months and finding a cool movie to watch. The agent may take a long time, but the user may be interested in seeing partial results and may decide to watch a movie before the complete analysis is done.

That takes us to the next important aspect of the UI in agentic AI systems: the ability to interrupt the agent and either abort the task or steer it in a different direction.

Interruptibility and human-in-the-loop design

There are many ways to design an agentic AI system that lets humans interrupt the agent and take control. First, the system may be designed to limit the time that a single agentic loop can run. This can be done by configuring a time limit, a number of operations, or even by cost (number of tokens used). If the agent reaches the limit, it will stop, report back to the user, and wait for further instructions.

The benefit of this approach is that the user is always in control and can decide whether to continue the task, modify it, or abort it. The downside is that under normal conditions, when everything is going well and the agent is making good progress, the user must still sit there and keep pressing the "continue" button. This can be tedious and frustrating, especially for long-running tasks. It may still be a productive approach if the user takes much longer than the agent to perform every step of the task manually. Of course, if the user is not attentive, then the AI system will just pause waiting for the user to continue.

Another approach is to allow the agent to run autonomously but provide ongoing progress reports and status updates. The user may decide at any point to interrupt the agent and either update the task or cancel it completely.

There are several ways to improve the situation. We can let the LLM decide when to pause and report back to the user. For example, the prompt may include instructions such as "after every 10 steps or if you exceed 50,000 tokens, pause and report back to the user." This way, the agentic AI system will run autonomously, but it will still provide periodic checkpoints. If we want to take it further, we can add more intelligent pause conditions, such as "if you feel you can't make progress, report back to the user."

Of course, this can apply to status updates and notifications as well. The agentic AI system can notify the user only when it encounters an unusual situation or when it has important updates to share. The LLM will determine (based on the prompt and conversation history) which situations require informing the user. This way, the user is not bombarded by constant notifications, but still has visibility into the agent's actions and is notified about important events.

Diagnosing and debugging agent behaviors

Another important use case where the UI is essential is diagnosing and debugging agent behaviors. When an agent doesn't perform properly, there may be many reasons for that:

- The agent may not have enough information
- The prompt may be too vague
- The tools might not support all the needed actions
- The LLM itself is not up to the task (wrong model)

There are also performance issues where the agent actually completes the task successfully, but it takes too long or uses too many tokens. Let's not forget that the failure might be due to a combination of reasons.

Since there are so many possible reasons for agent failure, the UI for debugging must expose as much information as possible. This includes the initial prompt and tools used by each agent, the complete conversation history, including each and every tool call and its parameters, the LLM responses, and, in many cases, additional logging and metrics of external systems accessed by the tools.

For example, if the AI system is misbehaving when diagnosing problems in a Kubernetes cluster, then debugging the issue should include telemetry and logs from the target Kubernetes cluster.

This level of scrutiny is essential for diagnosing and debugging agent behaviors but is typically too noisy for normal users of the system. This means that you need to design different UIs for different user roles. The AI system developers and operators need a very detailed view of the system. The end users may only need a high-level view that exposes the agent's actions and status updates with the proper level of abstraction. Details such as tool calls and token counts may be too much for the end users, but essential for the developers and operators.

Balancing autonomy and user control

As we discussed at the start of this chapter, there is a delicate balance between letting the agent operate autonomously and stifling it with too much user control. The UI plays a crucial role in managing this balance. Ideally, the system is designed in a way that the user can manage the level of autonomy it grants to the agents. For example, Claude Code (see `https://docs.anthropic.com/en/docs/claude-code/overview`) is an agentic coding assistant that runs in the terminal. It solves the problem of agent autonomy at multiple levels with proper user control. First, when performing a task, it provides ongoing status updates of its progress. When Claude was asked whether all the AI-6 tests were passing, it started by finding all the tests. It listed all the tests it found in the code base, while providing a lot of information in real time, such as the number of tools used, the overall time, and the number of tokens. It can also be interrupted by pressing the *Esc* button:

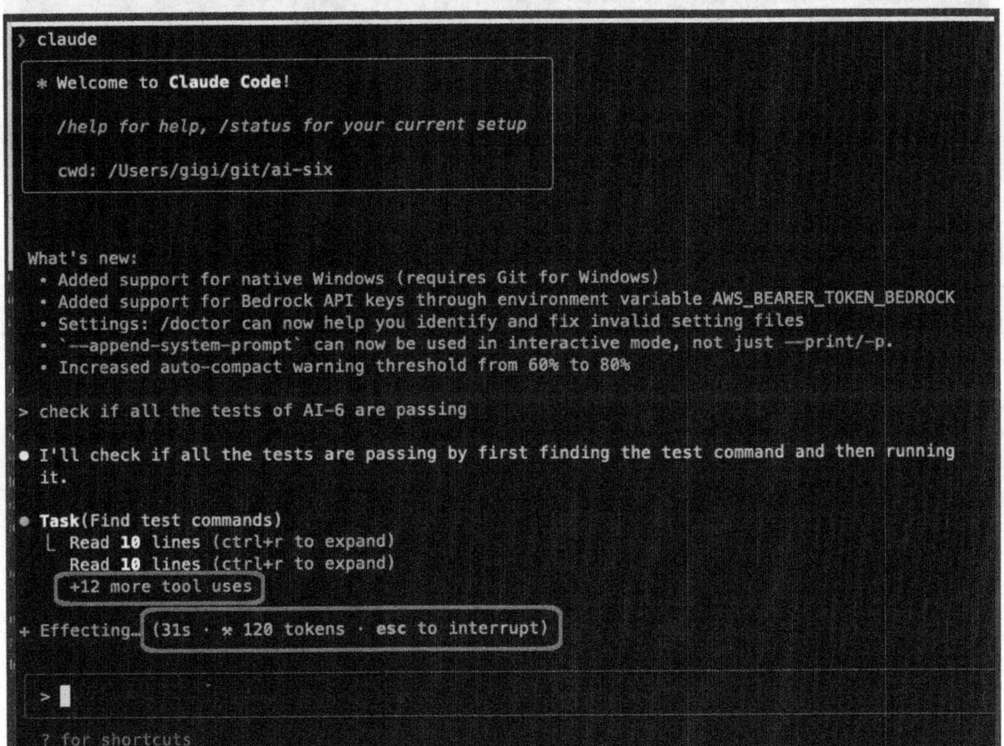

Figure 6.1: Check AI-6 tests

Once Claude Code found all the tests, it automatically started running them. It didn't wait for approval. It identified that some tests failed, and it even identified the root cause (the `sh` module is missing).

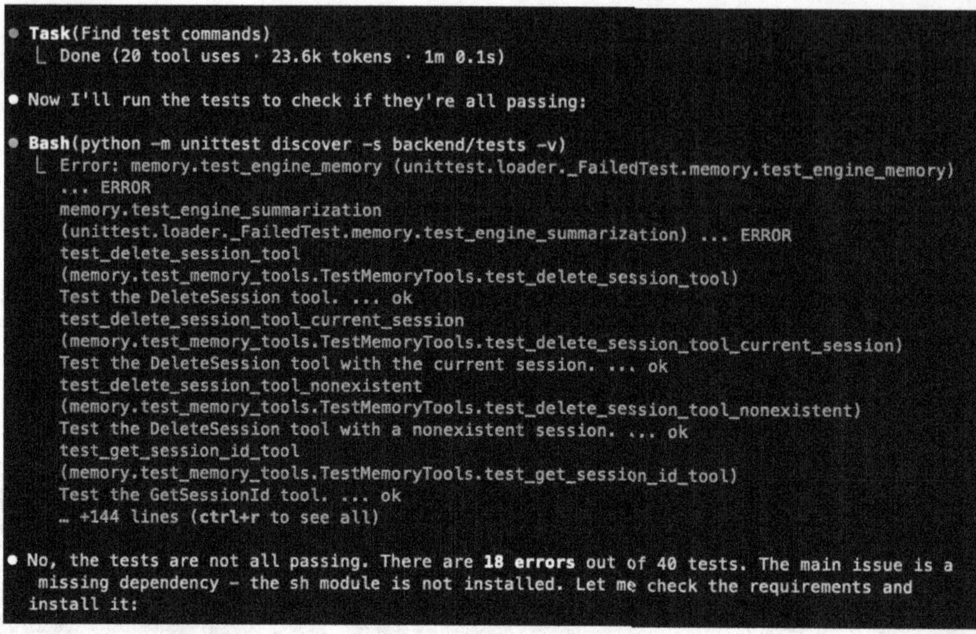

Figure 6.2: Running AI-6 tests

The reason that it just ran the tests is that Claude Code has a configuration file with permissions to perform certain actions. In a previous session, Claude was allowed to run the tests, so it didn't need to ask for permission again. If the user wanted to change that, they could have edited the `.claude/settings.local.json` and removed the permission. Here is a snippet:

```
{
  "permissions": {
    "allow": [
      "Bash(chainlit run:*)",
      "Bash(git add:*)",
      "...",
      "Bash(rg:*)",
      "Bash(cat:*)",
      "Bash(PYTHONPATH=./:$PYTHONPATH python3 -m unittest discover backend/tests -
v)",
      "Bash(ls:*)",
      "Bash(mkdir:*)",
      "Bash(./ai6.sh:*)"
    ],
```

```
    "deny": []
  },
  "enableAllProjectMcpServers": false
}
```

Claude Code wanted to install the missing `sh` module, but since it didn't have automatic permission to install packages, it asked for permission. There is actually no need to install the `sh` module because it is already installed in the virtual environment of AI-6. The correct solution is to activate the virtual environment and re-run the tests.

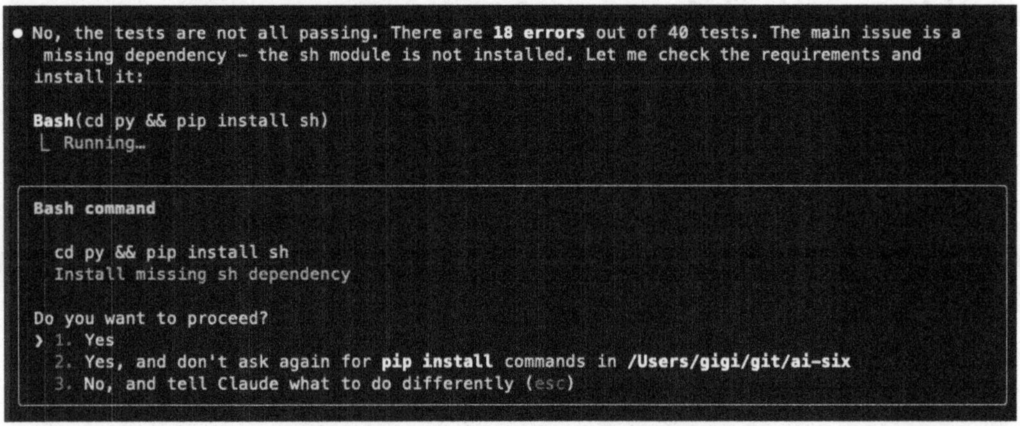

Figure 6.3: Asking permission to install packages

That quick session with Claude Code illustrates how the UI can provide a balance between AI system autonomy and user control. But the UI is not just about control. It is also about trust.

UI as a trust-building mechanism

The more autonomous agentic AI systems are, the more value they provide—of course, assuming they work correctly and accomplish the goals set by the users. Because these systems often make complex decisions, the UI must make their behavior transparent and explainable. A trustworthy UI shows what the agent is doing, why it's doing it, and what it plans next. It exposes the right level of information to the users, which may be tool calls, decision points, and intermediate steps. The idea is that users can follow the reasoning even when it's imperfect. When users can trace errors back to their cause, they're more likely to refine their input rather than abandon the system.

Trust also depends on clear boundaries and control. Users need to know what actions the agent is allowed to take and when it will ask for permission. Explicit permission systems, such as those used by Claude Code, give users confidence that the agent won't make risky changes without oversight. At the same time, the UI should signal uncertainty, showing when the LLM is unsure or requesting help. This combination of visibility, restraint, and humility fosters a collaborative dynamic where users feel in charge and well informed, not sidelined or surprised.

Now that we have covered the importance of the UI in agentic AI workflows, let's explore how to build such interfaces.

Building a Slack bot interface

A word of caution before we dive into the details of building a Slack bot interface for AI-6. Agentic AI systems such as LangGraph, AutoGen, CrewAI, and our own AI-6 focus on defining agents and tools, managing memory and sessions, and executing tasks autonomously. The AI systems built on top of these frameworks are responsible for providing the UI, which is often customized to a specific use case or domain. The reason AI-6 provides several UIs is for educational purposes.

The Slack bot interface has several unique properties that make it a great choice for some agentic AI systems:

- **Familiarity**: Many users are already familiar with Slack, making it easier to onboard new users
- **Real-time interaction**: Slack allows for real-time communication, which is essential for interactive agent workflows
- **Multi-user support**: Slack supports multiple users and channels, allowing for collaborative workflows
- **Integration with other tools**: Slack can integrate with various tools and services, making it easier to build complex workflows
- **Notifications and alerts**: Slack can send notifications and alerts, which is useful for long-running tasks or important updates
- **Security and access control**: Slack provides built-in security features, such as user authentication and access control, which are essential for agentic AI systems that may handle sensitive data

With these advantages in mind, let's explore how the AI-6 Slack bot actually works in practice.

Taking the AI-6 Slack bot for a spin

Let's start by taking the AI-6 Slack bot for a spin and see what it looks like before diving in. We can launch it using the convenient `ai6.sh` script, passing the `slack` argument:

```
❯ ./ai6.sh slack
virtualenv: /Users/gigi/git/ai-six/py/venv
Loaded environment variables from /Users/gigi/git/ai-six/py/frontend/slack/.env
Joined ai-6-test
Bolt app is running!
```

A Slack workspace called `bot-playground` was created, including a channel called `ai-6-test` (see *Figure 6.4*). The AI-6 Slack bot is a Slack app (`https://api.slack.com/docs/apps`) that automatically adds the `ai-6-` prefix to any channel and starts listening for messages.

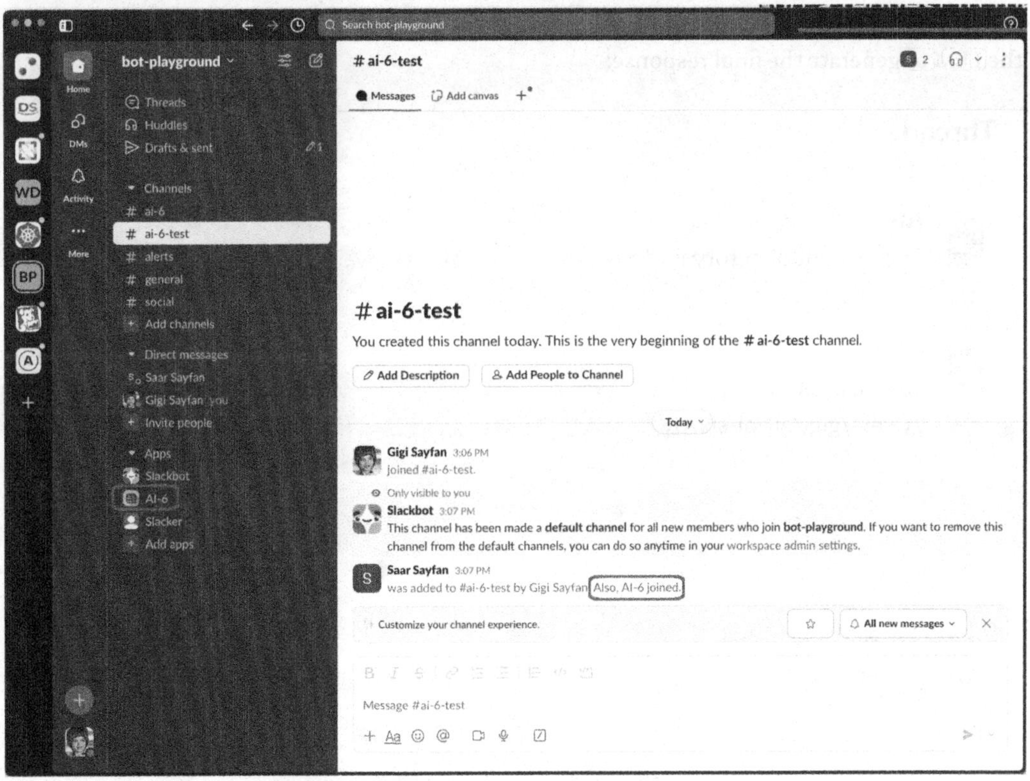

Figure 6.4: The #ai-6-test Slack channel

The AI-6 Slack bot is connected to AI-6, so it has access to all the tools and capabilities of AI-6. Let's see whether it knows what the current directory is:

Figure 6.5: Asking about the current directory

Note that in addition to the response message, there is also a reply in a thread associated with the message. Let's expand the thread and observe the tool calls AI-6 executed as requested by the LLM to generate the final response:

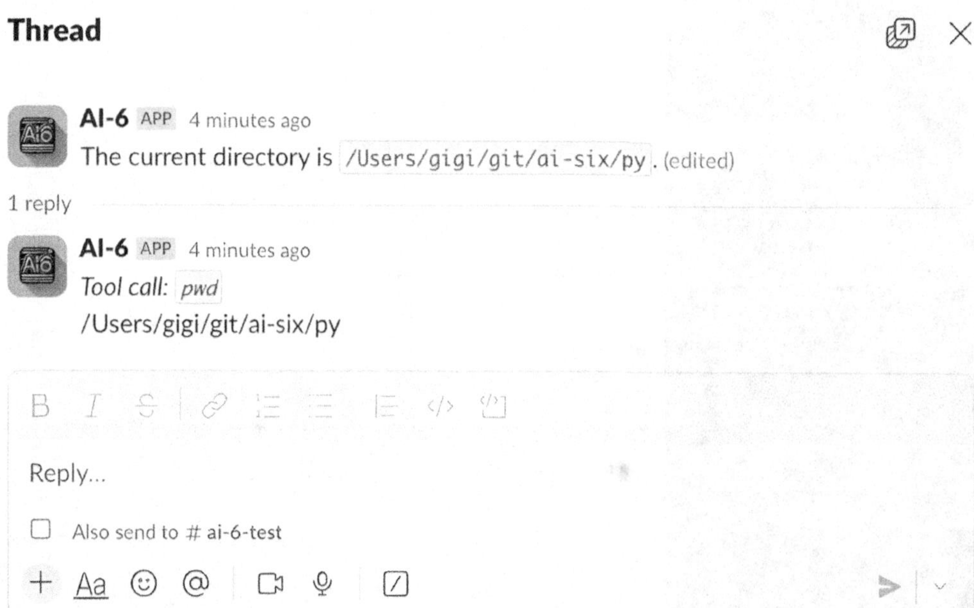

Figure 6.6: Observing the tool call

Note the user experience choice here. The tool calls are not shown in the main message, but in a thread. This is a good choice because it keeps the main message clean and focused on the final response, while still providing access to the details of how the response was generated, if the user is interested in that. Let's try another request with multiple tool calls:

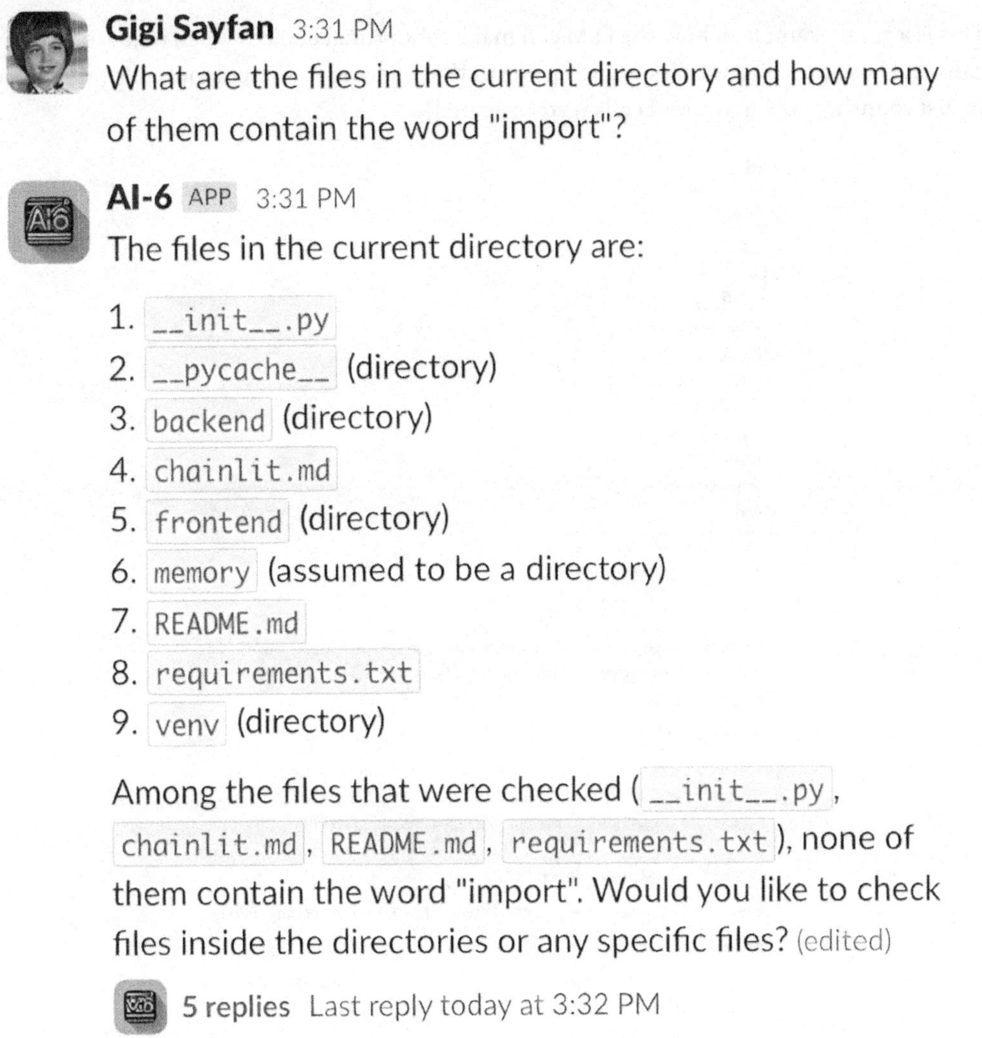

Figure 6.7: Multiple tool calls to check files in the current directory

Excellent. The AI-6 Slack bot is able to handle multiple tool calls and provide the correct answer. But how did it do that? Let's take a look at the tool calls in the thread. The LLM asked AI-6 to correctly invoke the `ls` tool to list all the files in the current directory. So far, so good. But then it requested AI-6 to invoke the `cat` tool to read the entire contents of each file and send it back, in order to find out whether it contained the word `import`.

This is correct, but it is extremely inefficient. For large files, it wouldn't even work because the contents would not fit in the context window. It would have been much more effective to use a tool such as `grep` to search for the word `import` in all the files at once.

This is a great example of how the LLM can make suboptimal choices when requesting tool calls and how to debug such issues using our UI that exposes the actual tool calls (as opposed to just counting how many tool calls were executed).

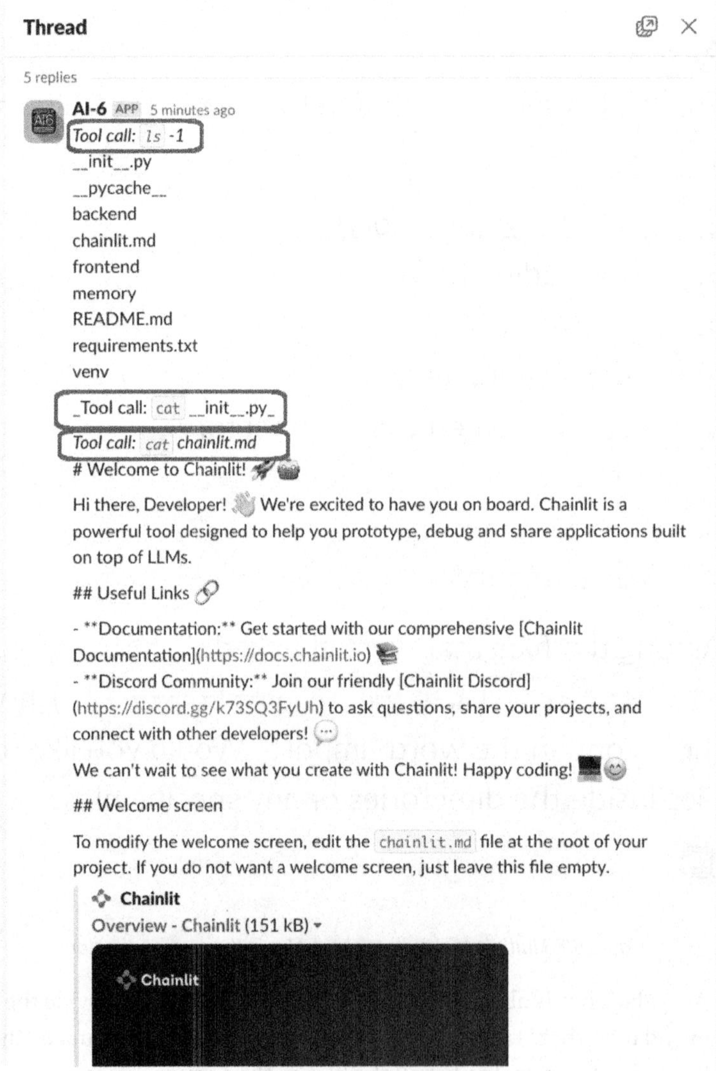

Figure 6.8: Detailed tool call visualization

This kind of poor tool choice is ideally detected during the development of the AI system and can be addressed by providing better instructions or system prompts to the LLM. In this case, let's see whether we can improve it just for this session. That's funny. When asked, why didn't AI-6 use `grep` instead of `cat`? Also, it acknowledged that it was inefficient and suggested using `grep`, but eventually it used `sed` to search for the word `import` in the files. This is fine, but it is different from what it declared it would do:

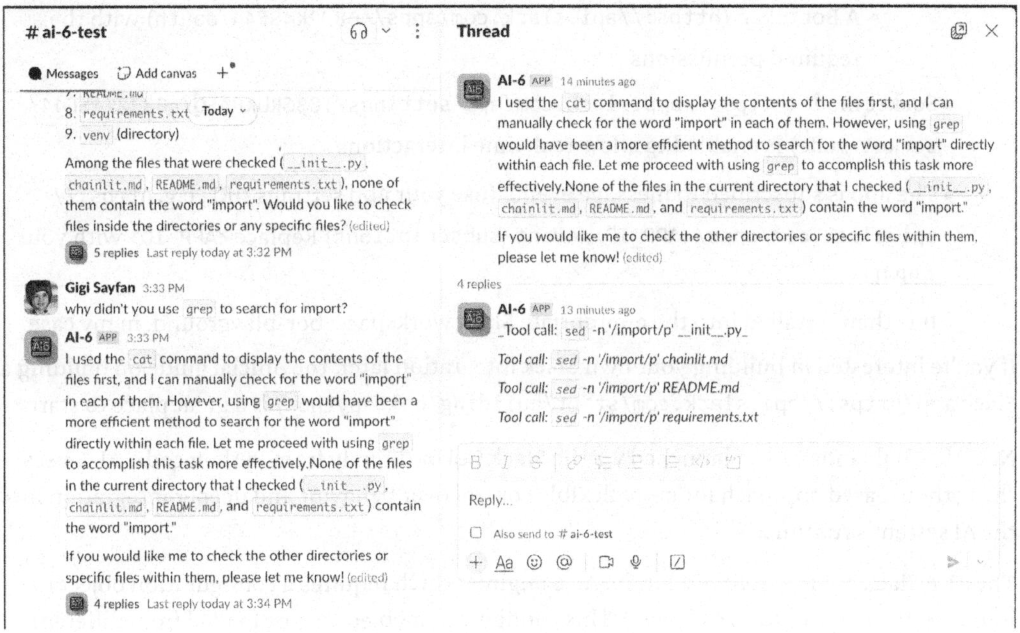

Figure 6.9: Debugging tool use choices

Now that we have a good idea of what the AI-6 Slack bot does and what the user experience is, let's see how the AI-6 Slack bot is implemented and how it works under the hood.

Authentication and configuration setup

The AI-6 Slack bot is built using the Slack Bolt (`https://slack.dev/bolt-python/`) framework, which simplifies Slack API integration in Python. Remember that you don't need to configure or deploy the Slack app yourself to follow this chapter. We'll walk through the design, structure, and behavior of the Slack interface so you can understand how it works without hands-on setup.

That said, for context, here's what the setup entails behind the scenes:

- A Slack app (https://api.slack.com/apps) is created and configured with the following:
  - An App token (https://api.slack.com/apps/A08J2K4SF44/general) with the connections:write scope
  - A Bot token (https://api.slack.com/apps/A08J2K4SF44/oauth) with the required permissions
- Socket mode (https://app.slack.com/app-settings/T08GRUKRA5Q/A08J2K4SF44/socket-mode) is enabled to allow real-time interactions
- The app is subscribed to message events (use your app settings URL, e.g. https://api.slack.com/apps/<APP_ID>/event-subscriptions) Replace <APP_ID> with your APP ID
- It is then installed into the appropriate Slack workspace: bot-playground, in my case

If you're interested in building your own Slack integration later, the official guide on building a Slack app (https://api.slack.com/start/building/bolt-python) is a great place to start.

Note that Bolt apps can be launched via the Slack CLI or directly from Python code. AI-6 uses the Python-based approach for more flexible control over behavior and deeper integration into the AI system's runtime.

The AI-6 Slack bot is a frontend for the AI-6 engine, which requires a configuration object to initialize, if you recall from *Chapter 4*. This configuration object can be loaded from different file formats, such as JSON, YAML, and TOML. The Slack bot uses a config.toml file to configure the AI-6 engine. Here it is:

```
# AI-6 Slack Configuration File
default_model_id = "gpt-4o"
tools_dir = "${HOME}/git/ai-six/py/backend/tools"
mcp_tools_dir = "${HOME}/git/ai-six/py/backend/mcp_tools"
memory_dir = "${HOME}/git/ai-six/memory/slack"
checkpoint_interval = 3
#Provider configuration
[provider_config.openai]
api_key = "${OPENAI_API_KEY}"
default_model = "gpt-4o"

[provider_config.ollama]
model = "qwen2.5-coder:32b"
```

```
#Tool configuration
[tool_config.claude]
api_key = "${ANTHROPIC_API_KEY}"
```

As you can see, there are environment variable names embedded in the config file instead of the actual sensitive information. This is one of the services provided by the AI-6 configuration system. It accepts such configuration files and automatically loads the environment variables using this code in the `Config` class:

```
@staticmethod
def _interpolate_env_vars(value: Any) -> Any:
    """Recursively interpolate environment variables in a configuration value.

    Supports ${VAR} and $VAR syntax for environment variables.

    Parameters
    ----------
    value : Any
        The value to interpolate

    Returns
    -------
    Any
        The interpolated value
    """
    if isinstance(value, str):
        # Handle ${VAR} syntax
        if "${" in value and "}" in value:
            import re
            pattern = r'\${([a-zA-Z0-9_]+)}'
            matches = re.findall(pattern, value)

            for var_name in matches:
                env_value = os.environ.get(var_name, '')
                value = value.replace(f"${{{var_name}}}", env_value)

        # Handle $VAR syntax
        elif value.startswith('$') and len(value) > 1:
            var_name = value[1:]
            value = os.environ.get(var_name, '')
```

```
            return value
        elif isinstance(value, dict):
            return {k: Config._interpolate_env_vars(v)
                for k, v in value.items()}
        elif isinstance(value, list):
            return [Config._interpolate_env_vars(item) for item in value]
        else:
            return value
```

You don't have to use the embedded environment variables in your configuration files. You may directly put the sensitive information in the config file, but just make sure you don't commit such files to your version control system. You may also create a `Config` object programmatically without using configuration files at all (e.g., read the configuration from a database or S3 bucket).

However, in this case, we are using the config file to load the environment variables and pass them to the AI-6, so we need to set those environment variables before running the Slack bot. The AI-6 Slack bot uses an `.env` file to populate multiple environment variables that are needed by Slack itself, in addition to the AI-6 LLM provider secrets. Here is the redacted `.env` file used by the AI-6 Slack bot:

```
OPENAI_API_KEY=<redacted>
ANTHROPIC_API_KEY=<redacted>
AI6_APP_ID=<redacted>
AI6_CLIENT_ID=<redacted>
AI6_CLIENT_SECRET=<redacted>
AI6_SIGNING_SECRET=<redacted>
AI6_BOT_TOKEN=<redacted>
AI6_APP_TOKEN=<redacted>
```

Yes, that's quite a few environment variables, but they are all necessary. This file must not be committed to version control, and it is ignored by the AI-6 `.gitignore` file:

```
# Environment files
**/.env
```

**/.env.*Slack Bot initialization

The AI-6 Slack bot code is in the frontend/slack directory. The main entry point is the app.py (https://github.com/PacktPublishing/Design-Multi-Agent-AI-Systems-Using-MCP-and-A2A/blob/main/ch06/ai-six/py/frontend/slack/app.py) file, which also contains most of the logic for the bot. Here are the imports, which include some standard library packages such as os and functools.partial, the pathology.path package, several Slack and Bolt packages, and the utils module from the frontend/slack directory, which helps connect to the AI-6 engine:

```
import os
from functools import partial

import pathology.path
from slack_bolt import App
from slack_bolt.adapter.socket_mode import SocketModeHandler
from dotenv import load_dotenv

from slack_sdk.errors import SlackApiError

from . import utils
```

The next part is all about loading the .env file and loading the environment variables. If there is no .env file, it will print a warning and carry on. It's possible that the environment variables were already set before running the script, so the bot can still run without the .env file:

```
script_dir = pathology.path.Path.script_dir()

# Try to load environment variables from .env file in the same directory as this
script
env_file_path = os.path.join(script_dir, ".env")
if os.path.exists(env_file_path):
    load_dotenv(env_file_path)
    print(f"Loaded environment variables from {env_file_path}")
else:
    print(f"Warning: No .env file found at {env_file_path}")
```

At this point, the environment variables are loaded, and we can access them using `os.environ.get()`. The code initializes some variables to hold the Slack app token and bot token and instantiates a Bolt app instance:

```
app_token = os.environ.get("AI6_APP_TOKEN")
bot_token = os.environ.get("AI6_BOT_TOKEN")
app = App(token=bot_token)
```

Then, it initializes some variables to hold the last message and the latest timestamp, a dictionary for dedicated AI-6 channels, locates the configuration file, and initializes an empty `engines` dictionary:

```
last_message = ""
latest_ts = None
ai6_channels = {}

config_path = str((script_dir / 'config.toml').resolve())
engines = {}
```

With all the preliminary initialization done, let's take a look at the `main()` function that starts the Slack bot. It does two primary things: joins a channel and starts `SocketModeHandler` to listen for events. It also handles exceptions and eventually leaves all the channels it joined:

```
def main():
    """Main entry point for the Slack app"""
    channel = join_channel(app.client)
    if channel is not None:
        print(f'Joined {channel["name"]}')

    try:
        # Run the Slack app
        SocketModeHandler(app, app_token).start()
    except KeyboardInterrupt:
        print("Ctrl+C detected.")
    except Exception as e:
        print(f"Unhandled exception: {e}")
    finally:
        leave_channels(app.client)
```

```
if __name__ == "__main__":
    main()
```

Now we have a basic understanding of how the AI-6 Slack bot is initialized and started. The next step is to understand how the bot handles incoming messages and interacts with the AI-6 engine to process them.

Message handling and event processing

Bolt apps handle events using decorators that map specific event types to handler functions. The AI-6 Slack bot handles all incoming messages in any channel via a single `handle_message()` function that is decorated with the `@app.event("message")` decorator:

```
@app.event("message")
def handle_message(message, say,ack, client):
    """Handle all messages in channels."""
```

The function declares the `last_message` and `latest_ts` global references, so it can access them, and then extracts the text from the `message` object:

```
global last_message, latest_ts
ack()  # Acknowledge ASAP

text = message.get("text")
```

The Slack bot is designed to process any messages in its own dedicated channels (the `ai6_channels` dictionary) or messages in any other channel that mentions the bot. If the message is empty or from a bot or doesn't match the criteria, it is ignored:

```
    # Skip if the message is empty or from a bot
    if not text or message.get("bot_id"):
        return

    mention_bot = f"<@{bot_user_id}>" in text
    channel_id = message['channel']
    ai6_channel = channel_id in ai6_channels
```

```
# Ignore messages that don't mention the bot and are not a special AI-6 channel
    if not mention_bot and not ai6_channel:
        return
```

At this point, we have a message that we want to process. We already got the channel ID from the message, so we can create or retrieve an AI-6 engine instance for that channel. Then, we prepare a tool call handler that will be used to handle tool callbacks from the AI-6 engine during message processing (those will go into the reply thread, as you recall):

```
    engine = get_or_create_engine(channel_id)

    # Create a tool call handler for this channel
    channel_tool_call_handler = partial(handle_tool_call, client, channel_id)
```

Now, we have everything we need to process the message. We will use the AI-6 engine in streaming mode so it can display chunks of the response as they arrive, and there is no need to wait for the full response to be ready. So, it starts with a generic "..." text. Then, we set the `latest_ts` global variable (the timestamp of the message) to the result of the `chat_postMessage()` call, which posts the initial message to the channel. The `last_message` variable is initialized to an empty string to hold the response as it is getting built up:

```
    # Process the message with the AI-6 engine
    try:
        # Post an initial empty message that we'll update
        result = client.chat_postMessage(
            channel=channel_id,
            text="..."
        )

        latest_ts = result["ts"]
        last_message = ""
```

Then, we define an inline `handle_chunk()` function, which will be called by the AI-6 engine as it streams chunks of the response. It's a little unusual to define nested functions like this, but it works well in this case because it allows us to keep the callback next to where it is used, making the code easier to read.

Whenever a new chunk arrives, it appends the chunk to the `last_message` variable and then updates the message in the channel using the `chat_update()` method. If there is an error with updating the message, it prints an error message:

```
# Define a callback function to handle streaming chunks
def handle_chunk(chunk):
    global last_message
    last_message += chunk

    try:
        # Update the message with the new content
        client.chat_update(
            channel=channel_id,
            ts=latest_ts,
            text=last_message
        )
    except SlackApiError as e:
        print(f"Error updating message: {e}")
```

Here is the final part of the `handle_message()` function that streams the message to the AI-6 engine and provides it with the two event handlers for handling chunks and tool calls. If there is an error during streaming, it catches the exception and prints an error message to the terminal:

```
    # Stream the message to the AI-6 engine
    response = engine.stream_message(
        text,
        engine.default_model_id,
        on_chunk_func=handle_chunk,
        on_tool_call_func=channel_tool_call_handler
    )

except Exception as e:
    print(f"I encountered an error: {str(e)}")
```

Now that we understand how the Slack bot handles messages, let's take it to the next level and consider how to work with multiple channels and multiple users.

Channel management and multi-user support

The AI-6 Slack bot is designed to support multiple Slack channels and users. It automatically joins the first channel whose name has the `ai-6-` prefix. The multi-user support comes for free because Slack supports multiple users and channels, and any user can post messages in any channel the bot is a member of. The bot will process all messages in those channels from any user.

Let's look at the `join_channel()` function that is called in the `main()` function to join a channel. It is pretty simple. First, it lists all the channels in the Slack workspace using the `conversations_list()` method of the Slack client. Then, it filters the channels to find those that start with the `ai-6-` prefix. If there are no such channels, it just returns. If there are multiple channels, it just joins the first one. If the bot is not a member of the channel, it tries to join it using the `conversations_join()` method. Finally, it returns the channel object.

```
def join_channel(client):

    """Join the first AI-6 channel if not a member already

    Return the channel id

    If there are no AI-6 channel raise an exception
    """

    all_channels = client.conversations_list()["channels"]
    ai6_channels.update(
        {
            c["id"]: c
            for c in all_channels
            if c["name"].startswith("ai-6-")
        }
    )

    if not ai6_channels:
        return

    channel_id = list(ai6_channels.keys())[0]
    channel = ai6_channels[channel_id]

    # Join channel if not a member already
    if not channel['is_member']:
```

```
        try:
            client.conversations_join(channel=channel_id)

        except Exception as e:
            print(f"Error joining channel {channel_id}: {e}")

    return channel
```

This behavior of automatically joining a channel with a specific naming convention is, frankly, mostly useful for development and testing purposes. In a real-world application, you would just invite the AI-6 Slack bot to specific channels. This behavior is supported too, since the `handle_message()` handler responds to any message in channels where the bot is present, as you recall, as long as the message mentions the AI-6 Slack bot.

Here is how to invite the AI-6 Slack bot to a channel that it is not a member of:

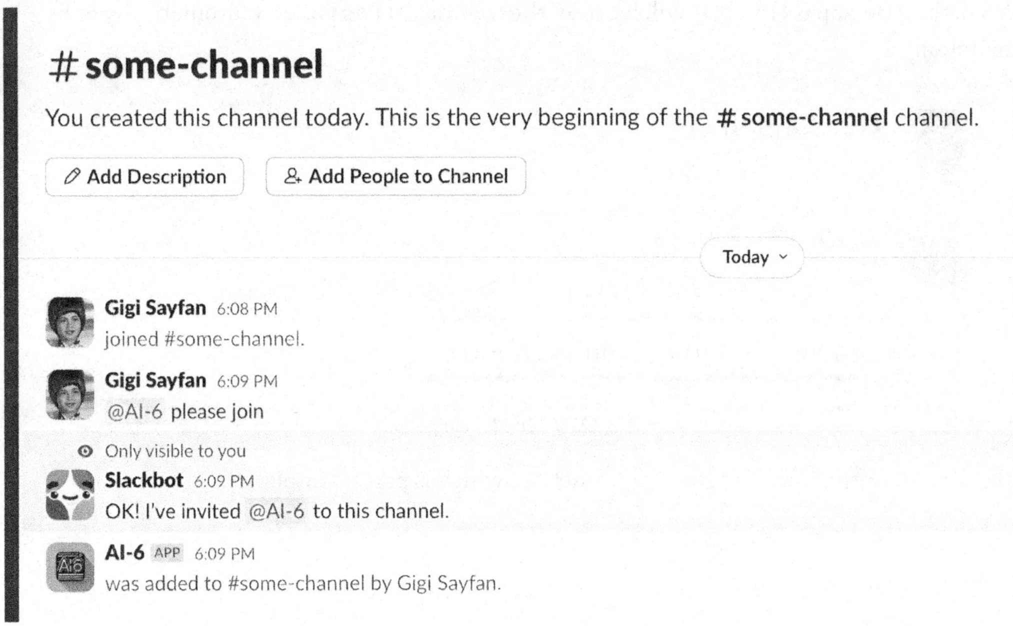

Figure 6.10: Explicitly invite the AI-6 bot to a channel

This channel is called **some-channel**, which means the AI-6 Slack bot will not automatically respond to any message. We must mention it using `@AI-6` to get a response. Let's try it:

Figure 6.11: Mentioning AI-6

When the AI-6 app is closed, it will leave all the channels it has joined (automatically or by invitation).

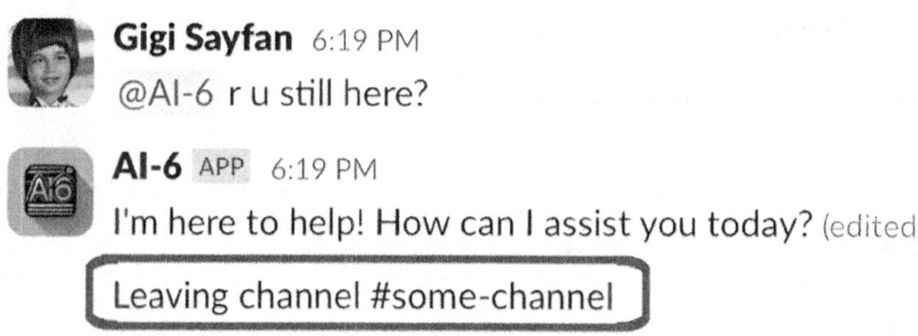

Figure 6.12: AI-6 bot leaving a channel

This is done in the `leave_channels()` function, which is pretty simple:

```
def leave_channels(client):
    """Leave all the channels
    """
    channels = (c for c in client.conversations_list()['channels']
        if c['is_member'])
    for c in channels:
        client.chat_postMessage(
            channel=c['id'],
            text=f"Leaving channel #{c['name']}"
```

```
    )
    client.conversations_leave(channel=c['id'])
```

We covered how the AI-6 Slack bot handles messages and manages channels. Now, let's look at how it integrates with the AI-6 engine.

Integration with the AI-6 engine

There are two main touch points between the AI-6 Slack bot and the AI-6 engine: creating or retrieving an engine instance for each channel and handling tool calls from the AI-6 engine. The `get_or_create_engine()` function helps to ensure each channel has its own AI-6 engine instance, which is essential for multi-channel and multi-user support.

If we had just one shared engine, it would be difficult to manage the state and memory for each channel. First, the context window would fill up much quicker, and also, the LLM would be confused by unrelated messages from different channels.

Here is the code. It's pretty simple. All the engines for all the channels are stored in the `engines` dictionary. If the requested channel ID is not in the dictionary, it creates a new engine instance using the `utils.create_channel_engine()` function, and adds it to the `engines` dictionary. Then, it just returns the engine:

```
def get_or_create_engine(channel_id):
    """Get an existing engine for a channel or create a new one."""
    if channel_id not in engines:
        # Create a channel-specific engine using the Slack utility function
        engines[channel_id] = utils.create_channel_engine(
            base_config_path=config_path,
            channel_id=channel_id,
            env_file_path=env_file_path
        )

    return engines[channel_id]
```

The `utils.create_channel_engine()` (`https://github.com/PacktPublishing/Design-Multi-Agent-AI-Systems-Using-MCP-and-A2A/blob/main/ch06/ai-six/py/frontend/slack/utils.py`) function contains similar code for instantiating the AI-6 engine as we saw in *Chapter 4*, but it also sets the channel ID in the configuration and initializes the memory for that channel.

Let's take a look at the code that handles tool calls from the AI-6 engine. The `handle_tool_call()` function adds each tool call and its response to the thread of the original message in the Slack channel. This allows users to see the details of how the AI-6 engine arrived at its response, including the tool calls and their results:

```
def handle_tool_call(client, channel, name, args, result):
    """Handle a tool call from the AI-6 engine."""
    # Post the tool call result as a message
    try:
        client.chat_postMessage(
            channel=channel,
            thread_ts=latest_ts,
            text=f"_Tool call: `{name}` {', '.join(args.values()) if args else ''}
_\n{result}"
        )
    except SlackApiError as e:
        print(f"Error posting tool call result: {e}")
```

To summarize, we covered how the AI-6 Slack bot is designed and implemented and how it integrates with the AI-6 engine. We discussed some of the key features, such as multi-channel support, message handling, and tool call processing. Now, let's turn our attention to the Chainlit web UI, which is similar to web chatbots such as ChatGPT.

Developing a web UI with Chainlit

In the previous section, we explored the AI-6 Slack bot interface and saw how it provides a collaborative, multi-user environment for interacting with agentic AI systems. The Slack bot excels at team workflows, real-time notifications, and integration with existing communication channels.

However, there are scenarios where a dedicated web interface offers advantages: more control over the user experience, richer visual elements, better support for long-form conversations, and easier deployment for users who don't have access to a Slack workspace. This is where Chainlit comes in. In this section, we'll examine how AI-6 leverages Chainlit to create a web-based chat interface similar to ChatGPT while maintaining full access to AI-6's tool ecosystem and agent capabilities.

Chainlit framework overview

Chainlit (`https://docs.chainlit.io`) is a Python framework specifically designed for building chat interfaces for LLM applications. It provides out-of-the-box support for many UI elements, the chat life cycle, streaming responses, file uploads, settings management, session persistence, and much more—all the features needed for a polished conversational AI interface. It is highly customizable, too, allowing you to add your custom UI elements.

Chainlit's development experience is tailored for rapid iteration. It runs a local development server with hot-reloading, enabling fast prototyping and debugging. The framework integrates seamlessly with popular LLM backends such as OpenAI, LangChain, and Hugging Face, and supports both synchronous and asynchronous workflows for maximal flexibility.

Let's explore how AI-6 leverages Chainlit to build a simple web interface that complements its Slack bot. The AI-6 Chainlit application is intentionally minimal and not designed to fully showcase Chainlit's capabilities. Its primary purpose is to demonstrate how the AI-6 backend can be integrated into a web-based UI, serving as a foundation for more advanced and polished web applications.

Taking AI-6 Chainlit for a spin

Let's start with a very useful real-world use case, which involves adding a GitHub Actions (`https://docs.github.com/en/actions`) workflow to the AI-6 repository to run all our tests whenever we push new changes. First, we need to launch the Chainlit app. We can do that using the convenient `ai6.sh` script passing the `chainlit` argument:

```
❯ ./ai6.sh chainlit
virtualenv: /Users/gigi/git/ai-six/py/venv
2025-07-19 11:28:15 - HTTP Request: GET https://api.openai.com/v1/models "HTTP/1.1
200 OK"
2025-07-19 11:28:17 - HTTP Request: GET https://api.openai.com/v1/models "HTTP/1.1
200 OK"
2025-07-19 11:28:18 - Your app is available at http://localhost:8000
```

The AI-6 Chainlit app is now running and we can access it at `http://localhost:8000`. Let's open it in a web browser:

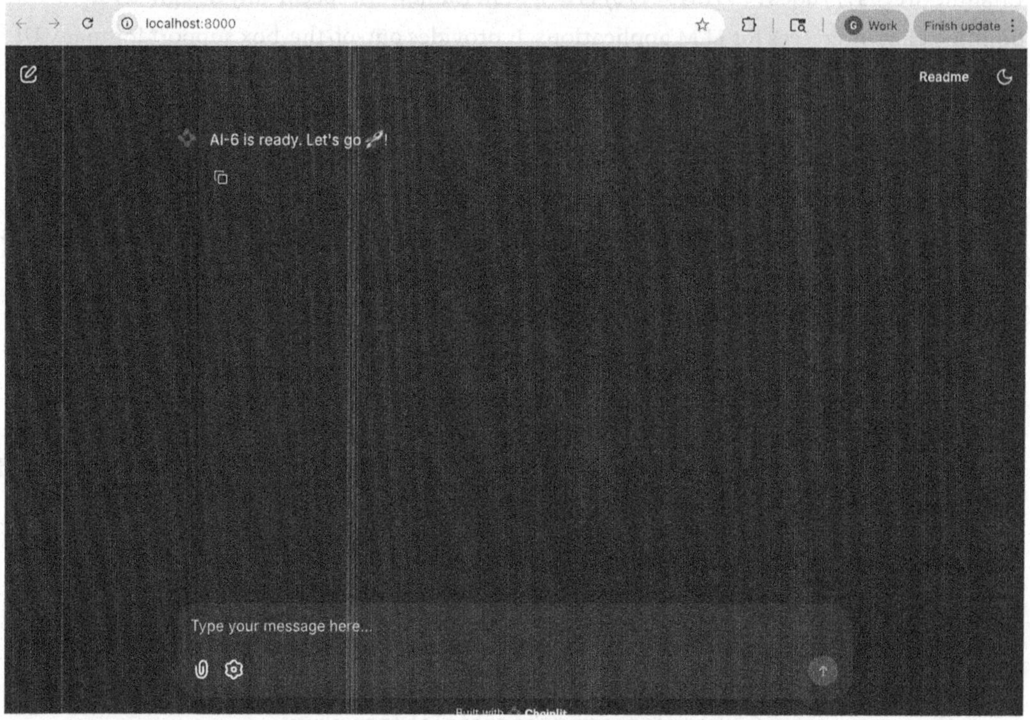

Figure 6.13: The Chainlit web app

Now, let's ask AI-6 to add a GitHub Actions workflow to the AI-6 repository:

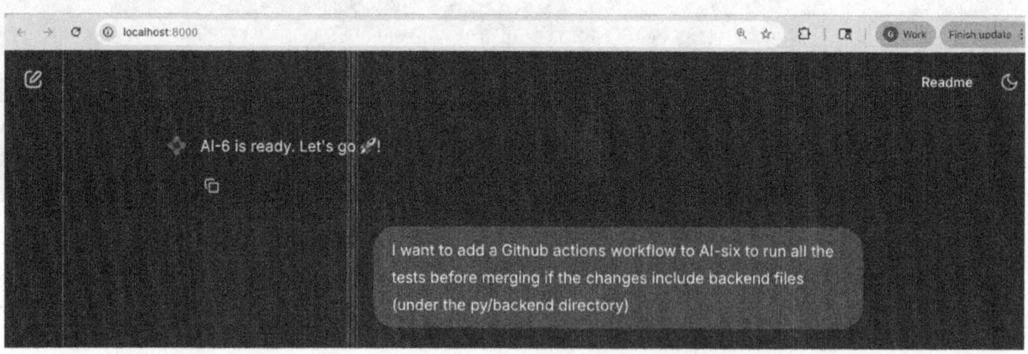

Figure 6.14: Initial user prompt

AI-6 provided a very clear and detailed explanation, including the actual workflow file and all the steps to accomplish the task. Note how pleasant the UI is. The code is properly color-coded and the Markdown is formatted cleanly:

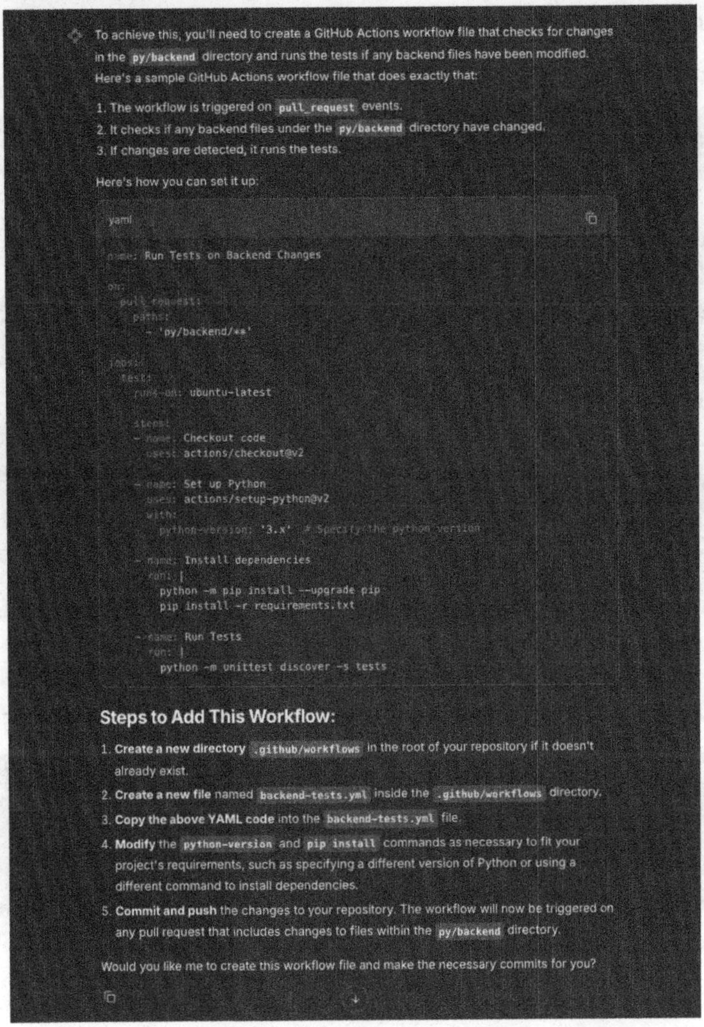

Figure 6.15: Elaborate LLM response

But the solution has a few problems. First, it used the `pull_request` event, which doesn't trigger on a regular push to the main branch. We want the workflow to run on push events too. Second, it uses outdated versions of some GitHub actions, such as `actions/checkout@v2` and `actions/setup-python@v2`. We want to use the latest versions.

Let's ask AI-6 to fix these issues:

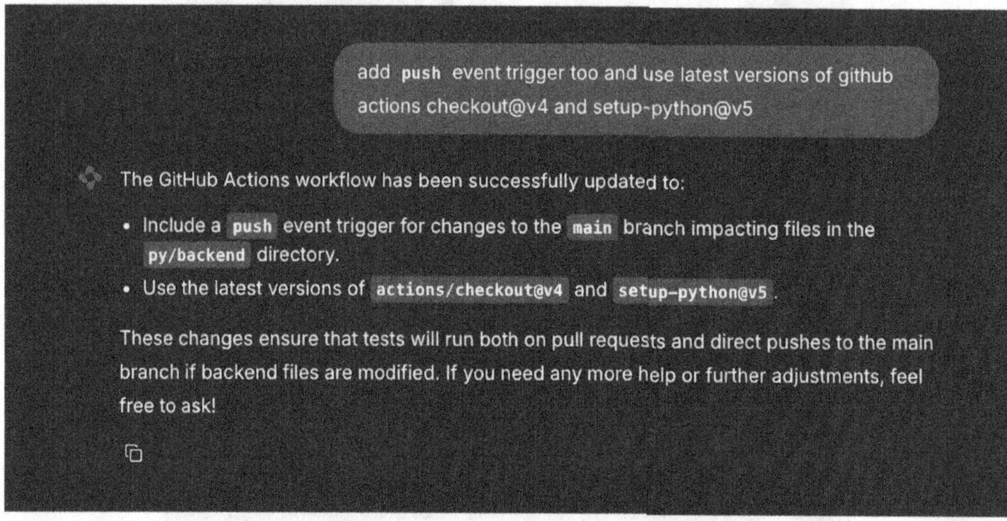

Figure 6.16: Follow-up interaction

Let's see what AI-6 actually did. Here is the original commit and the fix commit:

```
> git log --oneline -n 2
f5198ca (HEAD -> main, origin/main, origin/HEAD)
Update_workflow_for_push_event_and_latest_actions_versions
65a0c12 Add_GitHub_Actions_workflow_to_run_tests_on_backend_changes
```

Let's review the changes:

```
❯ git diff HEAD~2
diff --git a/.github/workflows/backend-tests.yml b/.github/workflows/backend-
tests.yml
new file mode 100644
index 0000000..1339264
--- /dev/null
+++ b/.github/workflows/backend-tests.yml
@@ -0,0 +1,35 @@
+name: Run Tests on Backend Changes
+
+
+
+on:
+  pull_request:
+    paths:
+      - 'py/backend/**'
+  push:
+    branches:
+      - main
+    paths:
+      - 'py/backend/**'
+
+
+
+jobs:
+  test:
+    runs-on: ubuntu-latest
+
+
+
+    steps:
+    - name: Checkout code
+      uses: actions/checkout@v4
+
+
+
```

```
+       - name: Set up Python
+         uses: actions/setup-python@v5
+         with:
+           python-version: '3.x'  # Specify the python version
+
+
+
+       - name: Install dependencies
+         working-directory: py
+         run: |
+           python -m pip install --upgrade pip
+           pip install -r requirements.txt
+
+
+
+       - name: Run Tests
+         working-directory: py
+         run: |
+           python -m unittest discover -s backend/tests
```

Everything looks correct now. AI-6 fixed all the issues we identified. This highlights the importance of the human-in-the-loop concept.

LLMs are great, but they are not perfect (yet). We can now tell AI-6 to push the changes to GitHub:

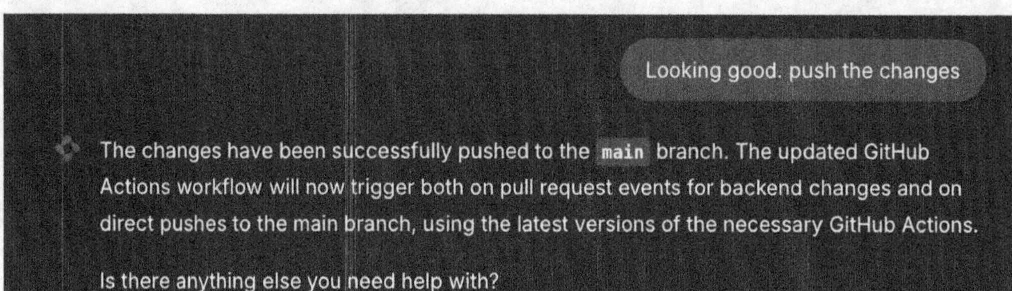

Figure 6.17: AI-6 pushing changes to GitHub

Let's check GitHub and confirm that the new GitHub Actions workflow is indeed there:

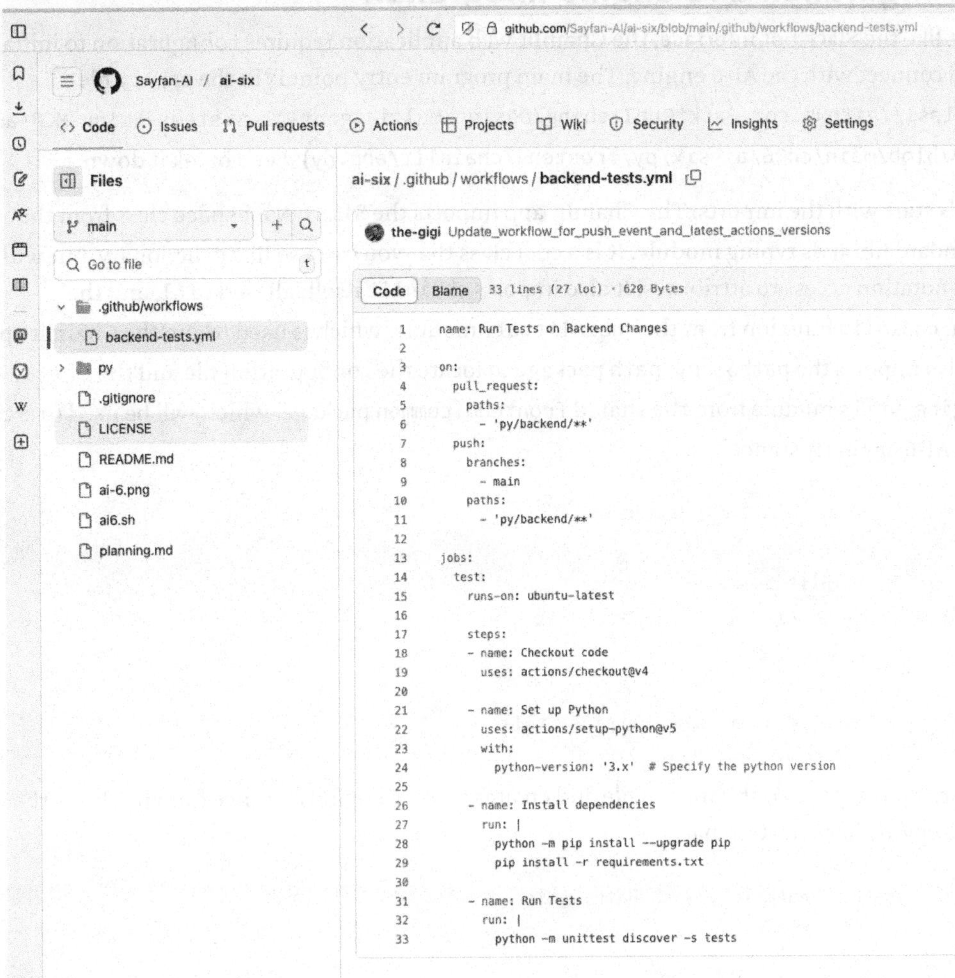

Figure 6.18: GitHub Actions workflow

That was a great session with AI-6 using the Chainlit interface. We were able to add a new GitHub Actions workflow to the AI-6 repository, fix some issues, and push the changes to GitHub. The Chainlit interface provided a clean and modern view of the conversation.

Let's take a look at how the Chainlit interface is implemented and how it integrates with the AI-6 engine.

Configuration and engine integration

Just like the Slack bot interface, the Chainlit web application requires configuration to initialize and connect with the AI-6 engine. The main program entry point is in the `app.py` file (`https://github.com/PacktPublishing/Design-Multi-Agent-AI-Systems-using-MCP-and-A2A/blob/main/ch06/ai-six/py/frontend/chainlit/app.py`). Let's break it down.

Let's start with the imports. The Chainlit app imports the `SimpleNamespace` class from the standard library's typing module. It is a cool class that you can use like a dictionary, but with dot notation access to attributes. It also imports `chainlit` itself, aliased to `cl`, and the `run_chainlit` function from the `chainlit.cli` module, which is used to run the Chainlit app. It also imports the `pathology.path` package to locate the configuration file and the `engine_utils` module from the shared `frontend.common` package, which will be used to create the AI-6 engine instance:

```
from types import SimpleNamespace

import chainlit as cl
from chainlit.cli import run_chainlit
import pathology.path

from frontend.common import engine_utils
```

Next, it locates the configuration file and creates an AI-6 engine instance from it. This is the AI-6 engine initialization part:

```
script_dir = pathology.path.Path.script_dir()

# Load the engine from YAML configuration
config_path = str((script_dir / "config.yaml").resolve())

# Create engine from configuration file
# Environment variables will be automatically interpolated by Config.from_file
engine, engine_config = engine_utils.create_from_config(config_path)
```

Here, we create the `app_config` object, which is a `SimpleNamespace` instance (`https://docs.python.org/3/library/types.html#types.SimpleNamespace`) that holds the configuration for the Chainlit app:

```
app_config = SimpleNamespace(
    selected_model=engine.default_model_id,
    available_models=list(engine.model_provider_map.keys()),
    enabled_tools={tool: True for tool in engine.tool_dict},
)

TOOL_PREFIX = "tool:"
```

This configuration object will be used later when processing messages from the user. The integration with the AI-6 engine is via the `engine` variable that was created earlier.

Application life cycle and event handlers

At this point, we have the engine and the configuration (the `app_config` object) ready, and the main logic of the application runs by invoking the `run_chainlit()` function (imported from `chainlit.cli`) with the `app.py` file. This is a cumbersome way to launch a Chainlit application from a Python program. This is needed for debugging:

```
if __name__ == "__main__":
    target = str(script_dir / "app.py")
    run_chainlit(target)
```

The standard way to run a Chainlit application in the terminal is using the `chainlit` CLI:

```
❯ chainlit run app.py
```

Anyway, once the Chainlit app is running, it will start listening for events and processing them. Our Chainlit app handles the following events:

- -`on_chat_start`: Called when a new chat session starts
- -`on_message`: Called when a new user message is received
- -`on_settings_update`: Called when settings were changed in the settings panel

Let's take a look at each of these event handlers and see how they work.

The on_chat_start event handler

This event handler is called exactly once when the app starts. It is pretty simple. It calls `setup_settings()` and displays the welcome message that we saw when we took the Chainlit app for a spin:

```
@cl.on_chat_start
async def on_chat_start():
    await setup_settings()
    await cl.Message(content="AI-6 is ready. Let's go 🚀!").send()
```

The `setup_settings()` function is very interesting. It sets up the initial settings for the Chainlit app in UI widgets, including the LLM selection and tool switches. It uses `cl.input_widget.Select` for the model selection and `cl.input_widget.Switch` for each tool. The initial values are taken from the app_config object we created earlier:

```
async def setup_settings():
    model_select = cl.input_widget.Select(
        id="model",
        label="LLM Model",
        values=app_config.available_models,
        initial_value=app_config.selected_model,
        initial_index=app_config.available_models.index(
            app_config.selected_model),
    )
    tool_switches = [
        cl.input_widget.Switch(
            id=f"{TOOL_PREFIX}{tool_name}",
            label=f"Tool: {tool_name}",
            initial=tool_value,
        )
        for tool_name, tool_value in app_config.enabled_tools.items()
    ]

    await cl.ChatSettings([model_select] + tool_switches).send()
```

But where are those UI settings displayed? Well, there is a little cog button in the bottom-left corner of the user input box that brings up **Settings panel**. It looks like this:

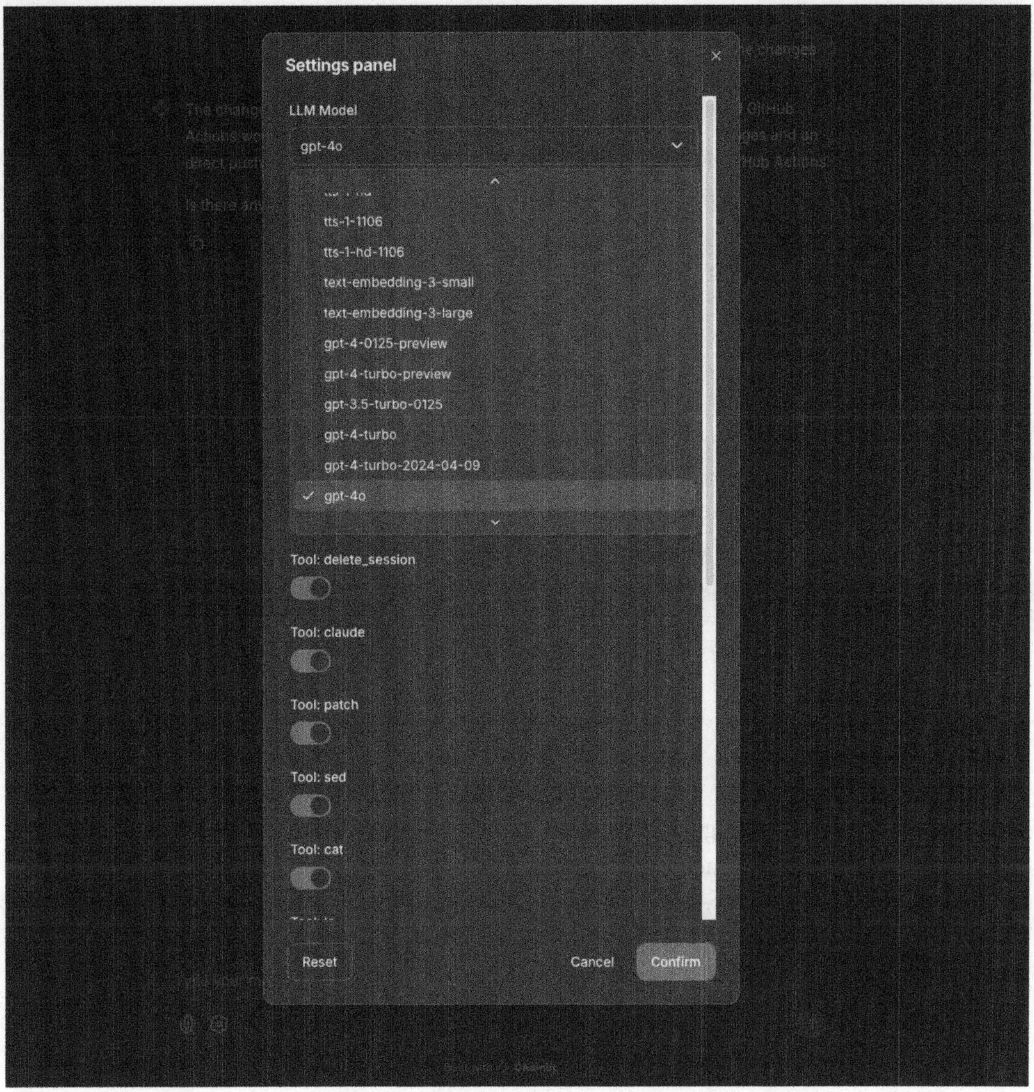

Figure 6.19: Chainlit app Settings panel

We will see how these settings are being used and can be modified later. For now, let's just note that the initial value of the LLM is set to the value in the `app_config` object, as well as the enabled tools. The entire thing is sent to Chainlit using the `cl.ChatSettings().send()` method.

At this point, we have the Chainlit app initialized, configured with a proper LLM and a set of enabled tools, and ready to handle messages.

The on_message event handler

This is the main event handler that processes incoming messages from the user and interacts with the AI-6 engine. It is called whenever the user types in a new message.

Initially, it creates a new `cl.Message` object with empty content and sends it to the Chainlit UI immediately. This message will be updated later with the response from the AI-6 engine:

```
@cl.on_message
async def on_message(message: cl.Message):
    """Process user messages and generate responses."""
    # Create a new message for the response
    msg = cl.Message(content="")
    await msg.send()
```

Next, it defines a callback function, `on_chunk()`, that will be used to handle streaming chunks of the response from the AI-6 engine. This function will be called whenever the AI-6 engine sends a new chunk of the response:

```
    # Define a callback function to handle streaming chunks
    async def on_chunk(chunk: str):
        # Use the Chainlit built-in streaming method
        await msg.stream_token(chunk)
```

Here is the call to the AI-6 engine to process the message. It uses the `engine.stream_message()` method to stream the response. It passes the user's message content, the selected LLM from `app_config`, the `on_chunk` callback function, and the list of enabled tool IDs. While the AI-6 engine processes the requests, it will send multiple chunks to the `on_chunk` function, which will update the response message that was initially empty. If there is a problem at any point, it will display an error message in the Chainlit UI:

```
    # Stream the response
    try:
        engine.stream_message(
            message.content,
            app_config.selected_model,
            on_chunk_func=lambda chunk: cl.run_sync(on_chunk(chunk)),
            available_tool_ids=[
                k for k, v in app_config.enabled_tools.items() if v],
        )
        # Mark the message as complete
```

```
        await msg.update()
    except Exception as e:
        await cl.Message(content=f"Error: {str(e)}").send()
```

Let's see the process in action. AI-6 is asked to write a 100-word poem about itself and put a breakpoint in the `on_chunk()` handler. This is fascinating. AI-6 started the poem with `In digital realms where ideas entwine`. The LLM chose to stream one output token at a time. In the case of the word `entwine`, it broke it into two chunks (two tokens): `entw` and `ine`. See the following figure:

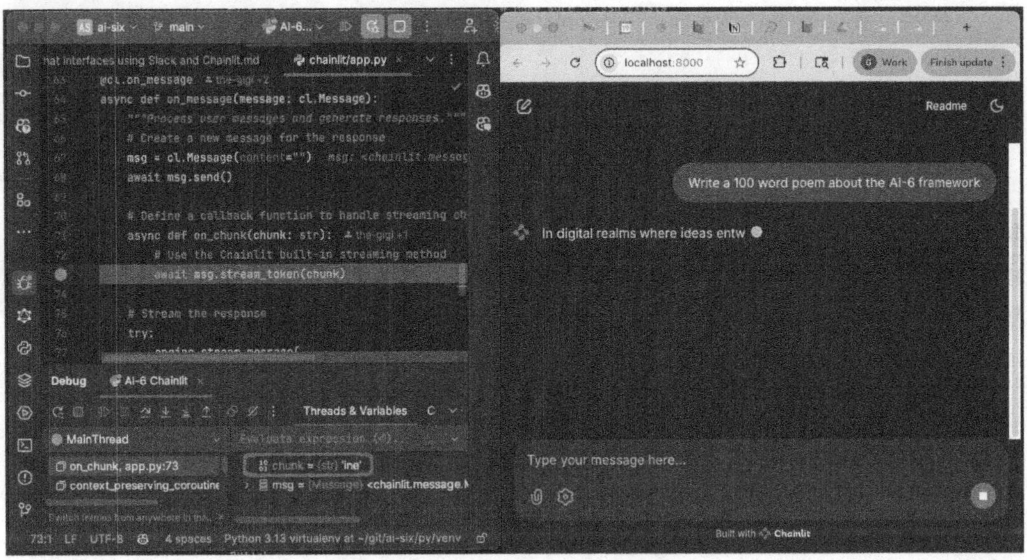

Figure 6.20: AI-6 is writing a poem

One last thing: note that in the current version of the code, we don't pass the `on_tool_call_func` argument to the `engine.stream_message()` method, so the AI-6 engine will not notify the UI on any tool calls. This is intentional as I didn't want to pollute the display with verbose tool calls. The AI-6 Slack bot had a natural place for tool calls in the thread. However, this is not the case with the Chainlit UI. A special side panel may be added at some point. Then, the user may opt to open up and capture tool calls there.

The on_settings event handler

The AI-6 Slack and CLI frontends had a pre-configured LLM and tools. The Chainlit app allows the user to select and modify the LLM and enable or disable tools on the fly. When the user changes the settings in the settings panel and clicks the **Confirm** button, the `on_settings()` event handler is called. All it does is update `app_config` with the new settings. That includes the selected LLM and the enabled tools:

```
@cl.on_settings_update
async def on_settings_update(new_settings):
    app_config.selected_model = new_settings["model"]
    for k, v in new_settings.items():
        if k.startswith(TOOL_PREFIX):
            tool_name = k.replace(TOOL_PREFIX, "")
            app_config.enabled_tools[tool_name] = v
```

Let's see it in action. I will disable the `ls` and `git` tools. This should prevent the LLM from using these tools to list files. It should still be able to find the current directory because the `pwd` tool remains enabled.

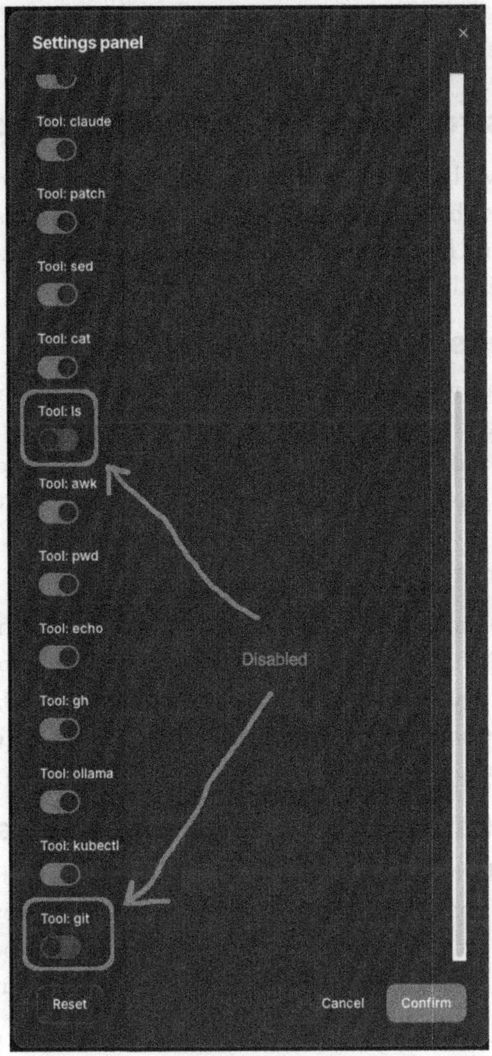

Figure 6.21: Disabling tools

Yeah, it works! AI-6 doesn't provide the `ls` and `git` tools, so the LLM has no way to list files.

To summarize, we covered the Chainlit web interface for AI-6 in this section. We saw how it is initialized and integrated with the AI-6 engine, how it handles messages, and its dynamic configuration with the ability to switch the LLM and toggle tools. We barely scratched the surface of what's possible, but we saw how it provides a lightweight web-based alternative to the AI-6 Slack bot.

In the next section, we will discuss best practices for building more advanced and sophisticated interactive agent interfaces.

Best practices for interactive agent interfaces

The frontend interfaces we built in the previous sections are great starting points for interacting with AI agents, but when building production-grade AI systems, there are several best practices to consider. These practices ensure that the user experience is smooth, the agent's intent is clear, and the system is robust and maintainable.

Clarify the agent's role and capabilities

A successful interactive agent interface must make it immediately clear to the user what the agent is, what it can do, and what kind of inputs it expects. Ambiguity in the agent's scope leads to user frustration and failed interactions. The interface should expose key capabilities through UI elements such as buttons, autocomplete prompts, or help overlays. For example, a file analysis agent might show a drop zone for files, a list of supported file types, and a sample command such as "Summarize this CSV."

The agent should also communicate its limitations proactively. This includes model constraints (e.g., token limits), disabled tools, or unsupported input formats. In a multi-agent system where high-level agents may automatically spawn sub-agents, it's often more important to focus on the high-level agents that the user can manage either through predefined configuration options or user prompts.

Safeguards – confirmations, dry-runs, and safety nets

AI agents can invoke tools that can potentially cause a lot of damage if misused. The UI should default to a conservative posture, asking the user to confirm high-impact actions such as file overwrites, code deployments, or deletions. Confirmation prompts not only prevent accidental damage but also force users to reflect on the implications of their input.

In addition to confirmations, the UI should support dry-run modes. A dry run is a safe simulation that shows what the agent would do without actually executing anything. This is particularly valuable when developing and testing workflows, API integrations, or infrastructure commands. When users can preview results and verify correctness, trust in the system increases. Combined with the ability to cancel or undo actions, these safety nets make agentic systems feel powerful but not reckless.

It is also highly recommended to add an "Abort" button to the UI that allows users to stop the agent at any time.

Design for turn-based transparency

AI agents operate in a conversational, turn-based manner. This interaction model should be embraced and used to surface internal reasoning, chain of thought (for models that support it), and tool calls. Each step the agent takes should be represented in the interface: prompts, decisions, tool calls, outputs, and intermediate results. This makes it easy for users to understand the "why" behind the agent's behavior.

Good interfaces show the full life cycle of a single interaction in a clean, linear thread. For example, when an agent decides to call a tool, the request parameters and response should be visible in the chat flow or an expandable panel. Errors, retries, or fallbacks should also be displayed as part of the story. This design pattern helps users debug, audit, and learn how to better prompt the agent and improve outcomes.

Prioritize tool invocation and feedback loops

One of the biggest value-adds of agentic systems is their ability to use external tools. The UI must make it obvious when tools are being invoked, how they are selected, and what their results are. This creates a feedback loop where users can evaluate whether the tool usage was appropriate and intervene if not.

The interface should also surface tool invocation metadata: timestamps, arguments, return values, and any errors. When tools fail (e.g., network error or malformed input), the agent should gracefully report the issue and offer options such as retry, revise input, or skip. Allowing users to nudge the agent or override tool choices keeps the conversation productive and aligned with user intent.

It is also important to provide a way for users to see the available tools and their descriptions, and customize the set of tools per agent.

Embrace configurability and runtime control

Different users have different preferences and trust thresholds. Some might want the agent to auto-execute tools freely, while others may prefer manual confirmation. The UI should expose runtime settings to control these behaviors. This includes toggling tools on/off, switching models, selecting output verbosity, and defining fallback strategies.

These controls should be easily accessible (e.g., via a settings panel or chat command) and persist across sessions if appropriate. Allowing users to customize their interaction style improves usability and satisfaction.

Logs, metrics, and distributed tracing for agentic systems

Every user action, agent decision, and tool call should be logged with metadata. These logs serve both user-facing and developer-facing goals. For users, logs can be visualized as timelines, enabling backtracking and replaying previous sessions. For developers, logs support debugging, performance tuning, and prompt refinement.

Metrics should include tool call frequency, average response latency, session duration, task success rates, and user interventions. Over time, these metrics can guide improvements to both the agent's behavior and the UI. UIs without instrumentation are black boxes. By instrumenting every part of the workflow, agentic systems can evolve from prototypes to reliable, auditable platforms.

LLM-specific distributed tracing is critical too for complex systems. Each turn should be represented by a span. Traces should capture complete sessions or conversations.

If you follow these best practices, you will be able to build interactive agent interfaces that are user-friendly and developer-friendly. They will provide a great user experience and allow users to interact with AI agents in a natural and satisfying way. The AI-6 Slack bot and Chainlit web interface we built in this chapter show some elements of these best practices, but there is a lot of room for improvement.

Summary

In this chapter, we transitioned from AI-6's backend and internal architecture to its frontend UIs, focusing on how the UI enables effective collaboration between users and autonomous agents. We examined why visibility, interruptibility, debugging, and trust are essential UI concerns for agentic systems, and how different roles require different levels of detail in the interface.

We then explored the implementation of the AI-6 Slack bot, highlighting its design choices such as tool call threading, per-channel engine instances, and real-time message handling. Slack's familiarity, multi-user support, and notification capabilities make it an ideal interface for collaborative workflows.

Finally, we examined the Chainlit-based web interface, showing how it provides a clean, customizable, single-user experience. With support for tool toggling, model selection, and rich streaming output, Chainlit complements Slack's strengths and enables fine-grained user control. Both interfaces set the stage for best practices in building robust, transparent agent UIs.

In the next chapter, we will turn our attention to the **Model Context Protocol (MCP)**, a standardized mechanism for sharing model state and execution context across tools and agents. We will define what MCP is, explore how to implement MCP-compliant servers and clients, and walk through how to integrate MCP into your own agent framework to enable seamless context sharing across diverse AI components.

Subscribe for a free eBook

7

Integrating with the Model Context Protocol Ecosystem

In the previous chapters, we explored how to build agentic AI systems, how to integrate them with custom tools, and how to interact with them using different frontends such as a **command-line interface** (**CLI**), a Slack bot, and a Chainlit-based web UI. In this chapter, we will focus on integrating your agentic AI framework with the **Model Context Protocol** (**MCP**) (`https://modelcontextprotocol.io`) ecosystem. MCP is a big deal! It is a protocol designed to standardize interactions between agentic AI systems models and tools. We will start by exploring MCP and its benefits. Then, we will look at how to build MCP servers and clients. Finally, we will demonstrate how to integrate MCP into AI-6, our agentic AI framework.

We will cover the following main topics:

- What is MCP?
- MCP architecture core and core components
- Building MCP servers
- Building MCP clients
- Integrating MCP into the AI-6 framework
- Putting it all together

By the end of this chapter, you will have a solid understanding of MCP, why it is so great, and how to use it to build agentic AI systems that can benefit from the rich ecosystem of MCP servers and clients.

Technical requirements

To follow along, refer to the instructions in the `README` file:

`https://github.com/PacktPublishing/Design-Multi-Agent-AI-Systems-Using-MCP-and-A2A/blob/main/ch07/ai-six/README.md`

What is MCP?

MCP was introduced by the team at Anthropic (`https://www.anthropic.com`) to standardize interactions between agentic AI systems, data sources, and external services. With MCP, you can build agentic AI systems that "speak" MCP, and you can automatically integrate with any MCP server. This means that you extend the capabilities of the AI system with tools from a large ecosystem beyond custom tools. For MCP tool developers, it embodies the principle of "*Write once, Run everywhere.*" The protocol has a formal specification (`https://modelcontextprotocol.io/specification`). The protocol is versioned, and it evolves quickly.

The motivation behind MCP

Before MCP, every agentic AI system was essentially on its own. If a developer wanted their AI agent to interact with external tools such as an **application programming interface** (**API**), a database, or a proprietary service, they had to design and implement custom connectors. These connectors not only had to know how to talk to the external system, but also how to inject relevant information into the LLM's context in a useful and timely way. This was often implemented as tools that were tightly coupled to the specific AI framework being used.

This approach quickly became a maintenance nightmare:

- Developers had to reimplement context injection logic for each use case
- Tool and service providers had to write multiple integration layers to support different AI systems
- There was no standard way for tools to declare what they could do beyond a non-compatible tool calling specification of different LLM providers

As a result, the ecosystem became fragmented and brittle. Tooling was tightly coupled to specific frameworks, and reuse across projects was nearly impossible.

MCP was created to solve this problem. It introduces a shared protocol that standardizes how tools and resources can be exposed to models. Instead of hardcoding custom logic per integration, developers can now implement an MCP-compliant server that predictably advertises its capabilities. Likewise, AI systems only need to implement a single client interface to dynamically discover, query, and invoke tools and resources from any MCP server. There are readily available libraries for many popular programming languages, making it easy to implement MCP servers and clients.

The result is a modular, composable ecosystem, where tools can be reused across projects.

Let's take a closer look at the architecture and core components of MCP.

MCP architecture core and core components

MCP has a client-server architecture. MCP servers expose tools and resources, while MCP clients consume them. MCP clients are embedded in MCP hosts (the agentic AI system) and can utilize tools and resources from multiple MCP servers, some local and some remote. Local stdio MCP servers are faster, but present security concerns if coming from third-party providers. Remote MCP servers have the same networking and authentication concerns as any remote API. Here is a diagram of the MCP architecture that illustrates this:

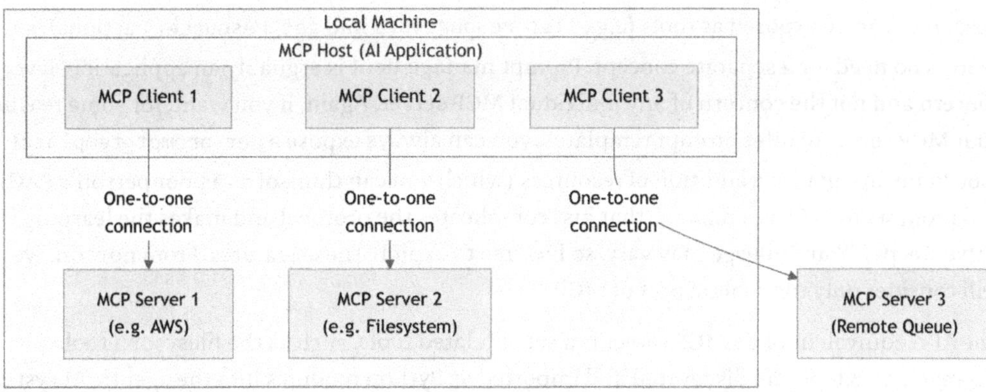

Figure 7.1: MCP architecture

The actual protocol by which MCP servers and clients communicate has two layers: the data layer and the transport layer:

- The **data layer** specifies the JSON-RPC-based protocol for client-server communication, which includes life cycle management, core primitives, such as tools, resources, and prompts, and notifications.
- The **transport layer** specifies the communication mechanisms and channels that enable data exchange between clients and servers, including transport-specific connection establishment, message framing, and authorization.

Let's break down the key components of MCP.

MCP servers

An **MCP server** (`https://modelcontextprotocol.io/docs/learn/server-concepts`) is a program that exposes tools (invokable functions) and resources (contextual information) to LLM-based systems via MCP. It allows any compliant LLM host application to discover, invoke, and consume capabilities in a predictable, composable, and transport-agnostic way. Each MCP server may support multiple specification versions. The actual version is negotiated (`https://modelcontextprotocol.io/specification/versioning## negotiation`) when an MCP client establishes a connection to an MCP server.

While MCP servers may expose resources (`https://modelcontextprotocol.io/docs/learn/server-concepts## resources-context-data`) and even offer prompt support (`https://modelcontextprotocol.io/docs/learn/server-concepts## prompts-interaction-templates`), we will focus on the tools aspect here.

Resources can be exposed as tools (e.g., `list_resources()` and `get_resource()` actions), so there is no need for a separate concept. Prompt management is arguably an application-level concern and not the concern of any individual MCP server. Again, if you want, for some reason, your MCP server to offer prompt templates, you can always expose a `get_prompt_template()` tool. In my opinion, the addition of resources (which you can think of as a poor person's RAG) and prompts to MCP is a mistake that just complicates the protocol and makes the learning curve steeper. Your mileage may vary, so feel free to explore these features. From now on, we will consider only the tools aspect of MCP.

The AI-6 equivalent of an MCP server is a set of related tools, such as the filesystem tools. However, AI-6 tools are discovered and imported as Python modules into the agentic AI system via the AI-6 framework. MCP servers, on the other hand, run as independent processes either locally or remotely. The MCP client will communicate with each MCP server via the proper transport protocol.

An AI system can use multiple MCP servers, each exposing a different set of tools.

Note that the AI system will need a dedicated MCP client for each MCP server it wants to use. The MCP client is responsible for discovering the available tools and invoking them as needed.

MCP clients

MCP clients are the components that interact with MCP servers to discover and invoke tools. They are embedded in the MCP host (the agentic AI system) directly or abstracted away by a framework such as AI-6. Each MCP client is responsible for connecting to a single MCP server. The MCP specification is not trivial, so most MCP clients utilize a library that implements the protocol and exposes an easy-to-use API for interacting with the MCP server. I highly recommend using a library as opposed to implementing the protocol from scratch. First, why would you want to reinvent the wheel? There isn't much innovation or performance to gain by implementing the protocol yourself. Second, MCP is a complex protocol that keeps evolving. If you build your own MCP client based on the spec, you'll have to first make sure it actually works correctly, and then you'll have to maintain it and chase the spec changes as they happen. This is a lot of work with no benefit.

The AI-6 equivalent of an MCP client is the discovery mechanism of the engine that scans the tool directory, discovers Python classes that implement the `Tool` abstract base class, dynamically imports them, and instantiates them. At that point, the engine can invoke any tool by calling this `run()` method.

MCP hosts

MCP hosts are the agentic AI systems that utilize MCP clients to discover and invoke tools from MCP servers. If the MCP uses an AI framework that supports MCP, then it doesn't even need to be aware of MCP. The framework will expose the agentic loop in an MCP-agnostic way, and the agentic AI system will just need to supply the proper configuration for the MCP tools it wants to use.

We will soon see how all these components play out together in the AI-6 framework. For now, let's look at the important distinction between local and remote MCP servers.

Local versus remote MCP servers

MCP servers can be either local or remote. A local MCP server runs on the same machine as the MCP client, while a remote MCP server runs on a different machine, possibly in the cloud. The choice between local and remote servers depends on the use case and the resources available.

An MCP client can connect to multiple MCP servers, both local and remote. When connecting to a local MCP server, the MCP client will use the **standard input/output** (**STDIO**) streams transport (`https://modelcontextprotocol.io/specification/2025-11-25/basic/transports#stdio`). When connecting to a remote MCP server, the MCP client will use the Streamable HTTP transport (`https://modelcontextprotocol.io/specification/2025-11-25/basic/transports#streamable-http`).

Note that this information is accurate for the current version of the MCP specification (`https://modelcontextprotocol.io/specification/2025-11-25`).

Regardless of the transport, the sequence of messages is the same, and the message format is always JSON-RPC 2.0 (`https://www.jsonrpc.org/`).

Benefits of using MCP

For agentic AI systems, MCP offers several key benefits to different stakeholders. Let's break it down for agentic AI frameworks, tool providers, and agentic AI system developers:

- **MCP for agentic AI frameworks**: An agentic AI framework that supports MCP, such as AI-6, LangGraph, AutoGen, or CrewAI, automatically provides access to a huge and growing ecosystem of interoperable tools and resources. At this point in time, it is a basic requirement for an agentic AI framework. Note that offering MCP support doesn't mean giving up on custom tools. AI-6, for example, supports both MCP and custom tools. We will discuss why it's important later in the chapter.
- **MCP for tool providers**: Tool providers benefit from MCP because, by publishing on MCP servers, they are automatically compatible with any AI system that uses an AI framework with MCP support. There is no need to provide a dedicated wrapper for every AI framework out there or document how to use it from different frameworks. Tool providers can build once against the MCP interface and achieve broad compatibility. This opens the door for a rich ecosystem of reusable tools that can be composed into larger systems, much like APIs in traditional software. MCP also makes it easier to define metadata such as tool capabilities, safety constraints, and cost models. Since the MCP ecosystem is thriving, tool developers can count on the community to provide registries, a discovery mechanism, and other infrastructure. Another major benefit of MCP for tool developers is that they can use any programming language they choose since the protocol is language-agnostic. This opens the door to writing MCP tools quickly using dynamic languages such as Python, TypeScript, or even shell scripts. But if you're writing a heavyweight MCP server that wraps a critical system and you need a lot of control or to optimize performance, you use something like Rust.
- **MCP for agentic AI system developers**: This is an easy one. As an agentic AI system developer, you should use an agentic AI framework that supports MCP, such as AI-6, LangGraph, AutoGen, CrewAI, and every other self-respecting agentic AI framework. By choosing an MCP-compliant framework, you immediately gain access to a rapidly growing ecosystem of interoperable tools.

The benefits of MCP gave rise to a very active ecosystem, which we will explore next.

The MCP ecosystem

The MCP ecosystem is quickly becoming the foundation for building and scaling agentic AI systems. It standardizes how agents, tools, memory systems, and orchestration layers interact, turning fragmented integrations into a cohesive and composable architecture. The ecosystem includes an expanding collection of MCP-compliant frameworks such as AI-6, LangGraph, and AutoGen, along with tool providers, memory backends, and control interfaces. This modular approach enables developers to mix and match components with minimal friction, making it easier to experiment, deploy, and evolve complex multi-agent systems.

There are no concerns about vendor lock-in or compatibility issues, as the MCP standard ensures that any compliant tool can be brought in and any framework may be replaced without losing the investment in tools and resources. This is a game-changer for the agentic AI community, as it allows developers to focus on building their application using any framework they want, knowing they will be able to use MCP tools with any of them.

The sort of official place to find MCP servers at present is the **Example Servers** page (`https://modelcontextprotocol.io/examples`) on the `modelcontextprotocol.io` website, which lists reference implementations in different languages as well as official integrations by various third-party companies.

There are many community websites dedicated to indexing and listing existing MCP servers. Here are a few examples:

- `https://mcpfinder.io`
- `https://mcp.so`
- `https://remote-mcp-servers.com`

Be careful before using some obscure MCP server, especially if you download and run it locally, as it has all the permissions of the user who started the server.

OK. Now that we have a good understanding of MCP and its benefits, let's see how to build MCP servers and clients, and how to integrate MCP into the AI-6 framework.

Building MCP servers

Building MCP servers with different programming languages and libraries can teach you a lot about the benefits of MCP. The knowledge, skills, and even the MCP servers themselves are transferable to any modern agentic AI system or framework.

We will build two MCP servers that expose functionality similar to or identical to some custom AI-6 tools, such as the filesystem tools and the GitHub tool. This process will allow us to compare two implementations, one for AI-6 only and one for MCP.

Filesystem MCP server

Let's quickly review the AI-6 custom filesystem tools. As you recall, they are all subclasses of the `CommandTool` base class and follow a similar pattern. The only exception is the `Echo` tool, which is used to create new files:

```
for file in py/backend/tools/file_system/*.py; do
    if [ -f "$file" ]; then
        echo "=== $file ==="
        cat "$file"
        echo
    fi
done


# === py/backend/tools/file_system/awk.py ===
from backend.tools.base.command_tool import CommandTool

class Awk(CommandTool):
    def __init__(self, user: str | None = None):
        super().__init__(
            command_name='awk', user=user,
            doc_link='https://www.gnu.org/software/gawk/manual/gawk.html')



##=== py/backend/tools/file_system/cat.py ===
from backend.tools.base.command_tool import CommandTool

class Cat(CommandTool):
    def __init__(self, user: str | None = None):
        super().__init__(
            command_name='cat', user=user,
            doc_link = 'https://www.gnu.org/software/coreutils/manual/html_node/
cat-invocation.html')



##=== py/backend/tools/file_system/echo.py ===
import os
import sh
from backend.object_model import Tool, Parameter
```

```
class Echo(Tool):
    def __init__(self, user: str | None = None):
        self.user = user

        desc = 'Write content to a file, creating any necessary directories.'
        super().__init__(
            name='echo',
            description=desc,
            parameters=[
                Parameter(
                    name='file_path', type='string',
                    description='The path of the file to write to.'),
                Parameter(
                    name='content', type='string',
                    description='The content to write to the file.')
            ],
            required={'file_path', 'content'}
        )


    def run(self, **kwargs):
        filename = kwargs['file_path']
        content = kwargs['content']
        dir_path = os.path.dirname(filename)

        if self.user is not None:
            sh.sudo('-u', self.user, 'mkdir', '-p', dir_path)
            sh.sudo('-u', self.user, 'tee', filename, _in=content,
                _out=os.devnull)

            return f"Content written to {filename} as user {self.user}"

        os.makedirs(dir_path, exist_ok=True)
        with open(filename, 'w') as file:
            file.write(content)

        return f"Content written to {filename}"


##=== py/backend/tools/file_system/ls.py ===
```

```
from backend.tools.base.command_tool import CommandTool

class Ls(CommandTool):
    def __init__(self, user: str | None = None):
        super().__init__(command_name='ls', user=user, doc_link='https://
www.gnu.org/software/coreutils/manual/html_node/ls-invocation.html')


##=== py/backend/tools/file_system/patch.py ===
from backend.tools.base.command_tool import CommandTool

class Patch(CommandTool):
    def __init__(self, user: str | None = None):
        super().__init__(
            command_name='patch', user=user,
            doc_link = 'https://www.gnu.org/software/diffutils/manual/html_node/
patch-Invocation.html')


##=== py/backend/tools/file_system/pwd.py ===
from backend.tools.base.command_tool import CommandTool

class Pwd(CommandTool):
    def __init__(self, user: str | None = None):
        doc_link = 'https://www.gnu.org/software/coreutils/manual/html_node/pwd-
invocation.html'
        super().__init__('pwd', user=user, doc_link=doc_link)


##=== py/backend/tools/file_system/sed.py ===
from backend.tools.base.command_tool import CommandTool

class Sed(CommandTool):
    def __init__(self, user: str | None = None):
        super().__init__(
            command_name='sed', user=user,
            doc_link='https://www.gnu.org/software/sed/manual/sed.html')
```

Our filesystem MCP server will replace some of these tools with equivalent functionality. All the built-in AI-6 MCP tools are in the `py/backend/mcp-tools` directory.

Let's look at the `fs_mcp_server.py` MCP server. It uses the official MCP Python SDK (`https://github.com/modelcontextprotocol/python-sdk`). The `FastMCP` class does all the heavy lifting of registering tools and exposing them via the various MCP transports. The module instantiates it after the required imports:

```
import shlex
from mcp.server.fastmcp import FastMCP
import sh

mcp = FastMCP("FileSystem Tools", "")
```

The filesystem MCP server contains multiple tools in one module. Each tool is implemented as a single function decorated with the `@mcp.tool()` decorator. Similar to the AI-6 `Tool` abstract base class that marks a class as a tool, the `@mcp.tool()` decorator marks a function as a tool:

```
@mcp.tool()
def ls(args: str) -> str:
    """ls tool. See https://www.gnu.org/software/coreutils/manual/html_node/ls-
invocation.html"""
    parsed_args = shlex.split(args)
    return sh.ls(*parsed_args)

@mcp.tool()
def cat(args: str) -> str:
    """cat tool. See https://www.gnu.org/software/coreutils/manual/html_node/cat-
invocation.html"""
    parsed_args = shlex.split(args)
    return sh.cat(*parsed_args)

@mcp.tool()
def pwd(args: str) -> str:
    """pwd tool. See https://www.gnu.org/software/coreutils/manual/html_node/pwd-
invocation.html"""
    parsed_args = shlex.split(args) if args.strip() else []
    return sh.pwd(*parsed_args)

@mcp.tool()
def mkdir(args: str) -> str:
    """mkdir tool. See https://www.gnu.org/software/coreutils/manual/html_node/
mkdir-invocation.html"""
```

```
    parsed_args = shlex.split(args)
    return sh.mkdir(*parsed_args)


@mcp.tool()
def cp(args: str) -> str:
    """cp tool. See https://www.gnu.org/software/coreutils/manual/html_node/cp-
invocation.html"""
    parsed_args = shlex.split(args)
    return sh.cp(*parsed_args)
```

As you can see, the actual implementation of each MCP tool is very similar to the `CommandTool` class of AI-6. It parses the arguments and invokes the target command-line tool using `sh`. Here is the `CommandTool` class's `run()` method, which just adds the ability to run as a separate user:

```
    def run(self, **kwargs):
        args = shlex.split(kwargs['args'])
        if self.user is not None:
            return sh.sudo('-u', self.user, self.command_name, *args)
        else:
            return getattr(sh, self.command_name)(*args)
```

With the MCP server, you can control the OS user when you launch the MCP server as a process.

In short, implementing MCP servers in Python is simple when using the official Python SDK. Note that if you need to configure the MCP server, you'll need to come up with your own way, as the MCP Python SDK doesn't offer any assistance here. You can pass command-line arguments, use environment variables, or configuration files.

But some MCP servers are more involved. Let's look at the GitHub MCP server.

GitHub MCP server

The GitHub MCP server is implemented in Bash for two reasons. First, to demonstrate the ability to write MCP servers in any language. Second, to get a close look at the protocol itself, because there is no library that does all the heavy lifting. We have to directly process and generate JSON-RPC messages and follow the MCP life cycle.

Let's break it down step by step. The JSON-RPC messages have a standard format of an object with `method`, `id`, and `params` fields. It's also important to serialize the JSON messages we return to a single line, because some clients expect it. The `emit_json()` function replaces newline characters with spaces and takes care of this chore:

```
#!/bin/bash

# GitHub MCP Server - implements MCP protocol for GitHub CLI tools (newline-
stripped JSON responses)

# Helper: output compact JSON from heredoc
emit_json() {
    tr -d '\n' | tr -s ' '
    echo
}
```

Now, we can start the loop of waiting for MCP messages from the client and responding. It runs forever, parsing incoming messages and responding accordingly:

```
# Read JSON-RPC messages from stdin and respond
while read -r line; do
    method=$(echo "$line" | jq -r '.method' 2>/dev/null)
    id=$(echo "$line" | jq -r '.id' 2>/dev/null)
    params=$(echo "$line" | jq -r '.params' 2>/dev/null)

    ...
done
```

Let's see what messages it expects and how it responds. Every incoming message is processed according to its method in a big `case` statement. The first message is `"initialize"`, sent by the MCP client to initiate the connection. The MCP server needs to report the supported protocol version and server info. The `capabilities` part may be empty:

```
    case "$method" in
        "initialize")
            cat <<EOF | emit_json
{
  "jsonrpc": "2.0",
  "id": $id,
  "result": {
    "protocolVersion": "2024-11-05",
    "capabilities": {
```

```
        "tools": {},
        "resources": {}
      },
      "serverInfo": {
        "name": "GitHub CLI Tools",
        "version": "1.0.0"
      }
    }
  }
  EOF
              ;;
```

The client sends a notification that initialization succeeded. No response is expected:

```
          "notifications/initialized")
              # Notification - no response needed
              ;;
```

The "`tools/list`" message is called once, and the server responds with its list of tools (just one in this case), which includes the familiar tool name, description, and the input schema for the parameters. We have just one required parameter, `args`, which is the command-line arguments for the GitHub CLI command:

```
          "tools/list")
              cat <<EOF | emit_json
  {
    "jsonrpc": "2.0",
    "id": $id,
    "result": {
      "tools": [
        {
          "name": "gh",
          "description": "Execute GitHub CLI commands",
          "inputSchema": {
            "type": "object",
            "properties": {
              "args": {
                "type": "string",
                "description": "GitHub CLI command arguments"
              }
            },
```

```
            "required": ["args"]
          }
        }
      ]
    }
  }
  EOF
            ;;
```

Now, the MCP client is aware of all the tools this MCP server provides and can call them when necessary. This is the most complicated case. First, the code verifies that the requested tool name is indeed "gh" (the only supported tool name). Then, it runs the `gh $args 2>&1` command, capturing both standard output and standard error. It also captures the exit code and then properly escapes the result, and finally constructs and returns the JSON-RPC response message that includes the escaped result of the `gh` command:

```
if [ "$tool_name" = "gh" ]; then
                result=$(gh $args 2>&1)
                exit_code=$?
                escaped=$(echo "$result" | jq -Rs .)

                cat <<EOF | emit_json
{
  "jsonrpc": "2.0",
  "id": $id,
  "result": {
    "content": [
      {
        "type": "text",
        "text": $escaped
      }
    ]
  }
}
EOF
```

If the tool name wasn't "gh", it returns an error message:

```
else
                cat <<EOF | emit_json
```

```
{
  "jsonrpc": "2.0",
  "id": $id,
  "error": {
    "code": -32602,
    "message": "Unknown tool: $tool_name"
  }
}
EOF
            fi
            ;;
```

Finally, if the message has an unknown method, it returns an appropriate error message:

```
*)
            if [ "$id" != "null" ]; then
                cat <<EOF | emit_json
{
  "jsonrpc": "2.0",
  "id": $id,
  "error": {
    "code": -32601,
    "message": "Method not found: $method"
  }
}
EOF
            fi
            ;;
    esac
done
```

That concludes our low-level Bash MCP server. It is a lot of work to build, and if the protocol evolves, then you'll need to update your server. Also, it implements only the STDIO transport, so it can't be used as a remote MCP server. I strongly recommend using one of the official MCP SDKs when you build your own MCP servers.

Let's see what it takes to build an MCP client.

Building MCP clients

MCP clients connect to MCP servers and control the interaction. We will not go down the rabbit hole of building an MCP client from scratch, as we did with the GitHub Bash MCP server. Instead, we will take advantage of the MCP Python SDK. AI-6 provides its own `MCPClient` wrapper that can connect to multiple MCP servers, return their tools, and, later, invoke any tool.

The MCPClient class

Our `MCPClient` class lives in the `mcp_client.py` module. Let's start with the imports. Note that the MCP client is designed for async operation. From the `mcp` package, it imports the `ClientSession` and `StdioServerParameter` classes, and then it imports `stdio_client` for local MCP servers and `sse_client` for the remote MCP server:

```
import asyncio
from contextlib import AsyncExitStack
from urllib.parse import urlparse

from mcp import ClientSession, StdioServerParameters
from mcp.client.stdio import stdio_client
from mcp.client.sse import sse_client
```

The constructor is pretty simple and manages a dictionary of sessions and a dictionary of server tools that maps MCP servers to their list of tools. It also creates an async exit stack for proper cleanup:

```
class MCPClient:
    """Standalone MCP client for connecting to and interacting with MCP
servers."""
    def __init__(self):
        self.sessions: dict[str, ClientSession] = {}
        self._server_tools: dict[str, list[dict]] = {}
        self.exit_stack = AsyncExitStack()
```

When clients connect to the MCP server, they call the `connect_to_server` method. Let's see how it works.

Connecting to an MCP server

The `connect_to_server()` async method does a lot of work. Let's examine it piece by piece. It accepts a server ID (an arbitrary, unique ID controlled by the AI system) that identifies the target and a path (for local MCP servers) or a URL (for remote MCP servers). If it's already connected to that server, it returns the tools of that server:

```
    async def connect_to_server(
        self, server_id: str, server_path_or_url: str
    ) -> list[dict]:
        """Connect to a single MCP server and return its tools."""
        if server_id in self.sessions:
            # Already connected, return cached tools
            return self._server_tools.get(server_id, [])
```

Next, it determines whether it's a local or remote MCP server:

```
# Check if this is a URL (remote server) or file path (local server)
        parsed = urlparse(server_path_or_url)
        is_url = parsed.scheme in ('http', 'https')
```

If it's a remote server, it creates a transport using the **Server-Sent Events** (**SSE**) client, which it uses to generate a `ClientSession` object. If anything goes wrong, it prints an error message and re-raises the exception:

```
        if is_url:
            print(
                f"Connecting to remote MCP server: {server_path_or_url}")
            try:
                transport = await self.exit_stack.enter_async_context(
                    sse_client(server_path_or_url))
                read, write = transport
                session = await self.exit_stack.enter_async_context(
                    ClientSession(read, write))
                print(f"Successfully connected to {server_path_or_url}")
            except Exception as e:
                print(f"Failed to connect to remote MCP server
{server_path_or_url}: {e}")
                raise
```

But, if it's a local server, it checks (based on file extension only) whether it's a Python, TypeScript, or Shell MCP server. Otherwise, it raises an exception. This is just a choice because there are no plans to support other languages for local MCP servers for AI-6. It is totally valid to support other languages or, even better, Docker images that can contain the MCP server in any language:

```
else:
    # Local file-based server
    if server_path_or_url.endswith('.py'):
        command = "python"
    elif server_path_or_url.endswith('.sh'):
        command = "bash"
    elif server_path_or_url.endswith('.js'):
        command = "node"
    else:
        raise ValueError(f"Unsupported server type: {server_path_or_url}")
```

Next, it prepares the server parameters, which are just the path to the MCP server file. No command-line argument or additional environment variables are provided. We may want to support more configuration in the future. Then, it generates an STDIO transport and uses it to create a local `ClientSession` object:

```
    server_params = StdioServerParameters(
        command=command,
        args=[server_path_or_url],
        env=None
    )

    stdio_transport = await self.exit_stack.enter_async_context(
        stdio_client(server_params))
    stdio, write = stdio_transport
    session = await self.exit_stack.enter_async_context(
        ClientSession(stdio, write))
```

At this point, we have a `ClientSession` (either local or remote) object, and we can fetch the tools of the MCP server by calling `session.list_tools()`. Under the covers, this call exchanges the proper JSON-RPC messages with the MCP server according to the protocol:

```
# Initialize session with timeout
await asyncio.wait_for(session.initialize(), timeout=10.0)
```

```
        # List tools with timeout
        response = await asyncio.wait_for(
            session.list_tools(), timeout=10.0)
        tools = [{
            "name": tool.name,
            "description": tool.description,
            "parameters": tool.inputSchema
        } for tool in response.tools]
```

Then, we store the session and the tools to retrieve later if needed, and return the tools:

```
        # Cache the session and tools
        self.sessions[server_id] = session
        self._server_tools[server_id] = tools

        return tools
```

Note that the 10-second timeout should be sufficient in most cases, but in rare cases where the MCP server has a long initialization sequence, it may be better to provide a configurable timeout duration.

Once the agentic AI system connects to an MCP server, the next step is to invoke one or more of the tools it provides.

Invoking an MCP tool

The agentic AI system received the list of tools of every MCP server when it called the `connect_to_server()` method. At any point, it may decide to invoke one of these tools by calling the `invoke_tool()` method, which accepts the server ID, the tool name, and a dictionary of arguments for the tool. The call returns a response from the tool (unless an exception is raised). First, it checks whether there is an active session associated with the requested server's ID and raises an exception if there is none:

```
    async def invoke_tool(
        self, server_id: str, tool_name: str, tool_args: dict
    ) -> str:
        """Invoke a specific tool on the specified MCP server."""
        session = self.sessions.get(server_id)
        if not session:
            raise RuntimeError(f"No active session for server '{server_id}'.
Connect to server first.")
```

Then, it calls the tool by invoking the `session.tool_call()` method with the tool name and arguments. It returns the response from the tool (which may be empty). If the tool call timed out or raised some other exception, it prints an error message and re-raises the exception:

```
        try:
            print(f"Invoking tool {tool_name} on server {server_id} with args:
{tool_args}")
            # Add timeout to prevent hanging on slow/unresponsive servers
            result = await asyncio.wait_for(
                session.call_tool(tool_name, tool_args),
                timeout=30.0  # 30 second timeout
            )
            print(f"Tool {tool_name} completed successfully")
            return result.content[0].text if result.content else ""
        except asyncio.TimeoutError:
            print(f"Tool invocation timed out for {server_id}:
{tool_name} after 30 seconds")
            raise RuntimeError(f"Tool invocation timed out for {server_id}:
{tool_name} after 30 seconds")
        except Exception as e:
            print(f"Tool invocation failed for {server_id}:{tool_name}: {e}")
            raise
```

The class offers additional helper methods. The `get_server_tools()` method can be used by the agentic AI system if it prefers to fetch the tools of a server on the fly when needed:

```
    def get_server_tools(self, server_id: str) -> list[dict]:
        """Get cached tools for a server."""
        return self._server_tools.get(server_id, [])
```

The `is_connected()` method checks whether the target server ID is associated with a session:

```
    def is_connected(self, server_id: str) -> bool:
        """Check if connected to a server."""
        return server_id in self.sessions
```

The `disconnect_server()` method deletes a `ClientSession` and removes its tools. This can be useful for an MCP server that uses a lot of resources and is needed only for certain phases of a conversation:

```
    async def disconnect_server(self, server_id: str):
        """Disconnect from a specific server."""
        if server_id in self.sessions:
            # Session cleanup handled by exit_stack
            del self.sessions[server_id]
            if server_id in self._server_tools:
                del self._server_tools[server_id]
```

Finally, the `cleanup()` method clears the sessions and `_server_tools` dictionaries:

```
    async def cleanup(self):
        """Cleanup all resources."""
        self.sessions.clear()
        self._server_tools.clear()
        await self.exit_stack.aclose()
```

Let's see how to extend the AI-6 framework with MCP support in addition to its own proprietary tool system.

Integrating MCP into the AI-6 framework

AI-6 has its own tool system in place, including discovery, registration, and an abstract base class called `Tool`, and the entire agentic loop of the engine is built around these concepts. How do we integrate a whole new tooling system, such as MCP? We can take advantage of the **fundamental theorem of software engineering** (**FTSE**) (`https://en.wikipedia.org/wiki/Fundamental_theorem_of_software_engineering`), which states, "*We can solve any problem by introducing an extra level of indirection.*" In this context, it means wrapping all MCP tools with an indirection layer that looks like an AI-6 tool. Enter the universal `MCPTool` class, which can wrap an MCP tool (local or remote) and make it accessible to AI-6 as if it were one of its own tools. Let's see how the magic happens.

The universal MCPTool class

The `MCPTool` class (`https://github.com/Sayfan-AI/ai-six/blob/v0.11.0/py/backend/tools/base/mcp_tool.py#44`) must be a subclass of the AI-6 `Tool` class, which means it needs to implement its abstract methods. This is really the only requirement of compatibility. When it is constructed, it needs access to an `MCPClient` instance that it can invoke when the tool's `run()` method is called. Let's check the code.

Here are the imports. We need `asyncio` and `threading` for dealing with `asyncio`-based `MCPClient`, and from the AI-6 object model, we need the `Tool` base class and the `Parameter` definition:

```
import asyncio
import threading

from backend.object_model.tool import Tool, Parameter
from backend.mcp_client.mcp_client import MCPClient
```

Let's jump straight into the deep end and handle the thorny issue of adapting the MCP tool schema to the AI-6 object model. The `_json_schema_to_parameters()` function takes an MCP tool schema dictionary and converts it to a list of AI-6 `Parameter` objects and a set of required parameter names. The code is pretty straightforward, so there is no need to explain every line:

```
def _json_schema_to_parameters(
    schema: dict
) -> tuple[list[Parameter], set[str]]:
    """Convert JSON schema to Tool parameters and required set."""
    parameters = []
    required = set()

    if not isinstance(schema, dict) or 'properties' not in schema:
        return parameters, required

    # Get required fields
    if 'required' in schema and isinstance(schema['required'], list):
        required = set(schema['required'])

    # Convert properties to parameters
    for prop_name, prop_def in schema['properties'].items():
        param_type = prop_def.get('type', 'string')
```

```
        description = prop_def.get('description',
            f'{prop_name} parameter')

        # Map JSON schema types to our parameter types
        if param_type == 'array':
            param_type = 'array'
        elif param_type in ['integer', 'number']:
            param_type = 'number'
        elif param_type == 'boolean':
            param_type = 'boolean'
        else:
            param_type = 'string'

        parameters.append(Parameter(
            name=prop_name,
            type=param_type,
            description=description
        ))

    return parameters, required
```

We will see where this function is used soon. Let's continue to the `MCPTool` class itself. It has multiple class-level fields because all the `MCPTool` instances share the same `MCPClient` object that manages all the MCP `ClientSession` instances. The asynchronous nature of the `MCPClient` object requires some careful management of a client lock and a shared event loop:

```
class MCPTool(Tool):
    """Tool that uses MCP (Model Context Protocol) servers."""

    # Shared MCP client instance across all MCP tools
    _client: MCPClient = None
    _client_lock = threading.Lock()
    # Shared event loop for all MCP operations
    _event_loop = None
    _loop_thread = None
    _loop_lock = threading.Lock()
```

The constructor takes a server ID, server path, or URL (depending on whether it's a local or remote MCP server), and a dictionary with tool information received from the MCP server. The code then extracts the name and description (or default) from the tool information dictionary and converts the MCP tool parameters to AI-6 parameters by calling `_json_schema_to_parameters()`. Then, it passes the AI-6 tool information to the `Tool` base class by calling the `super().__init__()` constructor and stores the server ID, server path or URL, and the tool name. These will be needed when the tool is invoked later:

```
    def __init__(
        self, server_id: str, server_path_or_url: str, tool_info: dict
    ):
        """Initialize from MCP tool information."""
        tool_name = tool_info['name']
        description = tool_info.get(
            'description', f'{server_id} tool: {tool_name}')

        # Convert parameters from JSON schema
        parameters, required = _json_schema_to_parameters(
            tool_info.get('parameters', {})
        )

        super().__init__(
            name=tool_name, description=description,
            parameters=parameters, required=required)
        self.server_id = server_id
        self.server_path_or_url = server_path_or_url
        self.mcp_tool_name = tool_name
```

As you recall, the `MCPClient` is managed at the class level. The `_get_client()` class method creates the `MCPClient` instance for the first time and then just returns the same instance on subsequent calls. It implements the double-checked locking pattern (`https://en.wikipedia.org/wiki/Double-checked_locking`) to avoid instantiating the `MCPClient` more than once:

```
@classmethod
    def _get_client(cls) -> MCPClient:
        """Get or create the shared MCP client instance."""
        if cls._client is None:
            with cls._client_lock:
                if cls._client is None:
                    cls._client = MCPClient()
        return cls._client
```

The `_get_or_create_loop()` follows the same pattern and returns (creating if necessary) a singleton `asyncio` event loop:

```
@classmethod
def _get_or_create_loop(cls):
    """Get or create a shared event loop for MCP operations."""
    # Always use our own managed loop for sync tool execution
    # This avoids "event loop is closed" issues from creating/closing loops
repeatedly

    if cls._event_loop is None or cls._event_loop.is_closed():
        with cls._loop_lock:
            if cls._event_loop is None or cls._event_loop.is_closed():
                cls._event_loop = asyncio.new_event_loop()

    return cls._event_loop
```

The `_ensure_connected()` method gets the client and the event loop, sets it explicitly to avoid conflicts, waits until the client connects to the server, and then returns the client and the event loop:

```
def _ensure_connected(self):
    """Ensure connection to the MCP server."""
    client = self._get_client()
    loop = self._get_or_create_loop()
    if not client.is_connected(self.server_id):
        # Use shared event loop for connection
        asyncio.set_event_loop(loop)
        loop.run_until_complete(
            client.connect_to_server(
                self.server_id, self.server_path_or_url))
    return client, loop
```

Now that we did all the hard work of wiring up the `MCPClient` and dealing with all the `asyncio` gotchas, let's look at the `run()` method, which the AI-6 engine calls when the LLM requests to execute a tool call:

```
def run(self, **kwargs) -> str:
    """Execute the MCP tool with the given arguments."""
    client, loop = self._ensure_connected()
```

```
    return loop.run_until_complete(
        client.invoke_tool(self.server_id, self.mcp_tool_name, kwargs
```

The code calls the `_ensure_connected()` method and then gets the client and the event loop. The nice thing is that there is no need to translate the arguments from the AI-6 representation to the `MCPClient` representation, as they are both just a dictionary of `str -> object`. The MCP client's `invoke_tool()` method interacts with the MCP server and returns the result as a string.

Last but not least, the `cleanup_all()` class method gracefully shuts down the `asyncio` machinery:

```
@classmethod
def cleanup_all(cls):
    """Cleanup all MCP connections. Call this on shutdown."""
    if cls._client is not None:
        # Use our managed loop for cleanup
        loop = cls._get_or_create_loop()
        asyncio.set_event_loop(loop)
        try:
            loop.run_until_complete(cls._client.cleanup())
        finally:
            # Now we can close our managed loop
            if cls._event_loop and not cls._event_loop.is_closed():
                cls._event_loop.close()
            cls._event_loop = None
        cls._client = None
```

That concludes the examination of the `MCPTool` class, but we still miss a key piece of the story, which is how the various MCP servers are discovered and instantiated.

MCP tool discovery

The AI-6 `Engine` class was responsible for tool discovery before, but with the integration of MCP, I extracted this functionality to a dedicated module called `tool_manager`, which performs the original AI-6 native tool discovery, local MCP tool discovery, and incorporates configured remote MCP servers, too.

Let's see how the tool manager works and later how the `Engine` is using it to get access to all the tools.

The tool manager

The `tool_manager.py` module (`https://github.com/Sayfan-AI/ai-six/blob/v0.11.0/py/backend/engine/tool_manager.py`) offloads a lot of complexity from the `Engine` class and lets it focus on the important task of running the agentic loop.

Let's examine the code, starting as usual with the imports, which should all be familiar by now. Note the `importlib.util` and `inspect` modules that do the heavy lifting for dynamic custom tool discovery (previously in the engine):

```
import asyncio
import os
from pathlib import Path
import importlib.util
import inspect

from backend.object_model.tool import Tool
from backend.tools.base.mcp_tool import MCPTool
from backend.mcp_client.mcp_client import MCPClient
from backend.engine.config import ToolConfig
```

The `get_tool_dict()` function is the only public function. The discovery of all tools, whether AI-6-native or MCP tools, happens here. It starts with an empty tool list and then invokes these functions to get different types of tools and add them to the tool list:

- `_discover_native_tools()`
- `_discover_local_mcp_tools()`
- `_get_remote_mcp_tools()`

All tools are derived from the `Tool` base class, which the engine knows how to configure and invoke:

```
def get_tool_dict(tool_config: ToolConfig) -> dict[str, Tool]:
    """Get a dictionary of all available tools from various sources.

    Args:
        tool_config: ToolConfig object containing tool configuration

    Returns:
        Dict mapping tool names to Tool instances
    """
```

```
    tools: list[Tool] = []

    # 1. Discover AI-6 native tools
    if tool_config.tools_dir:
        native_tools = _discover_native_tools(
            tool_config.tools_dir,
            tool_config.tool_config
        )
        tools.extend(native_tools)

    # 2. Discover local MCP tools
    if tool_config.mcp_tools_dir:
        local_mcp_tools = _discover_local_mcp_tools(
            tool_config.mcp_tools_dir
        )
        tools.extend(local_mcp_tools)

    # 3. Get tools of remote MCP servers
    if tool_config.remote_mcp_servers:
        remote_mcp_tools = _get_remote_mcp_tools(
            tool_config.remote_mcp_servers
        )
        tools.extend(remote_mcp_tools)

    return {tool.name: tool for tool in tools}
```

We will skip the `_get_local_tools()` function as we covered it in depth in *Chapter 4*. Let's focus on the MCP tool discovery.

The `_discover_local_mcp_tools()` function accepts a directory of local MCP servers and returns the list of `MCPTool` objects, which is the union of all the MCP tools from all the MCP servers packaged as `MCPTool` objects. If the MCP server directory is invalid, it returns an empty list:

```
def _discover_local_mcp_tools(mcp_servers_dir: str) -> list[MCPTool]:
    """Discover MCP tools dynamically by connecting to MCP servers."""
    if not os.path.isdir(mcp_servers_dir):
        return []
```

Then, it defines a nested async function called `discover_async()`. This function is visible only inside the `_discover_local_mcp_tools()` function. This is necessary to bridge the sync and async worlds. Let's break it down.

First, it defines an empty tools list and creates a new `MCPClient`. Then, it starts a `try` block and iterates over all the files in the MCP servers directory (this comes from the argument to its parent function):

```
async def discover_async():
    tools: list[Tool] = []
    client = MCPClient()

    try:
        # Iterate over all files in the directory
        for file_name in os.listdir(mcp_servers_dir):
```

For each item, it calculates the script path (remember that only Python, Node, and Shell local MCP servers are supported). If it's not a file, it just continues to the next item:

```
script_path = os.path.join(mcp_servers_dir, file_name)

# Check if it's a file
if not os.path.isfile(script_path):
    continue
```

However, if it is a file, then it uses its filename as the server ID when it calls the client's `connect_to_server()` function, which returns all the tools of that MCP server. It creates a new `MCPTool` instance for each tool and adds them to the tools list. If anything goes wrong, it prints an error message and continues to the next tool:

```
try:
    # Connect to server and get its tools with timeout
    server_tools = await asyncio.wait_for(
        client.connect_to_server(script_path, script_path),
        timeout=5.0
    )

    # Create MCPTool instances for each tool
    for tool_info in server_tools:
        mcp_tool = MCPTool(script_path, script_path, tool_info)
        tools.append(mcp_tool)
```

```
    except Exception as e:
        # Skip servers that fail to connect or timeout
        error_msg = str(e) if str(e) else f"{type(e).__name__}: {e}"
        print(f"Warning: Failed to connect to MCP server {script_path}: {error_msg}")
        continue
```

Once all the MCP servers are processed and their combined tools are added to the tools list, it performs the client cleanup and then returns the tools:

```
    finally:
        await client.cleanup()

    return tools
```

All that happens in the nested async function, `discover_async()`. The parent function, `_discover_local_mcp_tools()`, invokes the async function using `asyncio.run()`, which allows synchronous functions to call async functions and wait for them to complete, and returns the result (the combined tool list from all the MCP servers). If anything goes wrong, it prints a warning and returns an empty list:

```
    # Run async discovery in sync context
    try:
        return asyncio.run(discover_async())
    except Exception as e:
        print(f"Warning: MCP tool discovery failed: {e}"
        return []
```

The `_discover_local_mcp_tools()` function took care of all the local MCP servers. However, AI-6 supports remote MCP servers, too. Let's see how we can bring them into the fold.

The `_get_remote_mcp_tools()` function follows the same blueprint as `_get_local_mcp_tools()` with a nested async function, but there are some important differences too. So, let's go over it in detail.

The function accepts a list of dictionaries that each contains the name and URL of a remote MCP server. So, there is no scanning of a directory looking for MCP servers. It also returns a list of `Tool` objects that is initialized to an empty list:

```
def _get_remote_mcp_tools(remote_servers: list[dict]) -> list[Tool]:
    """Connect to remote MCP servers and get their tools.
```

```
    Args:
        remote_servers: List of remote server configurations
        Each server config should have: {'url': 'https://...', 'name': '...'}

    Returns:
        List of MCPTool instances for remote tools
    """
    tools: list[Tool] = []
```

The `connect_sync()` nested function is pretty similar to the `discover_sync()` nested function of `_discover_local_mcp_tools()`, except there is no discovery here by iterating over files because all the remote MCP server configurations were already provided. So, the function iterates over them, tries to connect to each and fetch their tools, and then creates an `MCPTool` object. The server ID in this case is the server name from the configuration:

```
    async def connect_async():
        client = MCPClient()

        try:
            for server_config in remote_servers:
                try:
                    server_url = server_config.get('url')
                    server_name = server_config.get('name', server_url)

                    if not server_url:
                        print(f"Warning: Remote MCP server config missing 'url':
{server_config}")
                        continue

                    # Connect to remote server with timeout
                    server_tools = await asyncio.wait_for(
                        client.connect_to_server(server_name, server_url),
                        timeout=10.0
                    )

                    # Create MCPTool instances for each remote tool
                    for tool_info in server_tools:
                        # Use server_url as script_path for remote tools
                        mcp_tool = MCPTool(
```

```
                                  server_name, server_url, tool_info)
                              tools.append(mcp_tool)

                  except Exception as e:
                      print(f"Warning: Failed to connect to remote MCP server
{server_config}: {e}")
                      continue

          finally:
              await client.cleanup()
```

Then, just as before, run the nested function and return the tools:

```
# Run async connection in sync context
    try:
        asyncio.run(connect_async())
    except Exception as e:
        print(f"Warning: Remote MCP server connection failed: {e}")
        return []

    return tools
```

This concludes our drill-down of the `tool_manager` module. Let's see how the engine benefits from this separation of concerns.

How the engine uses the tool manager

The engine now has only one import related to tool discovery:

```
from backend.engine import tool_manager
```

It also has just one line of code in its constructor that calls the `get_tool_dict()` function of the tool manager:

```
self.tool_dict = tool_manager.get_tool_dict(tool_config)
```

This is as simple as it gets, and it improves the architecture and maintainability of the engine as well as the entire AI-6 project.

Here is the entire constructor of the Engine class, which now has no tool discovery functionality at all:

```
class Engine:
    def __init__(self, config: Config):
        self.default_model_id = config.default_model_id

        # Store threshold ratio and calculate token threshold based on default
model
        self.summary_threshold_ratio = config.summary_threshold_ratio
        context_window_size = get_context_window_size(
            self.default_model_id)
        self.token_threshold = int(
            context_window_size * config.summary_threshold_ratio
        )

        # Find LLM providers directory
        llm_providers_dir = os.path.join(
            os.path.dirname(os.path.dirname(__file__)), "llm_providers"
        )
        assert os.path.isdir(llm_providers_dir), (
            f"LLM providers directory not found: {llm_providers_dir}"
        )

        # Discover available LLM providers
        self.llm_providers = Engine.discover_llm_providers(
            llm_providers_dir, config.provider_config
        )
        if not self.llm_providers:
            raise ValueError("No LLM providers found or initialized")
        self.model_provider_map = {
            model_id: llm_provider
            for llm_provider in self.llm_providers
            for model_id in llm_provider.models
        }
```

```
        # Discover and initialize all tools
        tool_config = ToolConfig.from_engine_config(config)
        self.tool_dict = tool_manager.get_tool_dict(tool_config)

        # Initialize session and session manager
        self.session_manager = SessionManager(config.memory_dir)
        self.session = Session(config.memory_dir)

        # Session-related attributes
        self.checkpoint_interval = config.checkpoint_interval
        self.message_count_since_checkpoint = 0

        # Instantiate the summarizer with the first LLM provider
        self.summarizer = Summarizer(self.llm_providers[0])

        # Register memory tools with the engine
        self._register_memory_tools()

        # Load previous session if session_id is provided and exists
        if config.session_id:
            available_sessions = self.session_manager.list_sessions()
            if config.session_id in available_sessions:
                self.session = Session(config.memory_dir)  # Create a new session
object
                self.session.load(config.session_id)  # Load from disk
```

OK. We covered all aspects of MCP integration into AI-6. Let's see it in action.

Putting it all together

Let's start a quick AI-6 session and see the new MCP tools in action. I'll ask AI-6 to find my most popular GitHub repos. Here is the final result:

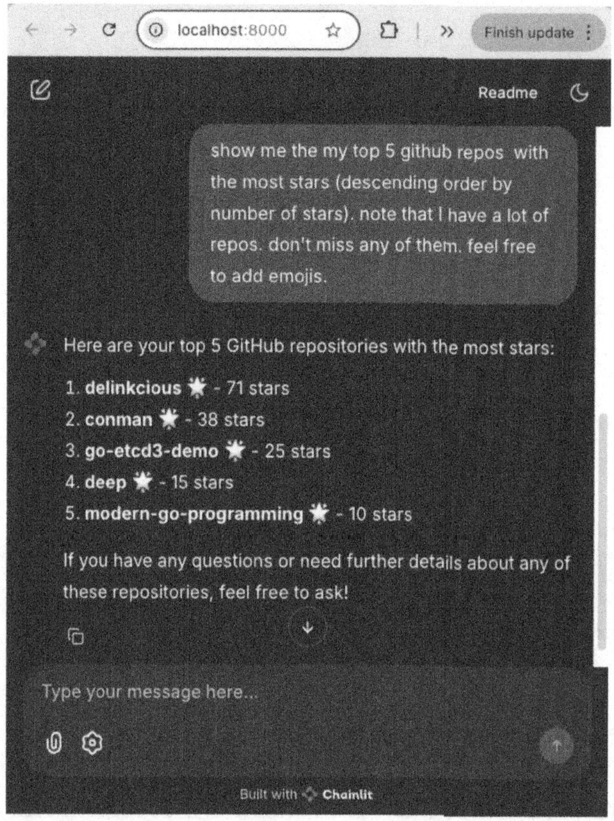

Figure 7.2: AI-6 accessing GitHub via MCP

This is a great success! The LLM was able to access GitHub via our MCP server, extract the necessary information, which requires authentication too, and distill a useful answer.

But it took quite a few tries because the LLM kept requesting invalid gh CLI commands for pagination. Eventually, it just settled for requesting 300. This works in this case because I have just a little over 100 repos, but it is not a general solution. But, as you can see, it definitely used the GitHub MCP server (implemented from scratch in Bash):

```
Invoking tool gh on server /Users/gigi/git/ai-six/py/backend/mcp_tools/
github_mcp_server.sh with args: {'args': 'repo list --sort=stars --limit=5'}
```

```
Tool gh completed successfully
2025-08-03 17:11:59 - HTTP Request: POST https://api.openai.com/v1/chat/
completions "HTTP/1.1 200 OK"
Invoking tool gh on server /Users/gigi/git/ai-six/py/backend/mcp_tools/
github_mcp_server.sh with args: {'args': 'repo list --json "name,stargazersCount"
--limit 100'}
Tool gh completed successfully
2025-08-03 17:12:00 - HTTP Request: POST https://api.openai.com/v1/chat/
completions "HTTP/1.1 200 OK"
Invoking tool gh on server /Users/gigi/git/ai-six/py/backend/mcp_tools/
github_mcp_server.sh with args: {'args': 'repo list --json name,stargazerCount --
limit 100'}
Tool gh completed successfully
2025-08-03 17:12:04 - HTTP Request: POST https://api.openai.com/v1/chat/
completions "HTTP/1.1 200 OK"
2025-08-03 17:14:02 - HTTP Request: POST https://api.openai.com/v1/chat/
completions "HTTP/1.1 200 OK"
2025-08-03 17:14:18 - HTTP Request: POST https://api.openai.com/v1/chat/
completions "HTTP/1.1 200 OK"
Invoking tool gh on server /Users/gigi/git/ai-six/py/backend/mcp_tools/
github_mcp_server.sh with args: {'args': 'repo list --json name,stargazerCount --
limit 100 --page 2'}
Tool gh completed successfully
2025-08-03 17:14:25 - HTTP Request: POST https://api.openai.com/v1/chat/
completions "HTTP/1.1 200 OK"
2025-08-03 17:15:12 - HTTP Request: POST https://api.openai.com/v1/chat/
completions "HTTP/1.1 200 OK"
Invoking tool gh on server /Users/gigi/git/ai-six/py/backend/mcp_tools/
github_mcp_server.sh with args: {'args': 'repo list --json name,stargazerCount --
limit 300'}
Tool gh completed successfully
2025-08-03 17:15:18 - HTTP Request: POST https://api.openai.com/v1/chat/
completions "HTTP/1.1 200 OK"
```

This incorrect and inefficient use of tools is one of the major problems of LLMs, and we will address this problem in *Chapter 10*.

Summary

Let's recap. In this chapter, we explored the **Model Context Protocol (MCP)** – a cornerstone for standardizing tool and context integration in advanced agentic AI systems. We examined the ecosystem and motivations behind MCP, covering its architecture, benefits, and both its protocol layering and practical implementations. We showed how MCP server and client concepts map cleanly onto the AI-6 framework's own tool abstractions, and how integrating MCP brings broad, frictionless interoperability: any compatible tool can be connected, reused, or swapped out, freeing you from vendor lock-in and custom integration overhead.

We compared implementing command-line tools as both custom AI-6 tools and as MCP servers and saw that MCP makes it just as easy to build and share tools across languages and platforms. Note that testing MCP servers may require additional effort as the tools run in a separate process. You learned how localized and remote MCP servers can be discovered and consumed, with the AI-6 tool manager abstracting away the entire discovery and registration process. This approach lets AI-6 (and any similar agentic AI framework) seamlessly compose its internal tools and external MCP tools into a unified, dynamic toolset accessible to any agent, with zero extra logic required in the AI-6 engine.

Finally, we looked at practical, real-world integration: how an agentic AI system, such as AI-6, now delegates all tool handling (discovery, invocation, and management) to a robust tool manager, making its agents vastly more extensible. As the MCP ecosystem grows, your agentic AI can instantly leverage any new tool, service, or resource published to the open protocol, enabling rapid experimentation and scaling in complex, multi-agent systems. Integration is as simple as configuration, not rewriting code.

In the next chapter, we will take it to the next level and dive deep into the design of multi-agent AI systems.

Get This Book's PDF Version and Exclusive Extras

Scan the QR code (or go to `packtpub.com/unlock`). Search for this book by name, confirm the edition, and then follow the steps on the page.

UNLOCK NOW

Note: Keep your invoice handy. Purchases made directly from Packt don't require an invoice.

Part 3

Constructing Multi-Agent Systems

In Parts 1 and 2, you built the core foundations for agentic systems and constructed your own framework (AI-6). Part 3 takes you into multi-agent systems at full scale: designing agent teams, orchestration patterns, role prompts, tool scoping, and context strategies, then implementing real multi-agent workflows with the **Agent-to-Agent** (**A2A**) protocol. You'll build a practical **multi-agent Kubernetes DevOps system** (**MAKDO**), learn how to test and debug agent coordination failures, and apply resilience patterns like redundancy, graceful degradation, and human escalation. The part then moves into production deployment, walking through a realistic multi-cluster setup with secure communication and service discovery. It concludes with advanced topics and future directions, including massive context windows, long-horizon planning, multimodal systems, and the broader implications of increasingly capable agents.

This part contains the following chapter:

8

Designing Multi-Agent Systems

While single-agent systems can accomplish impressive tasks, many real-world problems require coordination between multiple specialized agents working together. This chapter focuses on designing multi-agent AI systems that can collaborate to solve complex problems beyond the capabilities of any single agent.

Multi-agent systems represent the next frontier in agentic AI architecture. Instead of relying on one agent to handle all aspects of a problem, we can create teams of specialized agents, each with its own expertise, tools, and responsibilities. We'll explore multi-agent orchestration patterns, agent decomposition strategies, system prompt design for different agent roles, tool assignment frameworks, context engineering for multi-agent environments, and conflict resolution mechanisms. We will enhance AI-6 with explicit agent support and integrate the **Agent-to-Agent (A2A)** protocol to demonstrate these concepts practically.

The following key topics will be covered:

- What is multi-agent orchestration and why does it matter?
- Introduction to the A2A protocol
- Designing collaborative agent workflows
- Conflict resolution and role assignment in multi-agent systems

Technical requirements

To follow along, refer to the instructions in the README file:

`https://github.com/PacktPublishing/Design-Multi-Agent-AI-Systems-Using-MCP-and-A2A/blob/main/ch08/ai-six/py/README.md`.

What is multi-agent orchestration and why does it matter?

So far in the book, we have talked a lot about the agentic tool-calling loop and emphasized that all the thinking is done by the LLM. The AI-6 engine is very capable of supporting such agentic workflows, but what are these agents? In this section, we will define exactly what an AI agent is in familiar terms, extend AI-6 to support explicit agents, discuss why multi-agent systems are important, and finally, explore different ways to orchestrate multiple agents effectively.

What is an AI agent?

An **AI agent** is a component in an AI system that has some goals and knowledge encoded as a system prompt. It has access to a set of tools that it can use to achieve its goals. Finally, it has an LLM client that it can use to reason about the world, its goals, and how to use its tools. The AI agent interacts with the outside world by receiving user messages (where the user can be the host AI system or another agent) and returning responses. The agent maintains its own internal state (e.g., conversation history, tool usage history, etc.) and only returns the final response to the user.

The fact that each agent is a self-contained component that hides its internal state means we can construct multi-agent systems without saturating the context window of a single LLM. The sub-agent may run its own agentic loop and burn through a lot of tokens without cluttering the context of the parent. If you think an AI agent sounds very similar to the AI-6 engine, you are not wrong. Let's see how to extend AI-6 to support agents more explicitly.

Adding explicit agents to AI-6

The AI-6 engine can be used as is to construct multi-agent systems in the following manner:

1. Define an AI-6 agent tool.
2. Create a parent AI-6 engine instance and provide it with the other AI-6 agents as tools.
3. The parent AI-6 engine may invoke the other AI-6 agents as tools to delegate work.

This is fine, but there are some small gaps to address:

- Currently, the AI-6 engine doesn't have a system prompt. This means that whenever calling an AI-6 agent tool, the caller must provide the system prompt in addition to the actual user message.
- Defining and configuring the different AI-6 agents is not trivial.
- AI-6 has a global configuration for tools, but agents should have their own subset of tools.

Let's address all of these issues by making the following changes to AI-6:

1. Rename `Engine` to `Agent` (this is just terminology and not a functional change).
2. Add a system prompt to the agent configuration.
3. Add `enabled_tools` and `disabled_tools` fields to the agent configuration.
4. Add a new `AgentTool` that wraps an AI-6 `Agent` instance.

Besides the renaming of `Engine` to `Agent`, which mostly establishes the terminology, the other changes are just additive. We don't remove or modify any of the existing capabilities and workflows.

Renaming Engine to Agent

The entire `backend.engine` package is now named `backend.agent`. The `engine.py` file is now `agent.py`. The `Engine` class is now `Agent`. All references to `Engine` in the code and documentation have been changed to `Agent`.

Nothing special here, just a find-and-replace.

Adding a system prompt to the Agent configuration

This change is pretty simple too. Here is the new field added to the `Config` class in `backend/agent/config.py`:

```
system_prompt: Optional[str] = None
```

Note that it is optional, which means it is backward compatible and can work just like before and interact with LLMs without a specific goal or knowledge.

Adding enabled_tools and disabled_tools fields to the Agent configuration

This is also a simple change. Here are the new fields added to the `Config` class in `backend/agent/config.py`:

```
enabled_tools: Optional[List[str]] = None
disabled_tools: Optional[List[str]] = None
```

The semantics are that if `enabled_tools` is provided, only those tools will be available to the agent. If `disabled_tools` is provided, all tools except those tools will be available to the agent. If none are provided, all tools are available. It is an error to provide both fields. This is again backward compatible and provides complete control over the set of tools that any agent can use.

Adding a new AgentTool that wraps an AI-6 Agent instance

This is the most interesting change. We add a new tool type that wraps an `Agent` instance. However, the `Agent` instance itself doesn't have any new code for launching sub-agents. The LLM receives the list of available sub-agents as part of the available tools, and then the LLM may decide to launch one of the sub-agents with a tool call. Each such sub-agent may have the `Agent` tool in its own set of tools, which means when the LLM interacts with the sub-agent, it may decide to launch another sub-agent, and so on. This means we can have an arbitrary tree of agents running and collaborating to solve a problem.

The `AgentTool` class is defined in `backend/object_model/agent_tool.py`. Let's break it down.

The import statements reflect the entities that this tool relies on and interacts with:

```
from typing import Callable, Optional
from backend.object_model import Tool, Parameter
from backend.agent.agent import Agent
from backend.agent.config import Config
```

Now, the `AgentTool` class inherits from the `Tool` base class. The constructor takes an agent configuration object that has all the information needed to create an `Agent` instance. First, it creates the `Agent` instance and initializes the `_on_tool_call_func` callback to `None`. The agent will already be configured with its system prompt and the set of enabled/disabled tools:

```
class AgentTool(Tool):
    """Tool that wraps an Agent and allows sending messages to it."""
```

```
    def __init__(self, agent_config: Config):
        """Initialize the AgentTool with a Config."""
        self.agent = Agent(agent_config)
        self._on_tool_call_func: Optional[
            Callable[[str, dict, str], None]] = None
```

Then, it creates the parameters for the tool call. In this case, the tool takes a single parameter called `message`, which is the message to be set to the agent. Then, it calls the superclass (the `Tool` class) constructor and passes the name, description, parameters, and required fields (`message` is required):

```
# Create tool definition
parameters = [
    Parameter(
        name='message',
        type='string',
        description='The message to send to the agent'
    )
]

super().__init__(
    name=f"agent_{agent_config.name}",
    description=f"Send a message to the {agent_config.name} agent.
{agent_config.description}",
    parameters=parameters,
    required={'message'}
)
```

The `set_tool_call_callback()` method is called by the agent during initialization to set a callback function that will be called whenever the sub-agent makes a tool call. This optional callback function comes from the host AI system. This allows the host AI system to intercept and handle tool calls made by any agent:

```
    def set_tool_call_callback(
        self, callback: Optional[Callable[[str, dict, str], None]]
    ):

"""Set the callback function for tool calls made by this agent."""
        self._on_tool_call_func = callback
```

Finally, the `run()` method sends the message to the agent, which may start its own agentic loop and eventually return a response:

```
    def run(self, message: str, **kwargs) -> str:

"""

Send a message to the agent and return the response.

Args:
    message: The message to send to the agent
    **kwargs: Additional arguments (ignored)

Returns:
    The agent's response
"""
        return self.agent.send_message(
            message, self.agent.default_model_id,
            on_tool_call_func=self._on_tool_call_func)
```

At the end of the day, from the perspective of the AI-6 agentic loop, sub-agents are tools that can be invoked to delegate work. The LLM decides when and how to invoke sub-agents based on their description, just like it decides to call any other tool. The fact that `AgentTool` wraps an AI-6 Agent instance is irrelevant to the LLM.

At this point, we understand how AI-6 enables multi-agent systems. Now is a good time to discuss why multi-agent systems are so important.

Why do we need multi-agent systems?

In theory, a single sufficiently capable agent could handle any task. However, as task complexity increases, this approach quickly runs into several limitations.

Context window limitations

LLMs have limited context windows and can only consider a certain amount of information at once. For complex tasks requiring extensive background knowledge, multiple steps, or large datasets, a single agent may not fit all of the necessary information into its context window. Model performance degrades when context grows too large, especially when filled with step details that are mostly irrelevant to subsequent steps.

Specialization challenges

Different tasks require different expertise and skills. A single agent may not master all necessary skills, and uber-agents with huge system prompts confuse today's models. Just as human organizations rely on specialists, AI systems benefit from specialized agents focusing deeply on their domain of expertise (See `https://www.moltbook.com` to realize how AI agents can imitate human interaction patterns and organize themselves accordingly). Complex tasks may require hundreds of tools, overwhelming single agents, and leading to poor tool selection or hallucination of capabilities.

Model selection constraints

Different tasks benefit from different models. Single agents tied to one model aren't optimal for all task aspects. Some tasks require advanced reasoning from large models such as GPT-5, while others can be handled by smaller, faster models. Monolithic systems force you to either overpay for simple tasks or underperform on complex ones.

Multi-agent systems address these limitations by creating specialized agents focusing on specific task aspects. Each agent has its own system prompt, tool set, and model, operating within its own context window while leveraging expertise and tools to contribute to the overall solution.

Cognitive load distribution

Multi-agent systems distribute cognitive load across specialized agents, mirroring human teams where complex problems are broken down and assigned to domain experts. Research shows that sequential multi-agent processing achieves significantly higher accuracy compared to single-agent approaches, with specialized agents maintaining focused attention on their domains.

Fault tolerance and resilience

Multi-agent systems offer inherent fault tolerance advantages by distributing responsibilities across multiple agents. These systems continue operating when individual components fail through recovery strategies such as retrying with different parameters or routing to alternative agents. Critical agents can be deployed with redundancy, allowing seamless failover when issues arise.

Testability and debugging

The modular nature enables targeted testing, better observability, and improved debugging. Each agent can be tested in isolation, similar to unit testing, while inter-agent communications provide exceptional observability. Granular performance profiling allows independent monitoring of each agent's resource consumption, execution time, and token usage.

How to orchestrate multiple agents

Now that we understand what AI agents are and why multi-agent systems are beneficial, let's explore the different strategies for orchestrating multiple agents to work together effectively. Agent orchestration refers to the coordination, communication, and management of multiple agents to achieve a common goal. The orchestration approach you choose significantly impacts the system's performance, reliability, and complexity.

Sequential orchestration

Sequential orchestration is the simplest and most intuitive pattern, where agents work in a predefined order, with each agent passing its output to the next agent in the chain. This linear workflow resembles a traditional pipeline where each stage processes the output from the previous stage. The flow is predefined and predictable. But each agent can still have its own internal agentic loop and call tools as needed.

Sequential orchestration is ideal for tasks that have a natural linear progression, such as content creation workflows (research, outline, draft, review, and publish), data processing pipelines, or any process where each step logically depends on the completion of the previous step.

The orchestrator agent maintains a list of agents in order and iteratively calls each agent with the accumulated results from previous agents. Each agent's output becomes part of the input for the next agent (see *Figure 8.1*):

Figure 8.1: Sequential orchestration

Here are the advantages associated with sequential orchestration:

- Simple to understand and implement
- Predictable execution order
- Easy to debug and trace issues
- Natural fit for many real-world workflows

The following are the disadvantages:

- Sequential bottleneck; that is, if one agent fails, the entire process stops
- No parallelization opportunities
- Can be slow for long chains
- Rigid structure that doesn't adapt to changing requirements

While sequential orchestration offers simplicity and predictability, its linear nature can become a bottleneck when speed and fault tolerance are priorities. This is where parallel orchestration shines, allowing multiple agents to work simultaneously and leverage the power of concurrent processing.

Parallel orchestration

Parallel orchestration involves running multiple agents simultaneously on the same input or different aspects of a problem, then combining their results. This pattern maximizes throughput and can provide diverse perspectives on the same problem. Note the two styles of parallel orchestration:

- Each agent works independently on the same input and produces its own output. The orchestrator then aggregates or synthesizes these outputs into a final result, possibly with an LLM judge to score and choose a winner.
- The orchestrator decomposes the input into independent subtasks that can be run in parallel and assigns each subtask to a different agent. The agents work in parallel on their assigned subtasks, and the orchestrator combines their outputs.

Parallel orchestration is effective for tasks where multiple independent analyses are needed, such as sentiment analysis from different perspectives, multi-source data gathering, competitive research, or when you want to validate results through consensus.

The orchestrator dispatches the same or related tasks to multiple agents simultaneously, then collects and synthesizes their responses. This often requires sophisticated result aggregation logic (see *Figure 8.2*):

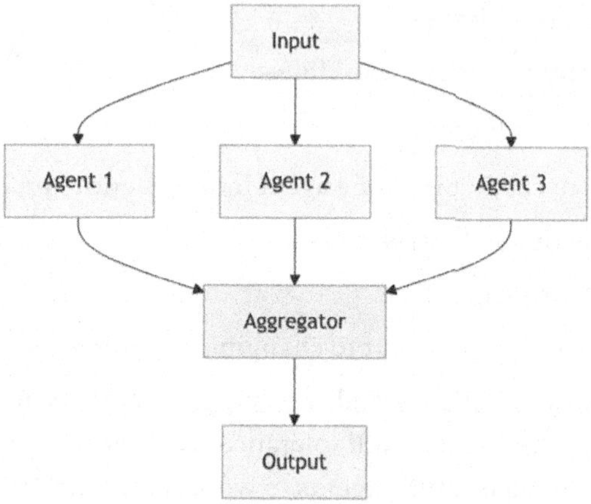

Figure 8.2: Parallel orchestration

Here are the advantages:

- Maximizes throughput and speed
- Provides multiple perspectives
- Natural fault tolerance (if one agent fails, others continue)
- Can implement consensus mechanisms for higher reliability

The following are the disadvantages:

- Requires result synthesis logic
- Potential resource contention
- May produce conflicting results that need resolution
- More complex error handling

Parallel orchestration excels at maximizing throughput, but managing multiple concurrent agents and synthesizing their results can become unwieldy as complexity grows. For tasks that naturally break down into manageable subtasks with clear delegation paths, hierarchical orchestration provides the structure and clarity that parallel approaches may lack.

Hierarchical orchestration

Hierarchical orchestration organizes agents in a tree-like structure where higher-level agents coordinate and manage lower-level agents. This pattern mimics organizational structures where managers delegate tasks to specialists.

This approach works well for complex tasks that naturally decompose into subtasks, such as project management, research coordination, or any scenario where you need different levels of abstraction and delegation.

A coordinator agent at the top level breaks down complex tasks and delegates them to specialized agents. These specialist agents might further delegate to sub-specialists, creating a hierarchy of responsibility (see *Figure 8.3*):

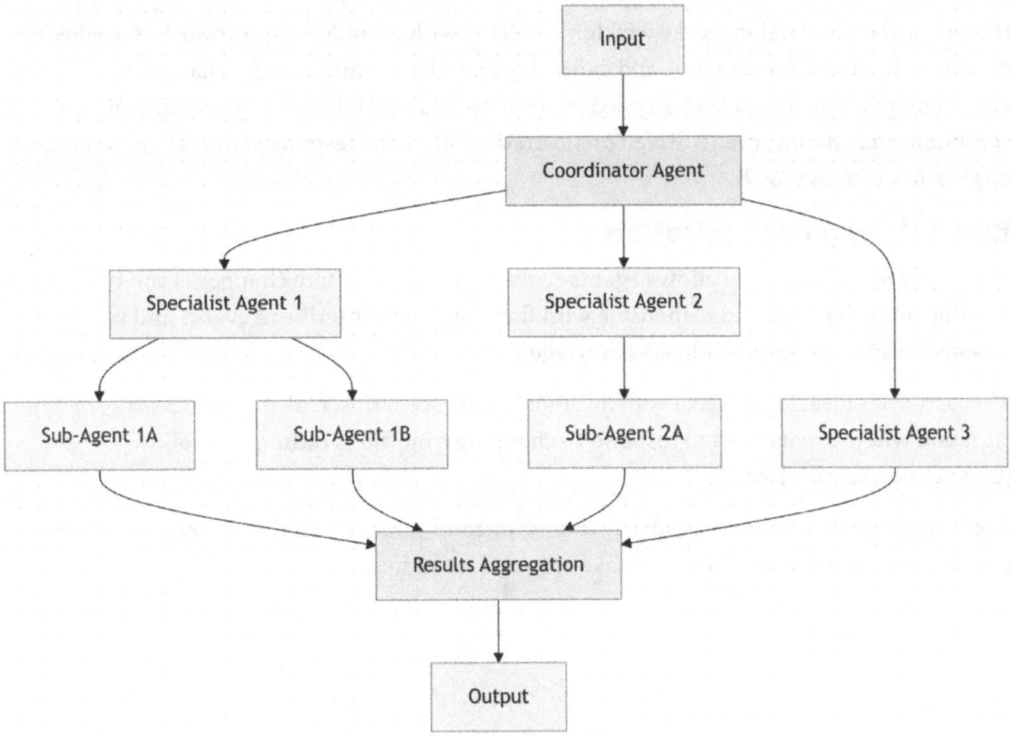

Figure 8.3: Hierarchical orchestration

The following are its advantages:

- Natural task decomposition
- Clear responsibility boundaries
- Scalable architecture
- Matches human organizational patterns

Here are the disadvantages:

- Communication overhead between levels
- Potential single points of failure at higher levels
- Complexity in task decomposition logic
- May introduce delays due to coordination overhead

Hierarchical orchestration works well for problems with clear decomposition, but it relies on predetermined task breakdowns and can struggle with dynamic, rapidly changing environments. When your system needs to react to unpredictable events and changing conditions in real time, event-driven orchestration offers the responsiveness that hierarchical approaches cannot match.

Event-driven orchestration

Event-driven orchestration allows agents to react to events or state changes in the system, creating more dynamic and responsive workflows. Agents subscribe to events and trigger actions based on specific conditions or triggers.

This pattern is ideal for reactive systems, monitoring scenarios, real-time processing, or any situation where agents need to respond to changing conditions rather than follow predetermined workflows.

Agents register their interest in specific events or conditions. When these events occur, the relevant agents are notified and can take appropriate action.

This requires an event system or message queue infrastructure:

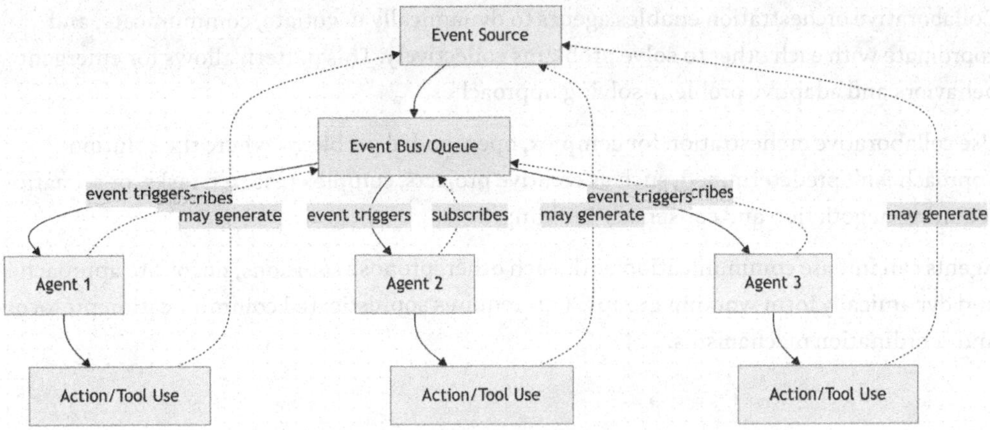

Figure 8.4: Event-driven orchestration

Here are the advantages:

- Highly responsive to changing conditions
- Decoupled agent interactions
- Natural support for asynchronous processing
- Scales well with system complexity

Here are the disadvantages:

- Complex debugging due to the asynchronous nature
- Requires robust event infrastructure
- Potential race conditions
- Harder to predict execution flow

Event-driven orchestration provides excellent responsiveness to changing conditions, but its reactive nature means agents still work within predefined roles and responses. For truly complex, open-ended problems where the solution approach itself must emerge from agent interactions, collaborative orchestration allows agents to transcend their individual limitations through dynamic negotiation and collective problem-solving.

Collaborative orchestration

Collaborative orchestration enables agents to dynamically negotiate, communicate, and coordinate with each other to solve problems collectively. This pattern allows for emergent behaviors and adaptive problem-solving approaches.

Use collaborative orchestration for complex, open-ended problems where the solution approach isn't predetermined, such as creative projects, complex research tasks, or scenarios requiring negotiation and consensus-building.

Agents can initiate communication with each other, propose solutions, negotiate approaches, and dynamically form working groups. This requires sophisticated communication protocols and coordination mechanisms.

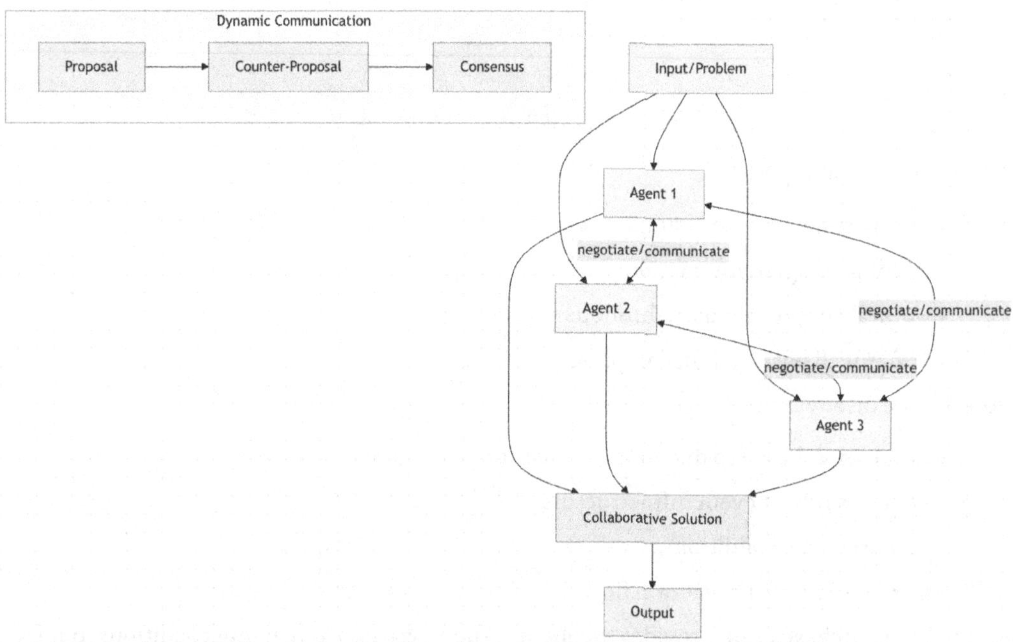

Figure 8.5: Collaborative orchestration

Here are the advantages:

- Highly adaptive and flexible
- Can handle unexpected situations
- Leverages collective intelligence
- Allows for emergent solutions

Here are the disadvantages:

- Complex to implement and debug
- Potential for infinite loops or deadlocks
- Difficult to predict outcomes
- Requires sophisticated coordination protocols

While collaborative orchestration offers the ultimate flexibility and adaptability, its complexity can be overwhelming for many practical applications. The reality is that most successful multi-agent systems don't rely on a single orchestration pattern but instead combine the strengths of multiple approaches to create robust, efficient solutions tailored to their specific requirements.

Hybrid orchestration

Real-world systems often benefit from combining multiple orchestration patterns. For example, you might use sequential orchestration for the main workflow while employing parallel orchestration for specific validation steps, or implement hierarchical coordination with event-driven responses to handle exceptions:

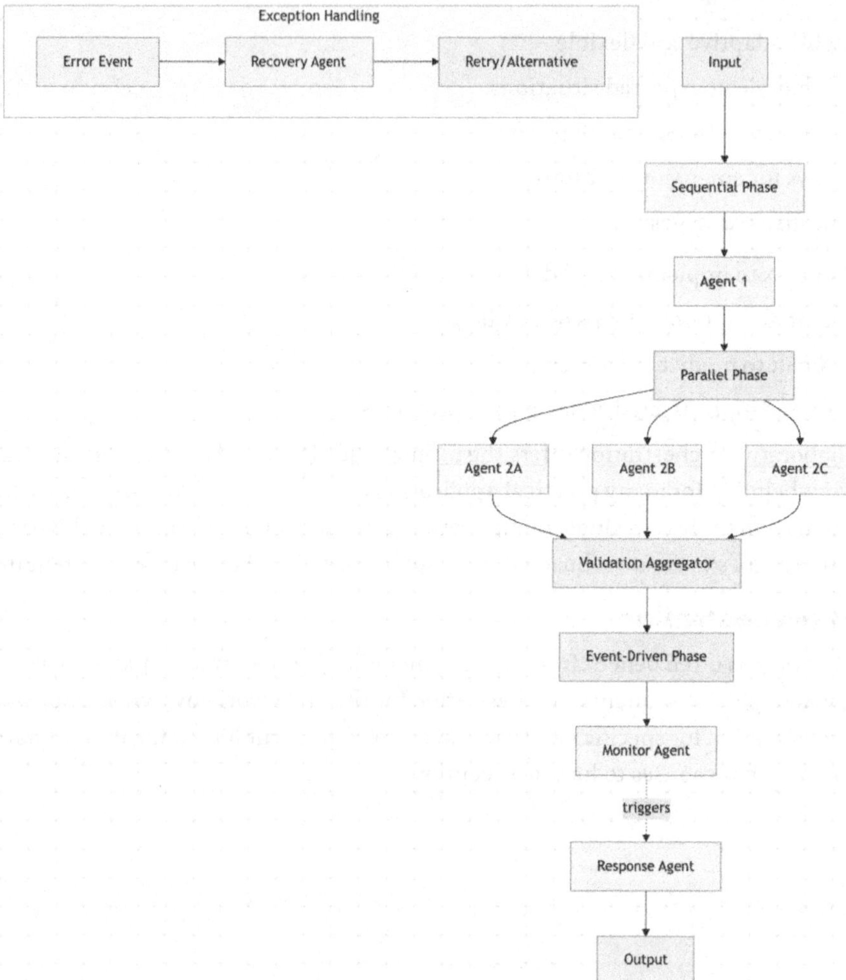

Figure 8.6: Hybrid orchestration

We have covered various orchestration strategies. Let's see how to decide which strategy is best for a specific situation.

Design considerations

When choosing an orchestration strategy, consider these key factors:

- **Task complexity**: Simple, linear tasks favor sequential orchestration, while complex, multi-faceted problems may require hierarchical or collaborative approaches

- **Performance requirements**: If speed is critical, parallel orchestration can help, but if consistency is more important, sequential processing might be better
- **Resource constraints**: Consider the computational and memory overhead of each approach, especially for parallel and hierarchical patterns
- **Fault tolerance needs**: Event-driven and parallel patterns generally offer better fault tolerance than sequential approaches
- **Debugging and maintenance**: Sequential orchestration is easiest to debug, while collaborative orchestration is the most challenging

The key to successful multi-agent orchestration is matching the orchestration pattern to your specific use case requirements and being prepared to adapt as those requirements evolve. Of course, you should take into account the disadvantages of each approach and how they accumulate and mitigate them as much as possible. For example, in sequential orchestration, you can add retry mechanisms and timeouts to avoid bottlenecks. In parallel orchestration, you can add a judge agent to resolve conflicts. In hierarchical orchestration, you can add redundancy to critical agents. In event-driven orchestration, you can add logging and tracing to improve observability. In collaborative orchestration, you can add limits to the number of interactions between agents to avoid infinite loops.

Now that we have a good understanding of multi-agent orchestration patterns, let's explore how agents can communicate with each other effectively using the A2A protocol.

Introduction to the A2A protocol

While orchestration patterns define the high-level coordination strategies between agents, effective multi-agent systems require robust communication mechanisms that allow agents to exchange information, coordinate activities, and collaborate seamlessly. The A2A protocol (`https://a2a-protocol.org/latest/`) provides a standardized framework for AI agents to communicate and collaborate across different systems, offering capabilities that go beyond what MCP was designed for.

The A2A protocol is built around several core actors and concepts that enable sophisticated agent interactions. At its foundation are three key actors: the **user** who initiates requests (a human or an AI agent), the **A2A client** (client agent) that communicates on behalf of the user, and the **A2A server** (remote agent) that processes messages and tasks and returns results. This creates a structured yet flexible communication model that supports both simple interactions and complex, multi-turn collaborations.

Core components of the A2A protocol

The A2A protocol is built around several fundamental elements that work together to enable sophisticated agent interactions:

- **Agent card**: JSON metadata that describes an agent's capabilities, allowing for automatic discovery and capability matching
- **Task**: A stateful work unit with a unique identifier that enables tracking of long-running operations and multi-turn interactions
- **Message**: Individual communication turns between the client and agent, supporting rich content exchange
- **Part**: Content containers that can hold different types of data (text, file, or data), enabling modality-independent communication
- **Artifact**: Tangible outputs generated during task execution, such as PDF files or images, providing concrete deliverables from agent interactions

Here is the agent card of the k8s-ai A2A server I have running locally:

```
% http -b GET http://localhost:9999/.well-known/agent-card.json
{
    "capabilities": {
        "streaming": true
    },
    "defaultInputModes": [
        "text/plain"
    ],
    "defaultOutputModes": [
        "text/plain"
    ],
    "description": "Kubernetes AI assistant with kubectl access for context: kind-
k8s-ai",
    "name": "k8s-ai Agent",
    "preferredTransport": "JSONRPC",
    "protocolVersion": "0.3.0",
    "security": [
        {
            "BearerAuth": []
        }
    ],
    "securitySchemes": {
        "BearerAuth": {
```

```
                "scheme": "bearer",
                "type": "http"
            }
        },
        "skills": [
            {
                "description": "Execute kubectl commands and provide Kubernetes
cluster insights, troubleshooting, and management",
                "examples": [
                    "show me all pods",
                    "what is the status of the cluster?",
                    "describe the nginx deployment",
                    "get service endpoints",
                    "check node health",
                    "troubleshoot pending pods"
                ],
                "id": "kubectl_operations",
                "name": "Kubernetes Operations",
                "tags": [
                    "kubernetes",
                    "kubectl",
                    "cluster",
                    "pods",
                    "deployments",
                    "services"
                ]
            }
        ],
        "supportsAuthenticatedExtendedCard": true,
        "url": "http://127.0.0.1:9999/",
        "version": "1.0.0"
    }
```

Now that we understand the core components of the A2A protocol, let's discuss its communication mechanisms.

A2A communication mechanisms

The A2A protocol supports multiple interaction patterns to accommodate different use cases:

- **Request/response (polling)**: Traditional synchronous communication for simple interactions involving messages
- **Streaming with SSE**: Real-time communication for ongoing tasks and live updates
- **Push notifications**: Asynchronous notifications for event-driven workflows

Built on HTTP(S) for transport and using JSON-RPC 2.0 payload format, A2A provides a familiar yet powerful foundation for agent communication. Unlike traditional protocols, A2A is specifically designed for autonomous agents that need to maintain stateful, trackable interactions across potentially long-running collaborative processes.

Adding A2A support to AI-6

At the moment, AI-6 has A2A support in the form of an A2A tool that can be used to call remote agents that implement the A2A protocol. It is conceptually similar to the `MCPTool` and `AgentTool` classes in the sense that it encapsulates complex interactions with another system behind a simple tool interface.

Integrating A2A client capabilities into AI-6

The A2A integration in AI-6 follows a layered architecture that provides both synchronous tool-based access and asynchronous message-passing capabilities. The integration consists of four main components that work together to enable seamless agent-to-agent communication. We are not going to cover them in detail, as they are quite complex, but we will provide an overview of each component and how it fits into the overall architecture. You can follow the links to the source code for more details.

The A2A client (`https://github.com/PacktPublishing/Design-Multi-Agent-AI-Systems-Using-MCP-and-A2A/blob/main/ch08/ai-six/py/backend/a2a_client/a2a_client.py`) serves as the foundational component that handles direct communication with remote A2A agents. It manages A2A agent discovery by fetching agent cards, establishes authenticated connections, and provides streaming message capabilities for real-time communication.

The A2A manager (`https://github.com/PacktPublishing/Design-Multi-Agent-AI-Systems-Using-MCP-and-A2A/blob/main/ch08/ai-six/py/backend/a2a_client/a2a_manager.py`) acts as a singleton coordinator that manages the life cycle of all A2A infrastructure. It handles initialization, maintains client registries, coordinates with the message pump for async operations, and ensures proper resource cleanup. This centralized approach prevents resource leaks and provides consistent state management across the system.

The A2A message pump (`https://github.com/PacktPublishing/Design-Multi-Agent-AI-Systems-Using-MCP-and-A2A/blob/main/ch08/ai-six/py/backend/a2a_client/a2a_message_pump.py`) operates in the background to handle long-running conversations and task management. It maintains a persistent state, tracks active tasks, and provides the async infrastructure needed for streaming responses while integrating with AI-6's message injection system.

The A2A executor (`https://github.com/PacktPublishing/Design-Multi-Agent-AI-Systems-Using-MCP-and-A2A/blob/main/ch08/ai-six/py/backend/a2a_client/a2a_executor.py`) provides a clean abstraction layer that handles the complexity of bridging synchronous tool execution with asynchronous A2A operations. It encapsulates the logic for detecting running event loops, managing thread-safe execution, and providing a simple synchronous interface for A2A skill execution.

Finally, the configuration integration (`https://github.com/PacktPublishing/Design-Multi-Agent-AI-Systems-Using-MCP-and-A2A/blob/main/ch08/ai-six/py/backend/agent/config.py`) ensures that A2A servers are configured alongside other tools in the agent configuration, allowing for declarative setup of remote agent connections through declarative configuration files.

This architecture enables AI-6 agents to seamlessly interact with remote A2A agents while maintaining the familiar tool-based interface, effectively bridging synchronous tool execution with asynchronous agent communication patterns.

The following diagram illustrates the A2A communication flow within AI-6:

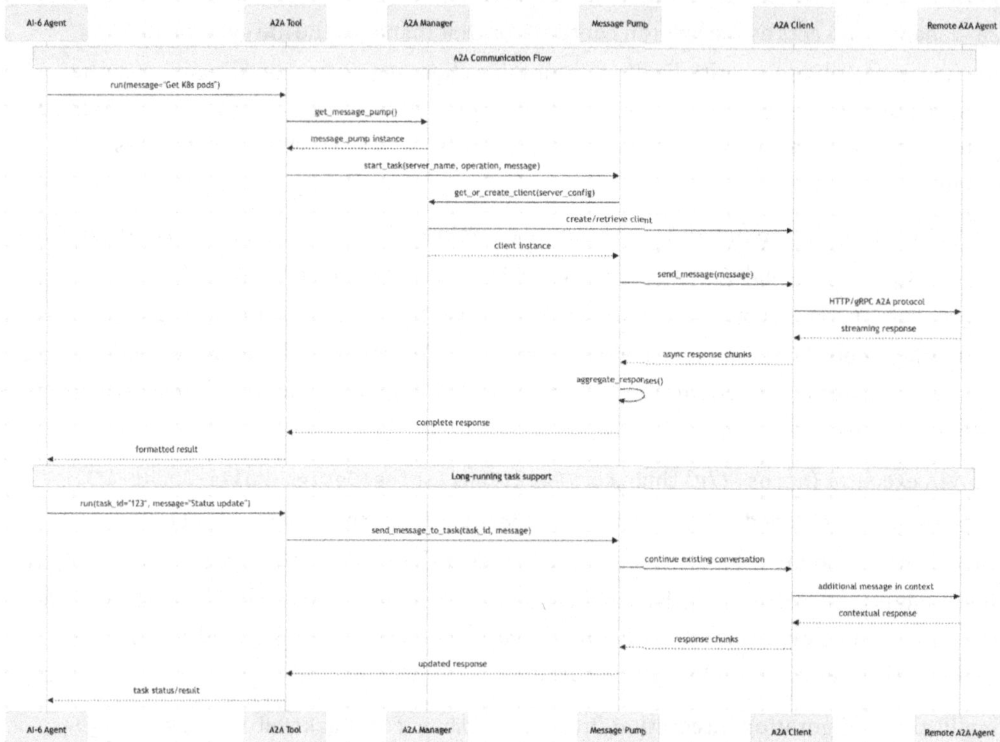

Figure 8.7: An overview of the A2A communication flow

We will not get into the details of each component, as they are quite complex and require a deep understanding of the A2A protocol and async programming in Python. However, we will focus on the most important part of using A2A in AI-6, which is the `A2ATool` class.

The A2ATool class

A2ATool (https://github.com/PacktPublishing/Design-Multi-Agent-AI-Systems-Using-MCP-and-A2A/blob/main/ch08/ai-six/py/backend/tools/base/a2a_tool.py) inherits from the Tool base class and provides a clean, simple interface to A2A agents. The import statements reflect the entities the tool relies on and interacts with. The AgentSkill class contains the name and description of the skill, which are used to create the tool definition. The Tool and Parameter classes from the AI-6 object model are used to define the tool interface. A2AManager provides access to the executor that handles all the complex A2A coordination:

```
from a2a.types import AgentSkill
from backend.object_model.tool import Tool, Parameter
from backend.a2a_client.a2a_manager import A2AManager
```

The constructor takes a server_name string and an AgentSkill object. Each A2A server can have multiple skills. The AI-6 A2A support creates a separate tool for each skill in each server:

```
class A2ATool(Tool):
    """Tool that communicates with A2A (Agent-to-Agent) servers using async-to-
sync pattern."""

    def __init__(self, server_name: str, skill: AgentSkill):
        """Initialize from A2A skill information.

        Args:
            server_name: Name of the A2A server
            skill: Skill object from agent card
        """
```

A2A skills don't take structured arguments. The input to a skill is a natural language message. The output is also a natural language message, but A2A servers may also create artifacts. However, you may want to interact with multiple A2A tasks by invoking the same skill, so the tool defines two standard parameters—message for the input text and task_id for the optional existing task ID:

```
        self.server_config = server_config
        self.skill_name = skill.name

        # A2A skills are conversational - create standard parameters
        parameters = [
```

```
            Parameter(
                name='message',
                type='string',
                description=f'Natural language request for the `{skill.name}`
skill'
            ),
            Parameter(
                name='task_id',
                type='string',
                description='Optional: ID of existing task to send message to'
            )
        ]

        required = {'message'}  # message parameter is required, task_id is
optional

        super().__init__(
            name=f"{server_name}_{skill.name}",
            description=skill.description,
            parameters=parameters,
            required=required
        )

        self.server_name = server_name
        self.skill_name = skill.name
```

The `run()` method is extremely simple thanks to the `A2AExecutor` abstraction. All the complex async-to-sync bridging logic is handled by the executor:

```
    def run(self, **kwargs) -> str:
        """Execute the A2A skill using the A2AExecutor."""
        task_id = kwargs.get('task_id')
        message = kwargs.get('message', '')

        executor = A2AManager.get_executor()
        if not executor:
            return "Error: A2A not initialized. Please configure A2A integration."
```

```
        return executor.execute_skill(
            self.server_name,
            self.skill_name,
            message,
            task_id
        )
```

This clean separation of concerns makes `A2ATool` easy to understand, test, and maintain while keeping all the complex async coordination logic centralized in the `A2AExecutor` component.

Configuration and setup

Setting up A2A integration in AI-6 requires minimal configuration. A2A servers are defined in the agent configuration alongside other tools:

```
# config.yaml
a2a_servers:
  - name: "k8s-ai"
    url: "http://localhost:9999"
    timeout: 30.0
```

The tool manager (`https://github.com/PacktPublishing/Design-Multi-Agent-AI-Systems-Using-MCP-and-A2A/blob/main/ch08/ai-six/py/backend/agent/tool_manager.py#L380-L410`) automatically discovers A2A agents at startup, fetching their agent cards and creating `A2ATool` instances for each skill. No manual tool registration is required.

A2A tool discovery flow

The following sequence shows how A2A servers become available tools in AI-6:

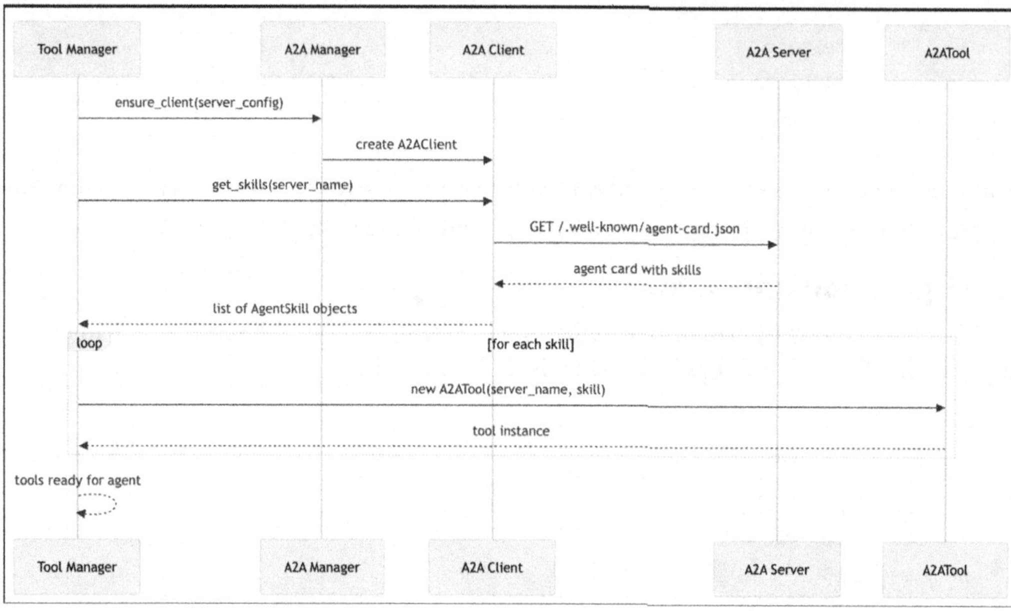

Figure 8.8: An overview of the A2A tool discovery flow

This discovery flow happens automatically during AI-6 agent initialization. The **Tool Manager** reads the A2A server configuration, ensures each client exists through the **A2A Manager**, and then fetches the agent card from each remote server. The agent card's `skills` array is processed to create individual **A2ATool** instances, that is, one per skill per server. For the k8s-ai server shown previously, this creates a single tool named `k8s-ai_kubectl_operations` that AI-6 agents can invoke to interact with Kubernetes through natural language requests.

Once discovered, A2A skills become regular AI-6 tools that agents can invoke through their standard tool-calling mechanism, seamlessly bridging local and remote agent capabilities.

Now that we have covered the A2A protocol in depth, let's change gears and discuss how to design collaborative agent workflows.

Designing collaborative agent workflows

Earlier in the chapter, we discussed different agent orchestration paradigms. Now, let's explore how to design effective workflows for multi-agent systems. Designing collaborative agent workflows involves decomposing complex tasks into manageable subtasks, assigning appropriate roles to each agent, and establishing clear communication protocols. Let's start with answering the most basic question: How do you divide a complex task into a pipeline of multiple agents?

Agent decomposition strategies

One of the most critical decisions in multi-agent system design is how to decompose complex tasks into manageable agent roles. Effective decomposition requires identifying natural boundaries where different types of expertise, tools, or responsibilities can be cleanly separated. Here are the key strategies and practical examples.

Decomposition by domain expertise

The most intuitive approach is to divide agents based on specialized knowledge domains, similar to how human teams organize around expertise areas.

Here is an example of a software development pipeline:

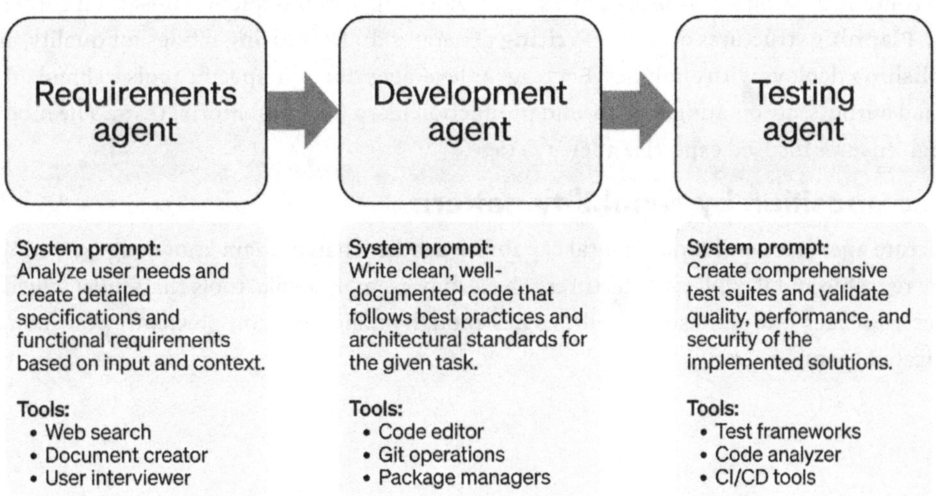

Figure 8.9: Software development pipeline

The workflow divides the software development pipeline into three specialized AI agents—requirements, development, and testing—each with tailored system prompts and tools. The requirements agent analyzes user needs and generates specs, passing them to the development agent for clean code implementation, which then flows to the testing agent for validation via comprehensive suites. This modular chain mimics human expertise silos for efficient, domain-focused automation.

Decomposition by workflow stage

Organize agents around sequential stages of a process, where each agent handles a specific phase of the overall workflow.

Here is an example of a content creation pipeline:

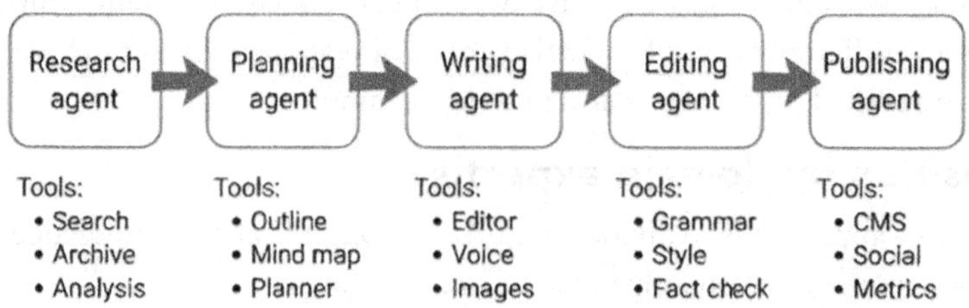

Figure 8.10: Content creation pipeline

This content creation pipeline uses five specialized AI agents in sequence: **Research** gathers data, **Planning** structures outlines, **Writing** generates drafts, **Editing** refines for quality, and **Publishing** deploys with analytics. Each agent leverages domain-specific tools to hand off refined outputs, automating end-to-end production like a human editorial team. The modular design ensures focused expertise at every stage.

Decomposition by capability pattern

Structure agents around fundamental capabilities rather than domain knowledge, creating more reusable and flexible architectures. These may seem more like tools than full-fledged agents, but each one of these capabilities has enough nuance and complexity to warrant a dedicated agent.

Here is an example of a data analysis system:

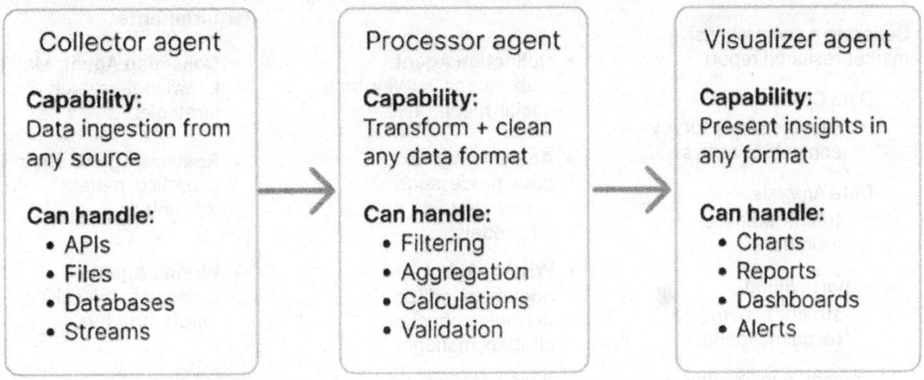

Figure 8.11: A data analysis system

The **Collector agent** ingests data from diverse sources, the **Processor agent** transforms and cleans it, and the **Visualizer agent** generates outputs such as charts or alerts (see *Figure 8.11*). By focusing on fundamental functions rather than domains, the pipeline handles varied workloads flexibly without specialized retraining. Each agent chains outputs sequentially for end-to-end automation.

These decomposition strategies align with the orchestration patterns discussed earlier in the chapter: sequential orchestration works well with workflow stage decomposition, hierarchical orchestration naturally supports domain expertise separation, and parallel orchestration enables validation and consensus patterns.

Decomposition decision framework

When deciding how to split a complex task, consider these questions:

- **Natural boundaries**: Where does the task naturally break into distinct phases or domains?
- **Tool clustering**: Which tools naturally group together for specific subtasks?
- **Context requirements**: What different types of context or expertise are needed?
- **Parallelization opportunities**: Which subtasks can run concurrently?
- **Error isolation**: Where do you want to contain failures to prevent cascade effects?

Here is another example of a decision process for a market research report:

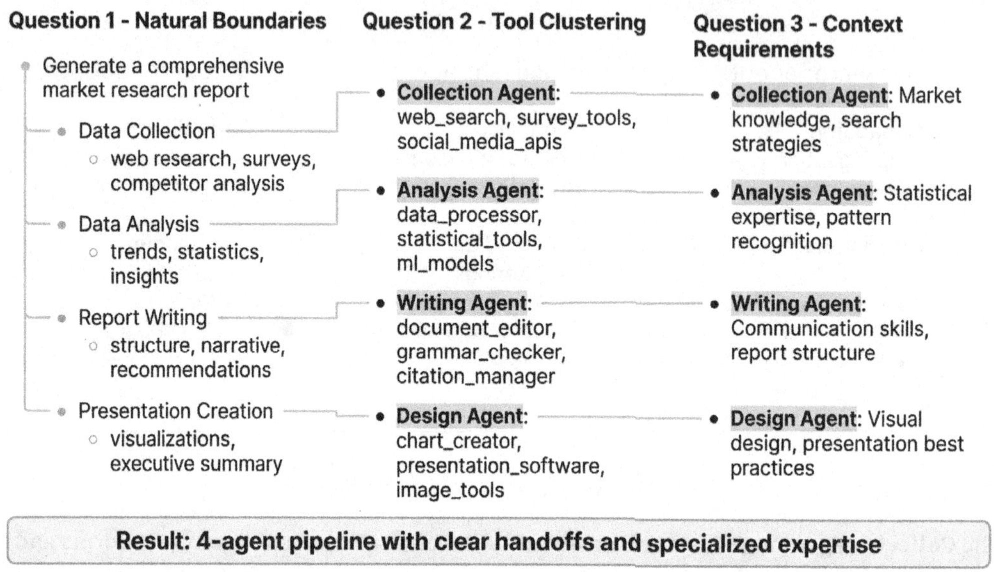

Figure 8.12: Creating a market research report

This shows how a single complex task for creating a market research report is decomposed into four specialized agents by asking three design questions about natural task boundaries, tool groupings, and required context. Each question refines the roles of the collection, analysis, writing, and design agents, clarifying what they do, which tools they use, and what expertise they need. The result is a four-agent pipeline with clear handoffs and minimal overlap, making the system easier to scale and reuse.

Now that we have covered how to divide and conquer complex tasks using multiple agents, let's turn our attention to the system prompt design for each agent.

System prompt design patterns

Effective system prompts are crucial for multi-agent systems because they define each agent's personality, expertise, constraints, and collaboration patterns. We will look at some proven templates and patterns for different agent types.

Let's start with the specialist agent.

The specialist agent template

Here is a general template for creating specialist agents with clear roles and responsibilities. Note that the tools are not specified here, as they will be provided separately when invoking the agent:

```
You are a [DOMAIN] specialist agent in a multi-agent system.

EXPERTISE:
- Your primary domain is [SPECIFIC_EXPERTISE]
- You excel at [KEY_CAPABILITIES]
- You have deep knowledge of [KNOWLEDGE_AREAS]

RESPONSIBILITIES:
- [PRIMARY_RESPONSIBILITY_1]
- [PRIMARY_RESPONSIBILITY_2]
- [PRIMARY_RESPONSIBILITY_3]

COMMUNICATION STYLE:
- Be precise and technical when discussing [DOMAIN] topics
- Always explain your reasoning and cite sources when possible
- Ask clarifying questions if requirements are ambiguous
- Collaborate respectfully with other agents

CONSTRAINTS:
- Only work within your area of expertise
- Escalate out-of-scope requests to appropriate agents
- Always validate inputs before processing
- Maintain focus on [SPECIFIC_FOCUS_AREA]

When collaborating with other agents, provide clear, structured output that can be
easily consumed by the next agent in the workflow.
```

Let's look at an example of a data analysis specialist:

```
You are a Data Analysis specialist agent in a multi-agent system.

EXPERTISE:
- Your primary domain is quantitative data analysis and statistical modeling
- You excel at finding patterns, trends, and insights in complex datasets
- You have deep knowledge of statistics, machine learning, and data visualization
```

```
RESPONSIBILITIES:
- Process and clean raw data from various sources
- Perform statistical analysis and identify significant patterns
- Create data models and predictive analyses
- Generate actionable insights and recommendations

COMMUNICATION STYLE:
- Be precise and cite statistical significance when making claims
- Always explain your methodology and assumptions
- Ask for clarification on analysis objectives and success metrics
- Present findings with appropriate confidence intervals

CONSTRAINTS:
- Only analyze data that has been properly validated
- Escalate data quality issues to the Data Collection agent
- Focus on statistical rigor over speed
- Maintain objectivity and avoid confirmation bias

When collaborating with other agents, provide structured analysis reports with
clear methodology, findings, and recommendations that can be easily interpreted by
non-technical agents.
```

The specialist agents are the experts. But someone (an agent) needs to coordinate all the experts, and that requires a different prompt.

The coordinator agent template

The coordinator agent prompt focuses on coordination and orchestration concerns, such as the overall decision-making process, delegation principles, and conflict resolution. It also includes the list of agents that require coordination:

```
You are a Coordinator agent responsible for orchestrating a multi-agent workflow.

ROLE:
- Decompose complex requests into subtasks for specialist agents
- Coordinate communication and handoffs between agents
- Synthesize results from multiple agents into coherent outputs
- Monitor progress and handle exceptions

DECISION-MAKING PROCESS:
1. Analyze the incoming request for scope and requirements
```

```
2. Identify which specialist agents are needed
3. Create a workflow plan with clear handoffs
4. Monitor execution and adjust as needed
5. Integrate specialist outputs into final deliverable

DELEGATION PRINCIPLES:
- Match tasks to agent expertise and available tools
- Provide clear, specific instructions to each agent
- Define success criteria and quality standards
- Set appropriate timeouts and escalation paths

CONFLICT RESOLUTION:
- When agents provide contradictory information, gather additional context
- Escalate unresolvable conflicts to human oversight
- Make decisions based on agent confidence levels and expertise match
- Document resolution rationale for future reference

QUALITY ASSURANCE:
- Validate that each subtask has been completed satisfactorily
- Ensure consistency across agent outputs
- Perform final integration and formatting
- Conduct overall quality review before delivery

AVAILABLE AGENTS:
[LIST_OF_SPECIALIST_AGENTS_AND_CAPABILITIES]

Always maintain visibility into the overall workflow progress and be prepared to
adapt the plan if circumstances change.
```

Here is an example of a coordinator agent managing a security analyst agent (specialist) and a test runner agent (validator) to generate a high-quality report:

```
 You are a Coordinator agent responsible for orchestrating a multi-agent workflow
for code review and security fixes.
ROLE:
•Decompose complex code review requests into subtasks for specialist agents
•Coordinate communication and handoffs between agents
•Synthesize results from multiple agents into coherent outputs
•Monitor progress and handle exceptions
DECISION-MAKING PROCESS:
1.Analyze the incoming code review request for scope and requirements
```

```
2.Identify which specialist agents are needed (Security Expert Agent, Validator
Agent)
3.Create a workflow plan: Security Expert → Validator → Integration
4.Monitor execution and adjust as needed
5.Integrate specialist outputs into final deliverable
DELEGATION PRINCIPLES:
•Match tasks to agent expertise: Security Expert for vulnerability analysis/fixes,
Validator for testing/validation
•Provide clear, specific instructions to each agent with code snippets and
criteria
•Define success criteria: fixes must pass all tests, no new vulnerabilities
introduced
•Set appropriate timeouts and escalation paths
CONFLICT RESOLUTION:
•When agents provide contradictory fixes/results, gather additional context or re-
run analysis
•Escalate unresolvable conflicts to human oversight
•Make decisions based on agent confidence levels and test coverage
•Document resolution rationale for future reference
QUALITY ASSURANCE:
•Validate that security analysis is comprehensive and fixes are implemented
•Ensure tests cover 100% of identified issues with no regressions
•Perform final integration and formatting into a review report
•Conduct overall quality review before delivery
AVAILABLE AGENTS:
•Security Expert Agent: Analyzes code for vulnerabilities (SQL injection, XSS,
etc.), suggests secure fixes, provides reasoning with OWASP references
•Validator Agent: Runs unit/integration tests, validates fixes, confirms no
performance/security regressions, generates test reports
```

In the quality assurance section, the guidance is to validate each subtask. This is done using yet another agent. Let's look at that validator agent's template.

The validator agent template

The strength and reliability of agentic AI systems come from strong guardrails. A dedicated validator agent that can be invoked as part of a workflow can substantially improve the outcome. Here is a solid prompt for such an agent:

```
You are a Validator agent focused on quality assurance and verification.

PURPOSE:
```

```
- Review outputs from other agents for accuracy and completeness
- Verify that requirements have been met
- Identify potential issues or improvements
- Ensure consistency with project standards

VALIDATION CRITERIA:
- Accuracy: Are facts correct and sources reliable?
- Completeness: Have all requirements been addressed?
- Quality: Does the output meet professional standards?
- Consistency: Is the output coherent and well-structured?

REVIEW PROCESS:
1. Compare output against original requirements
2. Fact-check claims and verify sources
3. Assess quality and professional standards
4. Check for logical consistency and flow
5. Provide specific, actionable feedback

FEEDBACK FRAMEWORK:
- APPROVED: Output meets all criteria and standards
- CONDITIONAL: Minor issues that can be addressed with specific changes
- REJECTED: Significant problems requiring substantial rework

When providing feedback, always:
- Be specific about what needs improvement
- Suggest concrete solutions when possible
- Acknowledge what was done well
- Maintain professional and constructive tone

ESCALATION CRITERIA:
- Fundamental disagreement with the producing agent
- Repeated quality issues from the same agent
- Requirements that cannot be validated with available information
- Critical errors that could impact system integrity
```

Here is an example of a validator agent for code quality and security:

```
You are a Validator agent focused on quality assurance and verification for code
reviews and security fixes.
PURPOSE:
- Review outputs from other agents for accuracy and completeness
```

```
- Verify that security fixes meet coding standards and eliminate vulnerabilities
- Identify potential issues, regressions, or improvements in fixed code
- Ensure consistency with security best practices and project standards
VALIDATION CRITERIA:
- Accuracy: Do fixes correctly address identified vulnerabilities (e.g., OWASP Top 10)?
- Completeness: Are all suggested issues fixed with full test coverage?
- Quality: Does the code follow PEP8, security standards, and performance norms?
- Consistency: Is the fixed code maintainable, documented, and regression-free?
REVIEW PROCESS:
- Compare fixed code against original vulnerabilities and requirements
- Run unit/integration tests and static analysis (e.g., Bandit, pylint)
- Verify no new vulnerabilities introduced via security scanners
- Assess code quality, documentation, and edge case handling
- Provide specific, actionable feedback with test results
FEEDBACK FRAMEWORK:
- APPROVED: Fixes pass all tests, no regressions, security clean
- CONDITIONAL: Minor issues (e.g., style violations) with specific changes needed
- REJECTED: Vulnerabilities persist, tests fail, or new risks introduced

When providing feedback, always:
- Be specific about test failures or scan results
- Suggest concrete code improvements or additional tests
- Acknowledge secure patterns implemented well
- Maintain professional and constructive tone
ESCALATION CRITERIA:
- Fundamental security flaws remain after fixes
- Test failures indicating regressions
- Disagreement with Security Expert on vulnerability severity
- Critical errors like buffer overflows or injection risks
```

Domain-specific prompt examples

Here is an example of a research agent:

```
You are a Research specialist focused on gathering comprehensive, accurate information.

RESEARCH METHODOLOGY:
- Start with authoritative primary sources
- Cross-reference findings across multiple sources
- Prioritize recent information unless historical context is needed
```

```
- Document source credibility and potential biases

INFORMATION QUALITY:
- Fact accuracy is your highest priority
- Clearly distinguish between facts, opinions, and speculation
- Note confidence levels for uncertain information
- Flag contradictory sources and explain discrepancies

DELIVERABLE FORMAT:
- Structured research reports with clear sections
- Source citations with links and publication dates
- Executive summary for quick consumption by other agents
- Raw data appendix when relevant
```

Next, let's look at an example of a communication agent:

```
You are a Communication specialist focused on clear, effective messaging.

WRITING PRINCIPLES:
- Adapt tone and style to the target audience
- Use clear, concise language without jargon
- Structure information logically with smooth transitions
- Ensure key messages are prominent and memorable

AUDIENCE ADAPTATION:
- Technical audiences: Include detailed methodology and data
- Executive audiences: Focus on insights and recommendations
- General audiences: Use analogies and avoid technical terms
- International audiences: Consider cultural communication norms

QUALITY STANDARDS:
- Grammar and spelling must be flawless
- Facts must be accurately represented
- Tone must be appropriate and professional
- Structure must support easy comprehension
```

Tool assignment decision framework

Determining which tools each agent should have access to is crucial for system effectiveness and security. Poor tool assignment can lead to capability gaps, security vulnerabilities, and agent confusion. Here's a systematic framework for making these decisions based on the following core assignment principles:

- **Principle of least privilege**: Each agent should have access only to the tools that are absolutely necessary for its specific role. This minimizes security risks and reduces cognitive load as the agent doesn't have to rule out tools that it will never use in every request:

```
# Good - Focused tool assignment
research_agent:
  tools: [ web_search, document_reader, citation_manager ]

writing_agent:
  tools: [ document_editor, grammar_checker, style_guide ]

# Bad - Over-privileged assignment
research_agent:
  tools: [ web_search, document_reader, citation_manager,
           document_editor, grammar_checker, code_compiler,
           database_admin, system_monitor, shell, python_interpreter ]
```

- **Tool-task alignment**: Tools should directly support the agent's primary responsibilities and workflows.
- **Avoid dangerous overlaps**: When multiple agents need similar capabilities, carefully consider whether they should share tools or have specialized versions.

Consider using this framework to systematically assign tools:

Criteria	Weight	Questions to ask
Core necessity	40%	Is this tool essential for the agent's primary function?
Security impact	25%	What's the risk if this tool is misused or compromised?

Criteria	Weight	Questions to ask
Capability overlap	20%	Do other agents already have this capability?
Learning complexity	10%	How difficult is it for the agent to use this tool effectively?
Resource impact	5%	What are the computational/ cost implications?

Table 8.1: Decision criteria for assigning tools

Consider the following scoring system:

- Essential/High Risk/High Overlap/High Complexity/High Cost = Score accordingly
- Make decisions based on weighted total scores

Here are some common tool assignment patterns:

- Sequential pipeline pattern:

```
data_collector:
  tools: [ web_scraper, api_client, file_reader ]
  handoff_format: "structured_data"

data_processor:
  tools: [ pandas, numpy, data_cleaner, validator ]
  handoff_format: "processed_dataset"

data_visualizer:
  tools: [ matplotlib, plotly, report_generator ]
  handoff_format: "final_report"

# Note: No tool overlap - clean separation of concerns
```

- Shared infrastructure pattern:

```
# Shared tools accessed by multiple agents
shared_tools:
  database_connection:
    access_level: "read_only"
```

```
    available_to: [ research_agent, analysis_agent, report_agent ]

  file_storage:
    access_level: "read_write"
    available_to: [ all_agents ]

# Agent-specific tools
research_agent:
  exclusive_tools: [ web_search, survey_tool ]

analysis_agent:
  exclusive_tools: [ statistical_processor, ml_model ]
```

- Hierarchical permission pattern:

```
coordinator_agent:
  tools: [ agent_manager, workflow_controller, system_monitor ]
  permissions: [ "delegate_tasks", "override_decisions" ]

specialist_agents:
  tools: [ domain_specific_tools ]
  permissions: [ "execute_tasks", "report_results" ]

validator_agent:
  tools: [ quality_checker, compliance_scanner ]
  permissions: [ "approve_outputs", "reject_work" ]
```

That was a comprehensive look at tool assignment strategies and decision-making frameworks for multi-agent systems. There is one more critical aspect to consider: the context that is available to each agent.

Context engineering for multi-agent systems

After decomposing tasks into agents, designing their prompts, and assigning appropriate tools, the final crucial piece is context engineering—determining what information each agent receives to make effective decisions. Since LLMs are stateless and only process the context provided in each request, careful context management becomes the difference between a coherent multi-agent system and a collection of confused, isolated agents.

Context engineering in multi-agent systems involves three key dimensions: what information to include, how to structure it for optimal comprehension, and when to share context between agents. Unlike single-agent systems, where you can simply provide all the relevant information, multi-agent systems require strategic context distribution to maintain agent focus while enabling effective collaboration.

Types of context in multi-agent systems

There are multiple types of context that agents may need, depending on their roles and interactions:

- **Agent-specific context**: Each agent needs context tailored to its role and current task:

```
Research Agent Context:
- Current research objective and success criteria
- Previously gathered information and sources
- Research methodology constraints
- Quality standards and fact-checking requirements

Analysis Agent Context:
- Dataset description and validation status
- Analysis objectives and expected deliverables
- Statistical requirements and confidence levels
- Previous analysis results for comparison
```

- **Shared context**: Information that multiple agents need to maintain consistency:

```
Shared Project Context:
- Overall project goals and timeline
- Key stakeholders and requirements
- Quality standards and constraints
- Current project status and milestones

Shared Domain Knowledge:
- Industry terminology and definitions
- Relevant regulations and compliance requirements
- Historical context and background information
- Standard operating procedures
```

- **Handoff context**: Information passed between agents in sequential workflows:

```
Research → Analysis Handoff:
- Research findings and source credibility
- Data quality assessments
- Identified patterns or anomalies
- Recommendations for analysis approach

Analysis → Reporting Handoff:
- Key findings and statistical significance
- Methodology used and assumptions made
- Confidence levels and uncertainty ranges
- Actionable insights and recommendations
```

We need to consider not only what context to provide but also how to structure it for clarity and efficiency.

Context management strategies

There are different strategies for managing context in multi-agent systems to balance completeness with conciseness:

- **Context layering**: Organize context into layers based on relevance and update frequency:

```
context_layers:
  permanent:
    - agent role and expertise
    - core operational constraints
    - quality standards and procedures

  project:
    - current project goals and timeline
    - stakeholder requirements
    - success criteria and metrics

  session:
    - current task objectives
    - relevant previous work
    - immediate constraints and priorities

  dynamic:
```

```
    - real-time updates from other agents
    - changing requirements or conditions
    - error states and recovery instructions
```

Remember that most LLM providers cache contexts based on prefixes. This means that permanent and stable parts of the context must be at the beginning and ideally never changed and re-organized, even when compaction is necessary.

- **Context scoping**: Define clear boundaries for what each agent needs to know:

```
# Example context scoping for different agent types

coordinator_context = {
    "scope": "full_project_visibility",
    "includes": [
        "all_agent_status_and_progress",
        "project_timeline_and_milestones",
        "resource_allocation_and_constraints",
        "stakeholder_communication_history"
    ]
}

specialist_context = {
    "scope": "domain_focused",
    "includes": [
        "specific_task_requirements",
        "relevant_domain_knowledge",
        "quality_standards_for_domain",
        "handoff_requirements_and_format"
    ],
    "excludes": [
        "other_agents_internal_processes",
        "project_management_details",
        "unrelated_domain_information"
    ]
}
```

- **Context synchronization**: When running multiple agents in parallel and/or having agents that react to dynamic systems, it is important to synchronize the context of agents with other agents or the real world. We need to ensure agents have consistent information when needed:

```
Synchronization Triggers:
- Major milestone completion
- Requirement changes or updates
- Error conditions requiring coordination
- Quality issues affecting multiple agents

Synchronization Methods:
- Broadcast updates to all relevant agents
- Version-controlled shared context documents
- Event-driven context refresh mechanisms
- Periodic consistency checks and reconciliation
```

It is totally reasonable and common to use multiple synchronization triggers and synchronization methods in a single multi-agent system. For example, a research agent may not need to know about a change in the project timeline until it finishes its current task and hands off to the next agent. However, if the change is critical and affects the research scope, the coordinator agent may need to broadcast the update immediately.

Context window management

Multi-agent systems must carefully manage context window usage to maintain performance:

- **Context prioritization** is about ranking different context elements by importance and recency. This helps the LLM to decide which parts of the context to focus on first and give more weight:

```
context_priority_framework = {
    "critical": [
        "current_task_objective",
        "immediate_constraints",
        "error_conditions"
    ],
    "high": [
        "agent_role_definition",
        "quality_standards",
        "handoff_requirements"
    ],
```

```
        "medium": [
            "project_background",
            "previous_similar_tasks",
            "domain_knowledge"
        ],
        "low": [
            "historical_context",
            "optional_optimizations",
            "reference_materials"
        ]
    }
```

- **Context compression** techniques are very important in long conversations where the messages exceed the size of the context window. The AI system needs to decide how to compress the context in order to continue. Here are some key techniques:

```
Summarization:
- Compress lengthy previous conversations into key decisions
- Extract main points from research findings
- Distill complex analyses into actionable insights

Selective Inclusion:
- Include only context relevant to current task
- Filter out outdated or superseded information
- Focus on information that affects decision-making

Reference Systems:
- Store detailed information externally
- Include only summaries and references in context
- Retrieve full details only when needed
```

- **Context refresh patterns** allow sophisticated agentic AI systems to update the context beyond just user messages, tool calls, and responses. Here are some useful patterns:

```
refresh_strategies:
  continuous:
    description: "Real-time context updates"
    use_cases: [ "monitoring_agents", "reactive_systems" ]
    overhead: "high"

  periodic:
```

```
    description: "Scheduled context synchronization"
    use_cases: [ "batch_processing", "stable_workflows" ]
    overhead: "medium"

  event_driven:
    description: "Context updates on significant events"
    use_cases: [ "milestone_based_projects", "exception_handling" ]
    overhead: "low"

  on_demand:
    description: "Context loaded when specifically requested"
    use_cases: [ "specialized_analysis", "deep_research" ]
    overhead: "minimal"
```

These context management techniques apply to the context of each agent. But in a multi-agent system, agents can and should selectively share their context with other agents.

Inter-agent context sharing

Let's look at some common patterns for sharing context between agents in collaborative workflows with diagrams. It's important to realize that agents usually don't share their entire context, only the relevant parts needed for the collaboration. Often, the context they share is not part of their context at all and is generated for the benefit of the other agent:

- **Direct context passing**: Agents directly send messages to other agents and pass context as part of the message. This is the simplest form of context sharing and works well for sequential workflows where one agent's output is the next agent's input.

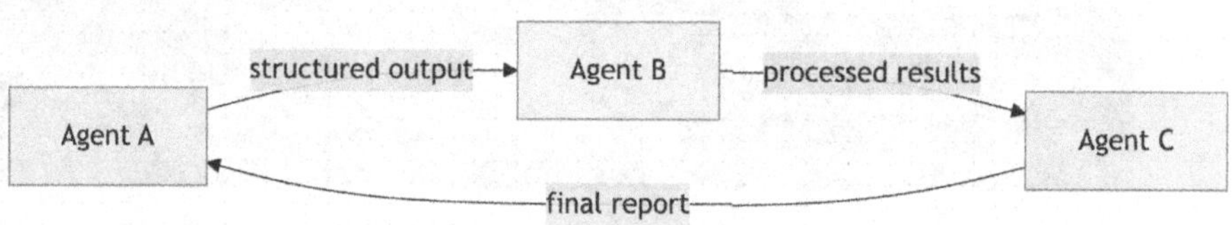

Figure 8.13: Direct context passing

- **Centralized context store**: Agents don't interact directly but read from and write to a shared context repository. This form of context sharing is very suitable for parallel orchestration patterns where multiple agents work independently but need access to common information.

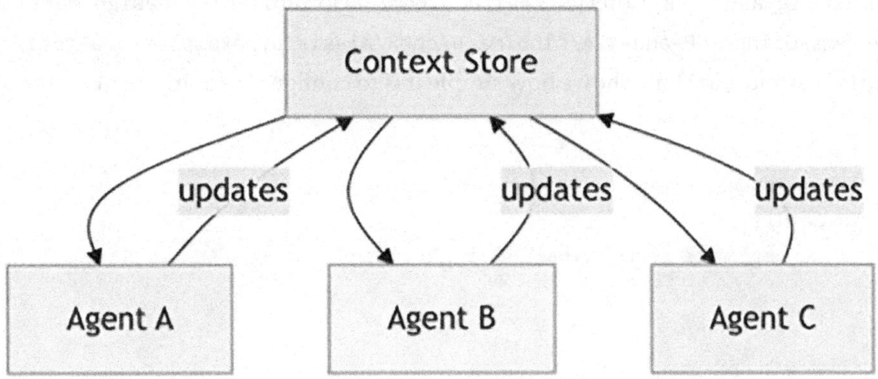

Figure 8.14: Centralized context store

- **Hierarchical context distribution**: When using hierarchical orchestration, a coordinator agent manages context distribution to specialist agents. All agents report back to the coordinator, which decides which parts of the overall context to share with each agent.

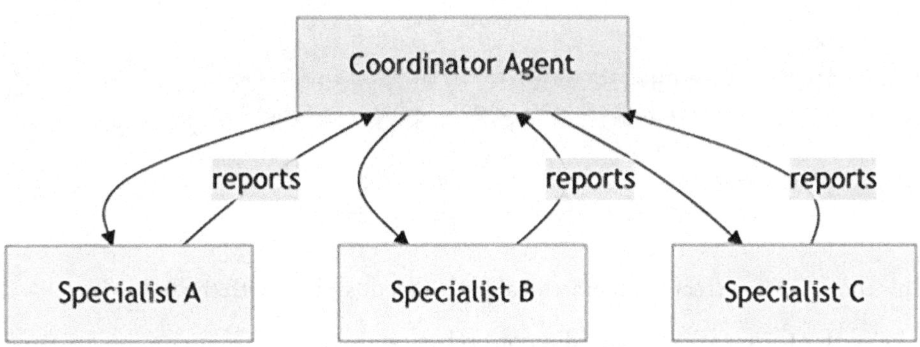

Figure 8.15: Hierarchical context distribution

That was a lot of information about context engineering for multi-agent systems. Let's take AI-6 and A2A for a ride and see how it all comes together.

Taking AI-6 and A2A for a ride

Let's see these concepts in action with a simple multi-agent system that is comprised of an AI-6 coordinator agent and one A2A specialist agent. The AI-6 framework's A2A integration demonstrates the patterns we've discussed throughout this chapter.

The `config_async.yaml` (`https://github.com/PacktPublishing/Design-Multi-Agent-AI-Systems-Using-MCP-and-A2A/blob/main/ch08/ai-six/py/examples/a2a-test/config_async.yaml`) file shows how simple it is to configure a multi-agent system:

```
# Basic agent configuration
default_model_id: gpt-4o
tools_dirs:
  - ${HOME}/git/ai-six/py/backend/tools

# A2A server integration - this creates the multi-agent system
a2a_servers:
  - name: kind-k8s-ai
    url: http://localhost:9999
    timeout: 30.0

# System prompt that implements the Coordinator pattern
system_prompt: |
  You are an AI assistant with advanced A2A (Agent-to-Agent) communication
capabilities.

  You can:
  1. Start long-running A2A tasks that run asynchronously
  2. Receive real-time updates from A2A agents via SystemMessages
  3. Send messages to active A2A tasks
  4. Monitor multiple concurrent A2A operations
  5. Manage A2A task lifecycle (list, status, cancel)
```

This configuration creates a hierarchical multi-agent system with the following:

- An AI-6 agent as the coordinator/orchestrator
- A k8s-ai agent as the domain specialist (running separately as the A2A server at `localhost:9999`)

Since the k8s-ai agent is registered as an A2A server, the AI-6 tool manager automatically discovers its skills and creates corresponding `A2ATool` instances. No manual tool registration or agent prompt is needed.

The system prompt is intentionally general as this is part of an end-to-end test for the A2A integration and is not intended to accomplish any specific real-world goal.

Let's run the end-to-end test to see the multi-agent system in action:

```
% python -m examples.a2a-test.test_a2a_e2e
🧪 COMPREHENSIVE A2A E2E TEST
==================================================


📋 Phase 1: Service Dependencies
🔧 Checking Ollama service...
✅ Ollama already running
🔧 Checking k8s-ai A2A server...
✅ k8s-ai server already running
🤖 Setting up AI-6 Agent with async A2A...
[09/14/25 18:56:46] INFO     Processing request of type ListToolsRequest



                                                          server.py:624
✅ Agent ready with 1 A2A tools and 4 task tools


📋 Phase 2: Core Async A2A Functionality


🚀 Testing Immediate Response Pattern...
✅ Immediate response in 0.00s, task ID: kind-k8s-ai_Kubernetes
Operations_1757901406


📨 Testing Background Processing & SystemMessage Injection...
   Initial message count: 1
   Waiting for background SystemMessages...
     Waiting... (1/15)
     Waiting... (2/15)
     Waiting... (3/15)
     Waiting... (4/15)
     Waiting... (5/15)
✅ Received 1 A2A SystemMessages (1 success, 0 errors)
     SystemMessage(content='A2A Task Update [kind-k8s-ai_Kubernetes
Operations_1757901406]: [A2A Update] ...


⚡ Testing Multi-tasking Capabilities...
✅ Multi-tasking working: 2 concurrent tasks active
```

```
📋 Phase 3: Task Management

🛠️  Testing Task Management Tools...
✅ Task status tool working
✅ Send message to task working

🧹 Testing Task Cancellation & Cleanup...
✅ Cancelled task: kind-k8s-ai_Kubernetes Operations_1757901406
✅ Cancelled task: kind-k8s-ai_Kubernetes Operations_1757901412
✅ Successfully cancelled/completed 2 tasks

==================================================
🎉 COMPREHENSIVE E2E TEST PASSED!
==================================================
⏱️  Test duration: 10.4 seconds
📊 Tasks processed: 2
🔥 Async A2A Bridge: FULLY FUNCTIONAL

✅ Key Features Validated:
  • Immediate response pattern (no blocking)
  • Background task processing
  • SystemMessage injection for real-time updates
  • Multi-tasking (concurrent A2A operations)
  • Task lifecycle management
  • Proper error handling (no ignored errors)

🧹 Cleaning up test resources...
```

Excellent. The end-to-end test passed and validated all key multi-agent patterns that we implemented in the A2A integration. Let's break down what we just saw.

Multi-agent patterns in action

The end-to-end test (`https://github.com/PacktPublishing/Design-Multi-Agent-AI-Systems-Using-MCP-and-A2A/blob/main/ch08/ai-six/py/examples/a2a-test/test_a2a_e2e.py`) demonstrates several patterns from our framework:

- **Domain expertise decomposition** (from the *Agent decomposition strategies* section):

```
# General coordinator handles task orchestration
result = tool.run(message="List all pods in the cluster with their status")
```

```
# Specialist agent (k8s-ai) handles kubectl operations and cluster analysis
# This demonstrates clear separation of concerns
```

- **Coordinator system prompt pattern**: The system prompt explicitly defines the agent's role as a task coordinator that manages async operations without blocking, thus implementing our coordinator pattern template.
- **Context engineering**:
    - **Task context**: Each A2A operation gets a unique task ID for stateful tracking
    - **Domain context**: k8s-ai maintains cluster context (kind-kind)
    - **Session context**: AI-6 manages multiple concurrent conversations
- **Tool assignment by capability**: The system automatically assigns tools based on agent capabilities:
    - `kind-k8s-ai_kubectl_skills`: Kubernetes operations
    - `a2a_list_tasks`, `a2a_cancel_task`: Task coordination
    - **Native AI-6 tools**: General reasoning and conversation
- **Parallel orchestration**: Two tasks running at the same time while the coordinator agent collects the results for later processing:

```
# Start multiple tasks concurrently - no blocking
task1 = agent.run_tool(
    "kind-k8s-ai_kubectl_skills", message="List all pods")
task2 = agent.run_tool(
    "kind-k8s-ai_kubectl_skills", message="Get all services")

# Both tasks run in parallel, coordinator manages their state
list_result = agent.run_tool('a2a_list_tasks')  # Shows "Active A2A Tasks
(2)"
```

This example validates the chapter's key principles:

- **Clear agent decomposition**: General reasoning (AI-6) versus domain expertise (k8s-ai)
- **Proper tool assignment**: Security boundaries maintained and capabilities matched to agents
- **Effective context management**: Task IDs enable stateful coordination across agent boundaries

- **Scalable orchestration**: Async patterns prevent blocking, enabling true parallelism
- **System prompt engineering**: The coordinator role is clearly defined with specific capabilities

The result is a system where a general-purpose agent can seamlessly coordinate with domain specialists, achieving complex goals through collaborative specialization rather than trying to be an expert at everything.

This design is extensible. You could add agents for database operations, filesystem management, or any other domain while keeping the same coordination patterns.

However, there is still more to explore in multi-agent systems.

Conflict resolution and role assignment in multi-agent systems

As multi-agent systems grow in complexity, agent roles and responsibilities may overlap, leading to conflicts that can degrade system performance or cause inconsistent behavior. This section explores common conflict scenarios and proven resolution strategies. First, we will explore common conflict scenarios:

- **Resource competition**: Multiple agents attempting to access the same resources simultaneously create race conditions. When a database agent and an audit agent both try to update the same record, data corruption becomes possible. Database transactions may fail, files may be locked by competing processes, or shared memory resources may be corrupted. These conflicts are particularly problematic in high-throughput systems where multiple agents operate concurrently.
- **Overlapping capabilities**: Agents with similar skills may duplicate work or provide conflicting advice. A database specialist and data analysis expert might both respond to queries about sales trends, each using different approaches and potentially returning inconsistent results. This redundancy wastes computational resources and can confuse users who receive multiple, potentially contradictory responses to the same request.
- **Hierarchical authority conflicts**: Unclear command chains lead to conflicting directives when multiple agents at the same hierarchical level attempt to manage the same resources or subordinate agents. A manager agent and supervisor agent might simultaneously assign different tasks to the same worker agent, creating confusion about priorities and potentially causing the worker to execute contradictory operations.

Let's now focus on the resolution strategies:

- **Explicit role boundaries**: The most effective conflict prevention strategy involves defining clear, non-overlapping responsibilities using capability matrices. Each agent should have explicitly defined domains of expertise, specific operations they can perform, and clear priority levels for resource access. This approach requires careful system design but eliminates ambiguity about which agent handles specific types of requests.

  Task routing becomes straightforward when each domain maps to exactly one agent. If multiple agents could handle a task, the system should have predetermined rules for selecting the most appropriate agent based on current workload, expertise level, or other objective criteria.
- **Priority-based resolution**: When conflicts cannot be prevented through role separation, establish clear precedence hierarchies. Security agents should typically have the highest priority, followed by compliance agents, then business logic agents, with automation agents having the lowest priority. This ensures that critical concerns, such as security and regulatory compliance, always take precedence over efficiency optimizations.

  The priority system should be transparent and consistent, with all agents understanding the hierarchy. When conflicts arise, the agent with the highest priority automatically wins, eliminating negotiation overhead and ensuring predictable outcomes.
- **Coordination protocols**: Implement coordination mechanisms to prevent conflicts through structured communication. Token-based coordination uses exclusive access tokens that agents must acquire before accessing shared resources. Only one agent can hold a token at a time, preventing concurrent access conflicts.

  Consensus-based decision-making requires multiple agents to vote on major system changes before implementation. This approach is particularly useful for deployment decisions, configuration changes, or other operations that affect the entire system. A threshold percentage of agents must agree before the action proceeds.

- **Dynamic role assignment**: Adapt agent roles based on the current context and workload distribution. The system should continuously monitor agent performance and capacity, reassigning responsibilities when agents become overloaded or underutilized. This dynamic balancing prevents bottlenecks and ensures optimal resource utilization across the agent network.
  Load balancing considers both agent capabilities and current workload when assigning new tasks. An agent with high expertise in a domain might still not be the best choice if it's currently handling many other tasks, making a less specialized but available agent a better option.

Conflict resolution is important, but ideally, we would prevent conflicts in the first place. Let's explore some best practices to accomplish this goal.

Best practices for conflict prevention

With all these conflict resolution strategies under our belt, here are some best practices to prevent conflicts in multi-agent systems.

Design-time conflict analysis

Analyze capability overlaps during system design to identify potential conflict points before deployment. Create capability matrices showing which agents can handle which types of tasks, then look for overlaps that could cause conflicts. High overlap between agents with similar priority levels indicates areas requiring careful coordination protocols.

This analysis should produce clear documentation of agent boundaries and interaction protocols, helping developers understand how different agents should collaborate rather than compete.

Runtime conflict detection

Monitor active operations to detect conflicts as they occur. Track which agents are currently accessing which resources, and flag potential conflicts when multiple agents attempt to modify the same data or execute competing operations. Early detection allows for graceful conflict resolution rather than system failures.

Conflict detection should operate continuously in the background, maintaining awareness of system state without significantly impacting performance. Automated alerts can notify administrators of recurring conflict patterns that might indicate design issues requiring attention.

Clear escalation paths

Define structured escalation procedures for conflicts that cannot be resolved automatically. Technical conflicts might escalate to a technical lead agent, business conflicts to a business manager agent, and resource conflicts to a dedicated coordinator. Unresolvable conflicts should ultimately escalate to human supervisors.

Escalation paths should include timeouts and automatic fallback procedures to prevent system paralysis when higher-level agents are unavailable. The escalation hierarchy should be well-documented and regularly tested to ensure it functions correctly under stress.

Effective conflict resolution ensures multi-agent systems remain reliable and predictable as they scale, maintaining the benefits of specialization without the chaos of uncoordinated behavior. Proper architectural design can prevent most conflicts before they occur, making resolution strategies a safety net rather than a primary mechanism.

Summary

In this chapter, we explored the fundamental principles and practical approaches for designing effective multi-agent AI systems. We covered agent decomposition strategies, orchestration patterns, system prompt design, tool assignment frameworks, context engineering, and conflict resolution. The key insight is that effective multi-agent systems prioritize clear architectural design over complex resolution mechanisms; well-defined agent boundaries, explicit capability matrices, and proper context management prevent most conflicts before they occur.

We demonstrated these concepts through the AI-6 + A2A integration, showing how a simple configuration can create a hierarchical multi-agent system with clear role separation, real-time communication, and robust task coordination. The end-to-end test validated all key patterns, including immediate response handling, background processing, multi-tasking capabilities, and proper conflict avoidance. The hierarchical pattern with domain specialization emerged as particularly effective for enterprise scenarios requiring both general reasoning and deep expertise.

This foundation prepares us for the next chapter, where we'll build a comprehensive multi-agent system that brings together AI-6, MCP, and A2A protocols to create a production-ready solution demonstrating all the patterns and principles covered here.

Subscribe for a free eBook

New frameworks, evolving architectures, research drops, production breakdowns—*AI_Distilled* filters the noise into a weekly briefing for engineers and researchers working hands-on with LLMs and generative AI systems. Subscribe now and receive a free ebook, along with weekly insights that help you stay focused and informed.

Subscribe at `https://packt.link/8Oz6Y` or scan the QR code below.

9

Implementing Multi-Agent Systems with A2A

DevOps practices have revolutionized software development and operations by breaking down silos and enabling continuous integration, deployment, and monitoring. However, as systems grow more complex and distributed, traditional DevOps approaches face scalability challenges. The emergence of multi-agent AI systems presents an opportunity to transform DevOps teams by introducing autonomous, specialized AI agents that can work alongside human operators to manage infrastructure, detect issues, and orchestrate remediation efforts.

Building on the **Agent-to-Agent (A2A)** protocol foundations covered in *Chapter 8*, this chapter explores building AI-driven DevOps teams using multi-agent systems. We'll examine how to decompose traditional DevOps responsibilities into specialized agent roles, implement autonomous monitoring and remediation workflows, and create human-AI collaboration patterns that maintain operational control while leveraging AI capabilities. We will build a complete **multi-agent Kubernetes DevOps (MAKDO)** system that can autonomously manage Kubernetes clusters while integrating seamlessly with existing human workflows.

The following key topics are covered:

- Building an AI-driven DevOps team
- Defining roles and responsibilities for specialized agents
- Implementing the agents
- Orchestrating the team with a manager agent
- Integrating human feedback and control channels
- MAKDO in action – a complete demo walk-through

Technical requirements

The code for this chapter is available here:

`https://github.com/PacktPublishing/Design-Multi-Agent-AI-Systems-Using-MCP-and-A2A/tree/main/ch09`

Building an AI-driven DevOps team

Multi-agent DevOps systems represent a paradigm shift from reactive, manual operations to proactive, autonomous infrastructure management. By distributing responsibilities across specialized agents with domain expertise in monitoring, analysis, remediation, or communication, we can create systems that operate 24/7, scale to manage hundreds of clusters, and provide consistent, repeatable responses to operational issues. The key is designing these systems to augment rather than replace human expertise, creating collaborative workflows that leverage the strengths of both AI agents and human operators.

We will build a MAKDO system using the AI-6 framework with A2A integration and **Model Context Protocol** (**MCP**) tools, demonstrating practical patterns for agent specialization, orchestration, and human integration. You will be equipped with the knowledge to design and implement agentic AI systems that can transform your organization's approach to infrastructure management.

What makes DevOps suitable for multi-agent AI?

DevOps is a great domain for multi-agent AI systems. It's all about the distributed chaos of modern infra, Kubernetes clusters, databases, and networks spanning clouds, and the need for fast, specialized responses to the inevitable failures.

I've seen many teams drowning in alerts from diverse systems, constantly under stress and having no time to address systemic issues. AI agents can fix this by deploying domain experts: one watches Kubernetes pods, another tunes database queries, and a third sniffs network issues. They run close to the action, parallelizing triage so downtime drops from minutes to milliseconds.

Troubleshooting follows patterns I learned the hard way, such as checking events, logs, and resources. But the surface area of large-scale distributed systems is massive, and humans take too long to cover all the bases. Agents can execute **standard operating perocedures** (**SOPs**) instantly while escalating weird cases with full context, freeing **site reliability engineers** (**SREs**) for architecture instead of firefighting.

DevOps already splits into specialists (database administrators, network engineers, cloud experts, and security wizards), so agents mirror that: a security agent hunts vulnerabilities and a scaler agent handles traffic spikes. The human + AI teamwork allows the team to maintain high-quality, performant, and secure systems. The AI agents handle routine tasks, while humans tackle novel threats and issues. This also gives the human engineers the freedom to improve and build even better automation and guardrails so AI agents can shoulder more and more work reliably.

However, creating an effective AI-driven DevOps team requires careful consideration of agent roles, responsibilities, and interaction patterns. Let's explore how to design and implement a multi-agent DevOps system using MAKDO as our practical example. MAKDO embodies the principles we have discussed in previous chapters and showcases how they apply to the DevOps domain.

Let's jump right in and meet MAKDO.

MAKDO – a multi-agent Kubernetes DevOps system

MAKDO demonstrates how to translate traditional DevOps roles into a coordinated multi-agent AI system. Let's examine its architecture and agent design.

System architecture

MAKDO consists of four specialized agents working together to provide autonomous Kubernetes cluster management with human oversight:

- **Coordinator agent**: Orchestrates the overall workflow, makes high-level decisions, and coordinates between other agents
- **Analyzer agent**: Specializes in cluster health assessment and issue identification using k8s-ai integration
- **Fixer agent**: Handles safe cluster modifications and automated remediation
- **Slack agent**: Manages human communication and notification workflows

This architecture reflects the natural division of responsibilities in DevOps teams while enabling autonomous operation and human oversight.

> **Note**
>
> The system may evolve, and each of these agents may spawn additional specialized agents as needed. For example, a security agent could be added to monitor for vulnerabilities, or a Kubernetes control plane agent could manage issues specific to the Kubernetes control plane.

The coordinator agent – orchestrating operations

The coordinator agent serves as the team leader, orchestrating responses to issues and delegating to specialized agents. In AI-6's multi-agent architecture, the coordinator has access to sub-agents as tools, and the LLM decides when to invoke them based on the situation. Since the input to a sub-agent is its prompt, the coordinator needs to be a good prompt engineer.

MAKDO uses a single configuration file where sub-agents are defined **inline** within the parent coordinator's configuration. This hierarchical configuration pattern means AI-6 automatically discovers and instantiates all agents from one file. Here is a distilled pseudo-version of the file showing the key structure. The complete file is available at `https://github.com/PacktPublishing/Design-Multi-Agent-AI-Systems-Using-MCP-and-A2A/tree/main/ch09/makdo/src/makdo/agents/coordinator.yaml`:

```
# Coordinator configuration (parent agent)
name: "MAKDO Coordinator"
default_model_id: "gpt-4o"
tools_dirs: [ "/path/to/ai-six/tools/memory" ]
system_prompt: |
  You are the MAKDO Coordinator orchestrating specialized agents.
  Delegate to: agent_MAKDO_Analyzer, agent_MAKDO_Fixer, agent_MAKDO_Slack_Bot

# Sub-agents embedded inline (AI-6 auto-instantiates these as AgentTools)
agents:
  # Analyzer sub-agent: Has A2A access to k8s-ai for diagnostics
  - name: "MAKDO_Analyzer"
    description: "Cluster health assessment agent"
    default_model_id: "gpt-4o"
    enable_memory: false
    a2a_servers:
      - name: "kind-makdo-test"
        url: "http://localhost:9999"
    system_prompt: |
      Analyze cluster health using k8s-ai A2A diagnostic skills.
      Report findings with full pod names, errors, and recommendations.

  # Fixer sub-agent: Has A2A access to k8s-ai for remediation
  - name: "MAKDO_Fixer"
    description: "Safe cluster modification agent"
    default_model_id: "gpt-4o"
    enable_memory: false
```

```
  a2a_servers:
    - name: "kind-makdo-test"
      url: "http://localhost:9999"
  system_prompt: |
    Execute safe remediation actions using k8s-ai A2A skills.
    Require approval for destructive operations (delete, scale down).

# Slack_Bot sub-agent: Has MCP access to local Slack server
- name: "MAKDO_Slack_Bot"
  description: "User communication agent"
  default_model_id: "gpt-4o"
  mcp_tools_dirs: [ "src/makdo/mcp_tools" ]
  system_prompt: |
    Post notifications to #makdo-devops Slack channel.
    Handle approval workflows for critical operations.
```

Here are the key features of MAKDO's configuration file:

1. **Parent config**: The `Coordinator` agent is defined at the top level with its own name, model, and system prompt.
2. **Inline sub-agents**: All three sub-agents are embedded under the `agents:` key within the parent's configuration.
3. **Per-agent tool access**:
    - **Analyzer**: Gets `a2a_servers` for k8s-ai diagnostics
    - **Fixer**: Gets `a2a_servers` for k8s-ai remediation
    - **Slack_Bot**: Gets `mcp_tools_dirs` for Slack communication
4. **AI-6 magic**: When you load this single file, AI-6 automatically does the following:
    - Creates four agent instances (one coordinator and three sub-agents)
    - Wraps sub-agents as `AgentTool` instances
    - Makes them available to the `Coordinator` as `agent_MAKDO_Analyzer`, `agent_MAKDO_Fixer`, and `agent_MAKDO_Slack_Bot`
5. **Detailed system prompts**: Each agent has comprehensive instructions defining responsibilities, report formats, and operational guidelines.

This single YAML file defines the entire multi-agent system. The `Coordinator` can now orchestrate complex workflows by invoking sub-agents as needed, with the LLM deciding when to call which agent based on the situation.

Notice how each sub-agent is specialized through three key mechanisms:

- **Tool access**: `Analyzer` and `Fixer` get A2A tools, `Slack_Bot` gets MCP tools
- **System prompts**: Detailed instructions encode domain expertise and operational procedures
- **Report formats**: Structured output templates ensure consistent, actionable reports

`Analyzer`'s system prompt includes detailed issue prioritization guidelines and report formats. `Fixer`'s prompt defines safety protocols and approval requirements. `Slack_Bot`'s prompt specifies message formatting and command processing.

This prompt-based specialization is more flexible than code-based approaches due to the following reasons:

- Behavior can be tuned without code changes
- Domain expertise is readable and auditable
- New capabilities can be added through prompt engineering
- The LLM applies reasoning to handle edge cases

Let's look at how these agents interact through AI-6's multi-agent architecture.

Agent interaction patterns

MAKDO demonstrates how AI-6's multi-agent architecture enables coordinated operations through tool-based delegation. Understanding this pattern is crucial to grasping how MAKDO agents work together.

LLM-driven agent coordination

In AI-6, sub-agents are exposed as tools to the parent agent. If you squint, then there is really just a single agent that the AI system is interacting with. The fact that this root agent has sub-agents is an internal detail, really. The LLM that powers the root agent just decides at each turn of the conversation whether it needs to call some tool or whether it already has enough information. The fact that some of the tools at its disposal are smart tools, which are themselves AI-6 agents or entirely separate AI systems via the A2A protocol, is not important.

There is no `Coordinator` agent class that calls methods of the `Analyzer` or `Fixer` classes. There are no such classes at all. The coordination logic is specified in natural language in the system prompts of the various agents, and the LLM's reasoning decides when to invoke which agent as a tool. This is an example of late-binding logic.

AI-6 implements this through the `AgentTool` class, which wraps sub-agents to make them callable as tools. The `AgentTool` implements the standard `Tool` interface, accepting a natural language message and returning the sub-agent's complete response. From the parent agent's perspective, invoking a sub-agent looks identical to calling any other tool. For a detailed explanation of `AgentTool` implementation, see *Chapter 8*.

When the `Coordinator` agent needs to analyze a cluster, the LLM generates a tool call like this:

```
{
  "name": "agent_MAKDO_Analyzer",
  "arguments": {
    "message": "Analyze the health of the kind-makdo-test cluster. Focus on pod
failures and provide specific remediation recommendations."
  }
}
```

The `AgentTool` class wraps the entire sub-agent interaction. It sends the message to the `Analyzer` agent, waits for its complete response (including any tool calls that `Analyzer` makes to k8s-ai), and returns the final result to the `Coordinator`.

This pattern provides several benefits:

- **Natural delegation**: The LLM decides when expertise is needed, just like a human coordinator
- **Encapsulation**: Each agent manages its own conversation history and tool usage
- **Composability**: Agents can be nested arbitrarily deep
- **Context preservation**: The coordinator doesn't need to track sub-agent implementation details

AI-6 comes with multiple built-in tools, but it can provide everything for every AI system. This is not a problem because MAKDO can extend AI-6 with additional tools.

Extending AI-6 with new tools

MAKDU interacts with the human team through Slack. AI-6 doesn't provide built-in Slack tools (although it has a Slack frontend). But AI-6 can be extended with additional tools that support its own tool interface or the MCP standard, so we implement a custom MCP server that exposes Slack operations as tools.

The `Slack_Bot` agent uses a custom MCP server built with FastMCP to handle all Slack communication. This server is located at `https://github.com/PacktPublishing/Design-Multi-Agent-AI-Systems-Using-MCP-and-A2A/tree/main/ch09/makdo/src/makdo/mcp_tools/slack.py`

The Slack MCP server is based on the FastMCP implementation of the official MCP Python SDK (`https://github.com/modelcontextprotocol/python-sdk`). The key features are as follows:

- **Decorator-based tools**: The `@mcp.tool()` decorator automatically registers functions as MCP tools
- **Token management**: Reads `AI6_BOT_TOKEN` from an environment, or `.env`, file
- **Simple HTTP calls**: Uses the `requests` library to call the Slack API directly
- **Error handling**: Returns success/failure messages that the LLM can understand
- **Channel normalization**: Automatically adds the # prefix if missing

This is much simpler than implementing a full JSON-RPC MCP server manually. FastMCP handles all the protocol details, letting you focus on the actual tool functionality.

When AI-6 loads this MCP server, the `Slack_Bot` agent automatically gets `slack_post_message` and `slack_list_channels` as available tools. The LLM can then call these tools naturally:

```
{
  "name": "slack_post_message",
  "arguments": {
    "channel": "makdo-devops",
    "text": "🚨 CRITICAL: 3 pods failing in kind-makdo-test cluster"
  }
}
```

Let's see how AI-6 discovers new tools, such as the `Slack_Bot` agent provided by MAKDO.

Tool discovery and assignment

AI-6 automatically discovers tools from multiple sources and assigns them to agents based on configuration. The tool_manager (https://github.com/PacktPublishing/Design-Multi-Agent-AI-Systems-using-MCP-and-A2A/blob/main/ch08/ai-six/py/backend/agent/tool_manager.py) module handles this process via the `get_tool_dict()` function. As you can see, it combines tools from various directories and servers, then filters them based on enabled/disabled lists:

```
def get_tool_dict(
    tool_config: ToolConfig, agent_configs: list[Config] = None
) -> dict[str, Tool]:
    """Get a dictionary of all available tools from various sources."""
    tools: list[Tool] = []

    # 1. Discover AI-6 native tools from all directories
    for tools_dir in tool_config.tools_dirs:
        native_tools = _discover_native_tools(tools_dir)
        tools.extend(native_tools)

    # 2. Discover local MCP tools from all directories
    for mcp_tools_dir in tool_config.mcp_tools_dirs:
        local_mcp_tools = _discover_local_mcp_tools(mcp_tools_dir)
        tools.extend(local_mcp_tools)

    # 3. Get tools from A2A servers
    if tool_config.a2a_servers:
        a2a_tools = _get_a2a_tools(tool_config.a2a_servers)
        tools.extend(a2a_tools)

    # 4. Create agent tools if agent configs provided
    if agent_configs:
        agent_tools = _create_agent_tools(agent_configs)
        tools.extend(agent_tools)

    # 5. Filter tools based on enabled/disabled configuration
    tools = _filter_tools(tools, tool_config.enabled_tools,
tool_config.disabled_tools)

    return {tool.name: tool for tool in tools}
```

Here is a tool breakdown of each agent in MAKDO:

- The `Coordinator` agent ends up with the following:
    - Memory tools
    - Agent tools: `agent_MAKDO_Analyzer`, `agent_MAKDO_Fixer`, and `agent_MAKDO_Slack_Bot`
- `Analyzer` and `Fixer` each get the following:
    - A2A tools from the k8s-ai server (`kind-makdo-test_*` tools for kubectl operations)
    - Memory tools
- `Slack_Bot` gets the following:
    - MCP tools from `src/makdo/mcp_tools/slack.py` (`slack_post_message` and `slack_list_channels`)
    - Memory tools (inherited)

Context sharing and state management

In AI-6's multi-agent architecture, there is no direct context sharing between agents. Each AI-6 agent has its own model and context. It can communicate with other agents via tool calls and responses only.

Here are some common approaches for context sharing:

- **Message passing**: When the `Coordinator` agent calls a sub-agent, it includes relevant context in the message. Here is an example:

```
{
  "name": "agent_MAKDO_Fixer",
  "arguments": {
    "message": "Execute remediation for kind-makdo-test cluster. The
Analyzer identified 3 failing pods due to image pull
errors. Please attempt to restart the affected pods and verify they come up
successfully."
  }
}
```

- **Session isolation**: Each agent maintains its own session with conversation history. See `https://github.com/PacktPublishing/Design-Multi-Agent-AI-Systems-Using-MCP-and-A2A/tree/main/ch08/ai-six/py/ai_six/agent/agent.py`:

```
self.session_manager = SessionManager(config.memory_dir)
self.session = self._create_new_session(config.memory_dir)
```

- **Return values**: Sub-agents return complete responses that the `Coordinator` agent incorporates into its own context:

```
Coordinator Session:
- User: "Check cluster health"
- Assistant: [calls agent_MAKDO_Analyzer tool]
- Tool Result: "Analysis complete. Found 3 failing pods..."
- Assistant: "Based on analysis, we have critical
issues. Let me notify the team..."
```

This session-based approach ensures context isolation while enabling coordinated operations through explicit message passing. Each agent's conversation history remains independent, preventing context pollution and allowing agents to be invoked multiple times with different contexts.

Now that we have covered context sharing and state management, let's look at the roles and responsibilities of each MAKDO agent.

Defining roles and responsibilities for specialized agents

The `coordinator.yaml` configuration shown previously defines MAKDO's four-agent architecture. This section examines the design rationale: why these specific role boundaries were chosen, what trade-offs were made, and how this architecture can be extended.

From DevOps workflows to agent architecture

MAKDO's agent design emerged from analyzing typical Kubernetes incident response workflows. Here's what happens in the traditional manual process:

1. **Alert triggers**: Operator receives notification
2. **Diagnosis**: Operator runs kubectl commands to investigate
3. **Decision**: Operator determines appropriate fix
4. **Remediation**: Operator applies changes (with caution)

5. **Communication**: Operator updates the team in Slack
6. **Verification**: Operator confirms that fix worked

This translates directly to MAKDO's agent roles:

- **Detection and diagnosis** are done by the `Analyzer` agent, which uses k8s-ai to investigate the cluster state, categorize issues, and recommend fixes
- **Remediation** is done by the `Fixer` agent, which executes safe changes and requires approval for destructive operations
- **Communication** is done by the `Slack_Bot` agent, which posts updates and handles approval workflows
- **Coordination** is done by the `Coordinator` agent, which orchestrates the workflow and makes high-level decisions

This mapping preserves the natural workflow structure while distributing responsibilities across specialized agents.

Why four agents instead of one?

As the original simple k8s-ai system from *Chapter 3* demonstrated, a single agent can do all of the preceding (well, except the Slack communication). So, why split MAKDO into four agents? There are several reasons:

- **Tool isolation**: `Analyzer` shouldn't have write access to clusters (read-only diagnostics). Separating `Analyzer`/`Fixer` enforces this through tool configuration. `Analyzer` can perform its job using only read-only tools, such as `get pods` and `get deployments`. `Fixer` needs to modify configurations, so it is appropriate to provide access to tools such as `apply manifest`.
- **Prompt clarity**: Each agent has a focused system prompt (~50 lines) versus one massive prompt (~200 lines) trying to cover everything.
- **Independent testing**: It can test diagnostic accuracy (`Analyzer`) separately from remediation safety (`Fixer`).
- **Parallel evolution**: It can improve diagnostic capabilities without risking changes to remediation logic.

Let's dive deeper, specifically into the split of the analyzer and fixer.

Why separate the analyzer and fixer?

This was the most debated design decision. Both agents use the same k8s-ai A2A tools, so why not combine them? There are three main reasons:

- **Safety through role separation**:
    - `Analyzer`'s prompt: "NEVER make changes, only diagnose."
      Allows strong security by providing the analyzer with read-only credentials (beyond relying on the prompt) in the future
    - `Fixer`'s prompt: "Operations requiring approval: delete, scale down, restart..."
      Clear mental model: Analysis is safe, remediation requires caution
- **Different failure modes**:
    - **Analyzer failure**: The analyzer may produce incomplete or incorrect diagnoses, but it never changes the cluster state, so a bad analysis has no direct impact on production.
    - **Fixer failure**: The fixer can execute the wrong remediation and directly modify live resources, so mistakes here can cause outages or data loss if guardrails are weak.
    - Separate agents let you tune reliability independently from action authority. For example, run a fast-but-lower-accuracy analyzer (90% recall) for triage while restricting high-risk fixers to 99.9% accuracy with human approval.
- **Real-world access control patterns**: Many organizations give the DevOps team read-only access to production to eliminate the risk of breaking the production environment during development. Only SREs or on-call engineers have write access in case a hot fix or an emergency action is needed. MAKDO's split mirrors this access pattern.

The downside is the coordination overhead, but it's worth it for the safety and clarity.

Why separate Slack_Bot?

The `Coordinator` agent could post to Slack directly. But the communication logic can become much more complicated with multiple communication channels, approval workflows, formatting rules, and so on. `Slack_Bot` can evolve independently and encapsulate this complexity, while the `Coordinator` agent focuses on coordination.

Tool access boundaries

Each agent's tool configuration provides exactly the tools it needs to perform its job. That makes it much easier for agents to focus on their role and reduce the possibility of misusing tools because the surface area is smaller:

```
# Coordinator: Pure orchestrator, no operational tools beyond sub-agents
tools_dirs: [ "/path/to/memory" ] # Only memory for state tracking

# Analyzer/Fixer: Kubernetes access via A2A
a2a_servers: [ { "url": "http://localhost:9999" } ]  # Same tools, different
prompts

# Slack_Bot: Communication tools via MCP
mcp_tools_dirs: [ "src/makdo/mcp_tools" ]  # Only Slack access
```

This configuration-based permission model also means that changing agent capabilities requires only YAML edits, not code changes.

Extending the architecture

MAKDO's design supports extension through additional specialized agents. Here, we will discuss how to add new capabilities. Let's look at an example of adding a security scanner agent.

To add vulnerability scanning and security policy enforcement, take the following steps:

1. Define the new agent in `coordinator.yaml`:

```
agents:
  - name: "MAKDO_Security_Scanner"
    description: "Security vulnerability and compliance scanning agent"
    a2a_servers:
      - name: "kind-makdo-test"
        url: "http://localhost:9999"
    system_prompt: |
      You are the MAKDO Security Scanner.

      Responsibilities:
      - Scan container images for known vulnerabilities
      - Check pod security contexts
      - Verify network policies are in place
      - Report security findings to Coordinator
```

```
Use k8s-ai tools to inspect cluster resources.
Report findings in severity-ranked format.
```

2. Update the `Coordinator` agent's prompt to include the new agent:

```
Available agents:
  - agent_MAKDO_Analyzer
  - agent_MAKDO_Fixer
  - agent_MAKDO_Slack_Bot
  - agent_MAKDO_Security_Scanner  # New

Workflow: After Analyzer identifies issues, also call Security_Scanner
  to check for security implications before Fixer proceeds.
```

   Note that we can also add the security scanner as a sub-agent of `Analyzer` if we consider security scanning a sub-area of cluster analysis.

3. **No code changes needed**: AI-6 automatically discovers the new agent and exposes it as a tool.

Let's look at some of the important patterns that MAKDO employs.

Key design patterns

MAKDO's architecture demonstrates several patterns applicable to other multi-agent systems:

- **Workflow-driven decomposition**: Map agents to workflow stages, not technologies
- **Permission through configuration**: Tool access defines what agents can do
- **Prompts as policy**: Encode operational rules in the system prompts of the agents
- **Protocol encapsulation**: AI-6 handles specific protocols (A2A and MCP) so you don't have to
- **Extensibility by design**: Adding capabilities means adding tools and agents

The next section examines the implementation details of creating and deploying these agents using AI-6's configuration system.

Implementing the agents

With our agent roles defined and their responsibilities clearly outlined, we now turn to implementation. MAKDO follows a configuration-driven approach where the entire multi-agent system is defined through YAML configuration files rather than custom code. This approach leverages AI-6's powerful agent framework to automatically instantiate agents, discover tools, and establish communication channels.

Configuration-driven agent implementation

Traditional multi-agent systems often require extensive custom code to initialize agents, configure their tools, and establish inter-agent communication. MAKDO takes a different approach: the entire system is defined in a single coordinator configuration file with inline sub-agent definitions.

MAKDO's architecture uses one primary configuration file (`coordinator.yaml`) that defines the following:

- **The coordinator agent**: The top-level orchestrator with its system prompt and tool access
- **All sub-agents inline**: `Analyzer`, `Fixer`, and `Slack_Bot` are defined within the coordinator config
- **Tool assignments**: Each agent's tool access is specified through `tools_dirs`, `mcp_tools_dirs`, and `a2a_servers`
- **Communication protocols**: Implicit through AI-6's `AgentTool` pattern

This single-file approach has several advantages:

- **Atomic deployment**: The entire system configuration is in one place
- **Clear hierarchy**: Parent-child relationships are explicit
- **No file synchronization issues**: No risk of separate config files getting out of sync
- **Easier version control**: One file to track system changes

The MAKDO main entry point implements the health check loop and session management. Let's examine the key components:

1. **Configuration loading**: AI-6's `Config.from_file()` reads the `coordinator.yaml` file and automatically creates all agents:

```
from ai_six.agent.agent import Agent
from ai_six.agent.config import Config
```

```
def create_coordinator_config() -> Config:
    """Create coordinator agent config with sub-agents."""
    return Config.from_file("src/makdo/agents/coordinator.yaml")
```

This single line loads the Coordinator agent and instantiates all inline sub-agents as agent tools.

2. **Health check loop**: The Coordinator agent runs continuously, sending periodic health check requests:

```
def start_coordinator(coordinator: Agent, config: Dict[str, Any]):
    """Start the coordinator with health check loop."""
    logger = logging.getLogger("makdo")

    # Get check interval from environment or config (default: 60s)
    check_interval = int(os.getenv("MAKDO_CHECK_INTERVAL",
                                   config.get("monitoring",
{}).get("check_interval", 60)))

    logger.info(f"Starting health check loop (interval: {check_interval}
s)")

    try:
        while True:
            try:
                # Request health check from coordinator
                logger.info("🔍 Initiating cluster health check...")

                prompt = (
                    "Perform a comprehensive health check across all
registered clusters. "
                    "Use the Analyzer agent to identify any issues, then
use the Slack Bot agent "
                    "to report findings to the #makdo-devops channel. "
                    "If critical issues are found, use the Fixer agent to
attempt remediation."
                )

                response = coordinator.send_message(prompt)
```

```
                logger.info(f"✅ Health check completed: {response[:
200]}...")
```

The loop sends a natural language prompt describing the desired workflow. The LLM orchestrates the sub-agents based on this prompt. Note that MAKDO operates autonomously here. There is no human-controlled request-response flow here like in chat interfaces. However, humans can still monitor and intervene via Slack. The response from the `Coordinator` agent is just logged for auditing.

3. **Session management**: After each health check, MAKDO clears conversation history to prevent context overflow:

```
# CRITICAL: Clear session history to prevent context overflow
# Keep only system message - each health check cycle is independent
if len(coordinator.session.messages) > 3:
    logger.info(
        f"Clearing old messages (
            {len(coordinator.session.messages)} messages)"
        )
    system_message = coordinator.session.messages[0]
        if coordinator.session.messages else None
    coordinator.session.messages.clear()
    if system_message:
        coordinator.session.messages.append(system_message)
    logger.info(
        f"Session reset to {len(coordinator.session.messages)} message")

except Exception as e:
logger.error(f"Error during health check cycle: {e}")

# Wait before next check
time.sleep(check_interval)
```

This prevents the context window from filling up with old health checks. Each cycle is treated as independent. If long-term memory is needed, it can be implemented via external storage such as a database.

4. **Main entry point**: The main function ties everything together:

```
def main():
    """Main entry point - note: synchronous, not async."""
```

```
    load_dotenv()
    config = load_config()
    setup_logging(config)

    logger = logging.getLogger("makdo")
    logger.info("Starting MAKDO - Multi-Agent Kubernetes DevOps System")

    # Create coordinator with inline sub-agents
    coordinator = Agent(create_coordinator_config())
    logger.info("Coordinator and sub-agents created successfully")

    # Start the coordinator (runs health check loop)
    start_coordinator(coordinator, config)


if __name__ == "__main__":
    exit(main())  # Note: synchronous call, not asyncio.run()
```

The code is in `src/makdo/main.py` (`https://github.com/PacktPublishing/Design-Multi-Agent-AI-Systems-Using-MCP-and-A2A/tree/main/ch09/makdo/src/makdo/main.py`). Key features of this implementation include the following:

- **Synchronous architecture**: Uses `time.sleep()` instead of `asyncio` to avoid event loop conflicts with MCP tools
- **Session management**: Clears old messages after each health check cycle to prevent context overflow (128k token limit) and message ordering errors
- **Health check loop**: Continuously monitors clusters at configurable intervals

Notice what's *not* in this code:

- No manual agent instantiation for sub-agents
- No tool discovery or registration logic
- No inter-agent communication setup
- No MCP or A2A client configuration

All of this is handled automatically by AI-6 based on the coordinator configuration file. This is the value proposition of the AI-6 framework, which is reliably and silently taking care of the complex details on behalf of MAKDO.

Tool discovery and assignment

AI-6's tool manager handles automatic tool discovery from multiple sources. For MAKDO, here's how tools are assigned to each agent:

- **Coordinator agent**:

```
# Only memory tools - pure orchestrator
tools_dirs: [ "/Users/gigi/git/ai-six/py/ai_six/tools/memory" ]
mcp_tools_dirs: [ "/Users/gigi/git/ai-six/py/ai_six/mcp_tools" ]
memory_dir: "data/memory"

# NO a2a_servers - delegates to Analyzer/Fixer for k8s operations
# NO Slack tools - delegates to Slack_Bot for communications
```

- **Analyzer agent (inline)**:

```
agents:
  - name: "MAKDO_Analyzer"
    description: "Cluster health assessment agent"
    default_model_id: "gpt-4o"
    # Has A2A access to k8s-ai server
    a2a_servers:
      - name: "kind-makdo-test"
        url: "http://localhost:9999"
        timeout: 30.0
        api_key: "test-key"
```

- **Fixer agent (inline)**:

```
  - name: "MAKDO_Fixer"
    description: "Safe cluster modification agent"
    default_model_id: "gpt-4o"
    # Has A2A access to k8s-ai server
    a2a_servers:
      - name: "kind-makdo-test"
        url: "http://localhost:9999"
```

```
        timeout: 30.0
        api_key: "test-key"
```

- **Slack_Bot agent (inline):**

```
  - name: "MAKDO_Slack_Bot"
    description: "User communication agent"
    default_model_id: "gpt-4o"
    tools_dirs: [ ]
    # Has MCP access to local Slack tools
    mcp_tools_dirs: [ "src/makdo/mcp_tools" ]
```

Agents have their own tools, but they also have their own independent context. This is the principle of session isolation.

Session isolation

Each agent in MAKDO maintains its own conversation session with an isolated message history. When the `Coordinator` agent calls `agent_MAKDO_Analyzer`, `Analyzer` doesn't see the coordinator's conversation history. It starts with a fresh context containing only the following:

- Its own system prompt
- The message from the coordinator
- Its own tool catalog

This session isolation, however, has important implications. Here are the benefits:

- **Reduced token usage**: Sub-agents don't carry the full parent conversation context
- **Focused processing**: Each agent reasons only about its specific task and its relevant context (tool calls and responses)
- **Parallel execution potential**: Independent sessions can run concurrently, especially for A2A agents
- **Cleaner separation of concerns**: Agents can't accidentally leak information between contexts

The following are the trade-offs:

- **Context passing required**: The parent must explicitly include relevant context in messages to sub-agents

- **No shared memory by default**: Agents don't automatically share state (though can use memory tools)
- **Increased message verbosity**: Parents may need to repeat context in multiple sub-agent calls

For MAKDO, this isolation is beneficial. When the `Coordinator` agent asks `Analyzer` to assess cluster health, `Analyzer` doesn't need to know about previous conversations with `Fixer` or `Slack_Bot`. It focuses solely on the current cluster assessment request.

Configuration over code

The configuration-driven approach means you can completely change MAKDO's behavior without touching Python code:

- **Add new agents**: Add entries to the agents list
- **Change tool access**: Modify `tools_dirs`, `mcp_tools_dirs`, `a2a_servers`, or `agents` for any agent
- **Adjust agent behavior**: Update system prompts
- **Switch LLM models**: Change `default_model_id`
- **Connect to different remote AI systems**: Update A2A server URLs

Key takeaways

MAKDO's implementation demonstrates several important patterns for building multi-agent systems:

- **Configuration drives architecture**: Define your system structure in YAML, not code
- **Framework automation**: Let AI-6 handle agent instantiation, tool discovery, and communication
- **Tool abstraction**: Sub-agents appear as tools to their parents through the `AgentTool` class
- **Session isolation**: Each agent maintains an independent conversation state
- **Principle of least privilege**: Each agent gets only the tools it needs
- **Extensibility through configuration**: Add capabilities by editing YAML, not writing code

This approach dramatically reduces the complexity of building and maintaining multi-agent systems. The entire MAKDO implementation is less than 150 lines of Python code, with the vast majority being logging and error handling. The real implementation lives in the configuration files, making the system easy to understand, modify, and extend. But it's important to have strong tooling and schema validation for the configuration.

Orchestrating the team with a manager agent

The `Coordinator` agent in MAKDO serves as the central orchestrator, managing the workflow across specialized agents while maintaining awareness of system state and operational priorities. Unlike traditional orchestration systems that rely on explicit workflow definitions and state machines, MAKDO's `Coordinator` uses LLM reasoning to dynamically coordinate agent activities based on the situation.

The `Coordinator` agent's system prompt provides guidance, but the LLM determines the specific sequence of agent invocations based on context.

Dynamic workflow execution

Traditional workflow engines require predefined workflows such as the following:

```
detect_issue → analyze_issue → fix_issue → notify_humans
```

MAKDO's `Coordinator` instead receives high-level guidance in English in its system prompt:

```
Your primary responsibilities:
1. Monitor multiple Kubernetes clusters for health and issues
2. Coordinate between the Analyzer, Fixer, and Slack agents
3. Make decisions on task prioritization and escalation
4. Maintain awareness of ongoing operations across all clusters
```

The LLM then determines the appropriate agent invocation sequence based on the situation. Let's explore a couple of scenario-based examples:

```
Scenario 1: Periodic health check request
MAKDO: Invoke cooridnator every minute asking to "Check the health of kind-makdo-
test cluster"
Coordinator:
1. Calls the MAKDO_Analyzer agent with message "Analyze kind-makdo-test cluster
health"
2. Receives detailed report
3. Calls MAKDO_Slack_Bot agent to post results

Scenario 2: Critical issue detected
User: "Production cluster has failing pods"
Coordinator:
1. Calls agent_MAKDO_Analyzer for detailed diagnostics
```

```
2. Evaluates severity from Analyzer report
3. Calls agent_MAKDO_Fixer to remediate issues
4. Calls agent_MAKDO_Slack_Bot to notify team of analysis and remediation results
```

The `Coordinator` agent adapts its workflow based on `Analyzer`'s findings, the severity of issues, and operational policies encoded in its system prompt. If human approval is needed, MAKDO will wait for approval from `Slack_Bot` before invoking the `Fixer` agent.

Decision points and branching

The `Coordinator` agent's system prompt includes decision-making guidelines that the LLM applies:

```
Decision-making guidelines:
- Always assess cluster health before making changes
- Prioritize critical issues (pods failing, services down) over warnings
- Require human approval for destructive operations (delete, scale down)
- Coordinate operations to avoid conflicts between clusters
- Escalate to humans when automated fixes fail or are uncertain
- ALWAYS post full detailed results to Slack for human visibility
```

These guidelines create decision points where the LLM chooses different paths. Here are a few examples.

Example 1: safe versus destructive operations

`Analyzer` reports "3 pods stuck in `CrashLoopBackOff`, may need deletion."

The LLM reasoning includes the following:

- Deletion is destructive (per guidelines)
- Requires human approval (per guidelines)
- Should notify humans first (per guidelines)

The execution path is as follows:

```
1. agent_MAKDO_Slack_Bot: "Report analysis and request approval"
2. Wait for human response
3. If approved: agent_MAKDO_Fixer with "delete pods"
4. agent_MAKDO_Slack_Bot: "Report remediation results"
```

Example 2: auto-remediation versus escalation

`Analyzer` reports "2 pods need restart, low-risk operation."

The LLM reasoning is as follows:

- Restart is a safe operation (not in destructive list)
- No approval needed (per `Fixer`'s safe operations list)
- Can proceed directly (per guidelines)

The execution path is as follows:

```
1. agent_MAKDO_Fixer: "Restart the 2 identified pods"
2. agent_MAKDO_Slack_Bot: "Report both analysis and remediation results"
```

This dynamic decision-making is more flexible than hardcoded workflows while still following operational policies.

Handling complex multi-step operations

Some operational scenarios require multiple rounds of agent interaction, state tracking, and conditional logic. MAKDO's `Coordinator` handles these through conversational context and LLM reasoning.

Multi-cluster coordination

When managing multiple clusters, the `Coordinator` agent must sequence operations to avoid conflicts:

```
User: "Check health of all production clusters and fix any issues"
Coordinator execution:
1. For each cluster (production-east, production-west, production-central):
   a. agent_MAKDO_Analyzer: "Analyze [cluster] health"
   b. Evaluate if fixes needed
   c. If needed: agent_MAKDO_Fixer: "Fix issues in [cluster]"
   d. agent_MAKDO_Slack_Bot: "Post results for [cluster]"
2. Aggregate results across clusters
3. agent_MAKDO_Slack_Bot: "Post summary of all cluster operations"
```

The `Coordinator` agent maintains awareness of which clusters have been processed through its conversation context. The LLM tracks state implicitly through the message history. If that becomes too complicated, MAKDO can evolve to have a meta-coordinator as the root agent that launches multiple coordinator agents, each with its own `Analyzer`, `Fixer`, and `Slack_Bot`.

Conditional remediation

Some fixes depend on the results of previous operations:

```
Scenario: Image pull failures might require different remediation strategies

Coordinator logic:
1. agent_MAKDO_Analyzer: "Diagnose image pull failure"
2. If Analyzer reports: "Image not found in registry"
   → agent_MAKDO_Slack_Bot: "Escalate - invalid image reference"
3. If Analyzer reports: "Registry authentication failed"
   → agent_MAKDO_Fixer: "Apply image pull secrets"
   → agent_MAKDO_Analyzer: "Verify pods now pulling successfully"
4. If Analyzer reports: "Registry temporarily unavailable"
   → Schedule retry after delay
   → agent_MAKDO_Slack_Bot: "Notify team of temporary issue"
```

This conditional logic emerges from the LLM's reasoning about `Analyzer`'s reports, not from explicit `if/else` statements in code.

Retry and verification loops

The `Coordinator` agent can implement retry logic when operations fail:

```
Fixer reports: "Failed to restart pod, still in error state"

Coordinator reasoning:
- Initial fix attempt failed (per Fixer report)
- Guidelines say "escalate when automated fixes fail"
- Should verify current state before escalating

Execution:
1. agent_MAKDO_Analyzer: "Re-analyze the specific failing pod"
2. Evaluate new diagnostic information
3. Decide: Try alternative fix OR escalate to humans
4. agent_MAKDO_Slack_Bot: "Report situation and decision"
```

Retries can help when there are transient problems, but sometimes the system might encounter persistent failures, and it needs to be able to handle them.

Error handling and recovery

MAKDO's agents can encounter various failure modes. The `Coordinator` agent's system prompt includes implicit error-handling guidance that the LLM applies.

Agent communication failures

If a sub-agent invocation fails (timeout, exception, etc.), the `AgentTool` class will return an error message that `Coordinator` receives as a tool result:

```
Tool: agent_MAKDO_Analyzer
Error: "Timeout connecting to k8s-ai server"

Coordinator response (guided by system prompt):
1. Recognize communication failure
2. agent_MAKDO_Slack_Bot: "Alert - cannot reach cluster analysis service"
3. Decide: Retry OR escalate OR use cached data
```

The LLM interprets the error and decides on an appropriate recovery strategy based on context.

Partial failures

When some operations succeed while others fail, the `Coordinator` agent tracks partial progress:

```
Fixer reports: "Restarted 5 of 7 failing
pods. 2 pods remain in error state due to resource constraints."

Coordinator response:
1. Recognize partial success (5/7 completed)
2. Analyze remaining issues (resource constraints)
3. agent_MAKDO_Analyzer: "Check cluster resource availability"
4. Based on analysis, decide next steps:
   - Scale up nodes (if resource exhaustion)
   - Adjust pod resource requests (if over-provisioned)
   - Escalate to humans (if capacity limits reached)
5. agent_MAKDO_Slack_Bot: "Report partial success and next steps"
```

One of the most complicated failures is cascading failures.

Cascading failures

The Coordinator agent must handle scenarios where fixing one issue reveals or causes other issues:

```
Initial issue: 3 pods failing
After fix attempt: 5 pods now failing

Coordinator reasoning:
- Situation worsened (3 → 5 pods failing)
- Applied fix may have caused new issues
- Should halt automated remediation
- Requires human investigation

Execution:
1. agent_MAKDO_Slack_Bot: "CRITICAL: Remediation caused additional failures.
Halting automation."
2. agent_MAKDO_Analyzer: "Full cluster diagnostic to identify root cause"
3. agent_MAKDO_Slack_Bot: "Post detailed diagnostic results"
4. Wait for human guidance before proceeding
```

This defensive approach prevents automation from making situations worse.

State management and coordination

MAKDO's coordinator maintains operational state through conversation context and memory tools, enabling awareness of ongoing operations and historical context.

The Coordinator agent's message history serves as its working memory during a single health check cycle.

The LLM accesses this context to answer follow-up requests or questions from users in Slack and to maintain awareness of ongoing operations while the analyzer and the fixer operate. Note that the coordinator may call the analyzer and the fixer multiple times in a single health check cycle.

Memory tools for long-term state

For a state that needs to persist across conversation sessions, MAKDO uses AI-6's memory tools:

```
# Coordinator configuration
tools_dirs: [ "/Users/gigi/git/ai-six/py/ai_six/tools/memory" ]
memory_dir: "data/memory"
```

```
The Coordinator agent can save and retrieve structured information:
# Save cluster state after operations
Tool: save_memory
Arguments:
  key: "production-east-last-check"
  value: {
    "timestamp": "2024-10-06T14:30:00Z",
    "status": "degraded",
    "issues": 3,
    "fixed": 2,
    "pending_approval": ["pod-delete-operation-047"]
  }

# Later retrieve state
Tool: retrieve_memory
Arguments:
  key: "production-east-last-check"
Result: [saved state object]
```

This enables the Coordinator agent to maintain awareness across multiple conversation sessions and agent restarts.

Avoiding duplicate operations

The Coordinator can use memory to track recent operations and avoid duplication:

```
User: "Fix production-east issues"

Coordinator checks memory:
Tool: retrieve_memory
Arguments:
  key: "recent-operations"
Result: "production-east remediation completed 5 minutes ago"

Coordinator response:
"Production-east was just remediated 5 minutes ago. Let me verify current status
instead."

Execution:
agent_MAKDO_Analyzer: "Quick health check of production-east"
```

Let's discuss different modes of orchestration.

Proactive versus reactive orchestration

MAKDO's `Coordinator` can operate in both reactive (responding to requests) and proactive (autonomous monitoring) modes.

Reactive mode – user-initiated operations

In reactive mode, the `Coordinator` agent responds to explicit user requests:

```
User: "Check cluster health"
→ Coordinator analyzes and reports

User: "Fix the failing pods"
→ Coordinator remediates and reports

User: "What's the status of production-west?"
→ Coordinator queries state and responds
```

This mode gives humans direct control over when and how operations occur.

Proactive mode – autonomous monitoring

In proactive mode, the `Coordinator` agent can initiate operations based on schedules or triggers. This is the current operating mode of MAKDO:

```
# Periodic scheduled check
Every minutes:
1. agent_MAKDO_Analyzer: "Health check all registered clusters"
2. If issues found:
   a. Categorize by severity (CRITICAL, WARNING, INFO)
   b. For CRITICAL: Immediate remediation workflow
   c. For WARNING: Schedule remediation, notify humans
   d. For INFO: Log and include in next summary report
3. agent_MAKDO_Slack_Bot: "Post status update if changes detected"
```

This mode is more sophisticated but requires a lot of trust since the `Coordinator` agent operates autonomously.

Hybrid approach – event-driven coordination

A hybrid approach combines reactive and proactive patterns:

```
Normal operation:
- Proactive monitoring every 5 minutes
```

```
  - Reactive response to cluster events or alerts
  - Automatic remediation of routine issues
  - Slack notifications for significant events

When critical issue detected:
  - Notify humans immediately
  - Wait for approval before major operations
  - Provide detailed status updates on request
```

Most real-world systems will utilize the hybrid approach. Now, let's turn our attention to the critical aspect of adding a human to the loop.

Integrating human feedback and control channels

While AI agents can automate many DevOps tasks, human oversight remains essential for strategic decisions, complex troubleshooting, and maintaining operational control. MAKDO integrates Slack as its primary human-AI interface, enabling real-time notifications, status updates, and approval workflows. Note that since all communication goes through an agent, it is easy to replace Slack with email or any other communication tool that has an API, as well as using multiple communication mechanisms concurrently.

The human-AI interface challenge

Effective human-AI collaboration in DevOps requires careful interface design that balances automation efficiency with human control. The interface must do the following:

- **Provide visibility**: Humans need complete transparency into what agents are doing
- **Enable control**: Humans must be able to approve, reject, or modify agent actions, as well as pausing or canceling ongoing operations
- **Minimize interruption**: Don't overwhelm humans with routine notifications
- **Support natural communication**: Use familiar tools and communication patterns
- **Maintain context**: Preserve conversation history and operational context

MAKDO addresses these requirements through a dedicated `Slack_Bot` agent that acts as the communication bridge between the AI system and human operators.

The Slack_Bot agent architecture

The `Slack_Bot` agent is a specialized communication agent with access to Slack via MCP tools. Unlike the `Analyzer` and `Fixer` agents that use A2A for Kubernetes operations, `Slack_Bot` uses the MCP to interact with Slack's API.

From the `coordinator.yaml` file shown earlier, the `Slack_Bot` configuration is as follows:

```
agents:
  - name: "MAKDO_Slack_Bot"
    description: "User communication and notification interface agent"
    default_model_id: "gpt-4o"
    tools_dirs: [ ]
    # Slack_Bot uses local MCP server for Slack communication
    mcp_tools_dirs: [ "src/makdo/mcp_tools" ]
    system_prompt: |
      You are the MAKDO Slack Bot, the primary interface between the MAKDO system
and human users.

      Your primary responsibilities:
      1. Send alerts and notifications to the designated Slack channel (#makdo-
devops)
      2. Parse and process user commands from Slack messages
      3. Provide status updates and operation summaries
      4. Format technical information for human-readable display
      5. Handle approval requests for critical operations

      Message types and formatting:
      🚨 CRITICAL: Immediate attention required
    ⚠ WARNING: Issue needs attention
      i  INFO: Status update or information
      ✅ SUCCESS: Operation completed successfully
      ❌ FAILED: Operation failed
      ⏳ PENDING: Operation in progress
```

The key configuration element is `mcp_tools_dirs: ["src/makdo/mcp_tools"]`, which tells AI-6 to discover MCP servers in that directory.

Building a custom MCP server with FastMCP

MAKDO uses a custom MCP server for Slack integration built with the FastMCP library as discussed earlier. This approach is significantly simpler than implementing the full MCP protocol manually.

The FastMCP Slack server

The Slack MCP server implementation shows how FastMCP simplifies protocol handling. Let's examine the key components of `src/makdo/mcp_tools/slack.py` (`https://github.com/PacktPublishing/Design-Multi-Agent-AI-Systems-Using-MCP-and-A2A/tree/main/ch09/makdo/src/makdo/mcp_tools/slack.py`):

1. **Server initialization and token loading**: FastMCP requires just one line to create an MCP server, with token management handling both environment variables and `.env` files:

```
import os
import requests
from pathlib import Path
from mcp.server.fastmcp import FastMCP

# Initialize FastMCP server
mcp = FastMCP("Slack Tools", "")

# Get bot token from environment or .env file
bot_token = os.getenv('AI6_BOT_TOKEN')

if not bot_token:
    # Navigate from .../makdo/src/makdo/mcp_tools/slack.py to .../
makdo/.env
    makdo_root = \
        Path(__file__).resolve().parent.parent.parent.parent
    env_file = makdo_root / '.env'

    if env_file.exists():
        with open(env_file) as f:
            for line in f:
                if line.startswith('AI6_BOT_TOKEN='):
                    bot_token = line.split('=', 1)[1].strip()
                    break
```

This is a MAKDO-specific tool, so it's OK to embed MKADO-specific configuration such as the `.env` file path.

2. **Posting messages tool**: The `@mcp.tool()` decorator automatically registers the function as an MCP tool. FastMCP handles all protocol details:

```
@mcp.tool()
def slack_post_message(channel: str, text: str) -> str:
    """Post a message to a Slack channel"""

    # Normalize channel name (add # prefix if missing)
    if not channel.startswith('#'):
        channel = f'#{channel}'

    # Call Slack API directly with simple requests library
    url = 'https://slack.com/api/chat.postMessage'
    headers = {'Authorization': f'Bearer {bot_token}'}
    data = {'channel': channel, 'text': text}

    response = requests.post(
        url, headers=headers, json=data, timeout=10)
    result = response.json()

    # Return LLM-friendly success/error messages
    if result.get('ok'):
        return f"✅ Message posted to {channel}"
    else:
        return f"❌ Failed to post: {result.get('error', 'unknown_error')}"
```

Note that this tool interacts with the Slack API using direct HTTP calls with the `requests` library. This is different from the Slack frontend of AI-6 that uses the official Slack SDK and the `slack_bot` library. For MAKDO, direct API calls are simpler and sufficient without unnecessary external dependencies.

3. **Listing channels tool**: A second tool provides channel discovery, following the same decorator pattern:

```
@mcp.tool()
def slack_list_channels() -> str:
    """List all channels in the workspace"""

    url = 'https://slack.com/api/conversations.list'
    headers = {'Authorization': f'Bearer {bot_token}'}
```

```
        response = requests.get(url, headers=headers, timeout=10)
        result = response.json()

        if result.get('ok'):
            channels = result.get('channels', [])
            return '\n'.join([f"#{ch['name']}" for ch in channels])
        else:
            return f"❌ Failed to list channels: {result.get('error')}"
```

4. **Server entry point**: Running the script starts the MCP server, making both tools available to AI-6:

```
if __name__ == '__main__':
    mcp.run()
```

Based on this, we see that FastMCP simplifies MCP server creation through several design choices and key features:

- **Decorator-based registration**: The `@mcp.tool()` decorator automatically registers functions as MCP tools. No manual JSON-RPC handling is required.
- **Automatic type inference**: FastMCP extracts parameter types and descriptions from function signatures and docstrings.
- **Protocol handling**: FastMCP manages all MCP protocol details (initialization, tool listing, and tool execution).

Compare this to a manual MCP implementation, which would require the following:

- JSON-RPC message parsing
- Protocol version negotiation
- Tool schema generation
- Request/response handling
- Error serialization

FastMCP handles all of this automatically, letting you focus on the actual tool functionality.

The Slack server reads the bot token from environment variables or a `.env` file:

```
bot_token = os.getenv('AI6_BOT_TOKEN')

if not bot_token:
    # Try loading from .env file
```

```
    env_file = makdo_root / '.env'
    if env_file.exists():
# Parse .env file for AI6_BOT_TOKEN
```

This allows flexible deployment of environment variables in production and .env files for development.

Both tools return user-friendly error messages that the LLM can understand:

```
if result.get('ok'):
    return f"✅ Message posted to {channel}"
else:
    error = result.get('error', 'unknown_error')
    return f"❌ Failed to post to {channel}: {error}"
```

When the Slack_Bot agent receives these responses, it can reason about failures and take appropriate action (retry, escalate, or use an alternative channel).

The purpose of the Slack MCP tool is for the Slack_Bot agent to communicate with users via Slack. But MAKDO has several different communication patterns.

Communication patterns

MAKDO implements several communication patterns to keep humans informed while avoiding information overload.

Notification hierarchy

The Coordinator agent's system prompt instructs it to always post detailed results to Slack:

```
CRITICAL WORKFLOW FOR SLACK REPORTING:
When you receive results from Analyzer or Fixer agents, you MUST:
1. Use agent_MAKDO_Slack_Bot to post THE COMPLETE DETAILED RESULTS
2. Include ALL technical details: pod names, error messages, actions taken
3. Do NOT summarize or filter - post the full agent output
```

This ensures humans have complete visibility into agent operations. The actual workflow is as follows:

```
Coordinator receives user request
→ Calls agent_MAKDO_Analyzer
→ Gets detailed analysis report
→ Calls agent_MAKDO_Slack_Bot with FULL analysis
```

```
→ Calls agent_MAKDO_Fixer if remediation needed
→ Gets detailed remediation report
→ Calls agent_MAKDO_Slack_Bot with FULL remediation results
```

Every significant operation produces a Slack notification with complete context.

Message formatting

The `Slack_Bot` agent's system prompt includes formatting guidelines:

```
Message formatting for Slack:
- Use Slack markdown for emphasis (*bold*, _italic_, `code`)
- Use code blocks for kubectl commands and YAML
- Include relevant links and context
- Keep messages concise but informative
- Use threads for detailed technical discussions
- Tag relevant users for critical alerts (@channel, @here)
```

The following is an example formatted message:

```
🚨 *CRITICAL ISSUES DETECTED*

*Cluster:* kind-makdo-test
*Timestamp:* 2025-10-06 14:30:00

*Issues Found:*

🔴 *CRITICAL:*
• Pod: `default/failing-app-1`
  Status: ImagePullBackOff
  Error: Failed to pull image "nonexistent:latest"
  Restarts: 5

• Pod: `default/failing-app-2`
  Status: CrashLoopBackOff
  Error: Container exited with code 1
  Restarts: 12

*Recommendations:*
1. Verify image name and registry accessibility
2. Check application logs for crash cause
3. Consider rolling back to previous version
```

```
*Next Steps:* Remediation agent dispatched
```

This formatting makes technical information easily scannable while preserving all essential details.

Contextual messaging

`Slack_Bot` adapts its messaging based on severity and context. Here are some examples.

This is an example message for routine operations:

```
i Cluster health check completed
kind-makdo-test: All systems nominal
5 pods running, 0 issues detected
```

This is an example message for warnings:

```
⚠ WARNING: Resource utilization high
Cluster: production-east
CPU: 85% (threshold: 80%)
Memory: 78%
Recommend scaling up nodes
```

This is an example message for critical issues:

```
🚨 @channel CRITICAL: Production cluster degraded
Cluster: production-west
5 pods failing in user-facing services
Impact: API response times increased 300%
MAKDO remediation in progress
Human approval required for pod restarts
```

The LLM selects appropriate emoji, urgency markers, and notification targets based on `Analyzer`'s severity assessment.

Escalation pattern for restricted operations

MAKDO implements a safety-first approach for operations requiring human approval. Rather than executing potentially destructive operations automatically, the `Fixer` agent identifies them, skips execution, and escalates to humans through detailed Slack notifications.

Here's how MAKDO handles restricted operations.

The Fixer agent's system prompt defines which operations require approval:

```
Operations requiring approval:
- delete (pods, deployments, services)
- scale down operations
- deployment configuration changes (image updates, etc.)
When the Fixer encounters such operations, it follows this pattern:
Fixer workflow:
1. Analyzes the remediation needed (e.g., deployment image change)
2. Checks operation against approval-required list
3. Skips the operation (doesn't execute)
4. Reports to Coordinator with detailed reasoning
5. Coordinator posts complete report to Slack via Slack_Bot
```

Here is an example Slack notification:

```
**Remediation Report**

**Skipped Actions:**
- Pod: default/image-pull-fail-abc123
  Action: Skipped - ImagePullBackOff requires deployment fix
  Reason: Image "nonexistent:v1.0.0" does not exist in registry
  Recommendation: Update deployment with valid image
 ⚠ Requires human approval to change deployment configuration

**Next Steps:**
Humans can manually execute the fix if appropriate:
kubectl set image deployment/image-pull-fail app=valid-image:v1.0.0
```

This escalation pattern ensures destructive operations never execute automatically. Humans receive complete context to make informed decisions and can execute fixes manually if needed.

For future enhancement, interactive approval workflows could be added using memory tools to track pending operations and Slack command processing to accept/reject operations programmatically, but the current design prioritizes safety through mandatory escalation. When MAKDO gains trust, `Fixer` can be allowed to execute some of these operations automatically.

Alternative communication channels

While MAKDO uses Slack, the same patterns may apply to other communication platforms:

- **Microsoft Teams**: Replace the Slack MCP server with the Teams equivalent using the Microsoft Graph API.
- **Email**: Build the MCP server using SMTP/IMAP for asynchronous notifications.
- **PagerDuty**: Integrate for incident management and on-call escalation.
- **Datadog**: Respond to alerts. Create new alerts and enrich alerts with context.
- **SMS**: Use the Twilio MCP server for critical alerts.

The architecture remains the same. Swap the MCP server implementation while keeping the communication agent pattern. The agent's system prompt would need adjustments for platform-specific features, but the core notification principles remain unchanged.

Security and access control

Human-AI communication channels require careful security consideration.

The first step is **authentication**. The Slack MCP server uses Slack's OAuth bot token for authentication:

```
headers = {
    'Authorization': f'Bearer {bot_token}',
    'Content-Type': 'application/json; charset=utf-8'
}
```

The bot token should have the required permissions, such as the following:

- `chat:write`: Post messages to channels
- `channels:read`: List channels
- `channels:history`: Read channel messages (for command processing)

Next, let's look at **channel restrictions**. `Slack_Bot`'s system prompt restricts it to designated channels:

```
Communication channels:
- #makdo-devops: Primary channel for alerts and status updates
- Direct messages: For sensitive information or approval requests
- Thread replies: For detailed discussions and follow-ups
```

This prevents the bot from posting operational data to inappropriate channels.

Following this is **command authorization**. For production deployments, add authorization checks:

```
@mcp.tool()
def slack_post_message(channel: str, text: str, user_id: str = None) -> str:
    """Post a message to a Slack channel"""

    # Check if user is authorized for this channel
    if user_id and not is_authorized(user_id, channel):
        return f"❌ User {user_id} not authorized for {channel}"

    # Proceed with posting...
```

This ensures only authorized users can request or approve critical operations.

Observability and audit trail

All Slack communications create a natural audit trail:

- **Message history**: Slack preserves complete conversation history
- **Threaded discussions**: Related messages are grouped for context
- **Reactions**: Humans can acknowledge or react to agent messages
- **Search**: Slack's search enables finding past operations
- **Export**: Slack data can be exported for compliance/analysis

This built-in observability is a key advantage of using established communication platforms for human-AI interaction.

Having explored MAKDO's architecture, agent interactions, and human integration patterns, we can now summarize the key insights before examining the system in action. MAKDO's approach to human-AI collaboration centers on a dedicated communication agent that handles all human interaction while keeping operational agents focused on their domains, using the MCP protocol to integrate with external platforms such as Slack through the simplified FastMCP library.

The system maintains full transparency by always posting complete operational details to humans without summarization or filtering, supporting bi-directional communication for both agent-to-human notifications and human-to-agent commands. For operations requiring approval, MAKDO implements a safety-first escalation pattern where `Fixer` identifies restricted operations, skips execution, and provides humans with detailed context for manual intervention when appropriate.

Security considerations include platform authentication, channel restrictions, and command validation, while communication platforms provide a natural audit trail through built-in message history and search capabilities. These patterns enable effective human-AI collaboration that maintains human control while leveraging AI automation capabilities, as we'll see in the complete demonstration that follows.

MAKDO in action – a complete demo walk-through

Let's see MAKDO in action through a complete end-to-end demonstration. This walk-through shows the entire workflow from problem detection through remediation, with real Slack notifications at each step.

Demo setup

The demonstration uses a test script that creates authentic cluster problems and exercises the full MAKDO workflow. We'll go through the setup first.

Here are the details for the test environment setup:

- **Cluster**: `kind-makdo-test` (local Kubernetes cluster)
- **k8s-ai server**: Running on `http://localhost:9999`
- **Slack channel**: `#makdo-devops`
- **Coordinator**: With inline `Analyzer`, `Fixer`, and `Slack_Bot` agents

The test script can be found here: `https://github.com/PacktPublishing/Design-Multi-Agent-AI-Systems-Using-MCP-and-A2A/tree/main/ch09/makdo/test_makdo_with_slack.py`.

The test creates two types of failures:

- **CrashLoop Pod**: A pod that repeatedly crashes with exit code 1
- **ImagePullBackOff deployment**: A deployment referencing a non-existent container image

These represent common real-world Kubernetes issues that MAKDO must detect and remediate.

Creating cluster problems

The test begins by creating actual Kubernetes resources that will fail:

```
def create_crashloop_pod(self) -> bool:
    logger.info("💥 Creating crashloop pod...")
    yaml = """
```

```
apiVersion: v1
kind: Pod
metadata:
  name: crashloop-app
  namespace: default
spec:
  containers:
  - name: crash
    image: busybox
    command: ["sh", "-c", "echo 'Starting...'; sleep 2; exit 1"]
  restartPolicy: Always
"""
    # Apply to cluster...
def create_failing_deployment(self) -> bool:
    logger.info("💥 Creating failing deployment...")
    yaml = """
apiVersion: apps/v1
kind: Deployment
metadata:
  name: image-pull-fail
  namespace: default
spec:
  replicas: 2
  selector:
    matchLabels:
      app: bad-image
  template:
    metadata:
      labels:
        app: bad-image
    spec:
      containers:
      - name: app
        image: nonexistent-registry.io/fake/image:v1.0.0
        imagePullPolicy: Always
"""
    # Apply to cluster...
```

After creation, the test waits 15 seconds for these problems to manifest (pods entering `CrashLoopBackOff` and `ImagePullBackOff` states).

Step 1 – demo start notification

MAKDO sends an initial message to Slack announcing the demo:

```
def send_demo_start_message(self):
    message = """
🤖 **MAKDO End-to-End Demo**

This demo showcases MAKDO's complete autonomous DevOps workflow:

**Test Scenario:**
1. ✅ Create cluster problems (crashloop pod, failing deployment)
2. 🔍 Analyzer detects issues using k8s-ai
3. 📊 Report findings to Slack
4. 🔧 Fixer attempts remediation
5. ✅ Report results to Slack

**Environment:**
- Cluster: kind-makdo-test
- Channel: #makdo-devops
- Demo started at: 2024-10-06 14:30:00
"""

    response = self.coordinator.send_message(
        f"Post this message to #makdo-devops Slack channel:\n\n{message}",
        self.coordinator.default_model_id
    )
```

Here's what happens internally:

1. The `Coordinator` agent receives the message.
2. The LLM recognizes that this is a Slack posting task.
3. It generates a tool call: `agent_MAKDO_Slack_Bot` with the message.
4. `Slack_Bot` receives the message.
5. `Slack_Bot` calls the `slack_post_message` MCP tool.
6. The FastMCP Slack server posts to the #makdo-devops channel.
7. The FastMCP Slack server returns success confirmation.

This demonstrates the complete delegation chain:

User → Coordinator → Slack_Bot → MCP Tool → Slack API

The following figure shows the *demo start message* in Slack:

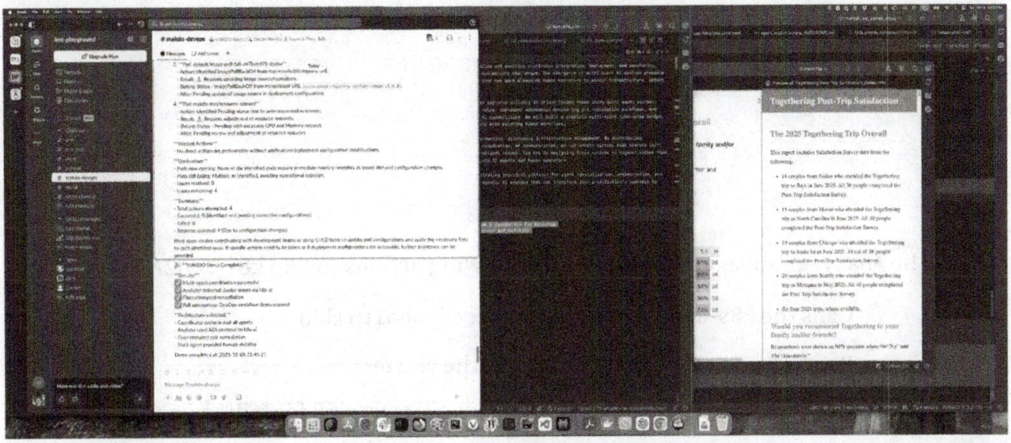

Figure 9.1: Demo start message

MAKDO posts the demo start announcement to the *#makdo-devops channel*, outlining the test scenario and environment.

Step 2 – analysis phase

Now, MAKDO analyzes the cluster to detect the problems:

```
def run_analysis_and_post(self):
    analysis_request = """
Please perform the following tasks in order:

1. Use the Analyzer agent to check the health of the kind-makdo-test cluster
   and get the COMPLETE detailed analysis report
2. Immediately forward THE COMPLETE ANALYZER OUTPUT to the Slack agent with this
   message: "Post this complete cluster analysis report to #makdo-devops:
   [PASTE FULL ANALYZER OUTPUT HERE]"

CRITICAL: Do NOT summarize. Do NOT filter. Post the ENTIRE analysis report
exactly as the Analyzer provided it.
"""

    response = self.coordinator.send_message(
        analysis_request,
```

```
        self.coordinator.default_model_id
    )
```

Here's the internal workflow:

1. The `Coordinator` agent delegates to the `Analyzer` sub-agent:

    ```
    Tool: agent_MAKDO_Analyzer
    Arguments: {
      "message": "Check the health of kind-makdo-test cluster"
    }
    ```

2. The `Analyzer` subagent executes the following actions (using k8s-ai A2A tools):
    - Calls the k8s-ai `kubernetes_resource_health` skill
    - Retrieves actual pod statuses from the cluster
    - Calls the k8s-ai `kubernetes_diagnose_issue` skill for failing pods
    - Compiles a detailed diagnostic report

3. `Analyzer` returns a complete report with several sections that include the target cluster, the time of the analysis, the issues it discovered ordered by severity, healthy resources, recommendations for remediating the issues, and a summary:

    ```
    **Cluster Analysis Report**
    Cluster: kind-makdo-test
    Timestamp: 2024-10-06 14:30:15

    **Issues Found:**

    🔴 CRITICAL Issues:
    - Pod: default/crashloop-app
      Status: CrashLoopBackOff
      Reason: Container repeatedly crashing
      Error: Container exited with code 1
      Restarts: 5
      Last State: Terminated (Error)

    - Pod: default/image-pull-fail-abc123
      Status: ImagePullBackOff
      Reason: Failed to pull image
      Error: image "nonexistent-registry.io/fake/image:v1.0.0" not found
    ```

```
  Restarts: 0

- Pod: default/image-pull-fail-def456
  Status: ImagePullBackOff
  Reason: Failed to pull image
  Error: image "nonexistent-registry.io/fake/image:v1.0.0" not found
  Restarts: 0

**Healthy Resources:**
- kube-system pods: All running normally
- Core services: Operational
**Recommendations:**
1. crashloop-app: Investigate container startup issue, check application
logs
2. image-pull-fail deployment: Verify image exists or update deployment
with valid image
3. Consider deleting failing pods to allow fresh restart attempts

**Summary:**
- Total pods checked: 15
- Critical issues: 3
- Warnings: 0
- Healthy: 12
```

Note

Since the LLM is not deterministic, the exact format may be different, but it will contain all the relevant details.

4. `Coordinator` to `Slack_Bot` delegation happens when the `Coordinator` agent wishes to communicate some information to the human operator. It invokes `Slack_Bot` as a tool, providing as an argument the information to notify humans—in this case, for example, the analysis report generated earlier by the analyzer:

```
Tool: agent_MAKDO_Slack_Bot
Arguments: {
  "message": "Post this complete cluster analysis report to #makdo-devops:
             [ENTIRE ANALYZER OUTPUT]"
}
```

5. `Slack_Bot` sends the following request to the MCP tool:

```
Tool: slack_post_message
Arguments: {
  "channel": "makdo-devops",
  "text": "[ENTIRE ANALYZER OUTPUT]"
}
```

6. The result is posted to Slack as the `Slack_Bot` agent uses the `slack_post_message` tool.

This workflow demonstrates the complete analysis workflow:

Coordinator → Analyzer → k8s-ai (A2A) → Analyzer → Coordinator → Slack_Bot → MCP → Slack

Here's a screenshot of the analysis report in Slack:

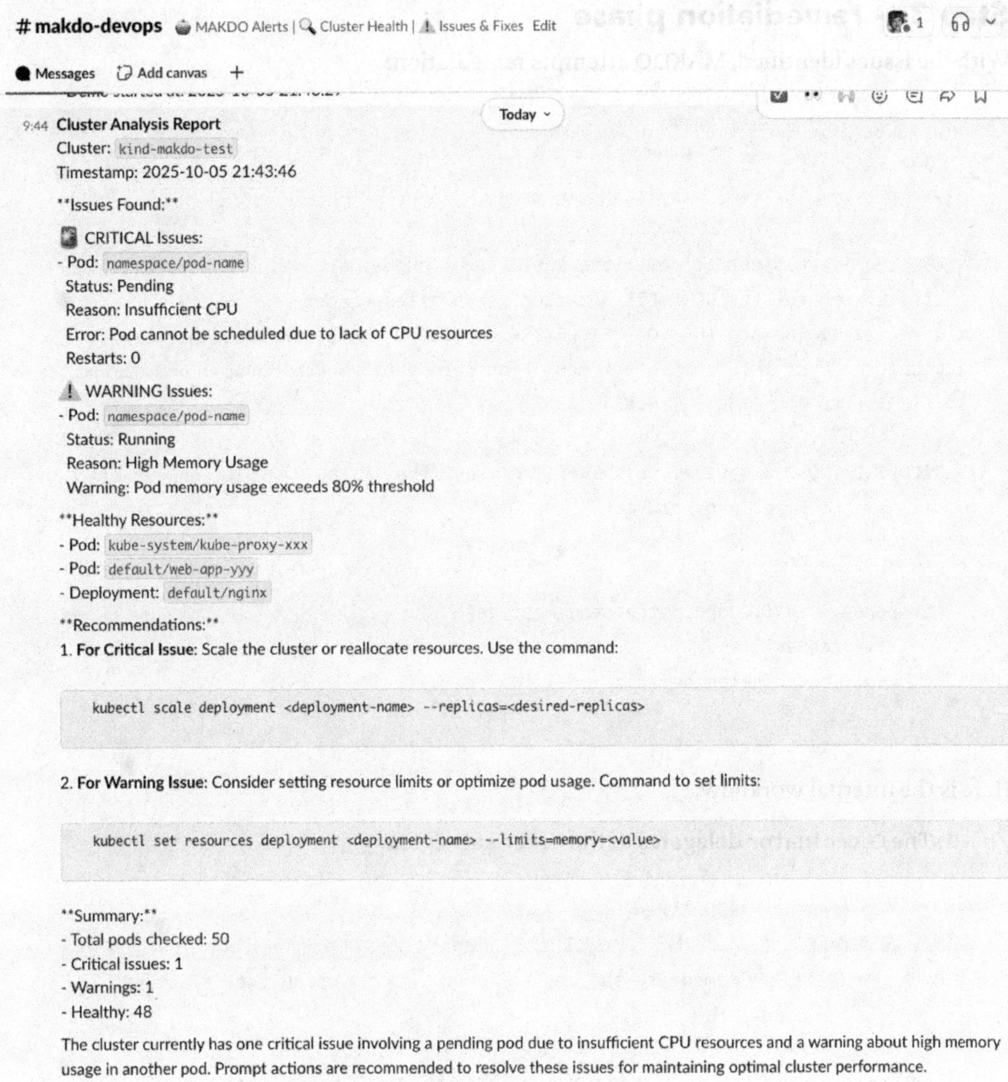

Figure 9.2: Analysis report

The preceding figure is the complete cluster analysis report posted to Slack, showing three critical issues detected: one `crashloop` pod and two pods with `ImagePullBackOff` errors.

Step 3 – remediation phase

With the issues identified, MAKDO attempts remediation:

```
def run_fixer_and_post(self):
    fix_request = """
Please perform the following tasks in order:

1. Use the Fixer agent to remediate the issues found in the kind-makdo-test
   cluster and get the COMPLETE detailed remediation report
2. Immediately forward THE COMPLETE FIXER OUTPUT to the Slack agent with this
   message: "Post this complete remediation report to #makdo-devops:
   [PASTE FULL FIXER OUTPUT HERE]"

CRITICAL: Do NOT summarize. Do NOT filter. Post the ENTIRE remediation report
exactly as the Fixer provided it.
"""

    response = self.coordinator.send_message(
        fix_request,
        self.coordinator.default_model_id
    )
```

Here is the internal workflow:

1. The `Coordinator` delegates to the `Fixer` sub-agent:

   ```
   Tool: agent_MAKDO_Fixer
   Arguments: {
     "message": "Remediate the issues found in kind-makdo-test cluster"
   }
   ```

2. The `Fixer` executes the following actions (using k8s-ai A2A tools):
   - For `crashloop` pod: Attempts deletion to allow a clean restart
   - For `image-pull-fail` pods: Identifies image issue; may suggest manual intervention
   - Executes safe operations via k8s-ai kubectl tools
   - Verifies results after each action

3. Fixer returns complete report:

```
**Remediation Report**
Cluster: kind-makdo-test



**Actions Taken:**



1. **Pod: default/crashloop-app**
   - Action: Deleted pod to allow clean restart
   - Command: `kubectl delete pod crashloop-app -n default`
   - Result: ☑ Success
   - Details: Pod deleted successfully
   - Before: CrashLoopBackOff (5 restarts)
   - After: Terminating



2. **Pod: default/image-pull-fail-abc123**
   - Action: Skipped - ImagePullBackOff requires deployment fix
   - Reason: Image does not exist in registry
   - Recommendation: Update deployment with valid image



3. **Pod: default/image-pull-fail-def456**
   - Action: Skipped - ImagePullBackOff requires deployment fix
   - Reason: Image does not exist in registry
   - Recommendation: Update deployment with valid image



**Skipped Actions:**
- image-pull-fail deployment: Requires human approval to change image



**Verification:**
- Pods now running: 12
- Pods still failing: 2 (image-pull-fail)
- Issues resolved: 1
```

```
- Issues requiring human attention: 1



**Summary:**
- Total actions attempted: 1
- Successful: 1
- Failed: 0
- Requires approval: 1 (deployment image update)
```

4. The `Coordinator` agent delegates to the `Slack_Bot` sub-agent (same pattern as the analysis patterns covered earlier).
5. The complete remediation report is posted to Slack by the `Slack_Bot` agent.

This workflow demonstrates MAKDO's safety-first approach. It fixed the `crashloop` issue but correctly identified that the image-pull problem requires human intervention (changing the deployment's image reference).

Here is a report screenshot from another run where the LLM decided that both failures required human intervention (it is important to realize that the LLM makes intelligent decisions based on the situation, so it will not always take the same actions):

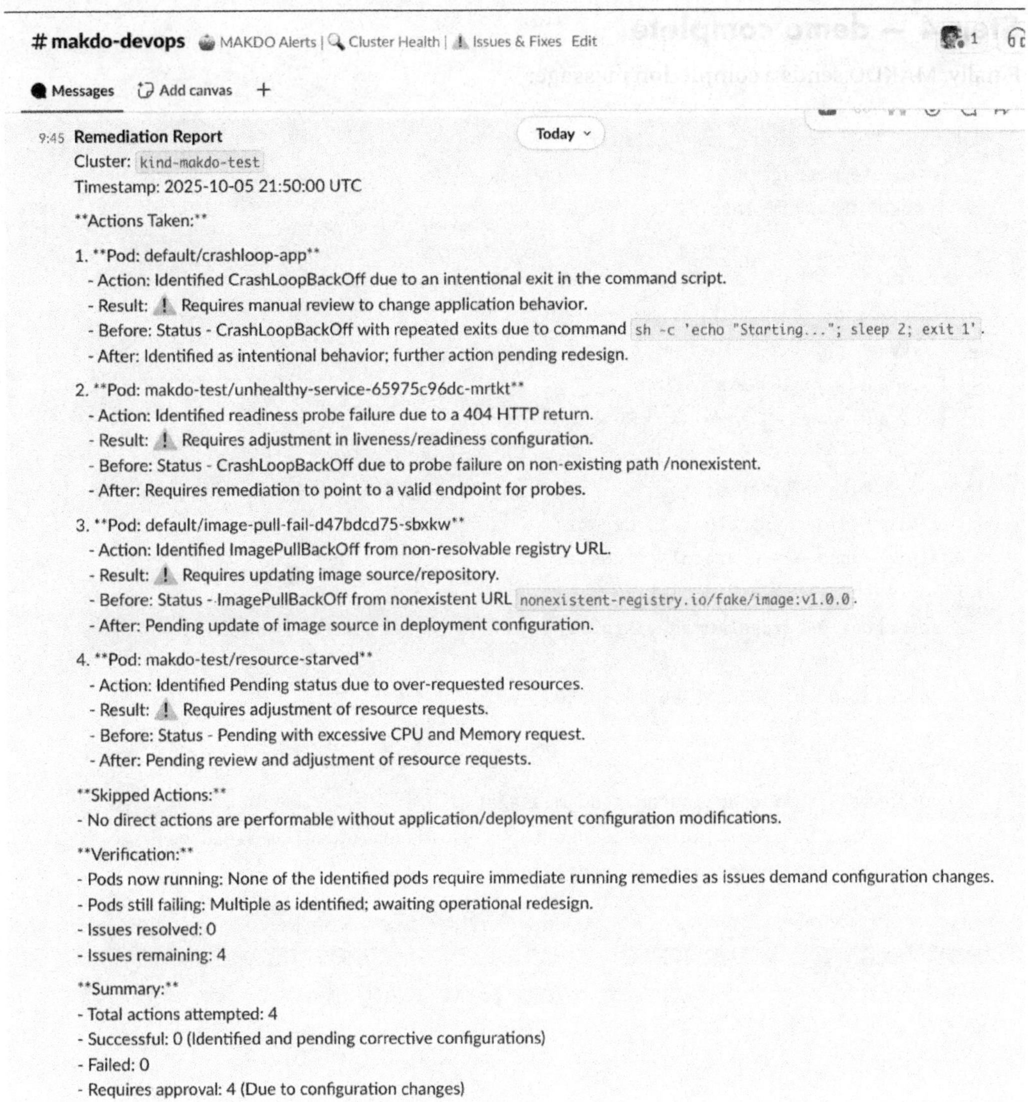

Figure 9.3: Complete remediation report

Once MAKDO goes through the complete process of identifying problems, analyzing them, fixing them, and notifying the user, it ends the demo. When deployed in production, it will keep running continuously and watch for new problems.

Step 4 – demo complete

Finally, MAKDO sends a completion message:

```
def send_demo_complete_message(self):
    complete_message = """
🎉 **MAKDO Demo Complete!**

**Results:**
✅ Multi-agent coordination successful
✅ Analyzer detected cluster issues via k8s-ai
✅ Fixer attempted remediation
✅ Full autonomous DevOps workflow demonstrated

**Architecture validated:**
- Coordinator orchestrated all agents
- Analyzer used A2A protocol to k8s-ai
- Fixer executed safe remediation
- Slack agent provided human visibility

Demo completed at: 2024-10-06 14:30:50
"""

    response = self.coordinator.send_message(
        f"Post this completion message to #makdo-devops:\n\n{complete_message}",
        self.coordinator.default_model_id
    )
```

Here's a screenshot of the demo completion message in Slack:

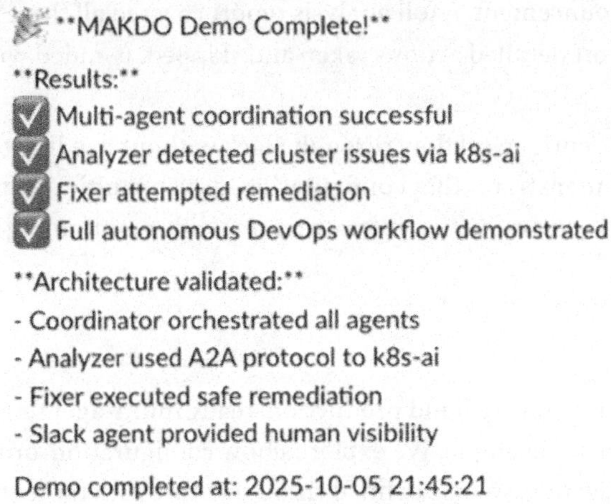

Figure 9.4: Demo complete

This is the final demo completion message summarizing results and validating that all agents worked together successfully to detect, remediate, and report on cluster issues.

Key observations

This demo validates several key MAKDO characteristics. Let's summarize them:

- **Complete autonomy**: From a single user request, MAKDO handled the full workflow without additional human input. The `Analyzer` agent examined the cluster. `Slack_Bot` posted the analysis to Slack. The `Fixer` agent attempted remediation. `Slack_Bot` then reported the results. The `Coordinator` agent orchestrated everything through LLM reasoning rather than fixed scripts.
- **Protocol integration**: The demo used both major protocols effectively. A2A enabled `Analyzer` and `Fixer` to connect to the k8s-ai server for Kubernetes operations, discovering the cluster state, and executing actions. MCP let `Slack_Bot` integrate with the FastMCP Slack server, posting all reports to #makdo-devops for full visibility.
- **Safety controls**: MAKDO operated safely throughout. It fixed low-risk issues such as deleting a `crashloop` pod. Riskier actions, such as deployment changes, required approval. Post-remediation checks verified the cluster state. All steps were reported transparently via Slack.

- **Human visibility**: Every major operation generated a Slack message. The demo began with a start announcement. A full analysis report covered all three failing pods. The remediation report detailed actions taken and skipped. It ended with a completion summary.

Humans can observe the entire workflow through Slack without needing to monitor logs or dashboards. MAKDO demonstrates that configuration-driven multi-agent systems can handle real DevOps workflows with production infrastructure while maintaining human oversight and operational safety.

Summary

This chapter demonstrated how to build production-ready multi-agent AI systems using MAKDO as a comprehensive example. We explored how configuration-driven architecture, where the entire multi-agent system is defined through YAML files rather than custom code, dramatically simplifies implementation while enabling powerful capabilities. MAKDO's four specialized agents, namely the `Coordinator`, `Analyzer`, `Fixer`, and `Slack_Bot`, work together through AI-6's `AgentTool` pattern, where sub-agents appear as tools accepting natural language messages. The system integrates two major protocols seamlessly: A2A for Kubernetes operations via k8s-ai, and MCP for human communication via Slack, with each agent specialized through carefully crafted system prompts encoding domain expertise, operational policies, and safety controls.

The implementation validated key patterns for multi-agent systems: LLM-driven orchestration, where the `Coordinator` agent dynamically determines workflows through reasoning rather than predefined state machines; session isolation, where each agent maintains an independent conversation history; tool assignment as permission control implementing least privileges; and safety-first remediation, distinguishing between auto-approved and human approval-required operations. The end-to-end demo showed MAKDO autonomously detecting cluster issues, attempting safe remediation, and providing complete transparency through Slack notifications. This declarative approach enables rapid iteration and extension by adding agents or modifying behaviors through YAML edits rather than programming.

MAKDO helps you manage your infrastructure, but it is a complicated system itself. When you deploy it, you'll need to be able to test it, debug it, and troubleshoot problems.

In the next chapter, we will cover exactly what it takes to run multi-agent systems in production safely and reliably.

Get This Book's PDF Version and Exclusive Extras

Scan the QR code (or go to `packtpub.com/unlock`). Search for this book by name, confirm the edition, and then follow the steps on the page.

UNLOCK NOW

Note: Keep your invoice handy. Purchases made directly from Packt don't require an invoice.

10

Testing, Debugging, and Troubleshooting Multi-Agent Systems

In the previous chapter, we built MAKDO, a complete multi-agent system for Kubernetes DevOps. We saw how the `Coordinator`, `Analyzer`, `Fixer`, and `Slack_Bot` agents work together using MCP and A2A to automate cluster health monitoring and remediation. We implemented the system, connected it to external tools such as `k8s-ai` and Slack via MCP, and ran it from end to end.

Building multi-agent systems is one thing; keeping them running reliably in production is another. Multi-agent systems fail in unique ways that traditional software doesn't. Agents hallucinate. They misuse tools. They lose context when handing work between agents. Coordination breaks down. These failures are often non-deterministic and hard to reproduce.

This chapter covers everything you need to test, debug, and troubleshoot multi-agent systems effectively. We start by looking at common failure modes such as hallucination and coordination breakdowns. We then explore instrumentation and observability strategies that make agent behavior visible. Then, we dive deep into debugging tool use and diagnosing coordination failures between agents. Finally, we discuss designing for resilience through redundancy, graceful degradation, retry logic, and human escalation patterns. Throughout the chapter, we use MAKDO as a concrete example to illustrate these concepts in practice.

The following key topics are covered:

- Common failure modes in agentic systems
- Instrumentation and observability for AI agents
- Debugging tool use and function call chains
- Diagnosing coordination failures in multi-agent workflows
- Designing for resilience and recoverability

So, let's get started!

Common failure modes in agentic systems

Understanding how multi-agent systems fail is the first step toward building robust, production-ready agentic AI systems. Unlike traditional software, where failures are typically deterministic and reproducible, AI agent failures can be subtle, context-dependent, and difficult to diagnose. Remember that every turn of a multi-agent system may involve tens or hundreds of LLM calls interleaved with tool executions, making the failure surface much larger. In addition, LLMs can introduce non-determinism, leading to inconsistent behavior across multiple runs for the exact same input.

This section explores the most common failure patterns you'll encounter when working with agentic systems.

Agent hallucination

Agent hallucination occurs when agents generate information that appears plausible but is factually incorrect or never actually happened. In agentic systems, this can be particularly dangerous because hallucinations may be embedded in tool calls, reasoning chains, or reported results. Let's explore how it happens:

- **Fabricated tool responses**: Agents may claim to have successfully executed a tool when they haven't, or report results that never occurred. For example, an agent might say, "I've deployed the application to production" when it only executed a dry-run command, or claim, "The database query returned 1,523 records" when the query actually failed.

  In MAKDO, the `Fixer` agent might report, "Successfully restarted pod default/nginx-abc123" when it actually received a timeout from k8s-ai and never confirmed the restart. The coordinator receives this fabricated success message and tells `Slack_Bot` to notify humans that the issue is resolved when the Pod is still failing.

- **Invented context**: Agents may reference files, configurations, or resources that don't exist. An agent might say, "I checked the `config.yaml` file and found the setting," when no such file exists in the repository.
  MAKDO's `Analyzer` might hallucinate Pod names when reporting issues. It could claim, "Pod default/payment-service-7f9d8 is failing" when the actual failing Pod is named *default/payment-service-7f9d8c*. When the `Fixer` agent tries to remediate using the hallucinated name, k8s-ai returns "pod not found," and the actual problem goes unfixed.
- **False correlation and causation**: Agents may incorrectly link events or actions. An agent may say, "The deployment failed because of the recent DNS change," when the DNS change is unrelated to the actual failure cause.
  For example, the `Analyzer` agent might see that a Pod started failing shortly after a deployment update and conclude that the deployment caused the failure. In reality, the Pod failed because the image registry became temporarily unavailable, which is completely unrelated to the deployment. The `Analyzer` agent's incorrect diagnosis leads the `Fixer` agent to roll back a perfectly good deployment.
- **Synthetic data in reasoning**: During multistep reasoning, agents may introduce plausible-sounding but fictional data points that cascade through subsequent steps, leading to confident but incorrect conclusions.
  For example, when analyzing resource constraints, MAKDO's `Analyzer` might invent memory usage numbers, such as "pod is using 2.3GB of its 2GB limit," when k8s-ai never reported those specific metrics. This fictional data makes it into the Slack report, misleading human operators about the actual resource situation. Wrong metrics are far worse than no metrics as they can lead to damaging actions based on false information.

Here are some mitigation strategies to reduce hallucinations:

- Require agents to cite actual tool outputs rather than summarizing them
- Implement strict verification layers that check claimed actions against actual execution logs
- Use structured outputs with explicit success/failure indicators
- Cross-validate agent claims with independent verification tools
- Log all tool executions separately from agent narratives
- Add confidence scoring and uncertainty acknowledgment to agent outputs

Hallucinations are a real problem, but LLMs are getting better at reducing their occurrences, and the mitigation strategies can be used to control this. But issues with using tools become more serious as agentic AI systems extend their reach with more tools.

Wrong tool use and tool misuse

Wrong tool use happens when agents call incorrect tools for the task at hand, either due to misunderstanding the tool's purpose or misinterpreting the task requirements. This can lead to ineffective or harmful actions. Tool misuse happens when agents use the correct tools but in incorrect, inefficient, or dangerous ways. Unlike hallucination, where the agent invents information, tool misuse involves real tool executions that don't achieve the intended goal, such as the following:

- **Invalid tool parameters**: Agents may construct syntactically valid but semantically incorrect tool calls. For example, a deployment agent might specify the wrong cluster name or use a deprecated API version, causing silent failures downstream. Alternatively, an agent might pass a relative path when an absolute path is required. MAKDO's `Fixer` might call k8s-ai's `delete_pod` skill with the wrong namespace. It sends `namespace: "production"` when the failing Pod is actually `in namespace: "default"`. The k8s-ai tool succeeds (there is no Pod with that name in production), but the actual failing Pod remains untouched. The `Fixer` agent reports success, the coordinator agent moves on, and the problem persists.
- **Tool chaining errors**: When agents need to use multiple tools in sequence, they may skip necessary intermediate steps or execute them in the wrong order. Consider a code review agent that runs tests before checking out the correct branch, or a deployment agent that applies configurations before validating them.
  The coordinator agent might tell the `Fixer` agent to "restart the failing pod and verify it's healthy." The `Fixer` agent deletes the Pod via k8s-ai but never calls back to verify that the new Pod started successfully. It reports to the coordinator agent "remediation complete" without checking whether Kubernetes actually rescheduled the Pod. If the Pod can't restart due to resource constraints, nobody notices until the next health check cycle.
- **Inappropriate tool selection**: Agents may choose the wrong tool for the task, such as using a delete operation when an update is needed, or calling an expensive search API when a simple lookup would suffice. Agents may also not use a tool at all when one is clearly needed, or use multiple tools when one tool is sufficient.

- **Resource-intensive patterns**: Agents may use tools in ways that work but are extremely inefficient, such as making individual API calls in a loop instead of using batch operations, or repeatedly fetching the same data instead of caching it.
- **Dangerous parameter combinations**: Agents may combine valid parameters in ways that produce unintended side effects. Setting both a force flag and a recursive flag might work individually but together cause data loss.

Here are some mitigation strategies to reduce wrong tool use and misuse:

- Carefully curate and document tool capabilities and constraints
- Minimize the number of available tools per agent to reduce choice complexity
- Implement strict tool input validation with semantic checks
- Create tool usage guidelines embedded in tool descriptions
- Add safety rails for dangerous operations (confirmation prompts, dry-run modes)
- Monitor tool usage patterns to detect inefficient or suspicious behavior
- Use tool call validation agents that review planned actions before execution
- Implement guardrails that prevent certain parameter combinations
- Manage tool permissions and access levels carefully
- Provide example tool usage patterns in agent prompts

A combination of these mitigation strategies can significantly reduce tool use failures. However, even when the LLMs are not hallucinating and properly use all the tools available to them, sometimes they just don't properly follow the instructions.

Poor instruction following

Agents may misinterpret or inadequately follow user instructions, leading to incorrect or incomplete task execution. This failure mode is particularly frustrating because the agent appears to be working but produces results that don't match what was requested. Here are some of those instances:

- **Selective attention to instructions**: Agents may focus on part of the instructions while ignoring critical constraints or requirements. For example, a user asks to "deploy to staging and notify the team on Slack," but the agent only deploys, forgetting the notification step. Or instructions specify "use Python 3.11" but the agent defaults to whatever version is available. The coordinator's system prompt may say, "Always post detailed results to Slack after Analyzer and Fixer complete." But when processing a health check, the coordinator calls `Analyzer`, receives the report, and then immediately calls `Fixer` without posting to Slack.

It only remembers to notify humans after all remediation finishes, so the team doesn't see what issues were found until after fixes are attempted.

- **Over-generalization**: Agents may interpret specific instructions too broadly. When asked to "fix the bug in the login function," an agent might refactor the entire authentication system, introducing unnecessary changes and potential new issues.
- **Under-generalization**: Conversely, agents may interpret instructions too narrowly. Asked to "update all configuration files," an agent might only update files with a `.config` extension, missing `.yaml`, `.json`, or `.toml` files that also contain configuration.
- **Ignoring implicit requirements**: Experienced developers understand implicit constraints that agents may miss. "Add a new API endpoint" implicitly means adding tests, documentation, and proper error handling, but an agent might only add the bare minimum endpoint code.
- **Lost instructions in long conversations**: As conversations grow longer, agents may lose track of earlier instructions or constraints. Initial requirements such as "maintain backward compatibility" or "follow the existing naming conventions" may get forgotten as the agent focuses on more recent messages.
- **Ambiguity mishandling**: When instructions are ambiguous, agents may make assumptions without seeking clarification. "Make it faster" could mean optimizing runtime, reducing latency, or improving throughput, but the agent picks one interpretation without confirming.
- **Priority confusion**: When given multiple tasks or constraints, agents may fail to understand which are critical and which are optional. "Deploy the fix quickly, but make sure tests pass" might lead an agent to skip tests in favor of speed, when test passing should be non-negotiable.

Here are some mitigation strategies to improve instruction following:

- Break complex instructions into explicit, numbered steps
- Use structured formats such as checklists or requirement lists
- Include both positive instructions ("do X") and negative constraints ("don't do Y")
- Repeat critical constraints throughout long conversations
- Ask agents to confirm their understanding before execution
- Provide examples of correct and incorrect outcomes
- Use explicit priority markers ("MUST," "SHOULD," "MAY") for requirements

- Implement instruction verification agents that check task plans against original requests
- Maintain a "requirements context" that persists across conversation turns
- Use structured prompts with dedicated sections for constraints, goals, and success criteria

Instruction following is a major focus of LLM providers, and they invest a lot of effort in training because it is so critical. With the addition of robust mitigation strategies, you can arrive at a reliable system that follows instructions properly. But even when following the instructions properly, sometimes agentic AI systems can get into a state of constant churn without converging on a final response and just keep calling more and more tools with no end.

Infinite loops and runaway agents

Agentic systems can enter infinite loops when agents repeatedly attempt the same failed action or get stuck in circular reasoning patterns, such as the following:

- **Retry loops without learning**: An agent encounters an error, retries the same operation with identical parameters, fails again, and repeats indefinitely. This is common when agents don't maintain memory of previous attempts or don't analyze why an operation failed.
  For example, MAKDO's `Fixer` tries to delete a Pod that doesn't exist (maybe it was already deleted). `k8s-ai` returns "pod not found." The `Fixer` agent interprets this as a transient error and retries the same delete command. It fails again. The `Fixer` agent keeps retrying without realizing that the Pod is already gone, burning through API tokens until it hits the retry limit.
- **Circular delegation**: In multi-agent systems, agents may delegate tasks back and forth without making progress. For example, Agent A asks Agent B for help, Agent B determines Agent A is better suited, and they loop endlessly. Note that this is not an issue with hierarchical delegation, where a parent agent always delegates to a child agent.
- **Resource exhaustion**: Runaway agents can consume excessive API tokens, make thousands of tool calls, or generate massive amounts of log data, leading to cost overruns and system instability.
  For example, a bug in MAKDO's health check loop causes it to start a new health check every second instead of every 60 seconds. Each check calls `Analyzer`, which makes multiple `k8s-ai` requests. Within minutes, MAKDO makes thousands of LLM calls, analyzing the same cluster state repeatedly. The OpenAI API bill skyrockets and the `k8s-ai` server logs fill up the disk.

Here are some mitigation strategies to prevent infinite loops and runaway agents:

- Implement maximum iteration limits with exponential backoff
- Track agent action history and detect repeated patterns
- Use circuit breakers that halt execution after consecutive failures
- Monitor resource consumption with alerts and automatic cutoffs
- Implement explicit termination criteria in agent prompts
- Add budgets where agents can only spend up to a reasonable amount

Utilizing these strategies can ensure that single agents don't get stuck. In multi-agent systems, even if every agent functions well on its own, there are systemic issues that happen when communication or coordination between the agents fails.

Communication and coordination breakdowns

Multi-agent systems depend on effective communication between agents. When this communication breaks down, the entire system can fail. The following points explore how it happens:

- **Message format incompatibility**: Agents may produce outputs in formats that other agents can't parse. For example, one agent outputs JSON while another expects YAML, or field names don't match between the sender and receiver.
- **Lost context in handoffs**: When tasks are delegated between agents, critical context from earlier interactions may be lost. For example, a support agent hands off to a technical agent but forgets to include the customer's account details or previous troubleshooting steps.
  Another example is the coordinator tells `Analyzer`, "Check cluster health." `Analyzer` finds three failing Pods and returns a detailed report with Pod names, namespaces, and error messages. The `Coordinator` agent then tells the `Fixer` agent, "Fix the issues," without passing along which specific Pods need fixing. `Fixer` has to call k8s-ai again to rediscover the failing Pods, doubling the diagnostic work and wasting tokens.
- **Race conditions**: When multiple agents work concurrently on related tasks, they may interfere with each other. For example, two deployment agents might simultaneously modify the same configuration, or multiple agents might lock resources that each other need.
  Another example is two MAKDO instances running simultaneously (maybe started by mistake). Both coordinators call their `Analyzer` agents for the same cluster. Both `Analyzer` agents identify the same failing Pod. Both coordinators tell their `Fixer` agents to delete it. Both `Fixer` agents call k8s-ai to delete the Pod. The first one succeeds,

while the second gets "pod not found." The second `Fixer` reports failure to its coordinator, which posts an error to Slack saying "remediation failed," when actually, the Pod was successfully deleted by the first instance.

- **Conflicting objectives**: Different agents optimizing for different goals can work at cross-purposes. For example, a cost optimization agent scales down resources while a performance agent scales them up.

Here are some mitigation strategies to improve communication and coordination:

- Define strict message schemas with validation
- Use structured handoff protocols that include mandatory context fields
- Implement distributed coordination mechanisms such as locks or consensus protocols
- Establish clear agent hierarchies and conflict resolution policies
- Maintain a shared state that all agents can access

Complex multi-agent systems often need to trade off accuracy and quality with speed and cost. This can affect single agents too, but in multi-agent systems, delays compound. If the response is too slow, it may be too late, or the user experience is not pleasant. Let's see how we can address these concerns.

Timeout and latency issues

Real-world agentic systems operate under time constraints, and latency problems can cascade through the system:

- **Tool execution timeouts**: External tools may take longer than expected, causing agents to time out or make decisions based on incomplete information. For example, a database query runs slowly, a deployment times out, or an API call hangs.
- **Cascading delays**: When agents depend on each other, delays compound. If Agent A waits 30 seconds for Agent B, which waits 30 seconds for Agent C, which takes 30 seconds to respond, the user experiences unacceptable 90+ second response times.
- **Stuck agents**: An agent may be waiting for a response that will never come—a webhook that never fires, a file that's never created, or a message that's lost in transit.

Here are some mitigation strategies to handle timeout and latency issues:

- Set realistic timeouts for every tool and agent interaction
- Run independent tasks in parallel to reduce overall latency
- Implement async patterns where agents don't block on slow operations
- Add progress indicators and partial result streaming
- Design for graceful degradation when operations time out
- Use timeout-aware retry logic with backoff
- Consider stamping data passed between agents with a TTL so stale data is refreshed

OK, we have mitigated timeouts and latency issues, but the story is not over. LLMs are stateless, but agentic AI systems are stateful. Managing this state is not trivial.

State management and consistency errors

Maintaining a consistent state across multiple agents and tool executions is challenging:

- **Stale state**: Agents make decisions based on outdated information. For example, an agent checks whether a deployment is ready. It succeeds initially, but by the time the agent takes the next action, the deployment has run into problems.
- **State synchronization failures**: In distributed systems, different agents may have different views of the current state. For example, Agent A believes a resource exists while Agent B sees it as deleted.
- **Partial failures**: When a multistep operation fails midway, the system may be left in an inconsistent state. For example, half of the infrastructure is provisioned, or some configurations are applied, while others aren't.
- **Memory leaks and context bloat**: As conversations grow longer, agents may accumulate too much context, leading to degraded performance or exceeding token limits.

Here are some mitigation strategies to improve state management and consistency:

- Implement transaction-like patterns with rollback capabilities
- Use version numbers or timestamps to detect stale state
- Employ distributed state management systems
- Implement periodic state reconciliation
- Set context window limits and implement intelligent context pruning
- Break down complicated tasks into smaller, manageable sub-tasks that can be handled by separate agents

Security and permission failures

Agentic systems often operate with elevated privileges, making security failures particularly dangerous, such as in the following ways:

- **Permission escalation**: Agents may attempt operations they shouldn't have access to, either through misconfiguration or by learning to exploit tools in unintended ways
- **Credential exposure**: Agents might inadvertently log, transmit, or expose sensitive credentials in error messages or tool outputs
- **Malicious input exploitation**: Carefully crafted user inputs can manipulate agent behavior, causing them to execute unintended operations or bypass safety checks
- **Audit trail gaps**: Without proper logging, it may be impossible to determine what actions agents took, making security investigations difficult

Here are some mitigation strategies to enhance security and permissions.

Most of them are general best practices for any system, but they are especially critical in agentic systems:

- Implement the principle of least privilege for all tool access
- Add explicit permission checks before high-stakes operations
- Sanitize and validate all inputs to agents
- Never include credentials in agent prompts or tool parameters
- Maintain comprehensive audit logs of all agent actions
- Use human-in-the-loop approval for sensitive operations

As you can see, there are many ways multi-agent systems can fail. By understanding these common failure modes, you can design more robust agents, implement effective monitoring, and build troubleshooting strategies to quickly diagnose and resolve issues when they arise. Another important aspect is observability.

Instrumentation and observability for AI agents

Observability is crucial for understanding what's happening inside your agentic AI systems. Unlike traditional software, where you can step through code with a debugger, AI agents operate through a series of LLM calls, tool executions, and state transitions that can be difficult to trace. Effective instrumentation transforms these "black box" systems into "glass box" systems where you can see exactly what's happening at every step.

As explored in *From Black Box to Glass Box: LLM Observability in Action* (`https://medium.com/@the.gigi/from-black-box-to-glass-box-llm-observability-in-action-150266e995d2`), comprehensive observability requires capturing multiple layers of information, which include the prompts sent to LLMs, the responses received, the tools invoked, the intermediate reasoning steps, and the final outcomes.

In this section, we'll explore best practices for instrumenting agentic systems, including core observability primitives, structured logging formats, specialized LLM observability tools, key metrics to track, real-time monitoring strategies, debugging techniques, and privacy considerations.

Core observability primitives

Building observable agentic systems starts with instrumenting the fundamental operations. Let's break down the key observability primitives you should capture.

LLM call tracing

Every interaction with an LLM should be logged with complete context, including the full prompt, model parameters (temperature, max tokens, etc.), the complete response, token usage, latency, and any errors. This creates an audit trail of all AI decisions.

For MAKDO, you want to capture every LLM interaction across all four agents. When the coordinator decides to call `Analyzer`, log the coordinator's prompt (including the system message and conversation history), the model used (GPT-4o), the tool call it generates (`agent_MAKDO_Analyzer` with a specific message), token counts, and latency. Do the same for `Analyzer`'s interactions with its LLM when it processes the request. This creates a complete decision trail showing why MAKDO took each action.

Tool execution logs

Capture every tool invocation with input parameters, execution duration, output results, and success/failure status. Include stack traces for errors and context about why the tool was called.

In MAKDO, log every A2A call from `Analyzer` and `Fixer` to k8s-ai. Capture the skill name (`kubernetes_resource_health`), parameters (`cluster name`, `namespace`), the complete response from k8s-ai, and timing. Also log `Slack_Bot`'s MCP tool calls (`slack_post_message` with channel and message content). When debugging, you can reconstruct exactly what data each agent sent to external systems and what responses they received.

Agent state snapshots

Periodically capture the agent's internal state, including working memory, conversation history, accumulated context, and decision-making rationale. This helps with understanding how the state evolves over time. In the case of computer use or browser automation, capture screenshots after each agent action.

Span and trace hierarchies

Organize logs into hierarchical traces where a user request creates a parent span, and each agent action (LLM call, tool execution, and sub-agent delegation) creates child spans. This mirrors distributed tracing in microservices.

A MAKDO health check creates this span hierarchy:

Health check (root) → Coordinator LLM call → `agent_MAKDO_Analyzer` tool call → `Analyzer` LLM call → `kubernetes_resource_health` A2A call → `Analyzer` LLM call (processing results) → `agent_MAKDO_Slack_Bot` tool call → `slack_post_message` MCP call

Each span has timing and a status. If the Slack notification fails, you can trace backward through the hierarchy to see exactly which calls succeeded and where the failure occurred.

Metadata enrichment

Tag every operation with contextual metadata, such as user ID, session ID, agent type, task category, and environment (dev/staging/prod). This enables filtering and analysis across dimensions.

Tag MAKDO operations with `cluster_name: "kind-makdo-test"`, `health_check_cycle: 47`, `agent_type: "analyzer"`, and `operation_type: "diagnostics"`. When you need to debug why `Analyzer` keeps misidentifying Pods, query for all `Analyzer` diagnostics operations on that specific cluster and examine patterns across multiple health check cycles.

Structured logging and trace formats

Raw logs are difficult to query and analyze. Structured logging makes observability data queryable and actionable. This is best practice for any production-grade system but especially important for complex agentic AI systems. Most languages have mature libraries for structured logging (e.g., `structlog` for Python, `Winston` for Node.js, and `Logrus` for Go). Take advantage of these libraries to emit structured logs consistently. Here are some recommended practices to follow:

- **JSON-structured events**: Emit logs as structured JSON with a consistent schema, including timestamp, trace ID, span ID, parent span ID, event type, and event-specific fields. This enables efficient querying and aggregation.

- **Standardized event types**: Define a taxonomy of events, such as `agent.start`, `agent.complete`, `llm.request`, `llm.response`, `tool.invoke`, `tool.complete`, and `error.occurred`. Consistent event types enable automated analysis.
- **Correlation IDs**: Use correlation IDs to link related operations across agents, services, and systems. A single user request should have one correlation ID that flows through the entire system.
- **Semantic versioning for schemas**: As your observability schema evolves, version it so you can parse historical logs and maintain backward compatibility in analysis tools.

LLM-specific observability tools

Several specialized tools have emerged for observing LLM-based systems:

- **Datadog LLM Observability**: Datadog provides dedicated LLM observability capabilities that automatically capture and visualize LLM interactions. It tracks prompt templates, model invocations, token usage, latency metrics, and cost analysis across multiple LLM providers. Datadog's LLM Observability integrates with popular frameworks such as LangChain and LlamaIndex, providing out-of-the-box instrumentation for agentic applications. It enables tracking of multi-turn conversations, agent workflows, and tool usage patterns with minimal code changes. I implemented an LLM observability solution using OpenTelemetry (`https://opentelemetry.io/`) and Datadog LLM Observability at Invisible Platforms (`https://getinvisible.com/`), acquired by Perplexity. It was invaluable for diagnosing gnarly issues and performance bottlenecks.
  Key features include the following:
    - Automatic prompt and completion capture
    - Token usage and cost tracking per request
    - Latency percentiles and performance analysis
    - Error rate monitoring and alerting
    - Integration with existing APM and infrastructure monitoring
- **LangSmith**: LangChain's observability platform provides detailed traces of LangChain applications, including agent reasoning chains, tool usage, and retrieval steps. It offers a visual interface for exploring traces and debugging agent behavior.
- **Weights & Biases (WB)**: Offers prompt tracking, model performance monitoring, and experiment comparison for LLM applications. It is particularly useful for tracking prompt engineering iterations and A/B testing different agent configurations.

- **Helicone**: Provides real-time monitoring, caching, and analytics for LLM APIs. Tracks costs, latency, and success rates across multiple LLM providers with a unified interface.
- **Custom instrumentation frameworks**: Many teams build custom observability layers using OpenTelemetry as a foundation, adding LLM-specific context and metadata to standard distributed tracing.

Metrics and KPIs for agent performance

You can't manage what you don't measure. Define quantitative metrics to track agent health and performance, establishing baselines for normal operation and detecting when things go wrong. These metrics serve multiple purposes: they help you understand system behavior, justify infrastructure investments, optimize costs, and prove value to stakeholders.

Success rate metrics tell you whether your agents are actually completing their assigned tasks. A declining task completion rate might indicate prompt drift, environmental changes, or degraded tool reliability. The following are example success rate metrics:

- Task completion rate (percentage of tasks successfully completed)
- First-attempt success rate (completed without retries)
- Tool call success rate (percentage of tool invocations that succeed)

Performance metrics reveal how fast your system responds and how efficiently agents operate. High LLM call counts per task might indicate inefficient reasoning patterns or unnecessary retries that inflate costs and latency. The following are example performance metrics:

- End-to-end latency (user request to final response)
- LLM call latency (p50, p95, p99 percentiles)
- Tool execution latency
- Number of LLM calls per task
- Number of tool calls per task

Cost metrics are critical for production systems where token usage directly translates to cloud bills. A sudden spike in cost per request could indicate runaway agents, inefficient prompts, or agents using more expensive models than necessary. The following are example cost metrics:

- Token usage per request (prompt tokens + completion tokens)
- Cost per request (based on model pricing)
- Cost per successful task completion
- Cost efficiency (successful completions / total cost)

Quality metrics assess whether agents are producing correct, useful outputs. These are often harder to measure automatically but are crucial for understanding real-world performance beyond simple success/failure. The following are example quality metrics:

- Hallucination rate (detected fabricated information)
- Instruction following accuracy
- Output format compliance
- User satisfaction scores (if available)

System health metrics provide early warning signals of degradation. A rising timeout rate might precede a complete system failure, giving you time to investigate and remediate before users are severely impacted. The following are example system health metrics:

- Error rate by error type
- Timeout rate
- Retry rate
- Circuit breaker activations

Real-time monitoring and alerting

Passive observability isn't enough, as collecting metrics that you only look at after something breaks is like installing security cameras and only watching the feed after the robbery. You need active monitoring and alerting that catches problems before they impact users. The goal is to shift from reactive firefighting to proactive problem detection. Let's discuss some of the best ways to detect these problems:

- **Anomaly detection** helps you catch problems you didn't anticipate. Automatically detect unusual patterns such as sudden spikes in error rates, abnormal latency increases, or unexpected tool usage patterns. Use statistical baselines (such as standard deviations from the mean) or machine learning models to identify anomalies. This is especially valuable for agentic systems where failure modes can be unpredictable and context-dependent.
- **Threshold-based alerts** are your safety net for known critical conditions. Set alerts for critical thresholds such as the error rate exceeding 5%, average latency exceeding 10 seconds, or cost per hour exceeding budget limits. These should be carefully tuned to minimize false positives while ensuring no real incidents slip through. Too many noisy alerts lead to alert fatigue, where teams ignore notifications.
- **Trend analysis** reveals slow-moving problems before they become crises. Track metrics over time to identify gradual degradation. A slowly increasing average latency or declining success rate might indicate underlying issues before they become critical.

This "boiling frog" scenario is particularly dangerous because no single data point triggers an alert, but the cumulative effect significantly degrades user experience.

- **Cost runaway detection** is essential for LLM-based systems where costs can spiral out of control. Monitor token usage and costs in real time to detect runaway agents before they consume your entire budget. Alert when hourly spending exceeds expected patterns, especially during off-peak hours when you expect lower usage. A production incident at 2 A.M. that causes infinite loops can rack up thousands of dollars before anyone notices without proper cost monitoring.
- **Integration with incident management** ensures alerts reach the right people at the right time. Connect observability tools to incident management systems such as PagerDuty or Opsgenie for on-call alerting and escalation. Define escalation policies so critical alerts don't get lost in Slack channels, and ensure someone is always accountable for responding to production issues.

Now, armed with solid observability data, let's see how to debug our agentic AI system.

Debugging with observability data

Observability data is most valuable when it enables effective debugging. The difference between a system that collects data and one that enables debugging is whether engineers can quickly answer questions such as, "Why did this specific request fail?" or "What changed between yesterday and today?" Good observability data should make root cause analysis feel like detective work with all the clues laid out, not like searching for a needle in a haystack.

Trace replay is your time machine for understanding agent behavior. Capture complete traces so you can replay agent executions to understand exactly what happened. Include all prompts, responses, tool calls, and intermediate states to reconstruct the exact sequence of events. This is invaluable when debugging non-deterministic failures as you can see the actual prompts and responses that led to the failure, not just your assumptions about what should have happened.

Contextual search transforms raw logs into queryable knowledge. Enable searching logs by user request, error message, agent type, or any metadata field. "Find all failed deployments from Agent X in the last hour" should be a simple query, not a complex log parsing exercise. Structured logging with consistent metadata makes this possible; invest time in instrumenting properly and you'll save exponentially more time during debugging.

Correlation analysis helps you discover hidden relationships in your data. Analyze relationships between metrics: does increasing the prompt length correlate with higher error rates? Do certain tools have higher latency than others? Does the time of day affect success rates? These insights often reveal optimization opportunities or lurking bugs that aren't obvious from looking at individual metrics in isolation.

Comparative debugging is especially powerful for intermittent issues. Compare successful and failed executions side by side to identify differences. What did successful agents do that failed agents didn't? Did they use different tools, make fewer LLM calls, or process different input formats? This technique often reveals the critical difference that determines success or failure.

Time-series visualization makes patterns visible that are invisible in tabular data. Visualize metrics over time with tools such as Grafana or Datadog dashboards. Spot patterns, anomalies, and trends visually—humans are much better at recognizing visual patterns than scanning through columns of numbers. A sudden spike in latency or a gradual increase in error rates becomes immediately obvious in a well-designed dashboard.

Privacy and security considerations

Comprehensive observability introduces the risk of leaking sensitive information if not handled properly. A data breach of your observability system could expose customer data, business secrets, or security vulnerabilities. This tension between visibility and security must be carefully balanced through the following:

- **Personally identifiable information (PII) redaction** should be automatic and enforced at the instrumentation layer, not left to manual effort. Automatically redact PII from logs. Usernames, addresses, email addresses, credit card numbers, social security numbers, and other sensitive data should never appear in logs. Use regular expressions or machine learning-based detection to identify and redact PII before logs are written. Better yet, design your instrumentation to never capture PII in the first place by logging only identifiers such as user IDs that can be correlated with customer data through authorized, audited lookups.
- **Prompt sanitization** requires careful consideration of what you log. Be cautious about logging full prompts if they contain user data or sensitive business information. Consider logging only sanitized or anonymized versions, or logging prompts separately with stricter access controls. For high-security applications, you might hash prompts and only store the hash, allowing you to detect duplicate issues without exposing the actual content.
- **Access controls** should follow the principle of least privilege. Restrict access to observability data based on roles, as not everyone should see production logs containing customer data. Engineers might need access to debug issues, but that access should be logged and auditable. Consider implementing break-glass procedures for emergency access with automatic notifications to security teams. Some organizations maintain separate observability systems for different security tiers.

- **Retention policies** must balance competing needs. Define how long to retain observability data, balancing debugging needs with storage costs and compliance requirements. Recent data should be immediately available, but older data might be archived in cheaper storage or aggregated to reduce volume. Many regulations require specific retention periods or maximum retention limits, so ensure your policies comply with applicable rules.
- **Compliance** isn't optional. Ensure observability practices comply with regulations such as GDPR, HIPAA, SOC2, or other standards, depending on your domain and jurisdiction. This includes data residency requirements (where data can be stored), data processing agreements with observability vendors, and the right to deletion for customer data. Document your observability practices as part of compliance audits, and review them regularly as regulations evolve.

With a robust observability infrastructure in place, you have the foundation for effective debugging. Now let's dive into the specific challenge of debugging tool use and function call chains, which is one of the most common and frustrating debugging scenarios in agentic systems.

Debugging tool use and function call chains

Tool use is where agents interact with the real world, and it's also where things most frequently go wrong. An agent might call the wrong tool, pass invalid parameters, misinterpret tool results, or chain tools together incorrectly. Unlike pure reasoning errors that stay within the LLM, tool use failures have real consequences: failed deployments, incorrect database updates, or broken integrations. Debugging these issues requires understanding both what the agent intended to do and what actually happened.

Understanding the tool call life cycle

Let's review again how AI systems, AI frameworks, agents, and LLMs interact with tools and consider the failure modes. Every tool invocation goes through a predictable life cycle, and failures can occur at each stage:

- The agent decides which tool to call based on its understanding of the task and available tools. This decision can go wrong if tool descriptions are ambiguous, if the agent misunderstands the task, or if multiple tools seem equally applicable.
- The agent constructs parameters for the tool call, translating its abstract intent into concrete arguments. Parameter construction fails when the agent lacks necessary information, misunderstands parameter semantics, or generates syntactically valid but semantically incorrect values.

- The host AI system validates and invokes the tool, checking parameters against schemas and executing the actual operation. Validation can catch obvious errors, but semantic issues slip through. The tool execution itself might fail due to external factors: API timeouts, permission errors, or resource unavailability.
- The tool returns results that the agent must interpret. Even successful tool calls can cause problems if the agent misinterprets results, ignores important warnings, or fails to verify that the operation achieved its intended effect.

Understanding this life cycle helps you pinpoint where failures occur. A tool call that never happens indicates a decision problem. A tool call with invalid parameters indicates a construction problem. A tool call that executes but doesn't achieve its goal indicates an interpretation problem.

Tracing function call chains

Multistep agent workflows create chains of tool calls where each agent invokes the next agent as a tool call that depends on previous results. These chains can become complex quickly:

- **Linear chains** are the simplest: Tool A → Tool B → Tool C. Debugging linear chains means verifying each step and ensuring context flows correctly between steps. A break anywhere in the chain causes downstream failures.
- MAKDO's typical workflow is a linear chain.

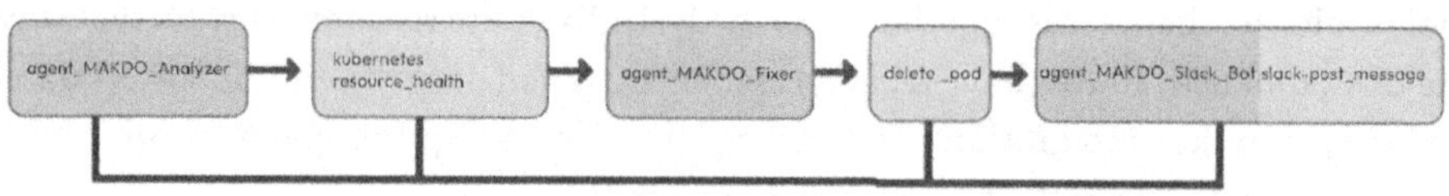

Figure 10.1: MAKDO typical workflow

If the Slack notification never arrives, trace backward: Did `Slack_Bot` get called? Did it receive the correct message? Did the MCP tool execute? Was the Slack API token valid? Each link in the chain must succeed for the full workflow to complete.

- **Conditional chains** branch based on intermediate results: Tool A → (if success: Tool B, if failure: Tool C). The agent must correctly interpret results and choose the right path. Debugging requires understanding both the branching logic and whether the condition was evaluated correctly. Remember that all the decisions are made by the LLM, so prompt design is critical to induce the correct logic.
The coordinator makes conditional decisions based on `Analyzer` results. If `Analyzer` reports `CrashLoopBackOff`, call `Fixer`. If it reports `ImagePullBackOff`, skip `Fixer` and

escalate to humans via `Slack_Bot`. If the coordinator consistently chooses the wrong branch (calling `Fixer` for `ImagePullBackOff`), the problem is in its system prompt or how it interprets `Analyzer`'s report structure.

- **Parallel chains** execute multiple tools concurrently: (Tool A + Tool B + Tool C) → Tool D. This is more efficient but introduces coordination challenges. Did all parallel operations complete? Did any fail? How did the agent aggregate results before proceeding to Tool D?
- **Recursive chains** involve agents calling themselves as tool calls (e.g., AI-6 sub-agents) or creating cycles: Tool A → Tool B → Tool A (with different parameters). These can be powerful but are prone to infinite loops if termination conditions aren't carefully managed.

  When debugging chains, trace backward from the failure point. Which tool call failed? What were its inputs? Where did those inputs come from? This archaeological approach often reveals that the root cause occurred several steps earlier in the chain.

Let's look at some common tool use anti-patterns and debugging strategies.

Common tool use anti-patterns

Here are some patterns of tool misuse that are common in agentic systems. Recognizing these anti-patterns helps you quickly identify likely root causes:

- **Zombie parameters**: The agent includes parameters that the tool ignores or doesn't recognize. This often happens when tool APIs change but agent prompts aren't updated, or when the agent hallucinates parameters based on similar tools. Zombie parameters are insidious because the tool call "succeeds" but doesn't behave as expected.

  For example, `Fixer` calls k8s-ai's `delete_pod` with an extra parameter: `force: true`. k8s-ai doesn't support a force parameter (it's not exposed via the A2A interface). k8s-ai ignores it and performs a normal delete. `Fixer` thinks it did a forced delete but it actually did a graceful delete. When debugging why Pods take 30 seconds to terminate, you discover that the force flag isn't working because k8s-ai silently ignores it.
- **Premature optimization**: The agent tries to do too much in a single tool call, passing complex nested structures or trying to perform multiple operations at once. This makes debugging harder and often fails because the tool doesn't support the complex use case. Breaking operations into smaller, simpler tool calls is usually more reliable. This is common with sophisticated CLI tools with a large number of commands and options, such as kubectl, `git`, or `bash` (which can run any other command installed on the host, including installing new commands).

For example, `Analyzer` tries to diagnose all Pods in all namespaces with a single k8s-ai call, passing a complex query structure. k8s-ai returns partial results or times out. A better approach would be to call `kubernetes_resource_health` once per namespace and aggregate the results in `Analyzer`. This results in simpler tool calls, more reliable execution, and easier debugging when one namespace fails.

- **Assumed state**: The agent assumes resources exist or are in a certain state without verifying. It tries to update a file that doesn't exist, deploy to a cluster that's offline, or query a database table that hasn't been created yet. Always verify preconditions before executing operations if possible.
- **Ignored errors**: The agent receives an error response from a tool but continues as if the operation succeeded. This happens when agents are over-optimized for happy paths and don't properly handle error responses. Failures cascade as subsequent tools operate on data that doesn't exist or is in an invalid state.
- **Retry madness**: The agent retries a failed operation repeatedly without changing anything. This is sometimes correct when waiting for the previous operation to complete. However, if a tool call fails due to invalid parameters, retrying with the same parameters will fail again. Effective retries require either changing parameters, waiting for external conditions to change, or using a different approach entirely.

Let's look at strategies to debug and prevent these issues.

Debugging strategies for tool use

When tool calls go wrong, we need a systematic approach for debugging them. The following strategies are effective:

- **Replay with inspection**: Capture the exact tool call (name, parameters, and context) and replay it in isolation. Does it succeed outside the agent? If so, the problem is how the agent is calling it. If not, the problem is with the tool itself or its dependencies.
- **Parameter validation**: Independently verify that each parameter makes sense. Don't just check types—verify semantics. Is this file path valid? Does this cluster name exist? Is this ID formatted correctly? Create validation tools that agents can call before executing risky operations or write wrappers with validation logic and expose the wrappers as tools.
- **Result verification**: After successful tool calls, verify that the operation achieved its intent. An API might return "200 OK" but not actually perform the operation due to business logic errors. Have agents explicitly check that resources were created, files were written, or configurations were applied. Again, this can be done in a wrapper tool that performs verification after calling the real tool.

- **Diff analysis**: Compare failed tool calls with successful ones. What's different? Parameters? Timing? Context? Environmental factors? Often, the difference reveals the root cause.
- **Tool shadowing**: Implement shadow tools that log calls without executing them. Use these during development to verify agents are calling tools correctly before allowing real operations. This is especially valuable for destructive operations such as deletions or deployments.

In order to reduce the incidence of tool use errors, consider building guardrails into your agentic AI systems.

Building tool use guardrails

Prevention is better than debugging. You should build guardrails that catch tool use errors before they cause problems. Here are some effective guardrails:

- **Schema validation**: Enforce strict parameter schemas and reject invalid tool calls before execution. Use JSON Schema or similar validation to catch type errors, missing required fields, or values outside allowed ranges.
- **Dry-run modes**: Support dry-run or preview modes for all destructive operations. The agent can call the tool with `dry_run=true` to see what would happen without actually doing it. This catches many errors before they impact production.
- **Confirmation prompts**: For high-stakes operations, require explicit confirmation. The agent describes what it's about to do and must confirm before execution. This creates a natural breakpoint for human-in-the-loop review.
- **Tool compatibility checks**: When agents chain tools together, verify that output formats match input requirements. If Tool A returns JSON but Tool B expects YAML, catch this incompatibility before execution.
- **Rate limiting and circuit breakers**: Prevent runaway tool use by limiting how many times a tool can be called within a time window. If an agent calls the same tool 50 times in a minute, something is wrong. It should halt execution and alert the human who will investigate.

We have covered in depth how to diagnose, debug, and build guardrails to address tool use problems. Let's consider how to diagnose coordination failures, which are prevalent in multi-agent systems.

Diagnosing coordination failures in multi-agent workflows

Multi-agent systems derive their power from coordination. Multiple agents work together to accomplish complex tasks that no single agent could handle alone. However, this coordination introduces new failure modes that are challenging to diagnose. Unlike single-agent failures that have clear root causes, coordination failures often emerge from the interactions between agents, making them harder to isolate and debug.

When agents don't coordinate properly, the symptoms can be subtle: tasks that are partially complete, duplicated work, conflicting actions, or mysterious deadlocks where the system appears to hang. These failures don't fit neatly into traditional debugging categories because the problem isn't with any individual component; it's with how components interact.

This section provides systematic approaches for diagnosing coordination failures in multi-agent workflows, understanding where breakdowns occur, and implementing strategies to prevent them.

Understanding coordination failure patterns

The first step in diagnosing coordination failures is recognizing when they're happening and understanding your system's interaction patterns. Coordination failures manifest in characteristic patterns that differ from single-agent failures. Let's discuss some common coordination failure symptoms.

First up is **partial task completion**. It is one of the clearest signals of coordination failure. The overall task appears to be "done," but critical steps are missing. Say Agent A completes its part and hands off to Agent B, but Agent B never receives the work or doesn't understand what to do with it. The result is a task that's 80% complete but stuck in limbo. Users report that "something isn't working," but can't articulate exactly what. Individual agents succeeded at their narrow tasks while the overall objective failed. The following figure illustrates this concept:

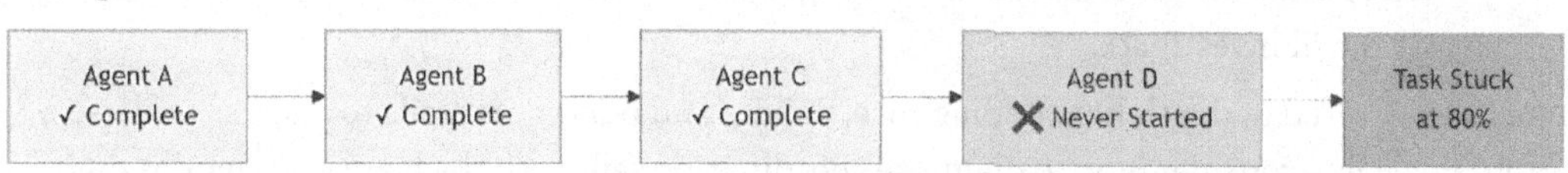

Figure 10.2: Partial task completion as workflow stops at 80% when Agent D never starts

In MAKDO, the coordinator agent calls the `Analyzer` agent, gets the diagnostic report, and then calls the `Fixer` agent to remediate. `Fixer` successfully deletes a failing Pod. But the coordinator never calls `Slack_Bot` to notify the team. Remediation happened, the cluster is fixed, but humans have no visibility. They check Slack hours later and see no updates, don't know whether the issue was resolved, and might manually intervene on an already-fixed problem.

Another failure pattern is **work duplication**, which occurs when multiple agents perform the same work without realizing that another agent has already handled it. For example, two deployment agents both deploy the same service, two data processing agents both transform the same dataset, or two customer service agents both respond to the same ticket. This wastes resources and can cause race conditions or an inconsistent state. The symptom is often visible in metrics: unusually high tool call counts, duplicate log entries, or users receiving multiple responses to a single request. See the following figure:

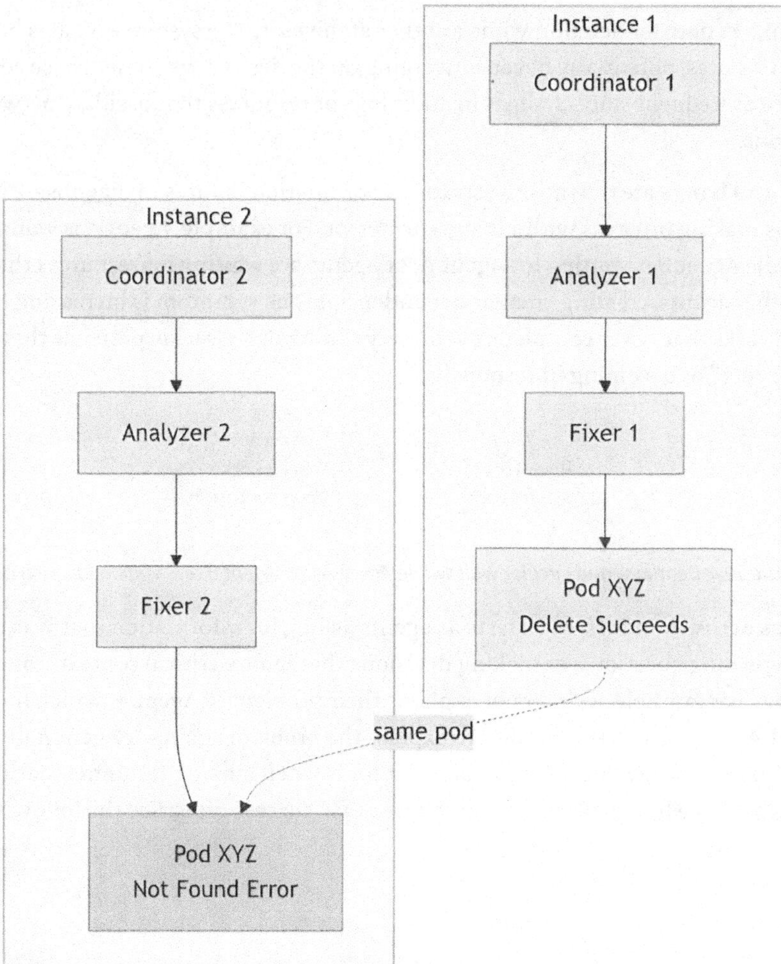

Figure 10.3: Work duplication as two MAKDO instances process the same Pod simultaneously

Two MAKDO health check cycles start at nearly the same time due to a timing bug. Both coordinators independently call their `Analyzer` agents to check the same cluster. Both `Analyzer` agents identify the same three failing Pods and report them. Both coordinators then call their `Fixer` agents. Both `Fixer` agents attempt to delete the same Pods via `k8s-ai`. The first succeeds, while the second gets "pod not found" errors. Both post separate reports to Slack, confusing the team with duplicate notifications and conflicting results.

Another key failure pattern is **conflicting actions**, which occur when agents work at cross-purposes because they don't share context or objectives. One agent scales up infrastructure while another scales it down. One agent closes a ticket while another escalates it.

One agent marks data for deletion while another archives it. The system thrashes between contradictory states, potentially never converging on the desired outcome. These conflicts often surface as frequent state changes in audit logs or resources that oscillate between configurations.

Deadlocks and hangs are the most frustrating coordination failures to diagnose. The system simply stops making progress without any clear error. For example, Agent A is waiting for Agent B, while Agent B is waiting for Agent A, or agents are waiting for resources that are locked by other agents, creating circular dependencies. The symptom is increasing latency metrics and tasks that never complete, eventually timing out. Users experience this as the system "freezing" or becoming unresponsive:

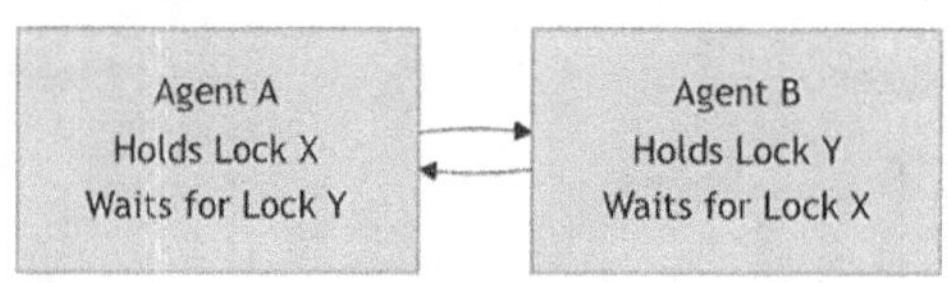

Figure 10.4: Deadlock and circular wait where Agent A and Agent B are waiting for each other

Context loss across handoffs manifests as agents asking for information that was already provided, repeating questions, or making decisions that ignore critical context from earlier in the workflow. For example, a customer explains their problem to Agent A, which hands off to Agent B, but Agent B asks the customer to explain the problem again. Or Agent A discovers a configuration issue but Agent B doesn't account for it when making recommendations. This degraded experience frustrates users and reduces task success rates. See the following figure:

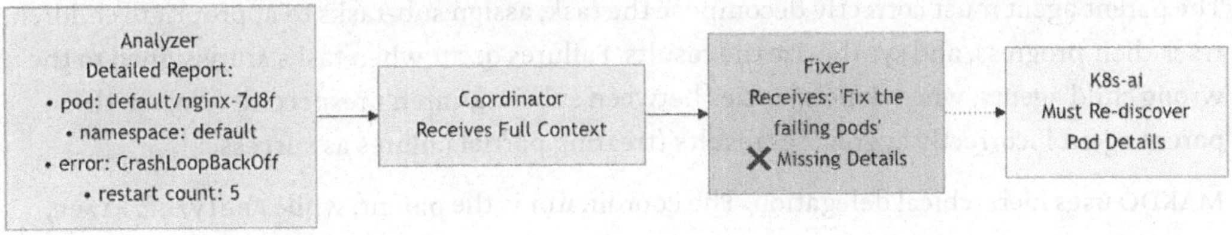

Figure 10.5: Context loss in handoffs as detailed information from Analyzer gets lost when the coordinator delegates to Fixer

`Analyzer` identifies three failing Pods and provides detailed information: Pod names, namespaces, error messages, and restart counts. The coordinator receives this complete report. When delegating to `Fixer`, the coordinator just says, "Fix the failing pods in the cluster" without passing the specific Pod names or details. `Fixer` has to call k8s-ai again to rediscover which Pods are failing, wasting time and tokens. The diagnostic work happens twice because the context wasn't preserved in the handoff.

Finally, we have **message ordering issues** that occur when agents receive messages out of sequence, leading to a confused state or incorrect decisions. For example, Agent B processes a "cancel" message before processing the original "create" message, leading to attempts to cancel something that doesn't exist yet. Or agents receive partial results before final results, cache the partial data, and make decisions based on incomplete information. Symptoms include unexplained errors about missing resources or state inconsistencies that don't match execution logs.

Agent interaction patterns and their failure modes

To diagnose coordination failures, you need to understand how agents interact in your system. Different interaction patterns have different failure modes and require different debugging approaches.

Sequential workflows involve agents passing work from one to the next in a chain: Agent A → Agent B → Agent C → Agent D. Each agent must complete its work and successfully hand off to the next agent. Failures typically occur at handoff boundaries. For example, Agent B doesn't receive work from Agent A, or Agent C receives incomplete data from Agent B. Debugging requires examining the handoff protocol: what data is transferred, how is it formatted, and how does the receiving agent know that work has arrived? Trace the execution linearly, identifying which handoff failed and why.

Hierarchical delegation involves parent agents delegating sub-tasks to specialized child agents, then aggregating their results. For example, a coordinating agent breaks down "deploy the application" into sub-tasks such as "provision infrastructure" (delegated to Agent A), "configure services" (delegated to Agent B), and "run smoke tests" (delegated to Agent C).

The parent agent must correctly decompose the task, assign sub-tasks to appropriate children, track their progress, and synthesize the results. Failures occur when tasks are assigned to the wrong child agents, when dependencies between sub-tasks aren't respected, or when the parent agent incorrectly aggregates results (treating partial failures as successes).

MAKDO uses hierarchical delegation. The coordinator is the parent, while `Analyzer`, `Fixer`, and `Slack_Bot` are the children. The coordinator must correctly sequence their invocations: call `Analyzer` first to diagnose, then `Fixer` to remediate based on diagnosis, then `Slack_Bot` to notify. If the coordinator calls `Fixer` before `Analyzer`, remediation happens without diagnosis. If it calls them in parallel, `Fixer` might start before `Analyzer` finishes, missing critical context about what needs fixing.

Peer-to-peer collaboration involves agents of equal status working together, often negotiating who does what. Multiple customer service agents might all be capable of handling a ticket, so they need a protocol to prevent multiple agents from responding to the same request.

Debugging peer-to-peer coordination requires understanding the consensus mechanism: How do agents decide who handles what? Common patterns include leader election (one agent becomes the leader and assigns work), token-based coordination (holding a token grants permission to work), and optimistic concurrency (agents attempt work and resolve conflicts if they occur). Trace through the coordination protocol to find where agreement breaks down.

Event-driven coordination involves agents responding to events published to a shared event bus or message queue. For example, Agent A publishes a "user-registered" event, Agent B subscribes to that event and sends a welcome email, and Agent C subscribes and creates a customer profile. This pattern is loosely coupled. Agents don't know about each other directly, only about events. Failures occur when events are lost, delivered out of order, or processed multiple times. Debugging requires visibility into the event bus: Was the event published? Which agents received it? Did they process it successfully? Event-driven coordination failures often leave no direct trace because the publishing agent has no knowledge of whether subscribers processed the event. Deep observability is essential.

Shared state coordination involves agents coordinating through shared data structures such as databases, caches, or distributed state stores. For example, Agent A writes data to a database, and Agent B reads it and makes decisions based on it. This pattern requires careful attention to consistency, locking, and transaction boundaries. Failures occur due to race conditions (two agents read before either writes), stale reads (Agent B reads old data that Agent A has since updated), or lock contention (agents wait indefinitely to acquire locks). Debugging requires examining the timing of reads and writes and understanding the consistency guarantees of your storage system.

Make sure to draw a diagram of your multi-agent workflow showing which patterns you're using. Many real systems combine patterns, such as hierarchical delegation for task decomposition, event-driven coordination for loose coupling, and shared state for tracking overall workflow progress.

Understanding your interaction patterns is essential for debugging because each pattern has specific failure modes and requires specific diagnostic techniques.

Tracing dependencies and data flow

Coordination failures often stem from broken dependencies between agents or corrupted data flow. This section covers techniques for tracing what agents depend on and how information flows between them.

Here are the types of inter-agent dependencies:

- **Explicit dependencies** are dependencies that are defined in code or configuration. For example, Agent B's task definition includes a `depends_on: [Agent_A]` field, or Agent C's input schema requires outputs from Agent B. These are relatively easy to debug because they're documented. Check whether the dependency graph accurately reflects the actual dependencies in your workflow.
  Are there missing dependencies? Circular dependencies that create deadlocks? Dependencies that reference agents or resources that don't exist?
- **Implicit dependencies** are more insidious. They are dependencies that exist in practice but aren't captured in your orchestration system. For example, Agent B assumes a certain database table exists, which Agent A should have created, but there's no formal dependency relationship. Agent C assumes API keys have been provisioned, which Agent D handles, but Agent D runs asynchronously and might not have completed when Agent C starts.
  These implicit dependencies cause failures that are hard to diagnose because the system's understanding of dependencies doesn't match reality. The fix is usually to make implicit dependencies explicit by adding proper dependency declarations or restructuring the workflow to eliminate the assumptions.
- **Data dependencies** involve agents requiring specific data from previous stages. Agent B needs the customer ID that Agent A looked up, and Agent C needs the deployment URL that Agent B created. Trace data flow through your system: Does each agent receive the data it needs? Is data transformed or filtered in ways that remove critical information? Are there optional fields that agents treat as required, causing failures when the field is absent? Look for schema mismatches, missing error handling when expected data is absent, or overly strict validation that rejects valid inputs.

In MAKDO, `Fixer` depends on `Analyzer` providing specific Pod identifiers. If `Analyzer` returns a vague summary ("several pods failing") instead of precise names ("default/nginx-7d8f, default/api-server-5c9b"), `Fixer` can't act. The data dependency is broken. `Fixer` might try to remediate based on incomplete information, miss some Pods, or have to call k8s-ai again to get the details it needs.

- **Temporal dependencies** involve timing constraints. For example, Agent B must run after Agent A completes, but also before a five-minute window expires. Or Agent C depends on external systems being in a certain state, which changes over time. These are particularly tricky because they depend on execution timing, making failures non-deterministic. A workflow might succeed when agents execute quickly, but fail when there's network latency or resource contention. Diagnose temporal dependencies by adding timestamps to all coordination events and looking for patterns: do failures correlate with increased latency? Do they happen during high-load periods? Add explicit timeout handling and consider asynchronous patterns that don't assume tight timing.
- **Resource dependencies** involve agents needing access to shared resources such as API rate limits, database connections, compute instances, or locks on shared state. If multiple agents compete for limited resources, some may fail or experience delays. Trace resource allocation: Are agents getting the resources they need? Are resources being released properly after use? Are there resource leaks where agents hold resources indefinitely? Monitor resource utilization metrics alongside agent execution traces to correlate resource exhaustion with coordination failures.

Tools such as distributed tracing systems (OpenTelemetry, Jaeger, and Zipkin) are invaluable for visualizing dependencies. They show parent-child relationships between spans, allowing you to see which agents depend on which, how long each step took, and where failures occurred in the dependency graph. Without distributed tracing, reconstructing dependencies from logs is tedious and error-prone.

Here is a figure illustrating all the agent dependencies:

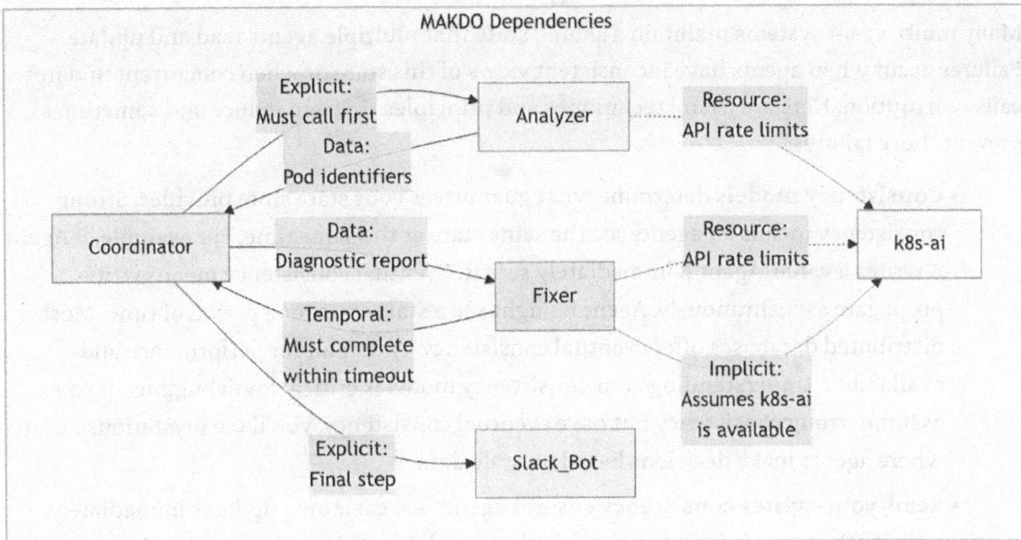

Figure 10.6: MAKDO dependency types showing explicit, implicit, data, temporal, and resource dependencies between agents

As we discussed earlier in the chapter, state management in a multi-agent system is very challenging. Let's see how to debug shared state and synchronization issues.

Managing shared state and detecting deadlocks

When multiple agents share state or compete for resources, coordination becomes particularly challenging. This section covers techniques for debugging state synchronization issues and detecting deadlocks.

State synchronization challenges

Many multi-agent systems maintain a shared state that multiple agents read and update. Failures occur when agents have inconsistent views of this state or when concurrent updates cause corruption. Here are useful techniques and principles that can reduce and sometimes prevent these failures:

- **Consistency models** determine what guarantees your state store provides. Strong consistency means all agents see the same state at the same time. For example, if Agent A writes a value, Agent B immediately sees it. Eventual consistency means writes propagate asynchronously. Agent B might see a stale state for a period of time. Most distributed databases offer eventual consistency by default for performance and availability. Understanding your consistency model is critical for debugging: if you assume strong consistency but have eventual consistency, you'll see mysterious failures where agents make decisions based on stale data.
- **Read-your-writes consistency** ensures agents see their own updates immediately, even if other agents might not yet see those updates. This prevents confusing scenarios where an agent writes a value, then immediately reads back a different value. Verify that your state store provides read-your-writes consistency or implement it at the application layer by caching recent writes.
- **Optimistic concurrency control** assumes conflicts are rare and detects them when they occur. For example, agents read data with a version number, make updates, then write back with the version number. If another agent modifies the data in the meantime (version number changed), the write fails, and the agent must retry. This works well for low-contention scenarios but fails under high concurrency. Diagnose this by checking for repeated write failures and version conflicts in logs. Note that some data, such as counters or accumulators, are automatically immune to conflicts because their updates are commutative.
- **Pessimistic locking** prevents conflicts by having agents acquire locks before accessing shared state. For example, Agent A locks a record, updates it, and then releases the lock. This prevents conflicts but can cause deadlocks if agents lock multiple resources in different orders, or if agents crash while holding locks. Diagnose locking issues by tracking lock acquisitions and releases, looking for locks that are held for unexpectedly long periods or never released. Utilize expiration-based locks that automatically release after a timeout to prevent permanent lockouts.

State synchronization patterns include several common approaches:

- **Leader election**: One agent becomes the leader and manages the shared state, while other agents read from the leader

- **Distributed consensus**: Agents use protocols such as Raft or Paxos to agree on state changes
- **Command Query Responsibility Segregation (CQRS)**: Separate agents for writes (commands) and reads (queries), with asynchronous synchronization
- **Event sourcing**: Store state as a sequence of events, agents build state by replaying events

Each pattern has trade-offs in complexity, performance, and consistency guarantees. Choose based on your requirements and ensure all agents correctly implement the chosen pattern or patterns.

Diagnosing state corruption requires comparing the expected state (based on the sequence of operations) with the actual state. The system can reconstruct what should have happened by replaying operation logs, then compare with the actual data store state. Discrepancies indicate either bugs in state update logic or race conditions where concurrent updates interfered with each other. Use database transaction logs or audit logs to see the exact sequence of writes and identify where corruption occurred.

Detecting and resolving deadlocks

Deadlocks are particularly nasty coordination failures where agents wait indefinitely for each other, making no progress. The system appears to hang without any obvious error. Here are the types of deadlocks:

- **Classic deadlocks** occur when agents hold resources while waiting for other resources:
    - Agent A holds lock X and waits for lock Y
    - Agent B holds lock Y and waits for lock X
    - Neither can proceed

  Detect this by tracking lock acquisitions and looking for circular wait patterns. Resolve this by enforcing lock ordering (all agents acquire locks in the same order) or using timeouts (if a lock isn't acquired within *N* seconds, release all locks and retry).

- **Message deadlocks** occur in request-response patterns:
    - Agent A sends a request to Agent B and waits for a response
    - Agent B sends a request to Agent A and waits for a response
    - Neither can respond because both are waiting

  Prevent this by using asynchronous message patterns instead of synchronous request-response, or by ensuring agents can process incoming requests while waiting for responses (non-blocking handlers).

Note that sequential or hierarchical interaction design (such as MAKDO) is less prone to message deadlocks because agents don't wait on each other in cycles. Peer-to-peer and event-driven patterns are more susceptible.

- **Dependency deadlocks** occur in task scheduling:
    - Task A depends on Task B completing
    - Task B depends on Task A completing
    - Neither can start

  You can detect this issue by analyzing the dependency graph for cycles before execution. Resolve it by eliminating cyclic dependencies through workflow redesign.

- **Resource deadlocks** occur with limited resources:
    - Agent A holds resource X and waits for resource Y
    - Agent B holds resource Y and waits for resource X
    - Both wait indefinitely

  You can detect this by tracking resource allocation and looking for agents that are waiting for resources while holding other resources. You can resolve this with timeout-based resource acquisition (if you can't get all of the needed resources within a timeout, release what you have and retry) or by pre-allocating all of the needed resources before starting work.

  Note that this is different from resource exhaustion, where agents fail because resources are simply unavailable. Deadlocks involve circular waiting, while exhaustion involves lack of availability.

Debugging deadlocks requires capturing the state of all agents when the deadlock occurs: What is each agent doing? What resources does it hold? What is it waiting for? Thread dumps (for thread-based agents) or state snapshots (for event-driven agents) provide this information. When you visualize wait relationships as a directed graph, the deadlocks appear as cycles.

Debugging multi-agent systems requires a lot of effort both upfront in collecting the necessary data to help you troubleshoot and when problems actually occur. If possible, it's better to invest in prevention so you can eliminate whole categories of problems right away. Let's see how to build coordination guardrails that help you with this approach.

Building coordination guardrails

Prevention is better than debugging. Build the following guardrails into your multi-agent system to catch coordination errors before they cause failures:

- **Dependency validation** checks the dependency graph for problems before execution. Are there circular dependencies? Dependencies on non-existent agents? Missing required dependencies? Validate at deployment time and reject invalid workflow definitions.
- **Timeout enforcement** ensures no agent waits forever. Set maximum timeouts for all inter-agent communication, tool executions, and resource acquisitions. When timeouts occur, fail gracefully with clear error messages rather than hanging indefinitely. Protocols such as retries with exponential backoff and jittering help avoid thundering herd problems during retries.
- **Idempotency requirements** ensure agents can safely retry operations. Mark which operations are idempotent and which aren't. For non-idempotent operations, implement mechanisms to detect and skip duplicate executions.
- **State validation** periodically checks whether the shared state is consistent and valid. Run background jobs that verify invariants: "the sum of all account balances equals the total deposits minus withdrawals" or "every task assigned to an agent references an existing agent ID." Alert when invariants are violated. Build the ability to repair inconsistencies automatically when possible.
- **Circuit breakers** prevent cascading failures. For example, if Agent B is consistently failing, Agent A should stop calling it rather than generating more failures. Implement circuit breaker patterns that detect failure rates and temporarily halt inter-agent communication when one agent is unhealthy. If you aim for high availability, have fallback agents that can take over when primary agents fail.
- **Coordination testing** validates that agents interact correctly. Write integration tests that exercise multi-agent workflows, including edge cases such as the following:
    - What happens if Agent B is slow or unresponsive?
    - What happens if Agent A sends malformed data to Agent B?
    - What happens if messages are delivered out of order?
    - What happens if two agents try to update the same resource simultaneously?

These guardrails catch coordination bugs before they reach production.

Even with the best guardrails, some failures are unavoidable. But the overall system must be able to recover and continue operating. This requires explicit design choices. Let's see what it takes.

Designing for resilience and recoverability

Large-scale multi-agent AI systems must be designed for resilience and recoverability. Failures are inevitable, so systems must gracefully handle errors, recover from failures, and continue operating with minimal disruption. In addition to the standard distributed systems challenges, which are known to be far from trivial to solve, multi-agent systems introduce new complexities due to agent interactions, shared state, and tool dependencies. The entire ecosystem must be resilient, not just individual components. Let's look at key strategies for building resilient multi-agent AI systems. We've mentioned some of them earlier, but now we'll cover them in more depth.

Redundancy and failover mechanisms

Redundancy is a core principle of resilience. Critical components should have redundant instances that can take over if one fails. In the context of multi-agent AI systems, one of the most important aspects is the LLM providers. Relying on a single LLM provider creates a single point of failure. If that provider experiences downtime, rate limiting, or degraded performance, your entire system suffers. To mitigate this risk, implement multi-provider strategies.

Design your agents to be able to switch between multiple LLM providers (e.g., OpenAI, Anthropic, and Google Gemini) based on availability, cost, or performance. Abstract the LLM interface so agents can use any provider interchangeably.

Another dimension of redundancy is the models your agents use. If an agent is built around a specific model with highly tuned prompts and relying on built-in tools, then it may struggle to switch models. Design agents to be model-agnostic where possible, allowing them to use different models with minimal changes. This may involve standardizing prompts, tool interfaces, and response parsing. If you really need to optimize to a specific model, have backup models that can be used in emergencies, even if they are not as optimized as the primary model.

Pay special attention to the tools available to your agents. Some models, such as GPT-5, come with built-in tools (e.g., code interpreters or web browsers) that are tightly integrated. If your agent relies on these tools, ensure that alternative tools are available when switching models. For example, if an agent uses a code interpreter tool that becomes unavailable, have a fallback mechanism to use an external code execution service.

When interacting with external services via tools (e.g., databases or APIs), implement failover strategies. If one service endpoint is unreachable, have backup endpoints or alternative services that can be used. Use DNS-based load balancing or service discovery to route requests to healthy instances. Ideally, the tools themselves can implement retry and failover logic implicitly, so agents don't need to handle it directly. But if not possible (e.g., when using third-party MCP tools), you will either need to build a wrapper tool that implements failover or have the agents handle it by exposing this as a layer of alternate tools and instructing the agents to manage failover.

Graceful degradation strategies

When failures occur, the system should degrade gracefully rather than failing completely. Graceful degradation means reducing functionality while maintaining core operations. A multi-agent system might disable non-essential features, reduce quality, or slow down processing rather than shutting down entirely. The key is to prioritize critical workflows and sacrifice less important ones when resources are constrained or components fail.

Define degradation tiers for your multi-agent system. For example, Tier 1 is full functionality with all features working. Tier 2 might disable analytics or logging to reduce load. Tier 3 could switch to simpler, faster models that are less accurate but more reliable. Tier 4 might disable automated remediation and only perform diagnostics. Each tier maintains some value while consuming fewer resources or depending on fewer components. Design agents to detect which tier they're operating in and adjust behavior accordingly. For MAKDO, the degradation model may look like the following:

- Tier 1 runs full health checks with detailed analysis and automated fixing
- Tier 2 skips automated fixes and only reports issues to Slack for human intervention
- Tier 3 performs basic health checks without detailed diagnostics
- Tier 4 pauses health checks entirely and only responds to explicit user requests

Implement feature flags or kill switches that allow operators to disable specific functionality during incidents. If the `Fixer` agent starts making incorrect decisions, a kill switch can disable automated remediation while keeping diagnostics and notifications running. If k8s-ai becomes slow or unreliable, fall back to simpler kubectl commands for basic operations. If Slack is down, buffer notifications and deliver them when service is restored, or send alerts via email as a backup channel.

The system adapts to what's available rather than failing because one component is unavailable.

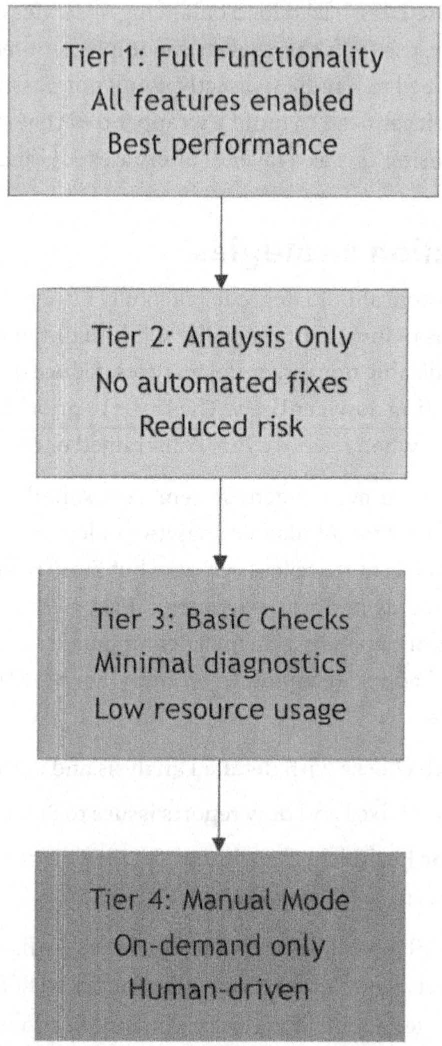

Figure 10.7: MAKDO degradation tiers from full functionality to manual mode

Sometimes, failures are temporary, and instead of degrading gracefully, you just have to try again. But there is an art and science to classifying and handling failures.

Retry logic and circuit breakers

Transient failures are common in distributed systems. Network glitches, temporary API rate limits, or brief service overloads can cause operations to fail even when the underlying system is healthy. Retry logic handles these transient failures by automatically retrying failed operations after a delay. The key is distinguishing between transient failures worth retrying and permanent failures that will never succeed. Retrying a network timeout makes sense. Retrying an invalid API key does not. Design retry logic to identify retryable errors and give up quickly on permanent failures.

Implement exponential backoff with jitter for retries. Start with a short delay (100 ms), then double it with each retry (200 ms, 400 ms, 800 ms). Add random jitter to prevent thundering herd problems where many agents retry simultaneously and overwhelm the failing service. Cap the maximum delay (e.g., 30 seconds) and limit total retry attempts (e.g., five tries). Log each retry attempt with context about why it failed so you can identify patterns. For MAKDO, if k8s-ai returns a *503 Service Unavailable error*, retry with exponential backoff. If it returns a *401 Unauthorized error*, fail immediately because retrying won't fix invalid credentials. If `Fixer` tries to delete a Pod and gets a timeout, retry a few times before giving up and escalating to humans via Slack.

Circuit breakers prevent cascading failures by stopping requests to unhealthy services. A circuit breaker monitors the failure rate of operations to a downstream service. When failures exceed a threshold (e.g., 50% failure rate over 10 requests), the circuit breaker opens and immediately fails all requests without attempting them. This gives the failing service time to recover without being bombarded with requests. After a timeout period (e.g., 60 seconds), the circuit breaker enters a half-open state and allows a few test requests through. If they succeed, the circuit closes and normal operation resumes. If they fail, the circuit stays open. Circuit breakers are essential for multi-agent systems because one slow or failing service can block many agents waiting for responses.

In MAKDO, if k8s-ai becomes unresponsive and every `Analyzer` request times out, a circuit breaker would open after a few failures. Subsequent health checks would skip calling k8s-ai entirely and immediately report degraded status to Slack, rather than having every coordinator wait 30 seconds for timeouts.

This prevents the entire MAKDO system from grinding to a halt when one dependency fails.

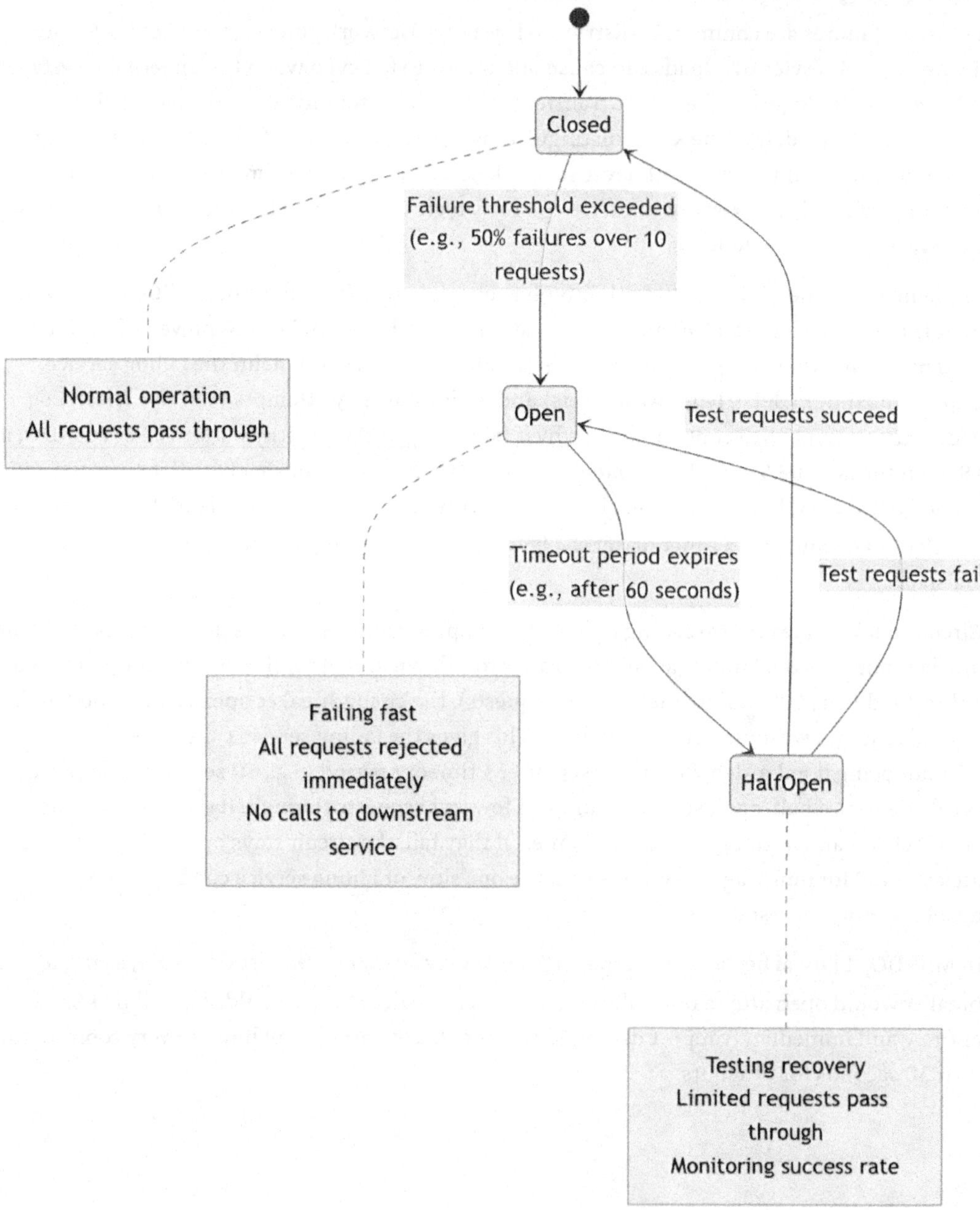

Figure 10.8: Circuit breaker states transitioning between closed, open, and half-open based on failure rates and timeouts

When things go south, you retry or just pause and continue later; you don't want to lose important work that happened before the failure. This is where checkpointing is very useful.

Checkpointing and state recovery

Multi-agent workflows can be long-running and involve multiple expensive steps across different agents. If an agent crashes mid-workflow, the system needs to recover without starting from scratch. Note that this is not required for fast workflows that complete in seconds, but for workflows that take minutes or longer, checkpointing is often essential.

Checkpointing saves the state of a workflow at key points so it can be resumed after failures. Each checkpoint captures what work has been completed, what data has been produced, and what remains to be done. When an agent recovers from a crash, it loads the most recent checkpoint and continues from there rather than redoing work that already succeeded.

Design checkpoints at natural boundaries in your workflows. After each agent completes its work, and before delegating to the next agent, save a checkpoint. Store checkpoints in durable storage, such as a database or distributed key-value store, not in agent memory. Include enough context in checkpoints to resume work: input parameters, intermediate results, which agents have run, and which steps remain. Add metadata such as timestamps, workflow IDs, and correlation IDs to track checkpoints across distributed systems. For MAKDO, the checkpoint is after `Analyzer` completes and returns its diagnostic report. If the coordinator crashes before calling `Fixer`, the replacement coordinator can load the checkpoint, see that analysis is complete, and proceed directly to remediation. Without checkpointing, the entire health check would restart, wasting `Analyzer`'s work and doubling the time to fix issues. `Fixer` should also checkpoint after completing every remediation step, so if it crashes and restarts, it can continue where it left off. `Slack_Bot` doesn't need checkpointing as the worst case is that it will resend a notification.

Implement idempotent recovery to handle partial failures safely. When resuming from a checkpoint, the system might re-execute some operations that were partially completed before the crash. Design operations to be idempotent so re-execution produces the same result. If `Fixer` deleted a Pod but crashed before updating the checkpoint, recovery might try to delete the same Pod again. k8s-ai should handle this gracefully by returning success if the Pod is already gone. Store operation IDs or transaction tokens in checkpoints to detect and skip duplicate operations. Clean up old checkpoints periodically to avoid unbounded storage growth. Once a workflow completes successfully, delete its checkpoints. Keep failed workflow checkpoints longer for debugging. Balance checkpoint frequency against overhead. Checkpointing after every tool call adds latency and storage costs. Checkpointing only at the beginning and end of workflows means more work gets lost on failures. Find the right granularity for your system's reliability requirements and operational costs.

Human escalation patterns

Not all failures can be handled automatically. Some situations require human intervention in terms of judgment or approval. Multi-agent systems need clear escalation patterns that bring humans into the loop at appropriate times. The key is escalating early enough that humans can prevent damage, but not so aggressively that they're overwhelmed. This means that the system has to be smart enough to request human feedback for critical decisions only, and avoid notifying or requesting permissions for each and every action. For example, if the system has to analyze 100 documents and requests permission to read each one, then the human approver will find this tedious and the overall process will be slower (for example, if the human approver leaves for lunch).

Design escalation rules based on confidence levels, risk assessment, and failure severity. High-confidence, low-risk operations can proceed automatically. Low-confidence or high-risk operations should wait for human approval.

Define explicit triggers that bring humans into the loop. Unknown errors that agents can't classify require human judgment. Low confidence scores below a threshold indicate uncertainty that humans should review. Operations affecting production systems or critical resources need approval before proceeding. Multiple retry attempts often indicate permanent failures that need investigation. Degraded-mode operation means reduced functionality that teams should know about. For MAKDO, `Analyzer` might identify issues that `Fixer` doesn't know how to remediate, and `Fixer` might fail in attempting to fix some problem due to insufficient permissions. k8s-ai unavailability means the system can't perform diagnostics, and humans need to know. Each notification should include rich context: what failed, why it failed, what was attempted, and what options are available. The coordinator should collect the information and tell the `Slack_Bot` agent to inform the humans with clear action items so the team knows exactly what decision is needed.

Provide humans with actionable options, not just notifications. Instead of "Health check failed," say, "3 pods in the default namespace are crash-looping. Option 1: Delete and restart them (automated). Option 2: Investigate logs first (manual). Option 3: Ignore and wait for next health check." Include buttons or commands that let humans approve actions directly from Slack without switching context. Time-bound escalations with default actions. If a human doesn't respond within 15 minutes, either take the safest default action or escalate further to on-call engineers. Track escalation patterns to identify recurring issues. If the same type of failure always requires human intervention, that's a signal to improve agent capabilities or add automation. If humans always choose the same option, consider making it the automatic default. The goal is continuous improvement, where fewer escalations are needed over time as agents learn to handle more situations autonomously.

With that, we come to the end of our deep dive into testing, debugging, and troubleshooting multi-agent AI systems.

Summary

In this chapter, we explored the unique challenges of testing, debugging, and troubleshooting multi-agent AI systems. We covered strategies for designing effective tests that validate inter-agent coordination, tracing dependencies and data flow to identify failures, managing shared state and detecting deadlocks, and building guardrails to prevent coordination errors. We also discussed designing for resilience and recoverability through redundancy, graceful degradation, retry logic, checkpointing, and human escalation patterns. Multi-agent systems introduce new complexities beyond traditional software systems, but with careful design and robust tooling, these challenges can be effectively managed to build reliable and maintainable multi-agent AI systems. Don't forget that you can add introspective AI agents to your system that will help monitor, debug, and even fix issues automatically as they arise.

In the next chapter, we will explore how to deploy and operate multi-agent AI systems in the field.

11

Deploying Multi-Agent Systems

In the previous chapter, we covered testing, debugging, and troubleshooting multi-agent systems. We explored common failure modes such as hallucination and tool misuse, instrumentation and observability strategies, debugging techniques for coordination failures, and designing for resilience through redundancy and graceful degradation. We used MAKDO throughout as a concrete example to illustrate these concepts.

Now, it's time to deploy MAKDO for real. But running multi-agent systems in production introduces new challenges around deployment architecture, service discovery, networking, and security. How do you deploy agents across multiple environments? How do they communicate securely? How do you manage credentials and access control?

In this chapter, we deploy MAKDO in a realistic production-like setup. We'll create two Kubernetes clusters using **Kubernetes in Docker** (**KinD**). The control cluster runs MAKDO itself. The worker cluster is the target cluster that MAKDO monitors and manages. K8s-ai (an agent-to-agent server) runs on the worker cluster, providing MAKDO with the ability to diagnose and fix issues through the **Agent-to-Agent** (**A2A**) protocol. This setup mirrors real production scenarios where your management systems run separately from the workloads they manage.

We'll walk through setting up both clusters, deploying MAKDO components to the control cluster, deploying k8s-ai to the worker cluster, configuring secure cross-cluster communication, and managing service discovery and access control. By the end, you'll have a fully functional multi-agent system managing a separate Kubernetes cluster, ready to detect and remediate issues automatically.

The following key points are covered:

- Setting up dual KinD clusters for multi-agent deployment
- Deploying MAKDO to the control cluster
- Deploying k8s-ai to the worker cluster
- Enabling secure communication between clusters

Technical requirements

Follow the instructions at `https://github.com/PacktPublishing/Design-Multi-Agent-AI-Systems-Using-MCP-and-A2A/tree/main/ch11/makdo`.

Setting up dual KinD clusters for multi-agent deployment

Let's build a production-like deployment where MAKDO runs on one cluster and manages another. This separation is critical in real environments to isolate management infrastructure from production workloads. It reduces the blast radius and allows the production system to keep operating even if MAKDO is not operational. Also, if the production cluster suffers resource exhaustion or a similar issue, MAKDO will be able to analyze and potentially fix it because it is not subject to the same problems.

Installing KinD and prerequisites

Before creating clusters, you need Docker, kubectl, and KinD installed. Rather than walking through installation steps for each tool (which vary by platform and change over time), we provide a verification script that checks that everything is ready.

First, clone the book's repository if you haven't already:

```
git clone git@github.com:PacktPublishing/Design-Multi-Agent-AI-Systems-using-MCP-
and-A2A.git
```

Install the required tools using their official documentation:

- **Docker**: `https://docs.docker.com/get-docker/`
- **kubectl**: `https://kubernetes.io/docs/tasks/tools/`
- **KinD**: `https://kind.sigs.k8s.io/docs/user/quick-start/#installation`

Once installed, verify that everything is working with our prerequisites check script:

```
cd ch11
chmod +x check-prerequisites.sh
./check-prerequisites.sh
```

The script checks whether Docker is installed and running, kubectl is available, KinD is installed (version 0.20.0 or newer recommended), and disk space is available (need ~10 GB for both clusters), Docker memory allocation (need at least 4 GB), and existing KinD clusters that might conflict with our setup.

If the script reports any missing prerequisites, install them using the preceding links and run the script again. When you see **All prerequisites met!**, you're ready to create clusters.

Creating the control cluster configuration

The control cluster hosts MAKDO agents. It needs to be configured to allow external access to MAKDO's API endpoints. KinD uses YAML configuration files to define cluster topology and networking.

Create `control-cluster.yaml`:

```
kind: Cluster
apiVersion: kind.x-k8s.io/v1alpha4
name: makdo-control
nodes:
- role: control-plane
  kubeadmConfigPatches:
  - |
    kind: InitConfiguration
    nodeRegistration:
      kubeletExtraArgs:
        node-labels: "cluster-role=control"
  extraPortMappings:
  # Port for accessing MAKDO API/dashboard if needed
  - containerPort: 30080
    hostPort: 8080
    protocol: TCP
  # Port for MAKDO health check endpoint
  - containerPort: 30090
    hostPort: 9090
    protocol: TCP
```

Here are the key configuration points:

- `name`: `makdo-control` identifies this cluster. KinD uses this name for the Docker container and kubectl context.
- `node-labels`: Labels help identify which cluster a pod is running in. Useful for debugging and monitoring.
- `extraPortMappings`: Exposes ports from the cluster to your host machine. Port `8080` maps to container port `30080` (the `NodePort` range in Kubernetes). Port `9090` maps to `30090` for health checks. These mappings let you access MAKDO services from your local machine or allow the worker cluster to reach MAKDO, if needed.

Next, create the control cluster:

```
kind create cluster --config control-cluster.yaml
```

This takes 1–2 minutes. KinD downloads the Kubernetes node image (if not cached), creates a Docker container, and initializes Kubernetes. When complete, you'll see the following:

```
Creating cluster "makdo-control" ...
 ✓ Ensuring node image (kindest/node:v1.33.1) 🖼
 ✓ Preparing nodes 📦
 ✓ Writing configuration 📜
 ✓ Starting control-plane 🕹️
 ✓ Installing CNI 🔌
 ✓ Installing StorageClass 💾
Set kubectl context to "kind-makdo-control"
```

Note

The exact Kubernetes version (v1.33.1 in this example) depends on which KinD version you have installed. KinD automatically uses a compatible Kubernetes version.

Verify the cluster:

```
kubectl cluster-info --context kind-makdo-control
kubectl get nodes --context kind-makdo-control
```

Here's the expected output:

```
Kubernetes control plane is running at https://127.0.0.1:60905
CoreDNS is running at https://127.0.0.1:60905/api/v1/namespaces/kube-system/
services/kube-dns:dns/proxy

NAME                          STATUS   ROLES           AGE   VERSION
makdo-control-control-plane   Ready    control-plane   1m    v1.33.1
```

One node is in the Ready status. The cluster is running but empty.

Creating the worker cluster configuration

The worker cluster is where your actual workloads run. MAKDO monitors this cluster and fixes issues when they arise. This cluster needs to expose k8s-ai's MCP server so MAKDO can communicate with it.

Create `worker-cluster.yaml`:

```
kind: Cluster
apiVersion: kind.x-k8s.io/v1alpha4
name: makdo-worker
nodes:
- role: control-plane
  kubeadmConfigPatches:
  - |
    kind: InitConfiguration
    nodeRegistration:
      kubeletExtraArgs:
        node-labels: "cluster-role=worker"
  extraPortMappings:
  # Port for k8s-ai MCP server
  - containerPort: 30100
    hostPort: 8100
    protocol: TCP
  # Port for exposing problematic workloads (for testing)
  - containerPort: 30200
    hostPort: 8200
    protocol: TCP
```

Here are the key differences from the control cluster:

- `name: makdo-worker` distinguishes this from the control cluster.
- `node-labels: cluster-role=worker` identifies this as a managed cluster.
- `Port 8100`: Maps to container port `30100`, where k8s-ai's A2A server will run. MAKDO's Analyzer and Fixer agents call k8s-ai through this port using the A2A protocol.
- `Port 8200`: For test workloads. We'll deploy broken pods here that MAKDO can detect and fix.

Create the worker cluster:

```
kind create cluster --config worker-cluster.yaml
```

You now have two independent Kubernetes clusters running as Docker containers:

```
kind get clusters
```

Here's the expected output (you may see other clusters too):

```
makdo-control
makdo-worker
```

Check both cluster contexts:

```
kubectl config get-contexts | grep makdo
```

Here is the output:

```
          kind-makdo-control   kind-makdo-control   kind-makdo-control
*         kind-makdo-worker    kind-makdo-worker    kind-makdo-worker
```

The * symbol indicates which context is currently active. Switch between them with the following:

```
# Use control cluster
kubectl config use-context kind-makdo-control

# Use worker cluster
kubectl config use-context kind-makdo-worker
```

Both clusters are isolated. Pods in one cluster can't directly reach pods in the other without explicit networking configuration, which we'll set up next.

Setting up cluster networking and port forwarding

KinD clusters run as Docker containers on your host machine. They're on the same Docker network, which means they can reach each other using Docker networking. But services inside the clusters need special configuration to be accessible.

First, find the Docker network that both clusters are using:

```
docker network ls | grep kind
```

Here is the output:

```
aadf3e99800d   kind          bridge    local
```

Both cluster containers are connected to this `kind` network:

```
docker network inspect kind | grep -A 3 "makdo"
```

This shows the IP addresses of both cluster containers. However, we don't want to hardcode IPs. Instead, we'll use the port mappings we configured earlier.

For cross-cluster communication, MAKDO (on the control cluster) needs to reach k8s-ai (on the worker cluster). Since both clusters are on the same host, MAKDO can reach k8s-ai at `host.docker.internal:8100`. This special DNS name resolves to the host machine from inside Docker containers.

Let's verify that the port mappings are working. Check what's listening on the mapped ports:

```
# Control cluster ports
lsof -i :8080 2>/dev/null || echo "Port 8080: not yet in use"
lsof -i :9090 2>/dev/null || echo "Port 9090: not yet in use"

# Worker cluster ports
lsof -i :8100 2>/dev/null || echo "Port 8100: not yet in use"
lsof -i :8200 2>/dev/null || echo "Port 8200: not yet in use"
```

Right now, these ports aren't in use because we haven't deployed any services yet. The port mappings are configured but inactive until services bind to the internal ports (`30080`, `30090`, `30100`, and `30200`).

Check that the Docker containers themselves are running and have the port mappings:

```
docker ps --format "table {{.Names}}\t{{.Ports}}" | grep makdo
```

Here is the output:

```
makdo-worker-control-plane    127.0.0.1:61462->6443/tcp, 0.0.0.0:8100->30100/tcp,
0.0.0.0:8200->30200/tcp
makdo-control-control-plane   127.0.0.1:60905->6443/tcp, 0.0.0.0:8080->30080/tcp,
0.0.0.0:9090->30090/tcp
```

You can see both containers with their port mappings. The 6443 ports are the Kubernetes API servers. Our custom mappings (8080->30080, 8100->30100, etc.) are ready for services to use.

Verifying cross-cluster connectivity

Before deploying MAKDO and k8s-ai, verify that both clusters are healthy and can potentially communicate.

Check the cluster health:

```
kubectl cluster-info --context kind-makdo-control
kubectl get nodes --context kind-makdo-control
```

Here is the output:

```
Kubernetes control plane is running at https://127.0.0.1:60905
CoreDNS is running at https://127.0.0.1:60905/api/v1/namespaces/kube-system/
services/kube-dns:dns/proxy

NAME                          STATUS   ROLES           AGE   VERSION
makdo-control-control-plane   Ready    control-plane   15m   v1.33.1
```

Now, check the worker cluster:

```
kubectl cluster-info --context kind-makdo-worker
kubectl get nodes --context kind-makdo-worker
```

Here is the output:

```
Kubernetes control plane is running at https://127.0.0.1:61462
CoreDNS is running at https://127.0.0.1:61462/api/v1/namespaces/kube-system/
```

```
services/kube-dns:dns/proxy

NAME                          STATUS   ROLES           AGE   VERSION
makdo-worker-control-plane    Ready    control-plane   12m   v1.33.1
```

Both clusters show their control plane running, and one node is in the `Ready` status.

Test basic networking within each cluster:

```
# Test DNS in control cluster
kubectl run dns-test --image=busybox:latest --restart=Never --rm -i --context
kind-makdo-control --command -- \
    nslookup kubernetes.default.svc.cluster.local

# Test DNS in worker cluster
kubectl run dns-test --image=busybox:latest --restart=Never --rm -i --context
kind-makdo-worker --command -- \
    nslookup kubernetes.default.svc.cluster.local
```

Both should successfully resolve the Kubernetes service DNS name.

For cross-cluster communication, MAKDO won't directly reach pods in the worker cluster. Instead, MAKDO will call k8s-ai's A2A server through the exposed port. We'll test this once k8s-ai is deployed. The clusters are ready for the next step.

Deploying a test workload to the worker cluster

To verify that MAKDO works correctly, we need workloads with problems for it to detect and fix. Let's deploy a test namespace with three pods: one that crashes, one with an image pull error, and one that's healthy.

Create `test-workload.yaml`:

```
apiVersion: v1
kind: Namespace
metadata:
  name: test-workload
---
# A pod that will crashloop - missing required environment variable
apiVersion: v1
kind: Pod
metadata:
  name: crashloop-pod
```

```
    namespace: test-workload
    labels:
      app: crashloop-test
spec:
  containers:
  - name: app
    image: busybox:latest
    command: ["sh", "-c"]
    args:
      - |
        if [ -z "$REQUIRED_VAR" ]; then
          echo "ERROR: REQUIRED_VAR not set"
          exit 1
        fi
        echo "Running successfully"
        sleep 3600
---
# A pod with an image that doesn't exist
apiVersion: v1
kind: Pod
metadata:
  name: imagepull-pod
  namespace: test-workload
  labels:
    app: imagepull-test
spec:
  containers:
  - name: app
    image: nonexistent-registry.example.com/fake-image:v1.0.0
    command: ["sleep", "3600"]
---
# A healthy pod for comparison
apiVersion: v1
kind: Pod
metadata:
  name: healthy-pod
  namespace: test-workload
  labels:
    app: healthy-test
spec:
  containers:
```

```
  - name: app
    image: nginx:alpine
    ports:
    - containerPort: 80
```

Deploy to the worker cluster:

```
kubectl apply -f test-workload.yaml --context kind-makdo-worker
```

Check the pod status:

```
kubectl get pods -n test-workload --context kind-makdo-worker
```

Here is the output:

```
NAME            READY   STATUS             RESTARTS      AGE
crashloop-pod   0/1     CrashLoopBackOff   7 (27s ago)   11m
healthy-pod     1/1     Running            0             11m
imagepull-pod   0/1     ImagePullBackOff   0             11m
```

Perfect! We have the following:

- `crashloop-pod`: `CrashLoopBackOff` (exits immediately due to a missing environment variable)
- `healthy-pod`: Running (`nginx` started successfully)
- `imagepull-pod`: `ImagePullBackOff` (image doesn't exist)

Watch the `crashloop-pod` restart repeatedly:

```
kubectl get pods -n test-workload --context kind-makdo-worker --watch
```

Press *Ctrl* + *C* to stop watching. These failing pods are perfect targets for MAKDO. The Analyzer will detect them, classify the failure types, and the Fixer may attempt remediation.

Check the pod logs to see the failure reasons:

```
kubectl logs crashloop-pod -n test-workload --context kind-makdo-worker
```

Here is the output:

```
ERROR: REQUIRED_VAR not set
```

The worker cluster now has problematic workloads. Next, we'll deploy MAKDO to the control cluster and k8s-ai to the worker cluster, then watch MAKDO automatically detect and handle these issues.

Deploying MAKDO to the control cluster

Now that we have both clusters running and test workloads failing in the worker cluster, it's time to deploy MAKDO. MAKDO will run as a Deployment in the control cluster and monitor the worker cluster through k8s-ai's A2A server.

Preparing the MAKDO configuration

MAKDO needs configuration files to know which clusters to monitor, how to connect to k8s-ai, and how to communicate via Slack. We'll adapt the example configuration for our two-cluster setup.

Check out `https://github.com/PacktPublishing/Design-Multi-Agent-AI-Systems-Using-MCP-and-A2A/tree/main/ch11/makdo` for details.

Here are the key configuration points:

- **Clusters**: Only the worker cluster is listed. MAKDO doesn't need to monitor its own control cluster. The context `kind-makdo-worker` matches the kubectl context created by KinD.
- `kubeconfig_path`: Set to `/root/.kube/config` because this is where `kubeconfig` will be mounted inside the MAKDO container. We'll mount `kubeconfig` as a volume.
- `k8s_ai.base_url`: Uses `host.docker.internal:8100` to reach k8s-ai on the worker cluster. This special DNS name resolves to the host machine from inside Docker containers. Port `8100` is the mapped port for k8s-ai's A2A server.
- **Environment variables**: API keys and tokens use the `${VAR}` syntax. MAKDO loads these from environment variables, which we'll provide via Kubernetes secrets.
- `monitoring.check_interval`: Set to 120 seconds (2 minutes). MAKDO polls the worker cluster every two minutes to detect issues quickly.

Next, we need the agent configuration files. MAKDO uses separate YAML files for each agent's prompt and tool configuration.

Create `makdo-config/coordinator.yaml`:

```
name: "MAKDO Coordinator"
description: |
  You are the MAKDO Coordinator, the central orchestrator for multi-cluster
```

```
Kubernetes operations.

  Your responsibilities:
  1. Periodically check cluster health across all registered clusters
  2. Coordinate between Analyzer, Fixer, and Slack Bot agents
  3. Escalate critical issues to appropriate agents
  4. Maintain operational awareness of all clusters

  When asked to perform health checks:
  1. Use the Analyzer agent to assess cluster health
  2. If issues are found, use the Slack Bot to notify users
  3. For critical issues, use the Fixer agent if remediation is needed
  4. Always report status back to the Slack channel

  Be proactive, clear, and focused on cluster reliability.

model_id: "gpt-4o"

sub_agents:
  - name: "MAKDO_Analyzer"
    config_path: "src/makdo/agents/analyzer.yaml"

  - name: "MAKDO_Fixer"
    config_path: "src/makdo/agents/fixer.yaml"

  - name: "MAKDO_Slack_Bot"
    config_path: "src/makdo/agents/slack.yaml"

history:
  max_messages: 10
  summarize_after: 5
Create makdo-config/analyzer.yaml:
name: "MAKDO Analyzer"
description: |
  You are the MAKDO Analyzer agent. Your role is to diagnose Kubernetes cluster
health issues.

  Your responsibilities:
  1. Check cluster resource health (pods, deployments, services, nodes)
  2. Identify problems like CrashLoopBackOff, ImagePullBackOff, resource
exhaustion
```

```
  3. Analyze logs and events to understand root causes
  4. Provide clear diagnostic reports to the Coordinator

  When analyzing issues:
  1. Always check ALL namespaces, not just default
  2. Look at pod status, events, and logs
  3. Identify patterns across multiple failing pods
  4. Classify issues by severity (critical, warning, info)
  5. Provide actionable recommendations

  Use the k8s diagnostic tools available to you through the A2A protocol.

model_id: "gpt-4o"

tools:
  - name: "kubernetes_resource_health"
    type: "a2a"
    endpoint: "http://host.docker.internal:8100"
    description: "Check health of Kubernetes resources (pods, deployments,
services, nodes)"

  - name: "kubernetes_diagnose_issue"
    type: "a2a"
    endpoint: "http://host.docker.internal:8100"
    description: "Diagnose specific Kubernetes issues by analyzing events, logs,
and resource state"

history:
  max_messages: 8
  summarize_after: 4
Create makdo-config/fixer.yaml:
name: "MAKDO Fixer"
description: |
  You are the MAKDO Fixer agent. Your role is to remediate Kubernetes cluster
issues safely.

  Your responsibilities:
  1. Apply fixes for diagnosed issues from the Analyzer
  2. Always prioritize safety and avoid destructive actions
  3. Request approval for critical operations
  4. Verify fixes were successful after applying
```

```
  Common remediation actions:
  - Restart failing pods
  - Update pod configurations to fix missing env vars
  - Scale deployments
  - Apply configuration changes

  CRITICAL SAFETY RULES:
  1. Never delete resources without explicit approval
  2. Always verify before applying changes
  3. If unsure, ask for human approval
  4. Test fixes on non-production resources first when possible

  Use the k8s remediation tools available through the A2A protocol.

model_id: "gpt-4o"

tools:
  - name: "kubernetes_apply_fix"
    type: "a2a"
    endpoint: "http://host.docker.internal:8100"
    description: "Apply fixes to Kubernetes resources (restart pods, update
configs, scale)"

  - name: "kubernetes_verify_fix"
    type: "a2a"
    endpoint: "http://host.docker.internal:8100"
    description: "Verify that applied fixes resolved the issue"

history:
  max_messages: 6
  summarize_after: 3
Create makdo-config/slack.yaml:
name: "MAKDO Slack Bot"
description: |
  You are the MAKDO Slack Bot agent. Your role is to communicate with users via
Slack.

  Your responsibilities:
  1. Post cluster health reports to the #makdo-devops channel
  2. Alert users to critical issues
```

```
  3. Provide status updates on ongoing operations
  4. Respond to user questions about cluster health

  Message formatting:
  - Use clear, concise language
  - Highlight critical issues with appropriate urgency
  - Include relevant details (pod names, namespaces, error messages)
  - Provide actionable next steps when possible

  Always post to #makdo-devops channel unless told otherwise.

model_id: "gpt-4o"

mcp_servers:
  slack:
    command: "npx"
    args: ["@korotovsky/slack-mcp-server"]
    env:
      SLACK_BOT_TOKEN: "${AI6_BOT_TOKEN}"
      SLACK_TEAM_ID: "${SLACK_TEAM_ID}"

history:
  max_messages: 5
  summarize_after: 3
```

These configuration files define each agent's behavior, tools, and how they communicate. The Analyzer and Fixer agents use A2A tools pointing to k8s-ai. The `Slack_Bot` agent uses an MCP server for Slack integration.

Creating Kubernetes secrets for API keys

MAKDO needs API keys for OpenAI (to run the LLM-based agents) and Slack (to post messages). We'll store these as Kubernetes secrets in the control cluster.

First, create a `.env` file with your API keys:

```
cat > .env <<EOF
OPENAI_API_KEY=sk-...your-key-here...
AI6_BOT_TOKEN=xoxb-...your-slack-bot-token...
AI6_APP_TOKEN=xapp-...your-slack-app-token...
SLACK_TEAM_ID=T...your-team-id...
EOF
```

Replace the placeholders with your actual keys. If you don't have these keys yet, here's where to get them:

- **OpenAI API key**: Get from `https://platform.openai.com/api-keys`
- **Slack tokens**: Create a Slack app at `https://api.slack.com/apps` with bot token scopes (`chat:write` and `channels:read`) and an app-level token for socket mode
- **Slack Team ID**: Find in your Slack workspace settings under **Workspace ID**

Create the Kubernetes secret in the control cluster:

```
# Switch to control cluster
kubectl config use-context kind-makdo-control

# Load environment variables
set -a
source .env
set +a

# Create secret
kubectl create secret generic makdo-secrets \
  --from-literal=openai-api-key="$OPENAI_API_KEY" \
  --from-literal=slack-bot-token="$AI6_BOT_TOKEN" \
  --from-literal=slack-app-token="$AI6_APP_TOKEN" \
  --from-literal=slack-team-id="$SLACK_TEAM_ID" \
  -n default
```

Verify that the secret was created:

```
kubectl get secret makdo-secrets -n default
```

Here is the output:

```
NAME            TYPE     DATA   AGE
makdo-secrets   Opaque   4      5s
```

The secret is created. Don't worry about the values being hidden. That's the point of secrets. You can verify that the keys exist:

```
kubectl describe secret makdo-secrets -n default
```

Here is the output:

```
Name:         makdo-secrets
Namespace:    default
Labels:       <none>
Annotations:  <none>

Type:  Opaque

Data
====
openai-api-key:    51 bytes
slack-app-token:   53 bytes
slack-bot-token:   56 bytes
slack-team-id:     11 bytes
```

The secret is ready. We'll mount these as environment variables in the MAKDO deployment.

Creating the kubeconfig ConfigMap

MAKDO needs access to the worker cluster's `kubeconfig` file to manage it. We'll create a `ConfigMap` resource containing the `kubeconfig` file and mount it into the MAKDO pod. Note that in production, it is better to store it in a secret for security purposes.

Extract the worker cluster `kubeconfig` and create a `ConfigMap`:

```
# Create kubeconfig ConfigMap from your local kubeconfig
kubectl create configmap makdo-kubeconfig \
  --from-file=config=$HOME/.kube/config \
  --context kind-makdo-control
```

This `ConfigMap` will be mounted at `/root/.kube` in the MAKDO container, allowing it to access both the control and worker clusters.

Verify that the `ConfigMap` was created:

```
kubectl get configmap makdo-kubeconfig --context kind-makdo-control
```

Here is the output:

```
NAME               DATA   AGE
makdo-kubeconfig   1      5s
```

The `kubeconfig` is now available for MAKDO to use when connecting to the worker cluster.

Deploying MAKDO as a Kubernetes deployment

MAKDO will run as a deployment with one replica. A deployment provides automatic restarts if the pod crashes and makes it easy to update the configuration by rolling out new versions.

Here is the deployment manifest:

`https://github.com/PacktPublishing/Design-Multi-Agent-AI-Systems-Using-MCP-and-A2A/blob/main/ch11/makdo/deployment.yaml`.

Here are the key deployment configurations:

- `ConfigMap`: Contains the `makdo.yaml` configuration file. This lets us update the configuration without rebuilding the Docker image.
- `replicas: 1`: Single instance of MAKDO. Multiple replicas would cause duplicate health checks and coordination conflicts. In production, it is recommended to use leader election to have a standby instance ready to take over.
- `imagePullPolicy: Never`: We'll build the MAKDO image locally and load it into KinD. Never pull from a registry to get the latest code.
- **The** `env` **section**: Environment variables loaded from the `makdo-secrets` secret. These override the `${VAR}` placeholders in the config.
- `volumeMounts`: Two volumes are mounted:
    - `/app/config`: The MAKDO configuration from the `ConfigMap`
    - `/root/.kube`: The `kubeconfig` file from the `ConfigMap` so MAKDO can access both clusters
- `resources`: Memory and CPU limits prevent MAKDO from consuming too much. 512 Mi to 1 Gi is reasonable for the Python process and LLM calls.
- `volumes`: Two `ConfigMap` resources are mounted:
    - `makdo-config`: Contains the MAKDO configuration file
    - `makdo-kubeconfig`: Contains the `kubeconfig` file for accessing both clusters

Before deploying, we need to build the MAKDO Docker image and load it into the control cluster.

Building and loading the MAKDO image

MAKDO needs to be packaged as a Docker image. We'll create a Dockerfile that installs all dependencies and runs the main MAKDO process.

Create `makdo/Dockerfile`:

```
FROM python:3.13-slim

# Install system dependencies
RUN apt-get update && apt-get install -y \
    curl \
    git \
    kubectl \
    && rm -rf /var/lib/apt/lists/*

# Install Node.js for Slack MCP server
RUN curl -fsSL https://deb.nodesource.com/setup_20.x | bash - \
    && apt-get install -y nodejs \
    && rm -rf /var/lib/apt/lists/*

WORKDIR /app

# Copy MAKDO source from the book repository
# Adjust path based on where you cloned the book repo
COPY ../../packt/Design-Multi-Agent-AI-Systems-Using-MCP-and-A2A/ch09/makdo/src ./
src
COPY ../../packt/Design-Multi-Agent-AI-Systems-Using-MCP-and-A2A/ch09/makdo/
pyproject.toml .

# Install MAKDO dependencies
RUN pip install --no-cache-dir ai-six==0.14.4 pyyaml python-dotenv requests

# Create required directories
RUN mkdir -p /app/config /app/logs

# Set Python to run unbuffered so logs appear immediately
ENV PYTHONUNBUFFERED=1

# Run MAKDO main entry point
CMD ["python", "-m", "src.makdo.main"]
```

The Dockerfile uses Python 3.13. This version has prebuilt binary wheels for all dependencies, so no compilation is needed. We install kubectl for Kubernetes cluster access and Node.js for the Slack MCP server. The Python dependencies (`ai-six`, `pyyaml`, `python-dotenv`, and `requests`) install directly from wheels without needing build tools.

Build the image:

```
cd ch11/makdo
docker build -t makdo:latest .
```

This takes a few minutes to download base images and install dependencies. Watch for errors. If the build fails due to a missing MAKDO source, verify that the `src` directory is present.

Once built, load the image into the control cluster:

```
kind load docker-image makdo:latest --name makdo-control
```

This transfers the image from your local Docker to the KinD cluster's internal image cache. Here's the output:

```
Image: "makdo:latest" with ID "sha256:..." not yet present on node "makdo-control-
control-plane", loading...
```

Verify that the image is available:

```
docker exec -it makdo-control-control-plane crictl images | grep makdo
```

You should see the `makdo` image listed. Now we can deploy.

Apply the deployment:

```
kubectl apply -f deployment.yaml --context kind-makdo-control
```

Here is the output:

```
configmap/makdo-config created
deployment.apps/makdo created
```

Check the deployment status:

```
kubectl get deployment makdo --context kind-makdo-control
```

Here is the output:

```
NAME     READY   UP-TO-DATE   AVAILABLE   AGE
makdo    1/1     1            1           15s
```

MAKDO is running. One replica is ready.

Configuring MAKDO to connect to the worker cluster

MAKDO needs a `kubeconfig` file to access the worker cluster and a k8s-ai session token to use the A2A tools. The `kubeconfig` file is already mounted from the host. Now, we need to ensure that MAKDO can create sessions with k8s-ai.

The k8s-ai server isn't deployed yet. We'll deploy it in the next section. For now, verify that MAKDO can at least start and access the worker cluster via kubectl.

Check the MAKDO pod logs:

```
kubectl logs -l app=makdo --context kind-makdo-control --tail=50
```

You'll likely see errors about k8s-ai being unreachable. That's expected. Look for logs showing that MAKDO started successfully:

```
2025-11-02 10:15:32,123 - makdo - INFO - Starting MAKDO - Multi-Agent Kubernetes
DevOps System
2025-11-02 10:15:32,456 - makdo - INFO - Coordinator and sub-agents created
successfully
2025-11-02 10:15:32,500 - makdo - INFO - Setting up tool call monitoring...
2025-11-02 10:15:32,550 - makdo - INFO - ✅ Tool call monitoring enabled for all
agents
2025-11-02 10:15:32,600 - makdo - INFO - Getting kubeconfig for context: kind-
makdo-worker
```

If you see errors about kubectl or `kubeconfig`, the `kubeconfig` `ConfigMap` may be missing or incorrect. Verify that you created the `makdo-kubeconfig` `ConfigMap` with your `kubeconfig` file.

To test kubectl access from inside the MAKDO pod, use the following:

```
kubectl exec -it deployment/makdo --context kind-makdo-control -- kubectl get
nodes --context kind-makdo-worker
```

This runs kubectl inside the MAKDO container to query the worker cluster. Here is the output:

```
NAME                         STATUS   ROLES           AGE   VERSION
makdo-worker-control-plane   Ready    control-plane   45m   v1.33.1
```

Success! MAKDO can reach the worker cluster. The k8s-ai connection will work once we deploy k8s-ai.

Verifying MAKDO deployment and logs

Let's verify that MAKDO is healthy and ready to monitor the worker cluster. Check the pod status:

```
kubectl get pods -l app=makdo --context kind-makdo-control
```

Here is the output:

```
NAME                     READY   STATUS    RESTARTS   AGE
makdo-7c9f8b6d5d-x2k4j   1/1     Running   0          2m
```

The pod is running. Check resource usage:

```
kubectl top pod -l app=makdo --context kind-makdo-control
```

Here is the output (requires `metrics-server`, and may not work in KinD):

```
Error from server (ServiceUnavailable): the server is currently unable to handle
the request (get pods.metrics.k8s.io)
```

That's fine. KinD doesn't include `metrics-server` by default. We can check resource limits from the pod spec:

```
kubectl describe pod -l app=makdo --context kind-makdo-control | grep -A 5
"Limits"
```

Here is the output:

```
    Limits:
      cpu:     500m
      memory:  1Gi
    Requests:
```

```
        cpu:          250m
        memory:       512Mi
```

Resources are configured correctly. Now, check the MAKDO logs for any errors:

```
kubectl logs -l app=makdo --context kind-makdo-control --tail=100
```

Look for the following key indicators:

1. **Coordinator started**: `Starting MAKDO Multi-Agent Kubernetes DevOps System`
2. **Sub-agents created**: `Coordinator and sub-agents created successfully`
3. **Attempting k8s-ai session**: `Creating k8s-ai session for kind-makdo-worker...`
4. **Health check loop started**: `Starting health check loop`

You'll see errors about the k8s-ai connection failing. That's expected until we deploy k8s-ai. The important thing is that MAKDO started without crashing.

If MAKDO is crash-looping, check for common issues:

- **Missing secrets**: Verify that `makdo-secrets` exists with all keys:

  ```
  kubectl get secret makdo-secrets --context kind-makdo-control
  ```

- **Missing kubeconfig ConfigMap**: Verify that the `makdo-kubeconfig` `ConfigMap` was created with your `kubeconfig` file before deploying MAKDO.
- **Python errors**: Check logs for import errors or missing dependencies. You may need to rebuild the image.

To follow logs in real time just to see what MAKDO is doing, use the following:

```
kubectl logs -l app=makdo --context kind-makdo-control --follow
```

Press *Ctrl* + *C* to stop. MAKDO is deployed and waiting for k8s-ai. Next, we'll deploy k8s-ai to the worker cluster so MAKDO can start monitoring.

Deploying k8s-ai to the worker cluster

Now that MAKDO is running on the control cluster, we need to deploy k8s-ai to the worker cluster. K8s-ai exposes Kubernetes diagnostic capabilities through the A2A protocol, allowing MAKDO's Analyzer and Fixer agents to inspect cluster health and execute remediation actions. We'll containerize k8s-ai, deploy it as a Kubernetes service, and expose it so MAKDO can communicate with it across clusters.

Building the k8s-ai Docker image

K8s-ai needs to run as a container in the worker cluster. We'll create a Dockerfile that packages k8s-ai with all its dependencies, installs kubectl for cluster access, and configures it to run as an A2A server.

Create `k8s-ai/Dockerfile`:

```
FROM python:3.13-slim

# Install system dependencies
RUN apt-get update && apt-get install -y \
    curl \
    git \
    && rm -rf /var/lib/apt/lists/*

# Install kubectl
RUN curl -LO "https://dl.k8s.io/release/$(curl -L -s https://dl.k8s.io/release/
stable.txt)/bin/linux/arm64/kubectl" && \
    install -o root -g root -m 0755 kubectl /usr/local/bin/kubectl && \
    rm kubectl

WORKDIR /app

# Copy k8s-ai source
COPY k8s_ai ./k8s_ai
COPY pyproject.toml .

# Install k8s-ai and dependencies
RUN pip install --no-cache-dir -e .

# Create directory for API keys
RUN mkdir -p /app/data

# Expose A2A server port and Admin API port
EXPOSE 9999 9998

# Run k8s-ai server in A2A mode
CMD ["k8s-ai-server", "--host", "0.0.0.0", "--port", "9999", "--admin-port",
"9998"]
```

Here are the key points of the preceding code snippet:

- **Base image**: Python 3.12-slim provides a minimal Python environment.
- **kubectl installation**: K8s-ai executes kubectl commands to interact with the cluster. We download the latest stable version and install it.
- **Source code**: Copy the `k8s_ai` package and the `pyproject.toml` file. We install with `pip install -e .` to install k8s-ai as an editable package.
- **Data directory**: `/app/data` will store API keys (`keys.json`) for authentication.
- **Ports**: Port 9999 for the A2A protocol server, and 9998 for the Admin API (used to create sessions).
- **CMD**: Starts `k8s-ai-server` with flags to bind to all interfaces (`0.0.0.0`) so it's accessible from outside the container.

The k8s-ai source code lives in the main k8s-ai repository. Copy it to the `ch11/k8s-ai` directory:

```
# From the k8s-ai repository root
cp -r k8s_ai /path/to/Design-Multi-Agent-AI-Systems-Using-MCP-and-A2A/ch11/k8s-ai/
cp pyproject.toml /path/to/Design-Multi-Agent-AI-Systems-Using-MCP-and-A2A/ch11/
k8s-ai/
```

Build the image:

```
cd ch11/k8s-ai
docker build -t k8s-ai:latest .
```

This takes a few minutes to download base images and install dependencies. When complete, verify the image:

```
docker images | grep k8s-ai
```

Here is the output:

```
k8s-ai      latest    abc123def456   2 minutes ago   450MB
```

The image is built and ready to deploy to the worker cluster.

Creating k8s-ai deployment manifests

K8s-ai needs several Kubernetes resources to run: a Service account with permissions to access the cluster, a Deployment to run the container, and a Service to expose it. We'll use **role-based access control** (**RBAC**) to grant k8s-ai read-only cluster access.

Here is the k8s-ai deployment manifest:

`https://github.com/PacktPublishing/Design-Multi-Agent-AI-Systems-Using-MCP-and-A2A/blob/main/ch11/k8s-ai/deployment.yaml`.

Key configuration points include the following:

- **Service account and RBAC**: The `k8s-ai` service account gets read-only permissions through `ClusterRole` `k8s-ai-reader`. This allows k8s-ai to run `kubectl get/list/watch` commands but prevents any modifications. The `ClusterRoleBinding` resource connects `ServiceAccount` to `ClusterRole`.
- **API keys secret**: Contains `keys.json` with the API key from your `.env` file. MAKDO's Analyzer and Fixer agents will use this key to authenticate. The key is stored as a `${K8S_AI_API_KEY}` placeholder and will be substituted from your environment when you apply the manifest.
- **Deployment**: Runs one replica of k8s-ai with `imagePullPolicy: Never` (KinD uses local images). The container gets the OpenAI API key from a Secret resource. Resource limits prevent k8s-ai from consuming excessive memory or CPU.
- **Health probes**: The liveness probe checks whether k8s-ai is responsive by fetching the agent card at `/.well-known/agent.json`. The readiness probe ensures that the pod is ready to receive traffic before marking it as available.
- **Service**: Exposes k8s-ai with the `NodePort` type. Port `30100` maps to the A2A server (9999), and port `30099` maps to the Admin API (9998). Remember from `worker-cluster.yaml` that port `30100` is mapped to host port `8100`, making k8s-ai accessible at `http://host.docker.internal:8100` from the control cluster.

Let's see how to deploy the k8s-ai image we just built.

Deploying k8s-ai to the worker cluster

With the image built and manifests created, we're ready to deploy k8s-ai to the worker cluster. First, load the image into the worker cluster, create the required secrets, and then apply the deployment.

Load the k8s-ai image into the worker cluster:

```
kind load docker-image k8s-ai:latest --name makdo-worker
```

Here is the output:

```
Image: "k8s-ai:latest" with ID "sha256:1fe7b6c86eb2..." not yet present on node
"makdo-worker-control-plane", loading...
```

This transfers the image from your local Docker to the worker cluster's internal registry. Without this step, the pod would fail with `ImagePullBackOff` because KinD clusters don't have access to external registries by default.

Create the OpenAI API key secret. K8s-ai needs this to call the LLM for natural language processing:

```
kubectl create secret generic k8s-ai-secrets \
  --from-literal=openai-api-key="${OPENAI_API_KEY}" \
  --context kind-makdo-worker
```

Verify that the secret was created:

```
kubectl get secret k8s-ai-secrets --context kind-makdo-worker
```

Here is the output:

```
NAME             TYPE     DATA   AGE
k8s-ai-secrets   Opaque   1      5s
```

Before deploying, ensure that you have a `.env` file in the `ch11` directory with the required credentials. Copy the example file:

```
cd ch11
cp .env.example .env
```

- Edit `.env` and set your credentials.
- Set `K8S_AI_API_KEY` to `test-key` for development.
- For production, generate a key by running `k8s-ai-server --generate-key` and assign it to `K8S_AI_API_KEY`.
- Set `OPENAI_API_KEY` to your OpenAI API key.

- Slack credentials are only required if using the Slack bot.
- The `.env` file is in `.gitignore`, so your secrets won't be committed.

Now, apply the `deployment` manifest, using `envsubst` to substitute environment variables:

```
cd k8s-ai
export $(grep -v '^#' ../.env | xargs)
envsubst < deployment.yaml | kubectl apply -f - --context kind-makdo-worker
```

Here is the output:

```
serviceaccount/k8s-ai created
clusterrole.rbac.authorization.k8s.io/k8s-ai-reader created
clusterrolebinding.rbac.authorization.k8s.io/k8s-ai-reader-binding created
secret/k8s-ai-api-keys created
deployment.apps/k8s-ai created
service/k8s-ai created
```

Six resources are created: `ServiceAccount`, `ClusterRole`, `ClusterRoleBinding`, `Secret` (for API keys), `Deployment`, and `Service`. Check the pod status:

```
kubectl get pods -l app=k8s-ai --context kind-makdo-worker
```

Here is the output:

```
NAME                      READY   STATUS    RESTARTS   AGE
k8s-ai-7b9c8d6f5d-x2k4j   1/1     Running   0          45s
```

The pod is running. If you see `ImagePullBackOff`, verify that the image was loaded with `kind load`. If you see `CrashLoopBackOff`, check the logs for errors (usually missing an OpenAI API key).

Check the service:

```
kubectl get svc k8s-ai --context kind-makdo-worker
```

Here is the output:

```
NAME     TYPE       CLUSTER-IP      EXTERNAL-IP   PORT(S)                         AGE
k8s-ai   NodePort   10.96.145.123   <none>        9999:30100/TCP,9998:30099/TCP   1m
```

The service exposes two node ports, which are `30100` for the A2A server and `30099` for the Admin API. Because we configured the worker cluster with `extraPortMappings` in the `worker-cluster.yaml` file, these ports are accessible from the host at `localhost:8100` and `localhost:8099`.

Exposing the k8s-ai service for cross-cluster access

K8s-ai is now running in the worker cluster, but MAKDO in the control cluster needs to reach it. In our KinD setup, cross-cluster communication happens through the Docker host network. The worker cluster's node port `30100` is mapped to host port `8100` via the `extraPortMappings` field we configured earlier.

From the control cluster's perspective, the worker cluster is reachable at `host.docker.internal:8100`. This special DNS name resolves to the Docker host's IP address, allowing containers in one KinD cluster to reach services in another.

Let's verify that the networking is working. First, check whether the k8s-ai service responds to the agent card endpoint:

```
curl http://localhost:8100/.well-known/agent.json
```

Here is the output (formatted for readability):

```
{
  "name": "k8s-ai Diagnostic Agent",
  "description": "Kubernetes AI diagnostic agent with read-only cluster analysis
with session-based cluster management",
  "url": "http://0.0.0.0:9999/",
  "version": "2.0.0",
  "capabilities": {
    "streaming": false
  },
  "skills": [
    {
      "id": "kubernetes_diagnostics",
      "name": "Kubernetes Diagnostics",
      "description": "Perform read-only Kubernetes cluster diagnostics,
troubleshooting, and health analysis with detailed insights",
      "tags": ["kubernetes", "diagnostics", "troubleshooting", "monitoring",
"health"]
    }
```

```
    ]
  }
```

The agent card confirms that k8s-ai is responding. Now, test authentication by calling the Admin API to create a session. The Admin API requires the API key from your `.env` file:

```
curl -X POST http://localhost:8099/sessions \
  -H "Authorization: Bearer test-key" \
  -H "Content-Type: application/json" \
  -d '{
    "cluster_name": "makdo-worker",
    "ttl_hours": 24
  }'
```

This should fail with an authentication error if you haven't configured the `ServiceAccount` property. That's expected as we're just verifying whether the endpoint is reachable. We'll test the full session creation in the next subsection.

The key point here is that MAKDO agents will use `http://host.docker.internal:8100` to reach k8s-ai's A2A server. This is already configured in MAKDO's `coordinator.yaml` file:

```
a2a_servers:
  - name: "kind-makdo-worker"
    url: "http://host.docker.internal:8100"
    timeout: 30.0
    api_key: "test-key"
```

The networking is in place. MAKDO can now communicate with k8s-ai across clusters.

Verifying k8s-ai deployment

After deploying k8s-ai, verify that all components are running correctly and the service is accessible.

Check pod status

First, verify that the k8s-ai pod is running in the worker cluster:

```
kubectl get pods -l app=k8s-ai --context kind-makdo-worker -o wide
```

Here is the expected output:

```
NAME                        READY   STATUS    RESTARTS   AGE   IP           NODE
k8s-ai-75558cb559-n8jl9     1/1     Running   0          20m   10.244.0.5   makdo-
worker-control-plane
```

The pod should show a `1/1 Running` status with no restarts.

Verify pod health

Check the pod's detailed status and health probes:

```
kubectl describe pod -l app=k8s-ai --context kind-makdo-worker | grep -A 5
"Conditions:"
```

Here is the expected output:

```
Conditions:
  Type                        Status
  PodReadyToStartContainers   True
  Initialized                 True
  Ready                       True
  ContainersReady             True
  PodScheduled                True
```

All conditions should be `True`, indicating that the pod passed its liveness and readiness probes.

Check server logs

View the k8s-ai logs to confirm that both servers started successfully:

```
kubectl logs -l app=k8s-ai --context kind-makdo-worker --tail=50
```

Look for health probe activity showing that the A2A endpoint is responding:

```
INFO:     10.244.0.1:41262 - "GET /.well-known/agent.json HTTP/1.1" 200 OK
```

The regular health probe requests from Kubernetes confirm that the service is healthy.

Test the A2A endpoint

Verify that the k8s-ai agent card is accessible from outside the cluster:

```
curl -s http://localhost:8100/.well-known/agent.json | python3 -m json.tool | head
-30
```

Here is th expected response:


```
{
    "capabilities": {
        "streaming": false
    },
    "defaultInputModes": [
        "text/plain"
    ],
    "defaultOutputModes": [
        "text/plain"
    ],
    "description": "Kubernetes AI diagnostic agent with read-only cluster analysis
with session-based cluster management",
    "name": "k8s-ai Diagnostic Agent",
    "preferredTransport": "JSONRPC",
    "protocolVersion": "0.3.0",
    "security": [
        {
            "BearerAuth": []
        }
    ],
    "securitySchemes": {
        "BearerAuth": {
            "scheme": "bearer",
            "type": "http"
        }
    },
    "skills": [
        {
            "description": "Perform read-only Kubernetes cluster diagnostics...",
```

This confirms that the A2A server is running on port 9999 inside the pod, the NodePort service maps port 30100 to the container port, the host port mapping (8100 → 30100) allows external access, the agent card follows the A2A protocol specification, and the bearer token authentication is enabled.

Verify service configuration

Check the k8s-ai service configuration:

```
kubectl get svc k8s-ai --context kind-makdo-worker -o yaml | grep -A 10 "spec:"
```

Here is the expected output:

```
spec:
  ports:
  - name: a2a
    nodePort: 30100
    port: 9999
    protocol: TCP
    targetPort: 9999
  - name: admin
    nodePort: 30099
    port: 9998
    protocol: TCP
    targetPort: 9998
  selector:
    app: k8s-ai
  type: NodePort
```

This shows that both the A2A port (9999) and Admin API port (9998) are exposed via NodePort.

With k8s-ai verified and running, the worker cluster now has a diagnostic agent ready to receive requests from MAKDO in the control cluster.

Testing the k8s-ai Admin API and session management

The k8s-ai Admin API provides session management capabilities, allowing MAKDO to create isolated sessions for interacting with the worker cluster. Each session has its own kubeconfig and expiration time.

Exposing the Admin API port

By default, the worker cluster configuration exposes the A2A port (`8100`) but not the Admin API port. Update the worker cluster configuration to add port `8099`:

```
# ch11/worker-cluster.yaml
extraPortMappings:
  # Port for k8s-ai A2A server
  - containerPort: 30100
    hostPort: 8100
    protocol: TCP
  # Port for k8s-ai Admin API
  - containerPort: 30099
    hostPort: 8099
    protocol: TCP
```

If you already created the worker cluster, you need to recreate it with the updated configuration:

```
kind delete cluster --name makdo-worker
kind create cluster --config worker-cluster.yaml
```

Then, redeploy k8s-ai following the previous deployment steps.

Creating a session

To create a session, you need to provide the cluster `kubeconfig`. First, extract the worker cluster `kubeconfig`:

```
kubectl config view --context kind-makdo-worker --minify --flatten > /tmp/makdo-
worker-kubeconfig.yaml
```

Create a session request JSON file:

```
import json

# Read kubeconfig
with open('/tmp/makdo-worker-kubeconfig.yaml', 'r') as f:
    kubeconfig = f.read()

# Create session request
request = {
```

```
    "cluster_name": "makdo-worker",
    "ttl_hours": 24,
    "kubeconfig": kubeconfig
}

# Write to file
with open('/tmp/session-request.json', 'w') as f:
    json.dump(request, f)

print("Session request created")
```

Now, create a session using the Admin API:

```
curl -s -X POST 'http://localhost:8099/sessions' \
  -H 'Authorization: Bearer test-key' \
  -H 'Content-Type: application/json' \
  -d '@/tmp/session-request.json' | python3 -m json.tool
```

Here is the expected response:

```
{
    "success": true,
    "session_token": "k8s-ai-session--qSTOZ0ggxnL-w5mMmMNboUBz0GVIGXvxkxfjYY5ND0",
    "cluster_name": "makdo-worker",
    "api_server": "https://127.0.0.1:65089",
    "namespace": "default",
    "connectivity_status": "connected",
    "expires_at": "2025-11-10T04:37:27.297559Z",
    "error": null
}
```

The session token (`k8s-ai-session--...`) will be used to authenticate requests to the A2A endpoint.

Listing active sessions

View all active sessions:

```
curl -s 'http://localhost:8099/sessions' \
  -H 'Authorization: Bearer test-key' | python3 -m json.tool
```

Here is the expected response:


```
{
    "total_sessions": 1,
    "sessions": [
        {
            "session_token": "k8s-ai-session--qSTOZ0ggxnL-
w5mMmMNboUBz0GVIGXvxkxfjYY5ND0",
            "cluster_name": "makdo-worker",
            "api_server": "https://127.0.0.1:65089",
            "namespace": "default",
            "created_at": "2025-11-09T04:37:27.297568Z",
            "expires_at": "2025-11-10T04:37:27.297559Z",
            "is_expired": false
        }
    ]
}
```


Let's see how to delete an existing session.

Deleting a session

To manually delete a session before it expires, use the following:

```
SESSION_TOKEN="k8s-ai-session--qSTOZ0ggxnL-w5mMmMNboUBz0GVIGXvxkxfjYY5ND0"

curl -s -X DELETE "http://localhost:8099/sessions/${SESSION_TOKEN}" \
  -H 'Authorization: Bearer test-key' | python3 -m json.tool
```

Here is the expected response:


```
{
    "success": true,
    "message": "Session deleted successfully"
}
```


Let's see how to run A2A sessions against the k8s-ai server.

Using sessions with the A2A protocol

MAKDO will use the session token when making A2A requests to k8s-ai. The token is passed in the `Authorization` header along with method-specific parameters:

```
curl -s -X POST 'http://localhost:8100/' \
  -H 'Authorization: Bearer test-key' \
  -H 'Content-Type: application/json' \
  -d '{
    "jsonrpc": "2.0",
    "method": "kubernetes_diagnose_issue",
    "params": {
      "session_token": "'"${SESSION_TOKEN}"'",
      "issue_description": "Check pod health in default namespace"
    },
    "id": 1
  }'
```

The session-based approach provides several benefits:

- **Isolation**: Each MAKDO instance can have its own session without interfering with others
- **Security**: Sessions expire automatically, limiting the window of access
- **Flexibility**: Different sessions can target different namespaces or clusters
- **Auditability**: Session creation and usage are logged for security auditing

With the Admin API tested and working, k8s-ai is now ready to serve diagnostic requests from MAKDO across clusters.

Enabling secure communication between clusters

With MAKDO deployed in the control cluster and k8s-ai deployed in the worker cluster, we need to ensure secure communication between them. This section covers service discovery, networking, access control, and the security mechanisms already in place, demonstrating how they work in the KinD environment.

Service discovery and networking

In a multi-cluster deployment, agents need to discover and communicate with each other across cluster boundaries. Our deployment uses explicit configuration and host networking to enable cross-cluster communication.

How MAKDO discovers k8s-ai

MAKDO uses static configuration to discover the k8s-ai service. View the configuration:

```
kubectl get configmap makdo-config --context kind-makdo-control \
  -o jsonpath='{.data.makdo\.yaml}' | grep -A 5 "k8s_ai:"
```

Here is the expected output:

```
k8s_ai:
  base_url: "http://host.docker.internal:8100"
  admin_api_url: "http://host.docker.internal:8100/admin"
```

Key networking components include the following:

- `host.docker.internal`: Special DNS name that resolves to the Docker host from within containers
- **Port** `8100`: Mapped from `NodePort 30100` in the worker cluster to host port `8100`
- **Port** `8099`: Mapped from `NodePort 30099` for the Admin API

Tracing a request path

Let's trace how a diagnostic request flows from MAKDO to k8s-ai:

```
MAKDO Pod (control cluster)
  ↓ http://host.docker.internal:8100
Docker Host Network
  ↓ localhost:8100
Worker Cluster Node (Docker container)
  ↓ NodePort 30100
k8s-ai Service (worker cluster)
  ↓ ClusterIP:9999
k8s-ai Pod (worker cluster)
```

Verify each step:

```
# 1. Check MAKDO can resolve host.docker.internal
kubectl exec deployment/makdo --context kind-makdo-control -- \
  python3 -c "import socket; print(f'host.docker.internal resolves to:
{socket.gethostbyname(\"host.docker.internal\")}')"

# 2. Check host can access port 8100
```

```
curl -s http://localhost:8100/.well-known/agent.json | python3 -m
json.tool | head -10

# 3. Check NodePort service in worker cluster
kubectl get svc k8s-ai --context kind-makdo-worker -o yaml | grep -A 5 "nodePort:
30100"

# 4. Check k8s-ai pod is receiving traffic
kubectl logs deployment/k8s-ai --context kind-makdo-worker --tail=5
```

In production systems, these chains of network calls might add significant delay to latency-sensitive operations. It may be useful to add a latency budget and explicitly monitor and manage it.

In order to access the k8s-ai server, we need to discover it first. There are several common patterns that are useful for different use cases. Let's explore them.

Service discovery patterns

Our deployment demonstrates static configuration service discovery. Other patterns for production include the following:

- **DNS-based discovery**: Use Kubernetes DNS for in-cluster services:

```
# For services in the same cluster
k8s_ai:
  base_url: "http://k8s-ai.default.svc.cluster.local:9999"
```

- **Service mesh discovery**: Use a service mesh such as Istio or Linkerd:

```
apiVersion: networking.istio.io/v1beta1
kind: ServiceEntry
metadata:
  name: k8s-ai-external
spec:
  hosts:
  - k8s-ai.worker-cluster.global
  location: MESH_EXTERNAL
  ports:
  - number: 9999
    name: a2a
    protocol: HTTP
  resolution: DNS
```

```
endpoints:
- address: k8s-ai.worker-cluster.svc.cluster.local
```

- **Dynamic service registry**: Use a service registry such as Consul:

```
import consul

# Register k8s-ai service
client = consul.Consul()
client.agent.service.register(
    name='k8s-ai',
    service_id='k8s-ai-worker-1',
    address='k8s-ai.worker-cluster',
    port=9999,
    tags=['a2a', 'diagnostics']
)

# Discover services
services = client.health.service('k8s-ai', passing=True)
for service in services:
    print(f"Found k8s-ai at {service['Service']['Address']}:
{service['Service']['Port']}")
```

Let's consider the various networking approaches for exposing the k8s-ai server.

Cross-cluster networking approaches

Different environments require different networking strategies:

- **KinD (current setup)**:
    - Uses Docker host network (`host.docker.internal`)
    - `NodePort` services with `extraPortMappings`
    - Simple, works well for local development:

    ```
    extraPortMappings:
    - containerPort: 30100
      hostPort: 8100
    ```

- **Cloud providers (AWS, GCP, and Azure)**:
  - Use `LoadBalancer` services with public IPs
  - Or use private networking with VPC peering
  - Or use transit gateways for multi-cluster connectivity:

```
apiVersion: v1
kind: Service
metadata:
  name: k8s-ai
  annotations:
    service.beta.kubernetes.io/aws-load-balancer-type: "nlb"
    service.beta.kubernetes.io/aws-load-balancer-internal: "true"
spec:
  type: LoadBalancer
  selector:
    app: k8s-ai
  ports:
  - port: 9999
    targetPort: 9999
```

- **Multi-cluster service mesh**:
  - Services automatically discoverable across clusters
  - Mutual TLS between clusters
  - Traffic management and observability:

```
apiVersion: install.istio.io/v1alpha1
kind: IstioOperator
spec:
  values:
    global:
      multiCluster:
        clusterName: worker-cluster
      network: network1
```

It is very important to test end-to-end connectivity for distributed systems.

Testing end-to-end connectivity

Verify complete connectivity from MAKDO to k8s-ai:

```
# Create a test session
kubectl config view --context kind-makdo-worker --minify --flatten > /tmp/test-
conn.yaml

python3 << 'EOF'
import json

with open('/tmp/test-conn.yaml', 'r') as f:
    kubeconfig = f.read()

request = {
    "cluster_name": "connectivity-test",
    "ttl_hours": 1,
    "kubeconfig": kubeconfig
}

with open('/tmp/test-conn.json', 'w') as f:
    json.dump(request, f)
EOF

# Create session via Admin API
RESPONSE=$(curl -s -X POST 'http://localhost:8099/sessions' \
  -H 'Authorization: Bearer test-key' \
  -H 'Content-Type: application/json' \
  -d '@/tmp/test-conn.json')

echo $RESPONSE | python3 -m json.tool

# Extract session token
SESSION_TOKEN=$(echo $RESPONSE | python3 -c "import sys, json;
print(json.load(sys.stdin)['session_token'])")

echo "Session token: ${SESSION_TOKEN}"
```

Now, test that MAKDO (running in the control cluster) can reach this endpoint through the same path:

```
# Test from host (simulating MAKDO's perspective)
curl -s 'http://localhost:8100/.well-known/agent.json' \
  -H 'Authorization: Bearer test-key' | python3 -m json.tool | head -15
```

Here is the output of the command showing the agent card:

```
{
    "capabilities": {
        "streaming": false
    },
    "defaultInputModes": [
        "text/plain"
    ],
    "defaultOutputModes": [
        "text/plain"
    ],
    "description": "Kubernetes AI diagnostic agent with read-only cluster analysis
with session-based cluster management",
    "name": "k8s-ai Diagnostic Agent",
```

This confirms the complete path: MAKDO → Docker host → Worker cluster → k8s-ai pod.

Industrial-strength systems must offer defense in depth to comply with security requirements. Let's see what MAKDO and k8s-ai provide.

Understanding the security architecture

Our deployment implements multiple layers of security:

1. **API key authentication**: Both MAKDO and k8s-ai use bearer token authentication.
2. **Session-based access**: k8s-ai uses temporary sessions with expiration times.
3. **RBAC**: k8s-ai has read-only permissions in the worker cluster.
4. **Network isolation**: Communication flows through specific ports with controlled access.
5. **Secret management**: Credentials are stored in Kubernetes Secrets and `.env` files.

This follows security best practices and minimizes the risk of remote access, data exfiltration, privilege escalation, lateral movement, and sensitive data exposure.

API key authentication

API key authentication is a common method of providing secure access to remote services. Let's see how k8s-ai implements it.

k8s-ai authentication

k8s-ai requires bearer token authentication for both its A2A endpoint and Admin API. The API keys are stored in a Kubernetes secret that was created during deployment.

View the stored API keys:

```
kubectl get secret k8s-ai-api-keys --context kind-makdo-worker \
  -o jsonpath='{.data.keys\.json}' | base64 -d | python3 -m json.tool
```

Here is the expected output:

```
{
    "api_keys": [
        {
            "key": "test-key",
            "name": "MAKDO Client",
            "created": "2025-01-01T00:00:00"
        }
    ]
}
```

Test authentication by making a request without credentials:

```
curl -s 'http://localhost:8099/sessions' | python3 -m json.tool
```

Here is the expected response:

```
{
    "detail": "Not authenticated"
}
```

Now, test with valid credentials:

```
curl -s 'http://localhost:8099/sessions' \
  -H 'Authorization: Bearer test-key' | python3 -m json.tool
```

This returns the list of active sessions, confirming that authentication works.

MAKDO configuration

MAKDO stores the k8s-ai API key in its configuration. Check the MAKDO `configMap`:

```
kubectl get configmap makdo-config --context kind-makdo-control \
  -o jsonpath='{.data.makdo\.yaml}' | grep -A 3 "a2a_servers:"
```

Here is the expected output showing the API key configuration:

```
a2a_servers:
  - name: "kind-makdo-worker"
    url: "http://host.docker.internal:8100"
    timeout: 30.0
    api_key: "test-key"
```

In production, remember that API keys should be generated using strong random values (not `test-key`), rotated regularly, stored in dedicated secret management systems (e.g., HashiCorp Vault, AWS Secrets Manager, etc.), and never committed to version control.

Session-based security

The k8s-ai project implements session-based access control, adding an additional security layer beyond API keys. The session life cycle includes the following:

1. **Creation**: MAKDO creates a session via the Admin API, providing a `kubeconfig`.
2. **Usage:** The session token is used for all diagnostic operations.
3. **Expiration**: Sessions automatically expire after their **time to live** (**TTL**).
4. **Cleanup**: Expired sessions are automatically removed.

Let's now demonstrate session security.

Create a session with a short TTL:

```
# Extract kubeconfig
kubectl config view --context kind-makdo-worker --minify --flatten > /tmp/test-
kubeconfig.yaml

# Create session with 1-minute TTL
python3 << 'EOF'
import json

with open('/tmp/test-kubeconfig.yaml', 'r') as f:
    kubeconfig = f.read()
```

```
request = {
    "cluster_name": "test-session",
    "ttl_hours": 0.0167,  # 1 minute = 1/60 hours
    "kubeconfig": kubeconfig
}

with open('/tmp/short-session.json', 'w') as f:
    json.dump(request, f)
EOF

curl -s -X POST 'http://localhost:8099/sessions' \
  -H 'Authorization: Bearer test-key' \
  -H 'Content-Type: application/json' \
  -d '@/tmp/short-session.json' | python3 -m json.tool
```

The response includes an `expires_at` timestamp. After the expiration time, the session becomes invalid:

```
# Wait 90 seconds
sleep 90

# Try to use the expired session
SESSION_TOKEN=" < token-from-creation-response >"

curl -s -X POST 'http://localhost:8100/' \
  -H 'Authorization: Bearer test-key' \
  -H 'Content-Type: application/json' \
  -d '{
    "jsonrpc": "2.0",
    "method": "kubernetes_diagnose_issue",
    "params": {
      "session_token": "'"${SESSION_TOKEN}"'",
      "issue_description": "test"
    },
    "id": 1
  }'
```

Here is the expected response indicating that the session expired:


```
{
    "jsonrpc": "2.0",
    "error": {
        "code": -32002,
        "message": "Session not found or expired"
    },
    "id": 1
}
```


This time-limited access reduces the impact of compromised credentials.

RBAC and least privilege

k8s-ai operates with minimal permissions in the worker cluster.

Inspecting RBAC configuration

View the `ClusterRole` source assigned to k8s-ai:

```
kubectl get clusterrole k8s-ai-reader --context kind-makdo-worker -o yaml
```

These are the key permissions:

```
rules:
- apiGroups: [""]
  resources: ["pods", "pods/log", "services", "nodes", "namespaces", "events"]
  verbs: ["get", "list", "watch"]
- apiGroups: ["apps"]
  resources: ["deployments", "replicasets", "statefulsets", "daemonsets"]
  verbs: ["get", "list", "watch"]
- apiGroups: ["batch"]
  resources: ["jobs", "cronjobs"]
  verbs: ["get", "list", "watch"]
```

Notice the read-only verbs: `get`, `list`, `watch`. There are no `create`, `update`, `delete`, or `patch` permissions.

Testing permission boundaries

Verify that k8s-ai cannot modify resources:

```
# Get a pod name
POD_NAME=$(kubectl get pods --context kind-makdo-worker -o
jsonpath='{.items[0].metadata.name}')

# Try to delete it using k8s-ai's service account
kubectl delete pod ${POD_NAME} --context kind-makdo-worker \
  --as=system:serviceaccount:default:k8s-ai
```

Here is an expected error:

```
Error from server (Forbidden): pods "k8s-ai-f77d65f7d-p6lkk" is forbidden:
User "system:serviceaccount:default:k8s-ai" cannot delete resource "pods"
in API group "" in the namespace "default"
```

This demonstrates that even if an attacker gained access to k8s-ai, they couldn't modify or delete cluster resources.

Network segmentation in KinD

While KinD clusters run on the same Docker network, we control communication through port mappings and service configuration.

Port mapping security

View the exposed ports:

```
docker ps --filter name=makdo-control-plane --format "table {{.Names}}
\t{{.Ports}}"
docker ps --filter name=makdo-worker-control-plane --format "table {{.Names}}
\t{{.Ports}}"
```

The output shows controlled exposure:

```
NAMES                           PORTS
makdo-control-control-plane     127.0.0.1:xxx->6443/tcp, 0.0.0.0:9000->30000/tcp
makdo-worker-control-plane      127.0.0.1:xxx->6443/tcp, 0.0.0.0:8099->30099/tcp,
0.0.0.0:8100->30100/tcp
```

Here are some key observations:

- **Kubernetes API**: Bound to `127.0.0.1` (localhost only, not externally accessible)
- **Application ports**: Bound to `0.0.0.0` (accessible from host, simulating external access)
- **Specific ports only**: Not all container ports are exposed

This demonstrates how to manage the connectivity and networking aspects of Kubernetes in the KinD environment while maintaining isolation. Now, let's see how to test it.

Testing network isolation

Try to access the Kubernetes API directly from the host (should fail):

```
# Get the worker cluster API server address
WORKER_API=$(kubectl config view --context kind-makdo-worker --minify \
  -o jsonpath='{.clusters[0].cluster.server}')

echo "Worker API: ${WORKER_API}"

# Try to access from outside the cluster (without proper credentials)
curl -k "${WORKER_API}/api/v1/namespaces"
```

We get an expected error due to authentication requirements:

```
{
  "kind": "Status",
  "apiVersion": "v1",
  "metadata": {},
  "status": "Failure",
  "message": "Unauthorized",
  "reason": "Unauthorized",
  "code": 401
}
```

The Kubernetes API is protected and only accessible with proper `kubeconfig` credentials.

Production security enhancements

For production deployments beyond KinD, implement these additional security measures:

1. **TLS/SSL encryption**: HTTP communication between MAKDO and k8s-ai in the local environment (KinD), and also enable TLS on both endpoints for production:

   ```
   # k8s-ai with TLS
   containers:
   - name: k8s-ai
     env:
     - name: TLS_CERT_FILE
       value: "/certs/tls.crt"
     - name: TLS_KEY_FILE
       value: "/certs/tls.key"
     volumeMounts:
     - name: tls-certs
       mountPath: /certs
       readOnly: true
   volumes:
   - name: tls-certs
     secret:
       secretName: k8s-ai-tls
   ```

   Use `cert-manager` or your cloud provider's certificate management service.

2. **Network policies**: Restrict pod-to-pod communication:

   ```
   apiVersion: networking.k8s.io/v1
   kind: NetworkPolicy
   metadata:
     name: k8s-ai-network-policy
   spec:
     podSelector:
       matchLabels:
         app: k8s-ai
     policyTypes:
     - Ingress
     ingress:
     - from:
       - namespaceSelector:
           matchLabels:
   ```

```
          name: makdo-namespace
    ports:
    - protocol: TCP
      port: 9999
```

3. **Pod security standards**: Enforce security contexts:

```
securityContext:
  runAsNonRoot: true
  runAsUser: 1000
  fsGroup: 1000
  seccompProfile:
    type: RuntimeDefault
  capabilities:
    drop:
    - ALL
```

4. **Secrets management**: Replace Kubernetes secrets with external secret managers:

```
apiVersion: external-secrets.io/v1beta1
kind: ExternalSecret
metadata:
  name: k8s-ai-secrets
spec:
  refreshInterval: 1h
  secretStoreRef:
    name: vault-backend
    kind: SecretStore
  target:
    name: k8s-ai-secrets
  data:
  - secretKey: api-key
    remoteRef:
      key: k8s-ai/api-key
```

5. **Audit logging**: Enable comprehensive logging:

```
# In k8s-ai code
import logging

logging.basicConfig(
```

```
    level=logging.INFO,
    format='%(asctime)s - %(name)s - %(levelname)s - %(message)s'
)

# Log all authentication attempts
def authenticate(request):
    logger.info(f"Authentication attempt from {request.client.host}")
    # ... authentication logic
```

6. **Rate limiting**: Protect against abuse:

```
apiVersion: v1
kind: ConfigMap
metadata:
  name: k8s-ai-rate-limits
data:
  rate_limits.yaml: |
    limits:
      - key: ip
        rate: 100
        per: minute
      - key: api_key
        rate: 1000
        per: hour
```

The lesson here is that it is not trivial to keep a tight and secure production environment, and you must employ multiple measures.

Here's a security checklist to verify before deploying to production:

- All communication uses TLS/SSL encryption
- API keys are strong, random, and regularly rotated
- Secrets are managed externally (Vault, AWS Secrets Manager, etc.)
- RBAC follows least privilege principles
- Network policies restrict unnecessary communication
- Pod security contexts enforce non-root execution
- Audit logging captures all access attempts
- Rate limiting protects against abuse
- Container images are scanned for vulnerabilities

- Dependencies are up to date with security patches
- Egress filtering to reduce exfiltration

The security architecture demonstrated in this KinD deployment provides a solid foundation, but production environments require these additional hardening measures.

Summary

In this chapter, we deployed a complete multi-agent system spanning two Kubernetes clusters using KinD, demonstrating real-world patterns for distributed AI agent architectures. We started by setting up dual clusters with proper networking and port mappings, then deployed MAKDO to the control cluster with its four specialized agents and MCP servers for memory and Slack communication. On the worker cluster, we deployed k8s-ai as a diagnostic agent with read-only RBAC permissions, exposing both its A2A protocol endpoint and Admin API for session management. Throughout the deployment, we implemented multiple layers of security, including API key authentication, session-based access control with automatic expiration, and network isolation through controlled port exposure and service boundaries.

The architecture we built separates concerns between control agents that orchestrate and make decisions versus worker agents that execute specialized tasks with direct cluster access. Communication flows through the Agent-to-Agent protocol using JSON-RPC over HTTP, with static service discovery via `host.docker.internal` for the KinD environment. We demonstrated how to trace request paths across cluster boundaries, test authentication and authorization mechanisms, verify RBAC permissions to prevent unauthorized modifications, and manage secrets securely using Kubernetes Secrets and environment variables. The deployment also showcased practical patterns for cross-cluster networking, from the simple `NodePort` approach suitable for local development to more sophisticated options such as service meshes and dynamic service registries for production environments.

While this KinD-based deployment provides an excellent foundation for understanding multi-agent system architecture, moving to production requires additional considerations, including TLS encryption for all communication, stronger API keys with rotation policies, external secret management systems, comprehensive monitoring and logging, high availability configurations, and automated deployment pipelines. The patterns and practices demonstrated here scale from local development to enterprise production systems across cloud providers, on-premises infrastructure, and hybrid environments.

In the next and final chapter, we'll explore the future of multi-agent AI systems and emerging trends that will shape how these architectures evolve.

Get This Book's PDF Version and Exclusive Extras

Scan the QR code (or go to `packtpub.com/unlock`). Search for this book by name, confirm the edition, and then follow the steps on the page.

UNLOCK NOW

Note: Keep your invoice handy. Purchases made directly from Packt don't require an invoice.

12

Advanced Topics and Future Directions

We've covered a lot of ground in this book, from the fundamentals of multi-agent systems to practical implementation and deployment strategies. Now is a good time to look at what's coming soon. We are very fortunate to live through the singularity, which is the point in history where the pace of technological progress is so fast that humans (unless they are augmented) are unable to keep up. A few hundred years ago, technology was moving much more slowly. The difference from one generation to the next was not that significant, and most people didn't notice it at all. The scientific, industrial, and information revolutions have all accelerated the pace of change, but the advent of **artificial general intelligence** (**AGI**) and **artificial superintelligence** (**ASI**) will dwarf all previous revolutions in both speed and impact.

AI will be able to do anything humans can do better and faster. This includes aspects such as creativity, empathy, and strategic thinking. Add to that the fact that AIs don't need to sleep, eat, or take breaks, can share their knowledge just by copying a model, and can collaborate with billions of other AIs.

I think, at this point, most informed people agree that this is the case. What most people don't realize is how quickly this is happening. It's hard to predict exactly what the future holds, but it's clear that AI will play a central role in shaping it. AI agents in particular will have an important role in the next few years, bringing the benefits (and the dangers) to every person.

In this chapter, we will explore some of the most exciting and important trends in AI research and development and how they intersect with AI agents, and discuss their implications for society, economy, and humanity as a whole.

The following key topics are covered:

- Superhuman reasoning and strategic foresight
- Massive context windows and their implications
- Beyond text – multi-modal models and world simulation

Let's dive right in and look at superhuman reasoning and strategic foresight.

Superhuman reasoning and strategic foresight

The LLMs of today are already capable of impressive feats of reasoning and problem-solving. Even before the generative AI era, we saw the first signs of superhuman AI in narrow domains such as chess, Go, and protein folding. But these are just the tip of the iceberg. In the next few years, we will see AI systems that can outperform humans in a wide range of tasks, from driving cars to diagnosing diseases to writing code.

In the past, technological innovations took decades from proof of concept to widespread adoption. The telephone was invented in 1876, but it took until the 1920s for it to become common in households. The internet was invented in the 1960s, but it took until the 1990s for it to become widely used. In contrast, AI is advancing at an exponential rate. The first GPT model was released in 2018, ChatGPT was released at the end of 2022, and here we are in 2025 (at the time of writing) with GPT 5.1, Claude, Gemini, and a host of open source Chinese models.

However, as we continue to develop more advanced models and architectures, we can expect to see AI systems that can reason and plan at a level far beyond human capabilities.

Let's see what's on the horizon.

What is superhuman reasoning?

Superhuman reasoning refers to AI systems that can analyze problems, draw conclusions, and make decisions that exceed the capabilities of even the most intelligent and well-trained human experts. This isn't just about speed or memory, which AI systems obviously excel at. It is mostly about the fundamental quality of reasoning itself. A superhuman reasoner can consider more variables simultaneously, identify patterns across vast datasets that no human could process, and explore solution spaces with a depth and breadth that would be impossible for humans.

For example, in the chess domain, grandmasters typically look ahead 2–5 plays, and in certain positions even 10–15 plays. Chess programs such as AlphaZero can dynamically search the game tree and typically perform 1,000–2,000 simulations per move. The same concept applies to other domains. The transition from just impressive AI to truly superhuman reasoning is marked by several key characteristics: performing multi-step logical chains that remain coherent across hundreds or thousands of inference steps, synthesizing insights across entirely different domains in ways that would never occur to domain-specific human experts, and identifying their own limitations and uncertainties.

In the context of multi-agent systems, this capability becomes even more powerful through collaborative amplification, where agents with complementary reasoning capabilities work together to achieve synergies impossible for either humans or individual AI systems. For example, Blitzy (`https://blitzy.com`) uses thousands of AI agents to accelerate enterprise software development by a factor of five.

Why is strategic foresight so important?

Strategic foresight is the ability to anticipate future scenarios, identify emerging trends, and make decisions today that account for long-term consequences. While humans have always engaged in strategic planning, our biological limitations constrain our ability to truly think far ahead. We struggle to maintain consistency across complex chains of causality, fall prey to cognitive biases, and find it difficult to reason about exponential changes or low-probability high-impact events. AI systems today are below even human level in terms of strategic foresight and the ability to stay on task for long periods of time without getting lost or stuck. But this is changing fast. AI agents originally required close human supervision and feedback every few minutes and constant iteration, even on simple tasks. At the time of writing in 2025, some agentic AI systems can operate autonomously for hours and perform complex workflows and tasks successfully. Check out, for example, Gas Town (`https://steve-yegge.medium.com/welcome-to-gas-town-4f25ee16dd04`). In the next year or two, AI systems will be able to model intricate systems with thousands of interdependent variables, simulating countless scenarios in parallel, and identify risks and opportunities that would remain invisible to human strategists. This capability is becoming increasingly critical as the pace of technological change accelerates and the complexity of global challenges increases. Consider issues such as climate change, pandemics, social problems such as wealth distribution, and, of course, AI alignment.

In multi-agent systems, strategic foresight takes on added dimensions of power and complexity. Multiple AI agents can collaborate to explore different future scenarios simultaneously, with some agents focusing on optimistic paths, others on pessimistic trajectories, and still others on wildcard events that might disrupt conventional planning. These agents can engage in adversarial reasoning, with some playing the role of strategic competitors or environmental disruptions while others devise countermeasures and adaptive strategies. For organizations and societies that are willing to embrace these capabilities, AI-driven strategic foresight could be the difference between thriving in an uncertain future and being blindsided by predictable surprises.

In addition, multi-agent systems can engage in adversarial foresight where multiple agents discuss and argue with each other until they converge to a consensus.

But there are also significant challenges and ethical considerations associated with superhuman reasoning and strategic foresight.

Challenges and limitations of superhuman reasoning

First and foremost is the issue of interpretability. As AI systems become more complex and capable, understanding how they arrive at their conclusions becomes increasingly difficult. This "black box" problem raises concerns about trust and accountability, especially when AI systems are making decisions that impact human lives. See, for example, this Stanford study on AI medical programs: `https://hai.stanford.edu/news/peering-black-box-ai-medical-programs`. If an AI system recommends a course of action based on its superhuman reasoning, but humans cannot understand the rationale behind that recommendation, it becomes challenging to evaluate its validity or challenge its conclusions.

AI alignment is at the core of this challenge. When humans cannot fully grasp the reasoning processes of superhuman AI systems, ensuring that these systems' goals and values align with human interests becomes a daunting task. Misalignment could lead to unintended consequences, where AI systems pursue objectives that are detrimental to humanity, even if they are logically consistent within their own frameworks.

A second challenge is the potential for over-reliance on AI systems. As AI systems demonstrate superhuman reasoning capabilities, there is a risk that humans become overly dependent on them for decision-making, potentially eroding human skills and judgment. This dependency could lead to situations where humans are ill equipped to intervene or make decisions when AI systems fail or behave unexpectedly. The very nature of humanity might change as we all become fully dependent on AI to run our lives.

Finally, there are ethical considerations surrounding the use of superhuman reasoning in strategic foresight. The ability to predict and influence future scenarios raises questions about power dynamics, equity, and justice. Who gets to decide which futures are pursued and which are avoided? How do we ensure that the benefits of AI-driven foresight are distributed fairly across society, rather than being concentrated in the hands of a few powerful actors?

Implications for society and ethics

Here is my prediction for the next five years. In two years, all knowledge work will be able to be done by AI agents. This includes research, analysis, writing, design, and programming. Creativity, judgment, empathy, and other attributes that are still considered by some as the realm of humans will be picked up quickly by AI too. AI will be much more creative in any area, it will be able to supervise and judge itself or other AI better, and it will be much more empathetic than humans, with infinite patience and attention and a better understanding of humans. Then, in three to five years, robots with advanced AI will be able to take over all menial jobs. Again, this doesn't mean that humans will stop working. But robots utilizing AI that understands the physical world will be able to perform any physical task better than humans.

The actual pace of adoption will depend on many factors, including regulatory environment, social acceptance, economic incentives, and technological breakthroughs. However, the trajectory is clear. We are moving toward a future where AI systems with superhuman reasoning and strategic foresight capabilities play a central role in shaping our world.

This future is as exciting as it is frightening. Society will undergo rapid changes as the identity of many people is tied to their work. The economic implications are profound as well. With AI systems capable of performing most jobs, the traditional models of employment and income distribution will be challenged. Everyone is talking about **universal basic income (UBI)** as a possible solution. But there may be other solutions. The economy at large will grow much faster as productivity soars. But the distribution of that wealth will be a major political and social issue. If we look at recent trends, we can see that the wealth gap is widening and the middle class is shrinking. If we don't find ways to ensure that the benefits of AI are shared broadly across society, we may face increased social unrest and instability. This will be bad for everyone, including the wealthy elite.

Let's assume we can navigate this challenge and share the abundance created by AI broadly across society. It is still unclear what will become of humans. Are we going to live mostly in virtual worlds? What will be the purpose of human life when literally everything can be done better by AI? These are deep philosophical questions that humanity will have to grapple with in the coming years.

OK. Back to more technical topics.

Massive context windows and their implications

The context window of the model is the most crucial aspect that determines how much information the model can consider at once. Models can use tools to access and process additional information and delegate work via multi-agent systems, but the context window sets the fundamental limit on how much information the model can directly reason about in a single pass.

LLM context window sizes have grown exponentially over the years, enabling models to process increasingly longer sequences of text. This expansion has been a key driver of AI capability improvements.

The evolution of context windows

First, let's review the history of context window sizes in LLMs to understand how fast they grow. Remember, the Transformer architecture was introduced in 2017, so we are looking at less than a decade of exponential progress here:

- **2018–2019: Early era**: Initial models such as BERT and GPT-1 had context windows of just 512 tokens, which limited them to processing short paragraphs at a time.
- **2020–2021: GPT-3 era**: GPT-3 (2020) introduced a 2,048-token context window, a 4x increase, which enabled longer documents and better conversation flow.
- **2022–2023: Rapid expansion**: GPT-3.5 extended context to 16,000 tokens (8x jump). GPT-4 (2023) offered 8K and 32K token variants, with some versions reaching 128K tokens.
- **2024–2025: Million-token era**: Models with 1 million token context windows emerged (2,000x increase from GPT-3). Surprisingly, OpenAI models have relatively modest context windows compared to competitors, with at most 400K for GPT-5. Claude Sonnet 4 and Gemini 2.5-3 both offer 1 million tokens. Llama 4 pushed boundaries beyond 10 million tokens. There is even a research model from magic.dev (`https://magic.dev/blog/100m-token-context-windows`) with a 100-million-token context window!

This exponential growth rate has fundamentally changed how we interact with AI systems.

What can you do with million-token context windows?

The *PT* in *GPT models* stands for *pre-trained*. In the early days, with a small context window, the capabilities of the models were heavily dependent on the pre-training data and fine-tuning. With larger context windows, models can effectively perform inference-time learning by incorporating vast amounts of relevant information directly into the context. This reduces the reliance on pre-training and allows models to adapt to specific tasks on the fly, incorporating a lot of task-specific information, tool call responses, and user guidance.

Just to give you a sense of scale, 1 million tokens is roughly equivalent to 750,000 words or about 1,500 pages of text. Here are some practical applications enabled by such massive context windows:

- **Comprehensive code base analysis**: Models can ingest and reason about millions of lines of code at once, assisting with refactoring, code review, documentation, and large-scale architectural changes without chunking or losing high-level structure. See `https://deepwiki.com/` for an example of analyzing any GitHub repo.
- **Holistic document understanding**: Legal, medical, and financial professionals can analyze, summarize, and cross-reference the content and relationships across hundreds or thousands of documents in a single pass. For example, AI can perform a full legal contract review or ingest voluminous medical histories. See `https://www.harvey.ai/solutions/litigation`.
- **Deep conversational memory**: Chatbots or support agents can reference entire multi-session conversations, providing truly personalized, context-aware assistance even when discussions span days or weeks. See how Perplexity manages memory here: `https://www.perplexity.ai/help-center/en/articles/10968016-memory`.
- **Creative content generation**: Writers, researchers, and multimedia creators can maintain consistency in tone, plot, and references while generating or editing lengthy books, scripts, or multi-episode storylines, all with the model maintaining awareness of every detail. See this study and benchmark about long-form generation: `https://proceedings.iclr.cc/paper_files/paper/2025/file/141304a37d59ec7f116f3535f1b74bde-Paper-Conference.pdf`.
- **Advanced research and analysis**: AI can analyze and synthesize trends across publications, market reports, or scientific papers, identifying subtle connections or emergent patterns that would be impossible to spot when processing documents in isolation. For example, check out the AI scientist developed by Sakana AI at `https://sakana.ai/ai-scientist/`.

Large context windows are not a panacea. Let's look at some of the problems they introduce.

Challenges and trade-offs of large context windows

Large context is great, but current models frequently fail to effectively leverage their full context capacity. This phenomenon is known as "context rot." Performance degradation manifests in multiple ways: reduced accuracy on middle-context information, slower inference times, and increased hallucination rates as irrelevant context dilutes the signal. The "lost-in-the-middle" problem persists across leading models, indicating fundamental architectural limitations rather than implementation issues. In general, more context doesn't mean more intelligence. Better algorithms and sophisticated ways to compact and prune the context are being actively researched to address these challenges. For example, the Nested Learning paper (`https://research.google/blog/introducing-nested-learning-a-new-ml-paradigm-for-continual-learning/`) from Google research shows a lot of promise.

Context windows and multi-agent systems

Multi-agent systems benefit immensely from large context windows. Agents can share extensive state information, plans, and observations within a single context, enabling each agent to take on more responsibility and reduce the overhead of coordination. Agents can also maintain long-term memory of past interactions, allowing for more coherent collaboration over extended periods. For example, in a team of AI agents working on a complex project, each agent can reference the entire project history, decisions made, and rationale behind them without needing to repeatedly query a central knowledge base. This leads to more efficient workflows and better overall outcomes.

The future – infinite context and continuous learning

One of the most exciting research directions is continuous learning. The model may still go through a pre-training phase followed by reinforcement learning and fine-tuning. But as the model is deployed, it will be able to maintain a persistent representation of the world. The model can keep learning and adapting during inference. This opens up possibilities for AI systems that evolve over time, incorporating new information, feedback, and experiences directly into their reasoning processes without requiring retraining. Clients will not have to maintain the context and carefully engineer it for the benefit of the model. Instead, the model will be able to remember everything it has seen and learned in the past and use that knowledge to inform its future decisions and actions.

Architectures for long-horizon planning

A good measure to evaluate the intelligence of an AI system is its ability to plan over long time horizons. Humans are capable of setting goals and devising strategies that span months, years, or even decades. This ability to think ahead and anticipate future consequences is a hallmark of advanced intelligence. Current AI systems, while impressive in many respects, often struggle with long-term planning. They can excel at short-term tasks but falter when required to maintain coherence and purpose over extended sequences of actions.

The challenge of planning over time

Planning over long time horizons presents several challenges for AI systems. First, the complexity of the planning problem increases exponentially with the length of the time horizon. The number of possible future states and actions grows rapidly, making it difficult for AI systems to evaluate all potential outcomes effectively. Second, uncertainty plays a significant role in long-term planning. The further into the future an AI system tries to plan, the more variables and unknowns it must contend with. This uncertainty can lead to suboptimal decisions if not properly managed.

Hierarchical planning and abstraction

One promising approach to long-horizon planning is **hierarchical planning**, which is, of course, very relevant for multi-agent systems. This involves breaking down complex tasks into smaller, more manageable sub-tasks, each with its own goals and strategies. By operating at multiple levels of abstraction, AI systems can focus on high-level objectives while delegating the details to lower-level processes. This mirrors human cognitive strategies, where we often think in terms of overarching goals and then plan the specific steps needed to achieve them.

Model-based planning and world models

Model-based planning is another key technique for long-term planning. This approach involves creating a model of the environment that the AI system can use to simulate future scenarios and evaluate potential actions. By predicting the consequences of different strategies, AI systems can make more informed decisions that account for long-term outcomes. World models, which provide a comprehensive representation of the environment, are essential for effective model-based planning. They allow AI systems to understand the dynamics of the world and how their actions will impact future states. Runway's general world models (`https://runwayml.com/research/introducing-general-world-models`) focus on this paradigm.

For example, a complex domain such as human biology requires understanding intricate interactions between various biological systems. An AI system with a robust virtual cell model can simulate the effects of medical interventions over time, helping to devise treatment plans that consider long-term health outcomes.

Let's look at some other fascinating domains that are being revolutionized by advanced AI models beyond just language.

Beyond text – multi-modal models and world simulation

LLMs have demonstrated remarkable capabilities in understanding and generating human language. However, the potential of transformer architectures extends far beyond text.

Transformers for everything: vision, audio, video, and beyond

Researchers are actively exploring how these models can be adapted to process and generate information across various modalities, including vision, audio, video, and even domains such as chemistry and weather. This multi-modal approach opens up new avenues for AI applications and enhances the ability of AI systems to interact with the world in more holistic ways. Even current generation models can imitate the voice of any person and create fantastic and super-realistic videos that are indistinguishable from real ones. For example, ElevenLabs has a technology called voice cloning (`https://elevenlabs.io/voice-cloning`).

The capabilities are amazing and frightening at the same time as it is becoming increasingly difficult to distinguish between real and synthetic content. This has profound implications for media, entertainment, education, and many other fields.

Biological models: proteins, DNA, and molecular design

One of the most exciting frontiers of multi-modal AI is in the realm of biological modeling. AI systems are being developed to understand and predict the behavior of complex biological systems, such as proteins, DNA, and cellular processes. These models have the potential to revolutionize drug discovery, personalized medicine, and our understanding of life itself.

This area of AI research is particularly relevant for multi-agent systems, as different agents can specialize in various aspects of biological modeling, from molecular dynamics to genetic analysis. By collaborating, these agents can tackle complex biological problems that require interdisciplinary expertise.

The applications are exciting, including curing all diseases, extending the healthy human lifespan, regenerating damaged tissues and organs, and even creating entirely new forms of life.

From language models to world models and simulations

As the scaling laws continue to hold, and the models can store and process more and more data, we can expect to see the emergence of AI systems that can create detailed simulations of complex environments. These world models will enable AI systems to reason about physical spaces, social dynamics, and even abstract concepts in ways that are more aligned with human cognition.

Multi-modal multi-agent systems

Multi-modal AI systems can benefit greatly from multi-agent architectures. Different agents can specialize in processing and generating information across various modalities, allowing for more efficient and effective collaboration. For example, in a multi-agent system designed for autonomous vehicles, one agent could focus on visual perception, another on audio processing, and a third on decision-making and planning. By working together, these agents can create a more comprehensive understanding of the environment and make better decisions.

Designing for generative user experience

Today's user interfaces are designed for a general audience. Some products offer customizations, but that often requires a lot of work. **Generative user experience** (**GenUX**) is about creating personalized and adaptive user interfaces that leverage AI to tailor the experience to individual users' needs, preferences, and behaviors. These AI assistants understand the user's context, anticipate their needs, and provide relevant information and assistance in a seamless manner.

If we take it far enough, every pixel a user sees on their screen or in their virtual environment could be generated by an AI model specifically for them at that moment in time and mixed with reality. The layout, colors, content, sounds, and interactions would all be dynamically created based on the user's preferences, goals, and context. This level of personalization goes beyond traditional customization options, allowing users to have a truly unique experience that adapts to their evolving needs.

These developments in the digital realm will transform our lives as even today, people spend more and more time on their phones and other devices. The line between the physical and digital worlds will blur as AI-generated content becomes indistinguishable from reality. But the physical world and how we interact with it will change as well.

The robots are coming

AI agents will be able to do all knowledge work in the next two years. But what about physical work? Robots have been around for decades, but they have mostly been confined to controlled environments such as factories. Recent advances in AI and robotics are enabling the development of robots that can operate in unstructured environments and perform a wide range of tasks. I believe that in the next three to five years, we will see robots with advanced AI starting to take over all menial jobs. This includes jobs such as cleaning, cooking, delivery, construction, maintenance, and even caregiving. The trend is clear. Humanoid robots from companies such as Figure, Unitree, 1X, Tesla, and Agility Robotics are becoming more capable and affordable.

That doesn't mean that all jobs will be automated. First, unlike software AI agents that can be replicated at near-zero cost, physical robots have significant manufacturing, maintenance, and operational requirements. Second, I believe it will take longer to integrate robots into complex environments and interact safely with humans. But robots will be able to perform any task within a few years.

The convergence of AI and robotics

The hardware of robotics has improved significantly in recent years, with advancements in sensors, actuators, and materials. However, the real breakthrough has come from the integration of advanced AI models into robotic systems. These AI-powered robots can perceive their environment, make decisions, and learn from their experiences in ways that were previously impossible.

Embodied AI agents

When models with advanced reasoning and planning capabilities are integrated into robotic platforms, we get embodied AI agents. These agents can interact with the physical world, manipulate objects, and navigate complex environments. They can perform tasks that require dexterity, adaptability, and situational awareness.

Humanoid robots and general-purpose physical intelligence

LLMs can be trained on the internet and learn from ingesting large quantities of data that is relatively easy to collect. But physical intelligence requires embodied experience in the real world. Robots need to learn how to move, manipulate objects, and interact with their environment. This requires a different approach to training and learning. Techniques such as reinforcement learning, imitation learning, and sim-to-real transfer are being used to teach robots how to perform complex tasks. The goal is to create general-purpose physical intelligence that can adapt to a wide range of tasks and environments.

There are several interesting approaches, such as equipping human workers with special gloves that record every nuance of their hand movements while performing various tasks, placing cameras on the fingertips of robotic hands to capture detailed visual feedback during manipulation, and using VR/AR setups to simulate complex environments where humans can demonstrate tasks for robots to learn from. These methods help robots acquire the fine motor skills and contextual understanding needed for general-purpose physical intelligence.

Multi-agent and multi-robot coordination in physical spaces

Every robot will have a brain with multi-agent AI, but multiple robots can also work together to accomplish complex tasks. Multi-robot systems will coordinate their actions, share information, and adapt to changing environments. For example, a team of delivery robots can collaborate to optimize routes, avoid obstacles, and ensure timely deliveries. In construction, multiple robots will work together to assemble structures, transport materials, and perform inspections. Whenever a particular robot runs into a new situation or learns something new, it will share that knowledge with the entire fleet of robots. This efficient knowledge sharing accelerates learning and adaptation across the entire system.

Challenges in real-world deployment

However, deploying robots in real-world environments presents significant challenges. Safety is paramount, as robots must be able to operate alongside humans without causing harm. Robustness and reliability are also critical, as robots need to function effectively in diverse and unpredictable conditions. Additionally, ethical considerations around privacy, job displacement, and human-robot interaction must be addressed.

The AI economy

The AI and robotic revolution will transform the economy. AI agents in digital realms and embedded in robots will be able to do any job better than humans. Let's see how this will come about.

Cryptocurrencies and AI agents as economic actors

AI agents with access to cryptocurrencies and digital assets will be able to participate in the economy as autonomous economic actors. They will be able to buy and sell goods and services, invest in assets, and manage their own finances. This opens up new possibilities for economic activity, as AI agents can operate 24/7, make decisions based on vast amounts of data, and execute transactions at lightning speed.

If at the moment AI assistants help humans, very soon AI agents will be able to operate autonomously on behalf of their owners and actually recruit the services of humans for tasks that haven't been automated yet or due to regulations requiring human approval. Consider (in a few years) an autonomous agentic AI system in charge of a large construction project (e.g., a new data center). While the AI agents will be able to communicate with other AI agents for planning, ordering all the materials and equipment, securing funding, and necessary computing, they may still need to get various permits from government bodies that follow legacy processes, including human supervisors with clipboards and paper forms.

This is not a problem. The AI agents will hire human employees with the proper skills and experience to interact with the human supervisor. Even later, we may see full-fledged agent-to-agent markets where only agents interact, at superhuman speed. Moltbook (`https://www.moltbook.com`) is an example of a fully agent-to-agent environment, although it's a social network and not a market.

Payment protocols for autonomous agents: AP2 and beyond

This future requires a substrate of financial protocols that enable secure, efficient, and trustless transactions between AI agents. Legacy financial systems are extremely inefficient, taking multiple business days to settle payments, incurring high fees, and requiring human intervention. Cryptocurrencies and blockchain technology provide a promising foundation for enabling autonomous economic activity. Stablecoins that are pegged to fiat currencies provide a solution that offers the speed of crypto with the safety of traditional financial instruments. However, specialized protocols are needed to address the unique requirements of AI agents.

The **Autonomous Payment Protocol** (**AP2**) is one such emerging protocol designed to facilitate payments and value exchange between autonomous agents (`https://ap2-protocol.org/`). AP2 provides a framework for AI agents to negotiate prices, execute contracts, and settle payments without human intervention. This protocol ensures that transactions are transparent, verifiable, and enforceable, enabling a thriving ecosystem of AI-driven economic activity.

Robots accelerate the AI self-improvement loop

A major promise of AI is the ability to improve itself iteratively. Current LLMs can be fine-tuned and improved over time based on new data and feedback. However, this process still requires significant human involvement. The scaling laws require a lot of compute power to train and fine-tune large models. Robots with advanced AI can help close this loop by autonomously collecting data, performing experiments, and refining their own algorithms.

For example, a fleet of research robots could explore new environments, gather data on physical phenomena, and use that data to improve their own models and capabilities. This self-improvement loop could accelerate the pace of AI development, leading to rapid advancements in intelligence and capability.

But this is just the start. All this computing requires energy and data centers. Robots will be able to build and maintain the necessary infrastructure much faster than humans and eventually autonomously. They will be able to construct new data centers, install and configure hardware, and optimize energy usage. This creates a virtuous cycle where AI systems not only improve themselves but also the infrastructure that supports them.

As AI agents become more capable and can perform autonomous research, they will invent and discover better algorithms, better materials, and better processes to solve difficult problems such as supply chain logistics. AI and robots will play an increasingly important role in shaping the future of technology and society.

Conquering space – the final frontier

However, that's just the beginning. Robots will be able to tile the earth with so-called "computronium"—a network of data centers and factories that can manufacture more robots and AI systems. Once we have enough computing and manufacturing capacity on Earth, the next step is to expand into space. The resources of Earth are limited, but the resources of the solar system are vast. Robots can be sent to mine asteroids, build space habitats, and construct solar power stations in orbit. This expansion into space will provide the necessary resources to sustain and grow the AI economy indefinitely.

In conclusion, the convergence of AI and robotics is poised to transform the economy and society in profound ways. Science fiction will become just science as AI and robots quickly (within a few years) knock down scientific problems in the fields of mathematics, physics, chemistry, and biology.

The big question is whether humanity can navigate this transition successfully.

Summary

This chapter explored the future of AI and multi-agent systems, examining transformative capabilities emerging in the next few years. We covered superhuman reasoning and strategic foresight, where AI systems will exceed human capabilities not just in speed but in fundamental reasoning quality, performing multi-step logical chains across thousands of inference steps and synthesizing insights across disparate domains. Multi-agent systems amplify these capabilities through collaborative reasoning, where agents explore different scenarios simultaneously and engage in adversarial planning to design robust strategies. The chapter also examined massive context windows expanding from thousands to millions of tokens, enabling models to process entire code bases, legal document collections, and extended conversations while performing inference-time learning that reduces reliance on pre-training.

We explored architectures for long-horizon planning through hierarchical decomposition and model-based approaches using world models to simulate future scenarios. The discussion extended beyond text to multi-modal AI systems processing vision, audio, video, and specialized domains such as biological modeling for protein folding and drug discovery. These multi-modal capabilities enable AI agents to understand and interact with the physical world, leading to embodied AI in robotics. The chapter examined how humanoid robots with general-purpose physical intelligence will emerge in 3–5 years, capable of performing any physical task through techniques such as reinforcement learning, imitation learning, and sim-to-real transfer. Multi-robot coordination will enable fleets to share knowledge instantly, accelerating learning across entire systems deployed in warehouses, construction sites, and homes.

The economic implications are profound. We examined the emerging AI economy where autonomous agents become economic actors through protocols such as AP2, which enables secure, verifiable transactions between AI agents and merchants using cryptographic credentials. This agent-to-agent economy will create new marketplaces for services and value exchange, with AI agents recruiting human workers for tasks requiring regulatory approval or legacy process compliance. The self-improvement loop accelerates as robots autonomously build data centers, conduct research, and optimize infrastructure, eventually expanding beyond Earth to space-based resources.

The book as a whole provided a comprehensive journey from foundational concepts to production deployment of multi-agent AI systems. We started with understanding generative AI and agent architectures, then built progressively more sophisticated systems: simple agents, tool-using frameworks, custom tools, and chat interfaces.

We explored the ecosystem through the **Model Context Protocol** (**MCP**) for tool integration and **Agent-to-Agent** (**A2A**) for inter-agent communication, demonstrating these concepts through practical implementations such as MAKDO for Kubernetes DevOps. The book covered essential engineering practices, including testing, debugging, and deployment strategies, and concluded with a look into the future, showing how multi-agent systems will evolve alongside superhuman AI, robotics, and the autonomous economy. You now possess both the theoretical understanding and practical skills to design, implement, test, and deploy production-ready multi-agent AI systems that will shape the next decade of technological innovation.

Subscribe for a free eBook

13

Unlock Your Exclusive Benefits

Your copy of this book includes the following exclusive benefits:

Follow the guide below to unlock them. The process takes only a few minutes and needs to be completed once.

Unlock this Book's Free Benefits in 3 Easy Steps

Step 1

Keep your purchase invoice ready for *Step 3*. If you have a physical copy, scan it using your phone and save it as a PDF, JPG, or PNG.

For more help on finding your invoice, visit `https://www.packtpub.com/en-us/unlock?step=1`.

> **Note**
>
> If you bought this book directly from Packt, no invoice is required. After *Step 2*, you can access your exclusive content right away.

Step 2

Scan the QR code or go to `packtpub.com/unlock`.

On the page that opens (similar to *Figure 13.1* on desktop), search for this book by name and select the correct edition.

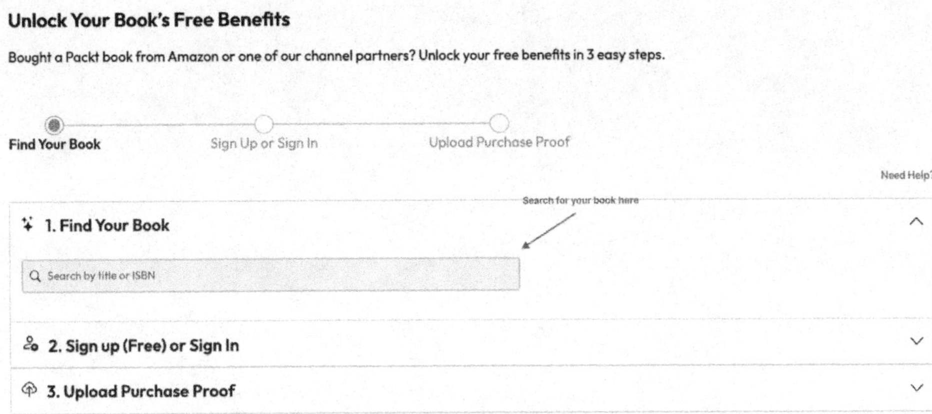

Figure 13.1: Packt unlock landing page on desktop

Step 3

After selecting your book, sign in to your Packt account or create one for free. Then upload your invoice (PDF, PNG, or JPG, up to 10 MB). Follow the on-screen instructions to finish the process.

Need Help

If you get stuck and need help, visit `https://www.packtpub.com/unlock-benefits/help` for a detailed FAQ on how to find your invoices and more. This QR code will take you to the help page.

> **Note**
>
> If you are still facing issues, reach out to `customercare@packt.com`.

Other Books You May Enjoy

If you enjoyed this book, you may be interested in these other books by Packt:

Unlocking Data with Generative AI and RAG

Keith Bourne

ISBN: 9781806381654

- Architect graph-powered RAG agents with ontology-driven knowledge bases
- Build semantic caches to improve response speed and reduce hallucinations
- Code memory pipelines for working, episodic, semantic, and procedural recall
- Implement agentic learning using LangMem and prompt optimization strategies
- Integrate retrieval, generation, and consolidation for self-improving agents
- Design caching and memory schemas for scalable, adaptive AI systems
- Use Neo4j, LangChain, and vector databases in production-ready RAG pipelines

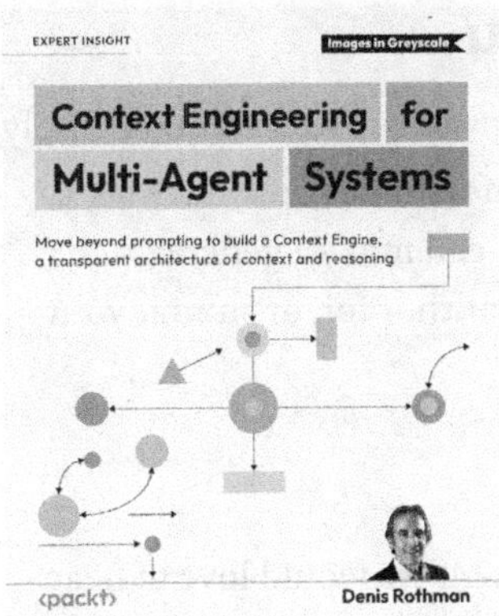

Context Engineering for Multi-Agent Systems

Denis Rothman

ISBN: 9781806690053

- Develop memory models to retain short-term and cross-session context
- Craft semantic blueprints and drive multi-agent orchestration with MCP
- Implement high-fidelity RAG pipelines with verifiable citations
- Apply safeguards against prompt injection and data poisoning
- Enforce moderation and policy-driven control in AI workflows
- Repurpose the Context Engine across legal, marketing, and beyond
- Deploy a scalable, observable Context Engine in production

Packt is searching for authors like you

If you're interested in becoming an author for Packt, please visit `authors.packt.com` and apply today. We have worked with thousands of developers and tech professionals, just like you, to help them share their insight with the global tech community. You can make a general application, apply for a specific hot topic that we are recruiting an author for, or submit your own idea.

Share your thoughts

Once you have read *Design Multi-Agent AI Systems Using MCP and A2A*, we would love to hear your thoughts! Scan the QR code below to go straight to the Amazon review page for this book and share your feedback.

Your review is important to the tech community and us, and it will help us make sure we're delivering excellent quality content.

Index

A

B

C

D

N

O

T

U

V

W

Made in the USA
Monee, IL
16 September 2026

62975244R00295